INDUSTRY, SOCIETY, AND CHANGE

A CASEBOOK

McGraw-Hill Series in Managem

CONSULTING EDITORS

Fred Luthans and Keith Davis

Also Available from McGraw-Hill

Schaum's Outline Series in Accounting, Business & Economics

Most outlines include basic theory, definitions, and hundreds of solved problems and supplementary problems with answers.

Titles on the Current List Include:

Available at your College Bookstore. A complete listing of Schaum titles may be obtained by writing to: Schaum Division
McGraw-Hill, Inc.
Princeton Road, S-1
Hightstown, NJ 08520

INDUSTRY, SOCIETY, AND CHANGE

A CASEBOOK

John F. Steiner

Professor of Management and Chair,
Department of Management
California State University, Los Angeles

McGRAW-HILL, INC.

New York St. Louis San Francisco Auckland Bogotá Caracas
Hamburg Lisbon London Madrid Mexico Milan Montreal New Delhi
Paris San Juan São Paulo Singapore Sydney Tokyo Toronto

This book was set in Times Roman by the College Composition Unit in cooperation with General Graphics Services, Inc.
The editors were Alan Sachs, Dan Alpert, and Ira C. Roberts; the production supervisor was Annette Mayeski.
The cover was designed by Karen K. Quigley.
R. R. Donnelley & Sons Company was printer and binder.

Cover photo: Inness, George. The Lackawanna Valley.
National Gallery of Art, Washington. Gift of Mrs. Huttleston Rogers.

INDUSTRY, SOCIETY, AND CHANGE
A Casebook

1 2 3 4 5 6 7 8 9 0 DOC DOC 9 0 9 8 7 6 5 4 3 2 1

ISBN 0-07-061174-2

Library of Congress Cataloging-in-Publication Data

Steiner, John F.
    Industry, society, and change: a casebook / John F. Steiner.
      p.   cm. — (McGraw-Hill series in management)
    Includes index.
    ISBN 0-07-061174-2 — ISBN 0-07-061177-7
(instructor's manual)
     1. Industry—Social aspects—United States—Case studies.
I. Title.   II. Series.
HD60.5.U5S85   1991
306.3′6—dc20   90-22648

To My Mother

ABOUT THE COVER

The Lackawanna Valley was painted by American artist George Inness (1825–1894). In 1855, Inness was given a commission of $75 by the president of the Delaware, Lackawanna & Western Railroad to paint a new roundhouse near Scranton, Pennsylvania. Inness was offended when he was required to add more tracks than existed. Even so, the work has such poetic beauty that it has become a masterpiece of American landscape painting. Note that *The Lackawanna Valley* is not a wilderness landscape. Rather, it is what Inness called a "civilized landscape," or a landscape in which nature was shaped to human purpose. Its dawning light captures an image of the fresh, enterprising spirit of nineteenth century industrialization. The relaxed onlooker near the tree is unconcerned about the changes being wrought. This is a moment in time when the themes of industry, society, and change—the elements in the title of this book—are joined in lyric harmony. The innocence of this moment was, of course, short-lived.

CONTENTS

kinder to their livestock, but consumers will have to pay premium prices or become vegetarians.

forces society to strike a balance between free commercial speech
and harm to public health.

PREFACE

The landscape of every modern society is shaped in large measure by the interaction between industry and social institutions. As industrial activity continues over time, the landscape changes. The title of this book, *Industry, Society, and Change,* acknowledges this reality.

There are thirteen case studies here. Each illustrates an important dimension of the field of business and society by telling the story of a specific company, industry, product, or industrial process. The business and society field is broad and eclectic. So no short collection of cases can completely encompass it. Hence, these cases are windows into a larger subject area; they are verbal portraits of a larger whole.

The cases recount incidents and events that will engage all readers with imagination and curiosity about the business world. Each contains central issues raised by the interaction between industry and society as both struggle toward mutual accommodation. The drama of these issues is interwoven with factual material on public policy, law, ethics, history, sociology, or science pertinent to each case. This didactic material serves as a backdrop for the narrative, just as scenery in a painting situates the subject matter in proper perspective.

There are many topics that could have been taken up in this book. But only a few are. Those selected have in common a focus on the interaction between managerial decisions and the social setting. And they illustrate the two great themes of this interaction: (1) the presence of trade-offs between profit making and the preservation of enduring social values such as truth, justice, virtue, love, and environmental quality; and (2) the sculpting of corporate strategic choice by historical forces and social mechanisms.

Within these broad themes the cases cover a range of issues. The lives of John D. Rockefeller and Huey Long are recounted to show how the industrial development of America after 1850 shaped the modern business environment. The ethical questions raised by Rockefeller's career are still central to the field of business ethics today. And the populist aspect of Huey Long's career still defines the basic themes of today's critics of business. The story of the deregulation of the airline industry illustrates the complex nature of business-government interaction today. The study of animal agriculture shows how new technology and widely divergent views about animals in society are complicating the environment of one of the world's oldest industries. Two cases, one on global warming trends and the other on environmental protesters, illustrate just how powerful the impact of business has been on the physical environment. Business-employee relations are at issue in stories about the Supreme Court affirmative action case, *Johnson* v. *Transportation Agency,* and paper-and-pencil honesty tests which raise questions about the ethics of both employers and employees. Consumer issues are discussed in the story of a Maryland man who sued the manufacturer of a handgun after being shot in a holdup and in "Selling Tobacco," a study of the power of advertising. The story of the KKR-RJR leveraged buyout, the largest of its kind to date, raises concerns over the future of our capitalist system. And the social responsibilities of multinational corporations are taken up—the role of U.S. corporations in world society is examined in a discussion of corporate involvement in South African society and in "Union Carbide and the Bhopal Plant Gas Leak."

I am grateful to those in the business community and the world of affairs who shared their expertise to assist in this project, including David W. Arnold, Reid Psychological Systems; Cathy Baldwin, Willamette Industries; John E. Benneth, American Forest Council; Kris, Earth First!; Richard Gardner, National Rifle Association; Judy Goldberg, American Civil Liberties Union; John W. Jones, London House Inc.; Kathryn Koenig, Bank Administration Institute; Olen J. Kelley, Safeway Stores; Barry Lacter, Louisiana-Pacific Corporation; Peter Lovenheim, attorney-at-law, Rochester, New York; Robert W. McCallum, Lucas Aerospace; Eric Shockman, Edmund G. "Pat" Brown Institute of Public Affairs; Howard L. Siegel, attorney-at-law, Rockville, Maryland; Glenys Simmons, Louisiana-Pacific Corporation; Michael Tiner, United Food and Commercial Workers International Union (AFL-CIO); and Jim Walls, Stanton Corporation.

Thanks are also due to my colleagues at California State University, Los Angeles, including Alan Stein, George Rollins, and Murray Ross at the John F. Kennedy Library, who were generous with their time; Mary Pat McEnrue of the Department of Management, who made helpful comments on part of the manuscript; and Charles J. Inacker, dean of the School of Business and Economics, who was supportive and encouraging. Li Zhou, an M.B.A. student, provided valuable research assistance.

George A. Steiner of UCLA made helpful suggestions for which I am grateful and contributed the story of the KKR-RJR leveraged buyout. I also express deep appreciation to Deborah K. Luedy for her assistance.

Laura Givner did an outstanding job on the copyediting as did Paul Sobel on the proofreading. At McGraw-Hill I am indebted to the editorial staff: Dan Alpert, George Hoffman, Kathleen Loy, Mimi Melek, Alan Sachs, Catherine Sauer, and June Smith for their stewardship of my efforts. A special acknowledgment of appreciation is due to Ira Roberts for his distinguished efforts in the production of the manuscript.

John F. Steiner

INDUSTRY, SOCIETY, AND CHANGE

A CASEBOOK

JOHN D. ROCKEFELLER AND THE STANDARD OIL TRUST

This is the story of John D. Rockefeller, founder of the Standard Oil Company. It is the story of a small-town boy who dominated the oil industry by dint of brilliant strategic insight and ruthless, methodical execution. He became the richest man in America and, for a time, one of the most hated.

Rockefeller's life spanned ninety-eight years. When he was born, Martin Van Buren was president, Andrew Jackson was the nation's preeminent hero, and settlers followed the Oregon Trail in covered wagons. He lived to see Franklin Roosevelt's New Deal, watch the rise of the Nazi party in Germany, and hear Frank Sinatra and *The Lone Ranger* on network radio.

The historical backdrop of this lifetime is an economy gripped by the fever of industrial progress. Rockefeller built his fortune in an era that lacked many ethical norms and legal restraints characteristic of contemporary business. Even so, his actions thrust business ethics into the realm of public debate for the first time in industrialized America. Revisiting Rockefeller at the helm of the Standard Oil Company is simultaneously a nostalgic historical adventure and a rediscovery of the origins of central questions that define the field of business ethics to this day. These are: (1) Is there a distinction between business and personal ethics? (2) What are the ethical consequences of competitive strategy? and (3) Does social responsibility exceed normal business productivity?

Since biographers characteristically seek auguries of future greatness in the early experiences of the famous, the story here begins with his boyhood.

THE FORMATIVE YEARS

John Davison Rockefeller was born on July 8, 1839, in the small village of Richford in southern New York. He was the second of six children and the oldest boy. His father, William Rockefeller, was an itinerant quack doctor and jack-of-all-trades who often left the family and traveled the country selling elixirs and patent medicines. On his business card he promised: "All Cases of Cancer CURED Unless Too Far Gone And Then They Can Be Greatly BENEFITED!"[1] In addition to his healing activities "Doc" Rockefeller engaged in a wide variety of businesses, including horse trading, lumbering, and moneylending. He had the jovial, irreverent personality of a slick operator; in business he was shrewd and cunning. He made enough money to keep the family in handsome style and always carried at least $1,000 on his person, a huge sum in those days.

John D.'s mother, Eliza, was opposite in temperament. She was a somber, religious woman who gave her children a strict upbringing emphasizing manners, church attendance, and the work ethic. As a fundamentalist Baptist she believed in literal interpretation of the Bible and a just God who rained fire and brimstone upon sinners. She exercised harsh discipline. Once she began to whip young John D. with a birch switch for misdeeds at school of which he was innocent. His protests finally convinced his mother he was not guilty, but she proceeded with the whipping anyway, explaining: "We have started on this whipping, and it will do for the next time."[2] She preached homilies such as "Willful waste makes woeful want." And she taught charity to the children; from an early age John D. made regular contributions to worthy causes.

When he was four, the family moved to the nearby village of Moravia. His father started a log hauling business and stayed at home until he was indicted by a local court for the rape of a young woman hired to work in the Rockefeller home. He fled the county to avoid arrest and visited only rarely and in the dark of night until moving his family to Owego, New York, in 1850, when John D. was eleven. With his family ensconced in a spacious house William Rockefeller resumed his traveling ways, returning home infrequently and for short periods. As the oldest boy, John D. had increased responsibility during his father's absences.

As a child John D. was not precocious. In school he was smart and hardworking, but never an exceptional student. His boyhood finances were ordinary. He was paid small sums for chores and once raised a flock of turkeys, which he sold. He exhibited notable thrift by saving money in a blue china bowl kept on the mantle. At the age of twelve he loaned $50 to a farmer at 7 percent interest and was impressed by the resultant income of $3.50, for which he did no physical labor. His older sister Lucy once remarked on his acquisitive dimension, saying: "When it's raining porridge you'll always find John's bowl right side up."[3]

---

[1]John K. Winkler. *John D.: A Portrait in Oils.* New York: Vanguard Press, 1929, p. 12.

[2]John D. Rockefeller. *Random Reminiscences of Men and Events.* New York: Arno Press, 1973, p. 34. This book was originally published in 1909 by Doubleday.

[3]Peter Collier and David Horowitz. *The Rockefellers: An American Dynasty.* New York: New American Library, 1976, p. 11.

During this period William Rockefeller taught his son the principles of business conduct. He reinforced his lessons with firsthand experience. To illustrate that sentimentality must not influence business transactions he loaned his sons money at the highest legal interest rate. "I cheat my boys every chance I get," he once said. "I want to make 'em sharp. I trade with the boys and skin 'em and I just beat 'em every time I can."[4] Apparently John D. took to the lessons because he later wrote: "By the time I was a man—long before it—I had learned the underlying principles of business and the rules of business as well as many men acquire them by the time they are forty.[5]

In 1854, when he was sixteen, John D. left home and moved into a boardinghouse in Cleveland, Ohio, where he attended Central High School for one year. There he showed himself to be a tenacious but uninspired student, little interested in books and ideas but willing to work hard. He had grown into a somber, intense lad nicknamed "the Deacon" by his classmates because of his faithful attendance at the Erie Street Baptist Church and his penchant for memorizing hymns. At the end of his first year he dropped out of high school, never to finish. That summer, with his father paying the tuition, he attended a three-month course at Folsom's Commercial College, where he learned accounting principles and the rudiments of banking and commercial law.

Upon graduation in September 1855 John D. hit the streets determined to place his feet on the first rung of the career ladder. In addition to his formal training he carried the contradictory temperaments of his parents—the wily, self-assured boldness of his father and the exacting, pietistic character of his mother. He internalized both, and the combination was to prove formidable. Here was a man with the precision of an accountant and the cunning of Cesare Borgia.

EARLY BUSINESS CAREER

Rockefeller's first job was that of assistant bookkeeper at Hewitt and Tuttle, a commodity brokerage firm in Cleveland. He worked in the main office, where he acquired some wisdom from the conversations of the partners. Put in charge of billing and collections, he worked tirelessly. He prided himself in detecting errors, and every bill and payment was meticulously audited. When he visited a neighboring business one day, he observed a local plumber present a long bill which was paid without inspection. But when the same plumber presented a bill to Rockefeller's company, he found several mistakes and corrected the man. There was no outward sign of avariciousness, but one day when Hewitt and Tuttle collected a $4,000 bank note, he repeatedly opened the office safe to gaze at it in wonderment.

His social life revolved around the Erie Street Baptist Church, where he

---

[4]Winkler, op. cit., p. 14.
[5]David Freeman Hawke. *John D.: The Founding Father of the Rockefellers*. New York: Harper & Row, 1980, p. 13.

spent Sundays and evenings listening to sermons. He began to keep the church's books and taught its largest Sunday school class. One Sunday the minister alarmed the congregation by announcing that the church's $2,000 mortgage was in danger of foreclosure. After the service Rockefeller stationed himself by the exits, notebook in hand, and asked each member to pledge money to save the church. He raised enough to pay the mortgage and when he became twenty-one was named one of the five church trustees, an unusual sign of respect for a young man.

At this time the thrifty Rockefeller began recording his personal income and expenditures in a small account book he called Ledger A. Its pages show that he saved most of his $25-a-month salary, paying $1 a week for board and $9.09 for clothing over a six-month period. His one extravagance was a pair of fur gloves costing $2.50. Despite his frugality he recorded continuous charitable contributions, giving away 10 percent of what he earned in his first four months of employment. Some of the entries included $0.10 for missionaries, $0.20 for the church poor, $0.25 to "a poor man in the church," and $0.50 to "a poor woman in the church." Ledger A, which became a cherished object in his old age, foreshadowed the coexisting parsimony and generosity that later characterized the millionaire.

In 1859, after $3\frac{1}{2}$ years at Hewitt and Tuttle, Rockefeller was earning $700 a year. Calculating exactly his worth to the company, he asked for a $100 raise. When he was turned down, he formed a partnership in the produce commission business with two others. He invested $2,000 in this enterprise—$1,000 borrowed from his father and $1,000 he had saved. Rockefeller kept meticulous books and records and calculated the exact value of the business at the end of each day, a practice he continued through his days with the Standard Oil Trust. He was also an intense negotiator of sales and commissions, once described by an acquaintance as a person "who can walk right up on a man's shirt bosom and sit down."[6]

The business was a success from the start due partly to the business boom brought about by the Civil War. The partners did a business of $450,000 in their first year supplying produce to the Union Army. Although in his early twenties at the time, the steady, unemotional lad was never touched by patriotic fervor. In those days the law permitted any man of means to pay for sending someone else to serve in his place, and this he did. Later in life Rockefeller claimed that he had outfitted as many as thirty soldiers to fight for the Union Army.

Profits from the produce business were so high that Rockefeller sought promising new investments. He soon found one—a petroleum refinery.

BEGINNINGS OF THE OIL BUSINESS

Petroleum production and refining at the time was an infant industry. In Rockefeller's youth the vast beds of liquid hydrocarbons beneath the earth's

---

[6]Jules Abels. *The Rockefeller Billions.* New York: Macmillan, 1965, p. 35.

surface lay untapped. The internal-combustion engine lay far in the future, and industry was powered by coal, wood, and muscle. Petroleum was collected from surface pools and used mainly in patent medicines of the kind sold by Rockefeller's father.

In 1854 a chemistry professor at Yale reported that the black oil freely oozing from the ground in northwest Pennsylvania could be refined into kerosene and lubricants.[7] Informed by this report, a group of investors hired an ex-railroad conductor, Edwin Drake, to drill for oil in the region. Drake borrowed technology from artesian well drillers and struck oil in Pennsylvania in 1859.

The major use for the newly discovered petroleum was home illumination. At the time, many people still used candles for household light after sunset. In the early 1700s huge whaling fleets had been built to capture sperm whales and refine their blubber for whale oil for use in lamps. Whale oil was expensive, however, and at the time of Rockefeller's birth only the wealthy used oil lamps. In the 1840s a process for distilling oil from coal was developed. This led to the marketing of a highly volatile kerosene that was only slightly less expensive, dangerously explosive, and prone to foul lamp wicks. Hence, before the discovery of underground petroleum deposits most Americans still rose with the sun and went to bed at nightfall. This simple pattern of life would soon seem primitive, its ancient premises overwhelmed by an industrializing society awash in oil.

The first oil strike set off a frenzied oil boom in rural Pennsylvania. Overnight the value of sleepy farmland skyrocketed. Flimsy drilling shacks crowded into pastures and refineries were built to process crude oil into kerosene, naphtha, lubricating oil, and petroleum jelly. The typical refinery of that day consisted of several large wooden vats for the stills in which crude oil was heated, a network of pipes, and some barrels to fill with the commercial products. It required only a small financial investment. In the heyday of the oil boom in the 1860s it was also a dangerous workplace, prone to fire and explosion.

THE RISE TO DOMINANCE

At this time the first oil refineries were set up in Cleveland, and Rockefeller invested $4,000 in a partnership with a young refinery operator and one of his partners from the produce business. He did not even want his name on the company—Andrews, Clark and Company—because he considered it a sideline. Soon, however, the refinery became his central interest, and he devoted his full energy to the oil business, dominating his partners through force of will and conforming the firm to his principles of parsimony. One of his basic principles was to avoid paying a profit to anyone where possible. For example, instead of buying barrels and paying the cooper $2.50 each, Rockefeller set up

---

[7]B. Silliman, Jr. *Report on the Rock Oil, or Petroleum, from Venango Co., Pennsylvania: With Special References to Its Use for Illumination and Other Purposes.* New Haven: J. H. Benham's Steam Power Press, 1855.

his own barrel-making factory and made them for $0.96. He even purchased a tract of forest and made the staves from his own trees. Another basic principle was methodical cost cutting. Lumber for barrel staves was kiln-dried before shipment to the cooperage plant, and because water evaporated from the wood, it became lighter and transportation costs were lower. Business consumed his life; success was his joy. An acquaintance told this story:

> The only time I ever saw John Rockefeller enthusiastic was when a report came in from the Creek that his buyer had secured a cargo of oil at a figure much below the market price. He bounded from his chair with a shout of joy, danced up and down, hugged me, threw up his hat, acted so like a madman that I have never forgotten it.[8]

During this period Rockefeller married Laura Spelman, a former classmate at Central High. The story of their courtship is told in his ledger, which contains entries for three courting bouquets at $0.50 cents each and $1.75 for a horse-drawn cab in which the couple rode one weekend. He entered $15.75 as the cost of a wedding ring. The couple married on September 8, 1864, and Rockefeller was back in the office the next day.

Though obsessed with details and small economies, Rockefeller also proved aggressive in larger plans. He borrowed heavily from banks to expand the refinery, taking risks that scared Maurice Clark, one of his partners. The two quarreled, and he bought out Clark in 1865, releasing one counterbalance on his audacity. Thus freed, he borrowed more to build a second refinery in Cleveland, and he incorporated an export sales company in New York.

Competitive and Economic Forces Shaping the Oil Industry

By the late 1860s the youthful industry was in a chaotic state. A basic cause was overproduction in the oil regions of Pennsylvania, which were the only source of crude oil. Prices fluctuated wildly as a consequence of overproduction. The price for a 42-gallon barrel of crude was $20.00 early in 1860 but fell to $0.10 by December. It rose to $14.00 in July 1864 and then fell to $4.00 in August 1865 and to $1.35 in December 1866. It went to $7.00 early in 1869 but fell as low as $2.70 in 1870.[9]

There were efforts to form producers associations to cut production at the wellhead, but successes were short-lived because of incentives to cheat. As prices fell, many drillers increased output to compensate. Since nobody knew how much oil was underground, many also feared that if they stopped pumping, neighboring wells would drain whole oil formations. The motive of most oil investors at the time was to get rich quickly before the oil fields dried up. During periods of oversupply, hired thugs roamed the oil fields beating up clandestine oil pumpers, but supply never stabilized.

---

[8]Ida M. Tarbell. *The History of the Standard Oil Company.* Gloucester, Mass.: Peter Smith, 1963, vol. I, p. 43.
[9]Abels, op. cit., p. 58.

Before the advent of refining methods that required expensive fractioning equipment, every drop in crude oil prices encouraged construction of new refineries. Hence, by the late 1860s refining capacity was three times greater than oil production, and refiners engaged in vicious price wars. The margin of profit on each gallon of refined oil dropped steadily from $1.00 in 1860 to as low as $0.16 early in 1869.[10] Because of technical innovations and cost cutting, Rockefeller's refineries were making money. But the workings of the free market were inexorably reducing profits.

An important cost to refiners was transportation. Refiners had to pay the railroads to ship in crude oil and ship out refined products such as kerosene and lubricating oil. In the 1860s the railroads were growing rapidly, borrowing money to lay new track, and fighting each other for business. Freight rates were altered to meet market conditions, and published rates were often only the starting point for negotiations. There were no regulatory restraints on railroad rates, and whatever the ethics of the situation, railroads in those days were under no legal obligation to serve as common carriers affording equal access and freight charges to all shippers.

Railroads often granted *rebates* to shippers; that is, they returned part of their freight charge after shipment. These rebates were usually secret and granted in return for the guarantee of future shipping business. The rebate system provided an incentive to increase volume, since larger shippers could always extract the highest rebates from the railroads. In the 1860s oil refineries often received rebates, and Rockefeller's firm was no exception. In 1868, for example, the Lake Shore Railroad gave Rockefeller a rebate of $0.65 cents a barrel on its regular rate of $2.40, reducing his shipping costs to $1.75.

Rockefeller's Competitive Strategies

Rockefeller was using a number of commonplace competitive strategies. He became a low-cost, high-volume producer. He used debt financing to expand. He also attempted to make his refined petroleum products of high and consistent quality, since fly-by-night refiners turned out inferior distillates, and cheap kerosene with a low ignition point had burned many a home after exploding in a wick lamp. In 1870 he reorganized the limited partnership by incorporating as the Standard Oil Company of Ohio; the name was intended to imply a "standard oil" of uniformly good quality. He engaged in vertical integration by making wooden barrels, thereby performing an operation earlier in the chain of production. As time went on, he also bought storage facilities and a fleet of tank cars. In furtherance of these strategies he used tactics common to the commercial environment of that time, including secret rebates.

He is described by biographers as being a prepossessing man with penetrat-

---

[10]These figures are from U.S. Bureau of Corporations. *Report of the Commission on the Petroleum Industry*, part II, "Prices and Profits." Washington, D.C.: Government Printing Office, 1907, p. 84, and ibid., p. 51.

ing eyes who drove a hard bargain. He would take the measure of a man with a withering stare, and few were his match. He was formidable in negotiations because he was invariably informed in detail about the other's business. But he was still a pious churchgoer who read the Bible every night before retiring and said that he never cheated anyone.

Late in 1871 Rockefeller hatched a brazen plan for stabilizing the oil industry at the refining level. In a series of clandestine meetings he worked out a rebate scheme between a few major refiners and the three railroads that connected to the oil regions in Pennsylvania. This was the South Improvement Plan. Under this plan the railroads agreed to a huge increase in rates for hauling oil. But Rockefeller's Cleveland refineries and a small number of major refineries in other states would be given large rebates on every barrel shipped. For example, the regular rate between the oil regions and Cleveland would be $0.80 a barrel and between Cleveland and New York $2.00 a barrel. It would cost a total of $2.80 per barrel for any other refinery in Cleveland to bring in a barrel of crude oil and ship a barrel of refined oil to New York for sale or export. Rockefeller, on the other hand, would be charged $2.80 but receive a rebate of $0.90. The other conspiring refineries got similar rebates.

In addition, the refineries participating in the South Improvement Plan received *drawbacks*, or payments made on the shipment of oil by competitors! Thus Rockefeller would receive a drawback of $0.40 on every barrel of crude oil his competitors shipped into Cleveland and one of $0.50 on every barrel of refined oil shipped to New York. Under this venal scheme the more a competitor shipped, the more Rockefeller's transportation costs were lowered. While competitors paid $2.80 for this critical transportation route (Pennsylvania oil regions–Cleveland–New York), Rockefeller paid only $1.00. Also nefarious was the requirement that railroads give the conspirators waybills detailing competitors' shipments—a more perfect espionage system could not be imagined.

Why did the railroads agree to this scheme? There were several reasons. First, it removed the uncertainty of cutthroat competition. Oil traffic was guaranteed in large volume and apportioned so that, for example, the Pennsylvania got 45 percent of eastbound shipments from the oil regions, the Erie 27.5 percent, and the New York Central 27.5 percent. Second, the refiners agreed to provide services to the railroads, such as tank cars, loading facilities, and insurance. And third, railroad executives were offered stock in the participating refineries. This gave them a large stake in their success.

The consequences of the South Improvement Plan were predictable. Nonparticipating refineries would face unreasonably high transportation costs and be noncompetitive with the conspirators. They would have two choices. Either they could sell to Rockefeller and his cohorts, or they could stand on principle and go bankrupt. The appeal of the former would encourage horizontal integration, the acquisition of other firms at the refining level. Refinery capacity would be limited and price stabilization would occur because a combination of refiners could keep down the price of crude. Rockefeller believed that the industry could thus be "rationalized."

The Oil War of 1872

Inevitably, such a vast conspiracy could not long be concealed. In February 1872 the new freight rates went into operation. Their advent was greeted by widespread and explosive rage in the industry, and the full outlines of the agreement were quickly revealed. Producers and refiners in the oil regions rebelled and boycotted the conspirators and the railroads. Rockefeller was correctly regarded as the prime mover behind the South Improvement Plan, and his reputation was scorched by public attacks throughout the Pennsylvania oil regions. His wife feared that Rockefeller's life was in danger, but he was steadfast in his belief that the plan was right. He said of the plan: "It was right. I knew it as a matter of conscience. It was right between me and my God."[11] Indeed, as historian Ida Tarbell noted, Rockefeller was not squeamish about such business affairs.

> Mr. Rockefeller was "good." There was no more faithful Baptist in Cleveland than he. Every enterprise of that church he had supported liberally from his youth. He gave to its poor. He visited its sick. He wept with its suffering. Moreover, he gave unostentatiously to many outside charities of whose worthiness he was satisfied. . . . Yet he was willing to strain every nerve to obtain for himself special and unjust privileges from the railroads which were bound to ruin every man in the oil business not sharing them with him.[12]

Within a month the weight of negative public opinion and loss of revenue caused the railroads to cave in. They rescinded the discriminatory rate structure. Some oil producers tried to boycott Rockefeller's refineries in Cleveland, but the effort soon faltered. Thus, the battle ended.

All appearances were of a Rockefeller defeat. But in this case appearances deceived. After the South Improvement Plan had been drawn up, but before it was exposed, Rockefeller quickly met one-by-one with rival refiners in Cleveland. Because of overcapacity and vicious price-cutting most were doing poorly. He explained the rebate scheme and its salutary effect on the industry and then asked to buy out his competitor. He offered the exact value of the business in cash or, preferably, in stock of the Standard Oil Company. In a few cases, strongly competent managers were asked to become Standard employees.

By the time the railroads reset their rates, Rockefeller had purchased twenty-one of his twenty-six Cleveland competitors. Some acquisitions were simply dismantled to reduce surplus capacity. He now dominated Cleveland, the country's largest refining center, and controlled over a quarter of U.S. ca-

---

[11]Collier and Horowitz, op. cit., pp. 24–25.
[12]Tarbell, op. cit., vol. I, p. 102.

pacity. Furthermore, he soon negotiated a secret new rebate agreement with Commodore Vanderbilt's Erie Railroad giving him renewed advantage in transportation costs. Of these actions Ida Tarbell noted sardonically: "He had a mind which, stopped by a wall, burrows under or creeps around."[13] If any circumstance cast a shadow over this striking victory, it was that public opinion had turned against him. Henceforth, he was reviled as an unfair competitor, hatred of him growing apace with his burgeoning wealth. He never understood why.

ONWARD THE COURSE OF EMPIRE

By this time Rockefeller, now thirty-three, was a wealthy man. But he drove on, compelled to finish a grand design, to spread his pattern over the entire industry landscape, to conform it to his vision.

He continued the strategy of horizontal integration at the refinery level by absorbing more and more of his competitors. Between 1872 and 1875 he branched out from Cleveland and purchased major refineries in the other refining centers—New York, Pittsburgh, Philadelphia, and the Pennsylvania oil regions. These acquisitions were the seeds of domination in each area. In assimilating the new refineries he recapitalized Standard Oil from $2,500,000 to $3,500,000, creating additional shares of stock to pay for even more acquisitions. He then began a relentless campaign to exterminate remaining competitors.

As the size of Standard Oil increased, Rockefeller gained added leverage over the railroads. At the time there were three competing railroads—the Erie, the New York Central, and the Pennsylvania—with routes between Cleveland, the Pennsylvania oil regions, and the East Coast. Like an orchestra conductor he played them against each other, granting shares of the oil traffic in return for rebates and drawbacks that gave him a decisive advantage over competitors.

Some competitors stubbornly clung to their businesses, but Rockefeller made them "sweat" and "feel sick" until they sold.[14] Some refiners were unable to obtain enough crude oil because tank cars owned by Standard were unavailable.[15] A lubricant manufacturer who had used 510 barrels of residuum weekly was cut to 72. Rockefeller kept many of his acquisitions a secret to conceal the full sweep of his drive to monopoly. These companies were the Trojan horses of Rockefeller's war against the independent refiners. They proclaimed opposition to Standard Oil and appeared independent but secretly conspired to undermine Standard's competitors. The conspiracy was elaborate, involving code words used in letters and telegrams such as "morose" for

---

[13]Ibid., p. 99.

[14]Abels, op. cit., p. 110.

[15]In *John D. Rockefeller's Secret Weapon,* his study of the Union Tank Car Company, Albert Z. Carr advances the thesis that control of tank cars was the crucial element in Rockefeller's blitzkrieg of independent refiners (New York: McGraw-Hill, 1962).

the Standard, "doubters" for refiners, "druggist" for Philadelphia, and "mixer" for railroad drawbacks. The phantom competitors bought refiners who refused in principle to sell out to Standard Oil. Their existence confronted independents with a dark, mysterious force that could not be brought into the light in order to be fought.

The Standard Oil Trust

By the late 1870s the Standard Oil Company had grown unusually large, and it soon pioneered a new method of organization. It was chartered as a stock corporation in Ohio, but Ohio and all other states prohibited one company from owning the stock of another. At first, Rockefeller had used two legal but awkward methods of binding his acquisitions into Standard Oil. He either let the firms remain independent while working for the interests of Standard Oil Company of Ohio or transferred all their stock to a Standard executive, who then owned the subsidiary companies and operated them at Rockefeller's bidding. As Standard Oil grew, however, these methods of organization made centralized control increasingly difficult.

In 1879 a lawyer hired by Rockefeller suggested transferring stock in all the subsidiaries to three trustees, who would then manage them for the stockholders. This was done, and the three trustees were loyal managers of Standard Oil of Ohio. Rockefeller was not one of them. Technically, the companies would no longer belong to the Standard Oil Company of Ohio, and while the company operated under this trust agreement, Rockefeller gave sworn testimony that its subsidiaries were not under his control. This was a thin legal subterfuge. Although the trustees were legally charged with operating the companies in the trust for the benefit of stockholders of the Standard Oil Company of Ohio, behind the scenes Rockefeller and his top hands were very much in control.

In 1882 a more definitive trust arrangement was invented. In it, thirty-nine subsidiaries and Standard Oil of Ohio conveyed their stock to nine trustees— Rockefeller and eight of his cronies. The nine, in turn, issued trust certificates to the stockholders of participating companies and managed the companies. This was the Standard Oil Trust. It was conservatively capitalized at $70,000,000 and produced 90 percent of the nation's refining output. Its uniqueness was that it was an ordinary common-law trust, not a corporation chartered by any state. It became the model for trusts in other industries of that day and was an organizational form that perplexed critics and frustrated state regulators for years. In 1889 Rockefeller again reorganized Standard Oil as a holding company in New Jersey to keep one step ahead of the antitrust regulators.

Standard Oil was headquartered at 26 Broadway in New York, and it was from there that Rockefeller directed his far-flung empire. He worked with a loyal inner circle of managers. As he had absorbed his competitors, so had he co-opted the best business minds in the industry, and business historians attribute much of the Standard's success to this stellar supporting cast. Of them the great entrepreneur William Vanderbilt once said: "There is no question about it but these men are smarter than I am a great deal. . . . I never came in contact with any class of men as smart and able as they are in their business."[16] Though dominant, Rockefeller delegated great responsibility to his managers by running the giant company with a system of committees.

His management style was one of formal politeness. He never spoke harshly to any employee. The perfectionist instinct remained strong. He insisted on having a statement of the exact net worth of Standard Oil on his desk every morning. Oil prices were always calculated to three decimal places. On the way to work he penciled notes on the cuff of his sleeve. Each day he gathered all his managers in an elegant lunchroom at 26 Broadway. It was always a business lunch—another efficiency. At night he prowled the headquarters turning down oil lamps. His mind was tightly focused on business; he had little interest in the art, science, or philosophy of his era. He read the Bible daily but seldom any other book. His own biographical work, *Random Reminiscences,* is unnaturally shallow and simplistic, filled with homiletic wisdom and devoid of intellectual depth.[17] No Marcus Aurelius here. After business hours he returned home to be with his family. By now he had five children and spent considerable time with them, remembering, perhaps, the long absences of his own father.

Compared with other moguls of the Gilded Age he lived simply. He had a 79-acre estate in Cleveland and a New York mansion, but neither was overly ostentatious. Unlike other multimillionaires of the era he had no yacht. He continued to attend a Baptist church and exhibited large and small charities. He sent his old shoes to the poor, leaving them on doorsteps at night with a note about how to care for them. He tipped by extending a hand filled with coins and allowing the waiter or coachman to take what he wanted.

Extending Domination

By the 1880s Standard Oil had overwhelming market power. Its embrace of refining activity was virtually complete, though Rockefeller wisely left some competitors for two reasons. First, a few independent refiners who survived in prosperous markets could be made to reduce output in any economic downturn while the Standard continued to operate at full capacity. And second, state and federal antitrust statutes increasingly endangered large trusts which appeared to have no competitors. The Standard also engaged in backwards vertical integration, buying drilling operations, pipelines, and storage facilities. Through rebate agreements with the railroads it was quasi-vertically integrated in transportation.

Given Rockefeller's passion for completeness, it was inevitable that Stan-

---

[16]Collier and Horowitz, op. cit., pp. 37–38.
[17]New York: Doubleday, 1909.

dard Oil would attempt further forward integration into the marketing of re-fined products such as kerosene, paraffin, turpentine, varnish, benzine, naph-tha, asphalt, lubricants, and gasoline. By now the world was addicted to kerosene as a general illuminator and to other distillates for a variety of uses. Until the 1890s, when the development of oil deposits in Russia and the growth of the Royal Dutch Petroleum Company took away about 40 percent of the world market, virtually the only source of illuminant was the Pennsylvania crude refined by Standard Oil. U.S. exports of petroleum products rose from 80 million gallons in 1868 to 418 million gallons in 1879.[18] Rockefeller orga-nized overseas marketing arms and sales campaigns. In China and the East Indies, for example, Standard gave away small tin lamps, and oil product ex-ports jumped from 10 million gallons in 1877 to 25 million gallons in 1878.[19]

Standard Oil set up regional marketing companies in the United States. Each was ordered by 26 Broadway to dominate retail sales in its geographic area and to destroy most independent suppliers. To this end a distribution net-work of marvelous efficiency spread all the way to California. Standard sup-pliers pioneered fanatical customer service of the type trumpeted a century later in the book *In Search of Excellence*.[20] To suppress competition Rockefeller's agents characteristically used more questionable tactics as well.

The company perfected a competitor intelligence-gathering network. A bookkeeper at one independent refinery was offered $25 to pass information to Standard Oil. Railroad agents were turned into company detectives and bribed to misroute shipments. On many an occasion Standard Oil employees climbed atop a competitor's tank cars and examined the contents to see what was being shipped. Each Standard agent was required to submit a detailed report of com-petitor activity in the area.

A second weapon was price warfare. A competitor often found Standard selling oil at a price substantially below production cost. No competitor was too small to escape threats or retribution. In the 1890s, when oil was still sold from horse-drawn wagons, one driver in Ohio received the following note from a grocer who had been retailing his oil products.

> The Standard agent has repeatedly told me that if I continued buying oil and gasoline from your wagon they would have it retailed here for less than I could buy. I paid no attention to him, but yesterday their agent was here and asked me decidedly if I would continue buying oil and gasoline from your wagon. I told him I would do so: then he went and made arrangements with the dealers that handle their oil and gas-oline to retail it for seven cents.[21]

Of course, a pervasive scheme of rebates and drawbacks, unmatched by com-petitors, underlay the ability to undersell.

---

[18]Henry Demarest Lloyd, "Story of a Great Monopoloy," *The Atlantic,* March 1881, p. 320.
[19]Ibid. See also Ralph W. Hidy and Muriel E. Hidy. *Pioneering in Big Business: 1882–1911.* New York: Harper & Brothers, 1955, pp. 259 and 547.
[20]Thomas J. Peters and Robert H. Waterman, Jr. New York: Warner Books, 1982.
[21]Tarbell, op cit., vol. II, p. 49.

A third tactic was the use of phantom companies. Many oil retailers despised Standard Oil or rejected monopoly in principle. They would, even at great risk and trouble, buy from independents. These retailers would be approached by a company which claimed the ability to undercut the prices of the firm from which the dealer bought. Over time this new company, which was secretly affiliated with the Standard, would undercut its rivals and win the business. Then the front company and Standard Oil would raise prices in unison.

Independents probably used similar weapons against Standard from time to time, a relevant fact in assessing their ethical propriety. As one historian notes:

> . . .the circumambient ethics and morality in business practices of those days, or the lack of it, are not comparable with those of the present day. Men fought bare-fisted for business conquest, without benefit of Marquis of Queensberry rules, as they did in the prize ring. No quarter was given and none was expected; no one was expected to be his brother's keeper.[22]

Rockefeller himself was never proved to be personally involved in any flagrant misconduct. He blamed criminal and unethical actions on overzealous employee behavior. His critics said the strategy of suffocating small rivals and policies such as that requiring regular written intelligence reports encouraged degenerate ethics among his minions. Certainly, the Standard colossus operated by tactics that must have chilled the hearts of those who carried them out. A historian describes the debasing of the local Standard agent.

> Prodded constantly by letters and telegrams from superiors to secure the countermand of independent oil, confronted by statements of the amount of sales which have gotten away from him, information he knows only too well to have been secured by underhand means, obliged to explain why he cannot get this or that trade away from a rival salesman, he sinks into habits of bullying and wheedling utterly inconsistent with self-respect.[23]

Rockefeller, however, saw Standard Oil as a stabilizing force in the industry and as a righteous crusade to illuminate the world. How, as a good Christian devoted to the moral injunctions of the Bible, was Rockefeller able to suborn such vicious behavior in business? His biographer Allan Nevins gives one explanation:

> From a chaotic industry he was building an efficient industrial empire for what seemed to him the good not only of its heads but of the general public. If he relaxed his general methods of warfare . . . a multitude of small competitors would smash his empire and plunge the oil business back to chaos. He always believed in what William McKinley called "benevolent assimilation"; he preferred to buy out rivals on decent terms, and to employ the ablest competitors as helpers. It was when his terms were refused that he ruthlessly crushed the "outsiders." . . . It seemed to him

[22]Abels, op. cit., p. 92.
[23]Tarbell, op. cit., vol. II, pp. 56–57.

better that a limited number of small businesses should die than that the whole industry should go through a constant process of half-dying, reviving, and again half-dying.[24]

THE STANDARD OIL TRUST UNDER ATTACK

Standard Oil continued to grow. Total net assets doubled from $72 million in 1883 to $147 million in 1896 and then doubled again in less than ten years to $315 million in 1905.[25] But eventually its very size brought a flood of criticism that complicated operations. For example, because the Standard was battling antitrust regulators in Texas, it was largely excluded from early development of the massive southwestern deposits heralded by the Spindletop gusher in 1901. Competitors such as Gulf Oil Company became entrenched in this new oil field, grabbing stronger positions in production, refining, and marketing.

A Permissive Business Environment

The growth of Standard Oil from a Cleveland refinery to the nation's largest trust paralleled the explosive growth of the general economy after the end of the Civil War. After 1865 the existing economy of local markets, small businesses, and hand production rapidly evolved into one of national markets, asset-rich corporations, and mechanized production. Between 1860 and 1900 capital investment in manufacturing grew from $1 billion to $10 billion, those employed from 1.3 to 5.3 million, and the value of the annual product from $1.9 billion to $12 billion.[26] This dazzling commercial efflorescence, from which unfolded the great blossom of Rockefeller's Standard Oil Company, occurred in a societal environment that strongly supported industry.

The basic economic philosophy of this era was set forth by Adam Smith in his *Wealth of Nations* in 1776. Smith wrote that the common good was best served when individuals bought and sold in a free market. Unrestricted competition among buyers and sellers regulated supply and demand and protected all parties from harm or injustice. In the laissez-faire economy idealized by Smith government regulation of companies was sharply limited to maintaining impartial rules. Smith's view of economic life was widely accepted by both intellectuals and the common citizen.

To this permissive ideology was soon added another—social Darwinism. Social Darwinism was a theory popularized by the English philosopher Herbert Spencer. Spencer believed that societies and their subparts, such as the business system, were evolving toward greater perfection. This evolution

---

[24]Allan Nevins. *Study in Power: John D. Rockefeller.* New York: Charles Scribner's Sons, 1953, vol. II, p. 433.

[25]Ibid., vol. II, app. III, p. 478.

[26]Louis B. Wright et al. *The Democratic Experience.* Chicago: Scott, Foresman and Company, 1963, p. 238.

was based on a social mechanism similar to the biological mechanism of natural selection. There is, wrote Spencer, "a stern discipline, which is a little cruel that it may be very kind."[27] Stronger and superior elements of society were able to adapt to change, while weaker and inferior elements fell by the wayside. This was the normal course of social evolution, and the temporary suffering it caused was necessary to achieve ultimate perfection. Hence, when a large trust ingested smaller competitors, its gluttony furthered the course of evolution. A spinning-mill owner who forced women to work 18-hour days could be praised for weeding out the less fit. Spencer published his theory in 1850, nine years before Charles Darwin's *Origin of Species,* but Darwin's explanation of the biological laws of evolution, when published, gave Spencer's disciples added conviction.

During the so-called Gilded Age—the years of runaway industrial growth, materialism, and fortune accumulation between 1870 and the turn of the century—Spencer enjoyed an astonishing vogue in America. His theories sanctioned the raw competitive tactics of Rockefeller and his cohorts by making them appear part of a cosmic order that could be verified by science. Spencer made the free market predations of monopolists appear to be socially useful, and they embraced his philosophy. Railroad executive James J. Hill said that "the fortunes of railroad companies are determined by the law of survival of the fittest."[28] Andrew Carnegie exulted that when he first read Spencer, "I remember that light came in as a flood and all was clear."[29] By the time of Spencer's death in 1903 Americans had purchased 400,000 copies of his books, an unprecedented number for philosophical works. But because Rockefeller was a lifelong member of a fundamentalist Baptist church and believed in the inerrancy of the Bible, it is doubtful that he accepted the new theory of evolution. For this reason, and because he was disinterested in philosophy, it is unlikely that he ever embraced social Darwinism.[30] But its widespread acceptance during the years when he built Standard Oil enhanced tolerance of the tactics he used.

[27]*Social Statics.* New York: Robert Schalkenbach Foundation, 1970, p. 288. This book was first published in 1851.

[28]Quoted in Richard Hofstadter. *Social Darwinism in American Thought,* rev. ed. New York: George Braziller, Inc., 1955, p. 45.

[29]*Autobiography of Andrew Carnegie.* Boston: Houghton Mifflin, 1920, p. 327.

[30]A famous quotation allegedly made in a Sunday school class is often erroneously attributed to John D. Rockefeller:

> The growth of a large business is merely a survival of the fittest. . . . The American Beauty rose can be produced in the splendor and fragrance which bring cheer to its beholder only by sacrificing the early buds which grow up around it. This is not an evil tendency in business. It is merely the working-out of a law of nature and a law of God.

See, for example, Hofstadter, loc. cit. But this statement was actually made by his son, John D., Jr.

The Business Environment Changes

Even as Standard Oil and other trusts grew, however, their impact on society slowly eroded the permissive climate. Predatory monopoly was at odds with traditional assumptions about individual rights and free competition. Some great entrepreneurs were brazenly dishonest even by the standards of that day, bribing politicians, creating false balance sheets, and unconscionably abusing workers. As the factory system grew and created the great industrial cities, immigrants and laborers lived in parlous slums lacking sanitation, proper housing, and schools. The worst precincts were marred by festering poverty, disease, and crime. This human misery, a by-product of industrial growth, stood in poignant contrast to the consumptive displays of tycoons that characterized the Gilded Age. Andrew Carnegie shipped a castle over from Scotland, stone by stone. Others raided Europe, buying great works of art for astonishing prices. J. P. Morgan bought a Jan Vermeer oil painting one day for $100,000, even though he had never before heard of the artist. Pompous industrialists outdid each other with spectacular dinner parties. At one, guests were invited to dig emeralds and diamonds from a sandbox to take home as party favors. Another was given by a man for his dog's birthday. The dog received a $15,000 diamond-studded collar.[31]

A Whirlwind of Public Criticism

By the 1880s Rockefeller and the Standard Oil Company began to feel the sting of public calumny. The first stirrings of adversity were regulatory initiatives. In 1887 the Interstate Commerce Commission was established to regulate railroad rate structures, making them "reasonable and just." Initially, however, the commission lacked enforcement powers and was unable to curtail under-the-table rebates and drawbacks. In 1889 Kansas passed the first law designed to limit monopolistic practices, and by 1891 fifteen states had antitrust statutes. In 1892 the Supreme Court of Ohio declared Standard Oil to be in violation of its antitrust law and ordered dissolution, an order it was never able to enforce. In 1890 Congress passed the Sherman Act, which made illegal "every contract, combination in the form of trust or otherwise, or conspiracy in restraint of trade or commerce." This was the law that would ultimately dismember Standard Oil, but the Supreme Court, in the 1895 case of *United States* v. *E. C. Knight Co.*, temporarily gutted it by holding that manufacturing was not an interstate activity and, hence, not subject to federal regulation.[32]

Some of the muckraking masterpieces of this era are diatribes against Standard Oil. In 1881 the journalist Henry Demarest Lloyd scorched Standard Oil

---

[31]Matthew Josephson. *The Robber Barons: The Great American Capitalists 1861–1901*. New York: Harcourt, Brace & World, 1934, p. 338.
[32]*United States* v. *E. C. Knight Co.*, 156 U.S. 1 (1895).

as a company by whose acts "hundreds and thousands of men have been ruined."[33] In 1894 his fiery book *Wealth against Commonwealth,* pictured Standard as an irresponsible monopoly.[34] Lloyd's work was followed in 1902 by a two-year series of articles in *McClure's Magazine* by the historian Ida Tarbell. These articles, soon published in a book entitled *The History of the Standard Oil Company,* were meticulous, detailed, and unflattering narratives of Rockefeller's stratagems.[35] They further lowered his public image.

He was the personification of greed in political cartoons, and politicians attacked him to build their popularity. Huey Long, the subject of the next essay in this book, was one such politician. The most prominent was Theodore Roosevelt, who was reelected to the presidency in 1904 after widespread attacks on Standard Oil and other trusts. Robert M. La Follette called him "the greatest criminal of the age."[36] Other politicians did Rockefeller's bidding. In 1908 newspaper publisher William Randolph Hearst printed letters from a top Standard Oil executive to Senator Joseph B. Foraker (R-Ohio) that caused a sensation. One letter requested action on legislation and was accompanied by a $15,000 check. Undoubtedly, this bribe was only one of many. The Standard Oil Company had, as was customary in those days, lubricated the palms of many politicians. Rockefeller himself gave huge sums to the Republican party in presidential election years—$250,000 in 1896, $250,000 in 1900, and $125,000 in 1904.

Rockefeller, by now the richest man in the nation, was shaken by public hatred. Feeling that his life was endangered, he hired bodyguards and slept with a revolver. At church on Sundays gawkers and shouters appeared, forcing the hiring of Pinkerton detectives to guard services. He developed a digestive disorder so severe that he could eat only a few bland foods, and upon his doctor's advice he stopped daily office work. By 1896 he appeared only rarely at 26 Broadway. Soon he was afflicted with a nervous disorder, generalized alopecia, and lost all of his hair. Pictures taken after 1904 show him hairless or wearing one of the hairpieces he bought to hide his condition. He had several, each a little longer, to simulate two weeks of natural hair growth.

In 1905 a controversy erupted over him. He had donated $100,000 for missionary work by the Congregational church, but thirty ministers objected, saying that Rockefeller offered "tainted money," or money not rightfully his because it had been dishonestly acquired. Debate raged for months. One minister called Rockefeller "an appalling revelation of the kind of monster that a human being may become."[37] Some defended the contribution, noting that others' gifts were not similarly questioned. "If the gift is refused," said the *Missionary Review,* "every dollar thrown in the plate must be scrutinized and its

---

[33]Lloyd, op. cit., p. 327.
[34]New York: Harper & Bros., 1894.
[35]Tarbell, loc. cit.
[36]Nevins, op. cit., vol. II, p. 347.
[37]Collier and Horowitz, op. cit., p. 3.

John D. Rockefeller at age sixty-five. This photograph was taken shortly after a disease, generalized alopecia, caused him to lose his hair. (*Source: Library of Congress.*)

pedigree searched out. . . .''[38] The church kept the contribution, but Rockefeller was appalled by the national debate over his virtue.

Rockefeller maintained silence toward his critics, but ceaseless attacks convinced him of the need to defend himself lest he become an object of universal loathing. In 1906 Standard Oil hired one of the first corporate public relations experts in the country. This employee succeeded in planting many favorable stories about Rockefeller in the press. One of the methods used was to pay newspapers by the line to run stories written at 26 Broadway. Standard Oil also paid up to $3,000 for ''subscriptions'' to magazines which printed congenial stories.

As attacks on Rockefeller grew, the vise of government regulation slowly tightened on the company. Theodore Roosevelt's reelection in 1904 confirmed

---

[38]Abels, op cit., p. viii.

the tide of progressive reform and brought with it his pledge to break up large trusts. In 1906 the Hepburn Act corrected enforcement deficiencies plaguing the Interstate Commerce Commission and curtailed secret rebates for Standard Oil shipments. A swarm of lawsuits and legislative hearings hung about the company; there were twenty-three lawsuits brought by state governments alone. Rockefeller was often forced to testify. Characteristically, he gave parsimonious and bland responses exhibiting "an evasiveness that seemed to border on aphasia."[39]

Finally, on May 15, 1911, the Supreme Court reconsidered its position in the *Knight* case and in an 8-1 opinion ordered the breakup of Standard Oil Company.[40] The opinion, written by Chief Justice Edward White, held that Standard Oil's monopoly position in refining and pipeline transportation was an "undue" restraint on trade that violated the "standard of reason." The company was given six months to separate into thirty-nine independent firms and to distribute shares in each to stockholders. The breakup, which consisted mainly of moving the desks of managers at 26 Broadway and calculating share fractions for stockholders, was accomplished on time. Dismemberment was a financial windfall for Rockefeller. In 1911 he held 43 percent of the shares in the Standard Oil Company, and his shares were worth $190,000,000. There were 6,000 stockholders, but the shares were not traded on stock exchanges. After the breakup a frenzy for shares in the newly independent Standard Oil companies arose and drove up their prices. Within several months there were more than 300,000 stockholders, and their buying had increased the value of Rockefeller's holdings by $50,000,000.

At first the separate companies operated in tacit harmony; only gradually did competitive rifts arise among them. All prospered because of growth in demand for gasoline. Prior to 1911 kerosene sales had buoyed the company. But just as electric light bulbs were replacing oil lamps, the automobile gave a new jolt to demand for another petroleum distillate—gasoline. In 1900 only 8,000 automobiles were registered, but by 1910 the number had grown to 458,000, by 1915 to 2,491,000, and by 1925 to 19,941,000.[41] Rockefeller, who was seventy-one at the time of the breakup, would earn new fortunes simply by maintaining his equity in the separate companies. In fact, on just one day, September 29, 1916, rising oil-stock prices increased his wealth by $8,000,000!

THE GREAT ALMONER

Since childhood Rockefeller had made charitable donations, and as his fortune accumulated, he increased them. In 1855, the first year he worked, he gave

---

[39]Collier and Horowitz, op. cit., p. 42.
[40]*Standard Oil Company of New Jersey* v. *United States,* 31 U.S. 221.
[41]Hastings Wyman, Jr., "The Standard Oil Breakup of 1911 and Its Relevance Today," in Michael E. Canes, ed. *Witnesses for Oil: The Case against Dismemberment.* Washington, D.C.: American Petroleum Institute, 1976, pp. 72–73.

gifts of $2.77, and the total increased each year. By 1865 he gave over $1,000; by 1875, almost $5,000. After 1884 the total was never less than $100,000 a year, and after 1892 it was usually over $1,000,000 and sometimes far more. In his mind these benefactions were linked to his duty as a good Christian to uplift humanity. When Andrew Carnegie wrote an article in 1899 advocating that the rich should act as trustees for their wealth and scientifically donate to humanitarian causes, Rockefeller sent a letter of praise.[42] To a reporter he once said:

> I believe the power to make money is a gift from God—just as are the instincts for art, music, literature, the doctor's talent, yours—to be developed and used to the best of our ability for the good of mankind. Having been endowed with the gift I possess, I believe it is my duty to make money and still more money and to use the money I make for the good of my fellow-man according to the dictates of my conscience.[43]

Over his lifetime, Rockefeller gave gifts of approximately $550,000,000. He gave, for example, $8,200,000 for the construction of Peking Union Medical College in response to the need to educate doctors in China. He gave $50,000,000 to the University of Chicago. He created charitable trusts and endowed them with millions. One such trust was the General Education Board, set up in 1902, which started 1,600 new high schools. Another, the Rockefeller Sanitary Commission, succeeded in eradicating hookworm in the South. The largest was the Rockefeller Foundation, established in 1913 and endowed with $200,000,000. Its purpose was "to promote the well-being of mankind throughout the world." Rockefeller always said, however, that the greatest philanthropy of all was developing the earth's natural resources and employing people. Critics greeted his gifts with skepticism, thinking them atonement for years of plundering American society.

HIS LAST YEARS

Rockefeller lived twenty-six more years after the breakup of Standard Oil, most of them on his great Pocantico estate in New York, which had seventy-five buildings and 70 miles of roads. It was a placid existence. He lived by a strict routine, rising at 6:30 and following a precise schedule of meals and activities. The spacious house at Pocantico was designed so that the sun entered certain rooms at the hour he used them. Each day he golfed (even when snow had to be shoveled from the course), played a number-counting game called Numerica, and motored for two hours.

His business principles were never forsaken. He raised trees on the Pocantico estate and sold them at a profit to his other estates. When driving in

---

[42]The article, which has achieved lasting fame, is "Wealth," *North American Review*, July 1899.
[43]Quoted in Abels, op. cit., p. 280.

his car he picked out good tree specimens and bought them. A companion of his described the acquisition process.

> On his motor jaunts, he often comes across trees that he covets. He carefully notes the location and a few days later a poorly clad, farmer-like fellow appears and makes a bid. The owner, whether he refuses or accepts the offer, has not of course the slightest inkling that his splendid oak or maple is purposed to embellish the velvety expanse of Pocantico![44]

As years passed the public grew increasingly fond of Rockefeller. Memories of his early business career dimmed, and a new generation viewed him in the glow of his huge charitable contributions. He also continued to employ a top public relations manager. Perhaps at the behest of his groom for many years he carried shiny nickels and dimes in his pockets to give to children and well-wishers. On his eighty-sixth birthday he wrote the following verse:

I was early taught to work as well as play,
My life has been one long, happy holiday;
Full of work and full of play—
I dropped the worry on the way—
And God was good to me every day.

Rockefeller died suddenly of sclerotic myocarditis at the age of ninety-seven on May 23, 1937. His estate was valued at $26,410,837. He had given the rest away.

ASSESSING ROCKEFELLER'S LIFE

Rockefeller's remarkable career flamed like a meteor over a century of economic expansion, mixing strategic brilliance with ruthless ambition. Even his most competent biographers are unable to assess his achievements with finality. His nemesis, Ida Tarbell, concludes her book on Standard Oil with a chapter entitled "The Legitimate Greatness of the Company." The thorough and sympathetic biographer Allan Nevins calls attention to "the deadweight the Standard Oil hung upon business ethics."[45] Noted historian Daniel J. Boorstin calls him "a colossus of moral-legal ambiguity."[46]

Despite years of scholarship several questions continue to fascinate students of Rockefeller's life. First, how could he simultaneously be a devout Christian and a ruthless monopolist? Is there any contradiction between his personal and business ethics? Second, in the utilitarian sense of accomplishing the greatest benefit for society, was his creation of the Standard Oil monopoly a plus or minus? On balance, did the company meet its responsibilities to so-

---

[44]Winkler, op. cit., p. 242.
[45]Nevins, op. cit., vol. II, p. 433.
[46]In *The Americans: The Democratic Experience*. New York: Random House, 1973, p. 53.

ciety? And third, how would you evaluate his corporate strategy? Would any strategy aside from horizontal integration at the refining level have been as appropriate or successful? And could his strategy or another have been well implemented using "nicer" tactics?

MILESTONES IN THE LIFE OF JOHN D. ROCKEFELLER

1839	Born on July 8 in Richford, New York
1854	Moves to Cleveland, Ohio, to attend high school
1855	First job with Hewitt and Tuttle for $3.57 a week
1859	Enters into produce commission business with partners
1862	Invests with partner in a small refinery
1864	Marries Laura Spelman
1865	Buys out Clark for $72,500 and forms firm of Rockefeller and Andrews
1867	Buys out first competitive refinery
1868	Negotiates first secret rebates with railroads
1870	Incorporates Standard Oil Company, the largest refiner in America
1871	South Improvement Company formed at secret meeting
1872	Secret contracts signed with railroads, precipitating the "Oil War of 1872"
1881	Henry Demarest Lloyd makes first muckraking attack on Standard Oil in *The Atlantic*
1887	Interstate Commerce Commission begins railroad rate regulation
1889	Kansas passes first state antitrust law
1890	Congress passes the Sherman Act, making combinations in restraint of trade illegal
1894	Henry Demarest Lloyd publishes *Wealth against Commonwealth*
1904	Publication of Ida Tarbell's *The History of the Standard Oil Company.* In photos in the book Rockefeller is seen to have lost all his hair.
1905	"Tainted money" controversy with Congregational church
1906	Rockefeller hires a public relations consultant
1908	Rockefeller Sanitary Commission begins work to eradicate hookworm in South
1909	Rockefeller publishes *Random Reminiscences of Men and Events*
1911	Supreme Court breaks up the Standard Oil Company into thirty-nine separate companies
1913	Rockefeller Foundation chartered
1916	September 29, his wealth increases by $8 million in one day in the stock market
1937	Dies at ninety-seven years of age

EVERY MAN A KING: THE POPULISM OF HUEY LONG

This is the story of a remarkable life, a life buoyed by historical forces and molded by the American reform tradition.

In the 1920s Huey Long emerged from a backwoods parish to become virtual dictator of the state of Louisiana. His ironfisted tenure there would have earned him a permanent place in the annals of American politics. But ambition drove him onto the national scene as a U.S. senator in the depression era of the 1930s. Long advocated a plan to redistribute wealth from the rich to the poor and built a mass movement with millions of followers. Perhaps only fate released Franklin D. Roosevelt from the opportunistic devices which the ruthless Long had set in motion to end the New Deal and overthrow its chief architect.

Long had brilliance, lust for power, and excessive, neurotic energy. He was crude and audacious, caring little for the opinions of colleagues. By instinct he was a Machiavellian who reduced political opponents to inferiors. While he championed the cause of the common man, he was beyond the restraint of democratic institutions. By 1935 he dominated the Senate and was locked in mortal combat with Roosevelt. He was, in the words of a contemporary, "the pole-cat, wild ass, Messiah and enigma of American politics."[1]

The puzzle of how Long was able to grasp power in brazen defiance of democratic values and strong enemies is only partly solved by reference to his extraordinary personality. Full explanation requires an understanding of the deep

---

[1]Carleton Beals. *The Story of Huey P. Long*. Philadelphia: J. B. Lippincott Company, 1935, p. 14.

reform currents that he expertly rode to power and how the era of the Great Depression opened the door to its cynical exploitation.

Long built his early career around attacks on the Standard Oil Company. Later, he attacked other large corporations and family fortunes. The populist themes he brandished then are still used today against big business. Reconsideration of Huey Long and his era is a way of learning how these critical motifs arose and why they persist even today.

HUEY LONG: THE EARLY YEARS

Huey Pierce Long, Jr., was born in a rural agrarian area of northwest Louisiana on August 30, 1893, the eighth child of Huey and Caledonia Long. Although the Long family was financially secure and lived in a large house, deep poverty in Winn Parish surrounded Huey as he grew up (parish is the name given to counties in Louisiana). When he was eight years old, an impressionable Huey witnessed a farm auctioned away for debt. Prior to the sale the farmer pleaded with the crowd not to offer a bid for his place. As the parish sheriff opened the bidding, the crowd was silent. But finally, the man's creditor made an offer, and the farm was gone. In his autobiography Long recalled that "this marked the first sign, in my recollection, of a neighborhood, where the blessings of the Creator were shared one with the other, being transformed into a community yielding to commercial enticements."[2] It was a theme he would return to many times.

As a baby Huey was a whirlwind of energy, constantly in motion, crawling and wandering about, escaping his mother's watchful eye. Later, he ran to and from school. He earned average grades in the single-building schoolhouse he attended in the town of Winnfield. He liked reading and frequently memorized long passages. Once, he obtained an instructor's manual with an English translation of his Latin reader. He startled the teacher in class by reading and translating the day's lesson without any book on his desk. When asked how he did it, Huey impudently replied that he had X-ray vision. By all accounts, his favorite book was Alexander Dumas's *The Count of Monte Cristo*. This book, in which the hero makes bold revenge against his enemies after years of waiting, may have inspired the harsh treatment of his own political enemies later in life. He was also entranced by a biography of Napoleon. He was most familiar with the Bible, however, since his mother insisted it be studied and frequently read from it.

His brashness was renowned. While most Winnfield boys were trained to be silent in the company of adults, Huey frequently reduced his elders to spluttering with outspoken, pretentious advice on serious topics such as politics and checkers. When he was twelve, Huey scrutinized the seventh-grade courses at Winnfield elementary school and decided they were not worth his

[2]Huey P. Long. *Every Man a King: The Autobiography of Huey P. Long*. New Orleans: National Book Co., 1933, p. 4.

time. He determined to skip the seventh grade, and when school opened in the fall, he simply walked in and joined the eighth-grade class. The teacher accepted him. In high school, he thumbed his nose at community standards by conspicuously dating older women who were high school teachers in a nearby town. He signed his textbooks as the "Hon. Huey P. Long" and as a junior in high school announced that he was destined to be "Governor, Senator, and President of the United States."[3] During lunch hours he mounted a soapbox and declaimed rather than joining in games and conversation with other students.

As a high school junior Huey won a speech contest and was awarded a scholarship to Louisiana State University. He did not attend, however, because he had a disagreement with the principal at Winnfield over the need to complete a twelfth grade and never received a high school diploma.

Instead, Huey struck out on his own selling a cooking oil called Cottolene door-to-door. He proved himself to be a natural at sales and led the staff in orders. Years later he revealed the secrets of his dynamic sales pitch to a reporter.

> If I couldn't convince the woman no other way I'd go right into the kitchen and bake a cake for her, or cook supper for the family. I also used the Bible on them, showing where the Lord had forbidden the Israelites to use anything from the flesh of swine for food, and how cottonseed oil, seeing it was a vegetable product, was just bound to be pure.[4]

After several months selling Cottolene, Huey was laid off by the company and began a period of itinerate wandering and dead-end career initiatives. He worked as a stenographer, salesman for a meat packing company, and laborer at a railyard foundry. For a brief time he was so down on his luck that he slept on park benches in Memphis, Tennessee. Admitting failure, he contacted his family back in Louisiana and agreed, at his mother's request, that he should join his brother, a dentist in Shawnee, Oklahoma, and attend a Baptist seminary there.

Huey journeyed to Oklahoma with train fare wired by his brother and, apparently, enrolled at Oklahoma Baptist University. The school, however, has no record of his attendance, and it is uncertain where he spent his time. At the Christmas break, Huey announced that he wanted to be a lawyer rather than a minister and convinced his brother to give him enough money to enroll in law school at the University of Oklahoma in Norman. But on the trip to Norman he lost the money gambling and once again took a sales job to get some cash.

He worked successfully at sales while taking law classes at the university but became bored with school when he started earning a lot of money. He made average grades but so impressed his employer that he was promoted to head a sales division covering four states. He dropped out of law school at the

[3]T. Harry Williams. *Huey Long*. New York: Knopf, 1970, p. 39.
[4]Stan Opotowsky. *The Longs of Louisiana*. New York: E. P. Dutton & Co., 1960, p. 34.

end of the year. In 1913 he married Rose McConnell, a woman he had met in a baking contest sponsored by Cottolene. While courting her, Huey confided to the astonished Rose that he planned to be a minor state official, then Governor, Senator, and President of the United States. This information may have delayed rather than hastened the wedding day, as Rose was undecided about his mental stability for a time.

Shortly, Huey was laid off and jobless again. This time, on the promise of another brother to support him, he went to New Orleans and entered law school at Tulane University. Without a high school diploma he could not earn a degree, so he enrolled in a special category which permitted him to audit courses. He attended Tulane over the 1914–15 academic year, studying 16 to 20 hours a day to learn the three-year law curriculum in one year. He crammed and memorized. When he studied a book, he would read passages to Rose, who would type them for him. Then he would memorize the typed extract. In this way he learned enough law to pass an examination by a committee of lawyers and gain admittance to the bar, even though he had no law degree. The year was 1915. He was twenty-one years old.

LAW PRACTICE AND ENTRY INTO POLITICS

Huey returned to Winnfield, his boyhood home, and set out to build a law practice. His first office was a decrepit arrangement with two chairs, a table, and a kerosene lamp. His early cases were minor civil matters, but he earned the reputation of a defender of the poor.

The case that made his reputation was that of a widow who came to Huey because the Bank of Winnfield refused to pay her $276 embezzled by a bank officer. The widow had accepted a note promising repayment of this debt from the banker himself, but then he had fled the state. No other lawyer would touch the case. Her acceptance of the note placed her claim on weak legal ground, but more importantly, local lawyers were unwilling to alienate the town's powerful bankers. The widow came to Huey not knowing that the bank was owned by his uncle, George Long.

Huey, however, happened to be angered at his uncle because the bank had failed to honor a slight overdraft Huey had written. Huey, never one to forgive a slight, took the case and used the audacious tactics he frequently relied upon. He invited prospective jurors, strangers to him, to have dinner with him in public so that the bank's lawyers exercised their challenges on these "friends" of his who were seen with him. Huey then got the jury he wanted. He displayed the widow and her raggedly dressed children in the courtroom each day. He loudly and frequently accused the bank of being heartless and Uncle George of being greedy. The widow won. Huey made no money on this case, but in attacking and besting the most powerful institution in Winnfield, he elevated his standing and assured a busy law practice.

Shortly, Huey moved his office to Shreveport, where he worked at his office from five in the morning until after dark to build a new law practice. He specialized in workers' compensation and personal-injury lawsuits and continued to ably and successfully champion the disadvantaged. A biographer notes that he had a special weak spot for the poor.

> Once he and a friend passed on the street a poor woman and her ragged brood of children. He went on a few steps and then stopped. "That breaks my heart," he muttered. He went back and gave all the change in his pocket to the woman. At a conference in his office he became so affected by a client's recital of poverty that he broke down and wept before his partners, and then directed them to fight the case twice as hard for half the fee.[5]

At about this time Huey wrote a letter to the editor of the *New Orleans Item* in which he lamented the unfair distribution of wealth in the United States. He had found the theme that would define his political career.

> A conservative estimate is that about sixty-five or seventy per cent of the entire wealth of the United States is owned by two per cent of the people. Sixty-eight per cent of the whole people living in the United States own but two percent of its wealth. From the year 1890 to 1910, the wealth of this nation trebled, yet the masses owned less in 1910 than they did in 1890. . . . This is the problem that the good people of this country must consider.[6]

At one time Huey wrote amendments to the Louisiana workers' compensation law, and when a senate committee took them up, he traveled to the state capitol in Baton Rouge. He claimed to have met a mysterious man on his way to the capitol who informed him that the legislators were minions of big corporate interests, especially the Standard Oil Company of Louisiana. In the hearing, Huey was upset that the committee was not taking action on his amendments. He requested permission to speak but was denied. The chair ridiculed him, asking: "Whom do you represent?" "Several thousand common laborers," Huey replied. "Are they paying you anything?" "No," said Huey. "They seem to have good sense," retorted the senator.[7] Fuming, Huey waited until midnight, when the committee prepared to adjourn. He rose and could not be hushed. He accused the legislators of being "dominated by the henchmen and attorneys of the interests" and of ignoring the needs of families of injured laborers while fair-minded people "bowed their heads in regret and shame."[8] Huey was once again attacking a powerful target to draw attention to himself and win the admiration of common citizens. In the corrupt climate of Louisiana politics of that era his remarks were also accurate.

[5]Williams, op. cit., p. 96.
[6]In Long, op. cit., pp. 37–39.
[7]Ibid., p. 27.
[8]Ibid., p. 28.

Railroad Commissioner

After four years of law practice Huey decided to enter politics by running for railroad commissioner. He traveled in a shiny new car and spoke in white linen suits. Campaigning up to 20 hours a day, he often knocked on farmers' doors in the early morning hours to ask for a place to sleep. He was victorious by a small margin.

The Railroad Commission (later renamed the Public Service Commission) gave Huey a new platform to attack corporations. He began with an immediate attack on the Standard Oil Company of Louisiana, a wholly owned subsidiary of Standard Oil of New Jersey. During his political career Huey would attack Standard Oil over and over. His immediate grievance was personal. Several years before, Huey had invested in a small oil company which was soon bankrupted when Standard shut off pipeline services in an effort to drive independent companies out of business. Huey also knew that attacking the largest corporation in Louisiana would win votes.

As a railroad commissioner, he invited representatives of small oil companies to hearings to air their grievances. He created so much commotion that the business strategies and political influence of Standard Oil became a central issue in the Louisiana gubernatorial election of 1920. During the gubernatorial campaign Huey spoke at political rallies, declaring that Standard was an "octopus" and its executives "the nation's most notorious and leading criminals."[9] The winning candidate, John M. Parker, was forced to promise that as governor he would break Standard's pipeline monopoly in Louisiana oil fields and impose a fair tax on oil.

After Parker was elected, a new law was passed regulating Standard's pipeline operations and imposing a "temporary" tax on barrels of oil pumped from the ground. As it turned out, Parker had permitted Standard Oil lobbyists in New York to write the legislation, and this opened the door for the voluble Huey. When the legislature reconvened, each member found a mimeographed circular written by Huey on his desk. Huey proclaimed that Standard Oil had corruptly purchased the administration of Governor Parker and was controlling Louisiana politics from its headquarters at 26 Broadway in Manhattan. He asked if the legislators were "fallen chattels" under the control of Standard Oil.[10] The legislators were stunned by Huey's impudence, and the Louisiana House of Representatives threatened to remove Huey from his position as a railroad commissioner but failed to find a way. Governor Parker had Huey arrested and charged with criminal libel. At the trial he was convicted but fined only $1 by a sympathetic judge. Huey refused to pay the fine, so the judge and Huey's defense counsel each paid $0.50 for him. Thereafter, Huey's attacks on Standard continued unabated.

[9]Williams, op. cit., p. 128.
[10]Long, op. cit., p. 58.

Running for Governor against the Establishment

In 1923 Huey, at the age of thirty, ran for governor. In doing so he challenged the entrenched political machine in Louisiana. At the time, the politics of Louisiana was controlled by an economic oligarchy composed of an alliance between the old planter aristocracy and powerful industries such as oil, lumber, railroads, sugar, and banking, which dominated the state's economy. The presence of a similar, dominant coalition of interests was typical of many southern states in those days. But there were two differences in Louisiana.

First, since 1900 Louisiana had led the South in industrialization. A broad range of industries was economically important—a situation more typical of the states of the industrial North. The Standard Oil Company of Louisiana was, at the time, the largest corporation in any southern state, and its political influence was extensive. Economic interests were more politically active in Louisiana than elsewhere in the south and created a climate of conservatism. Taxes on business were among the lowest in the nation, and the poorly funded state government provided skimpy social services. Despite its strong economy, Louisiana in the 1920s ranked near the bottom of all forty-eight states in literacy, years of education, and average income.[11]

Second, the Louisiana elite had dominated state politics unchallenged longer than comparable oligarchies in other southern states. It was axiomatic that in these states populist demagogues emerged to challenge them. But in Louisiana the ruling oligarchy had ruthlessly suppressed opposition.[12] No significant left-wing challenge to its rule had been mounted since the 1830s. It had manipulated state elections for generations with a corrupt political machine in New Orleans that trafficked in false registration, vote buying, and intimidation. For example, citizens who voted against the machine would be arrested. Then witnesses to a trumped-up "crime" would materialize, and a jail term might follow.

Hence, at the time Huey entered the governor's race, Louisiana resembled more a feudal monarchy than a democratic polity. He would defy an elite that had wielded power for a century. He set out to forge a winning coalition of backwoods fur trappers, farmers, small merchants, and other forgotten people. He would arouse the ineffectual, the discouraged, and the have-nots. He would be, in the words of Arthur M. Schlesinger, Jr., "the Messiah of the Rednecks."[13]

He traveled the state in his automobile, campaigning with characteristic vigor. In each parish he attacked the boss who represented the machine, and he promised to release the average citizen from repression by wealthy interests. He promised "a new day in Louisiana." He accused Standard Oil of dominating state government and called his opponents minions of corporate

---

[11]Williams, op. cit., p. 186.
[12]V. O. Key. *Southern Politics in State and Nation*. New York: Random House, 1949, p. 160.
[13]*The Politics of Upheaval*. Boston: Houghton Mifflin, 1960, p. 42.

interests. His platform called for more social services, including construction of roads and highways, free textbooks for schoolchildren, and new mental institutions. He attacked concentrated wealth and the corruption of his machine-backed opponents. The election was marred by controversy over the Ku Klux Klan. Huey was not a race-baiting politician like many of his era, though he clearly held racist values. He considered race an extraneous and volatile issue to be avoided, but he tried to temporize on the issue and win voters on both sides. On election day he lost. He won the rural areas of the north, but not by enough to overcome the New Orleans vote turned against him by the machine.

Huey spent the next three years building political support and in 1927 again declared himself a candidate for governor. Again he threw himself into twenty hours a day of campaigning on the same issues. On the stump he spoke with feverish energy, dressed in a white linen suit with a diamond in the lapel. He attacked "corporate plutocrats" and promised better education and social services for the common citizen. He expertly ridiculed his two machine-backed opponents, describing them as two waiters serving different groups but adding that all the food came from the same kitchen.

He was ingenious in courting his constituency of commoners. During a fashionable luncheon at the home of wealthy supporters Huey startled everyone by suddenly sweeping his full silver place setting to the floor. He yelled: "Give me a knife and fork. I don't know how to handle all this cutlery."[14] Huey calculated that all the hillbillies who heard the story would warm to this mockery of wealth and vote for him. He reduced his audiences to tears of laughter with descriptions of the corrupt L. E. Thomas, mayor of Shreveport.

> You take a yearling and when he gets twelve or fourteen months old he gets ashamed of himself and weans himself automatically. You take the pig, even the hog is ashamed of himself and weans himself when he gets to be a good sized shoat. But you take a pie eater and trough feeder like L. E. Thomas who has been sucking the pap for thirty-five years. You cannot wean him at all.[15]

Huey won the election and became governor of Louisiana in 1928 at the age of thirty-five.

Governor Long

Huey was not immediately in a position of great power as governor because majorities in both houses of the state legislature opposed him. Nevertheless, he managed to pass legislation enacting some of his campaign promises with skillful use of political favors and the purchase of corrupt legislators. He built new highways into the country where previously farmers had traveled on mud trails. A program to give children free schoolbooks was begun. New bridges and tuberculosis hospitals were built.

---

[14]Quoted in Hermann B. Deutsch, "Prelude to a Heterocrat," *Saturday Evening Post,* September 1935, p. 86.
[15]In Williams, op. cit., p. 269.

He made strong use of political patronage, appointing loyal followers to positions around the state and building his own Long machine. Huey was without compunction in his use of patronage; even a hint of disloyalty could mean the loss of a job—not only for the individual but for friends and family as well. On one trip Huey stopped to converse with a bridge tender. Discovering that the man was friendly with a state senator who had turned disloyal, Huey saw to it that the man lost his job.[16] Huey had never shed his youthful audacity either. For example, when the legislature refused to appropriate money for a new governor's mansion, he waited for adjournment and then tore the old one down and built a new one without authorization. And he openly subsidized his political organization with widespread state employee paycheck deductions.

In his first year of office Huey consolidated power, but he made enemies. Early in the second legislative session of his term he made a rare mistake. Needing revenue for his programs and thinking that he had eclipsed the influence of his old whipping boy, Standard Oil, he proposed a new tax on each barrel of oil refined in the state. Although the initial tax was small, Standard perceived extreme danger in the precedent it would set. Covertly, company lobbyists crystallized anti-Long feeling, and a top lobbyist was sent from New York to spearhead a drive for his impeachment (though this was admitted only by the man's family after his death many years later). Shortly, the Louisiana House of Representatives passed a bill of impeachment stipulating nineteen charges, including bribing legislators, demolishing the governor's mansion, and suborning assassination of a state legislator. The Standard Oil Company band played at a big impeachment rally in New Orleans.

Some charges were false or trivial; others were accurate. But the Senate was never able to try them. First, Huey mounted a publicity campaign to get opinion on his side. He simplified the issue for the people. The moneyed interests, he said, were out to get him. One circular, passed out by state police, read: "I would rather go down to a thousand impeachments than to admit that I am the Governor of the State that does not dare to call the Standard Oil Company to account so that we can care for destitute, sick and afflicted."[17] Then, Huey summoned fifteen state senators, exactly the number needed to block impeachment, to the governor's mansion and made deals with them to sign a pledge not to impeach him. What he promised them remains secret to this day, but all were later appointed to high-paying state jobs. The failed impeachment left his opponents in disarray, and afterwards Long was ascendant in Louisiana politics.

LONG IN THE NATIONAL ARENA

Soon Huey declared that even though his term as governor would not end until 1932, he would run for the Senate in 1930. If he won, he promised to stay in

---

[16]Alan Brinkley. *Voices of Protest.* New York: Knopf, 1982, p. 26.
[17]Long, op. cit., p. 152.

Louisiana and complete his term before going to Washington, D.C. Outraged opponents attacked the plan as irresponsible, arguing that in the meantime the state would be underrepresented. Huey responded by attacking incumbent Senator Joseph Randsdall, a colorless drone of the New Orleans machine. "Vacant for a year or two? Why with Randsdall up there the Senate seat has been vacant for many years."[18] During the campaign Huey pinned the nickname "Feather Duster Randsdall" on his hapless opponent in reference to his goatee. The country folk laughed at this impertinence toward the staid aristocrat and gave Huey such a large majority in the Democratic primary that no runoff was necessary. After the election Huey kept his word and remained in the governor's job. When his term was about to expire, Huey picked O. K. Allen, a compliant old friend, to succeed him.

As he prepared to assume his Senate seat, Huey could point to a strong record of accomplishment as governor. His most visible legacy was in public works. Louisiana had 3,000 miles of new concrete and asphalt roads and thousands of additional miles of new gravel roads. The roads were crowned with twelve modern bridges, and a magnificent 7-mile seawall ran along the shores of Lake Pontchartrain. A new airport was under construction in New Orleans. In many other areas he also had kept his pledge to improve the lot of the commoner. A system of night schools improved literacy among adults. Children were given free school textbooks. General property taxes were reduced 20 percent and the poor exempted. The state had modernized sanitariums and a new medical school at Louisiana State University.

How had Louisiana paid for all this? Not by soaking the rich or redistributing wealth. During Huey's term the legislature levied thirty-five new taxes, but most were on consumer products. In addition, Huey freely and continuously issued revenue bonds and increased Louisiana's indebtedness from practically nothing at the start of his term to over $150 million in 1932. Most of the bond issues came due in twenty years, and later generations payed Huey's debts. At the time, the average Louisianan saw only the new roads and bridges and praised Huey.

The Great Depression

As Huey departed for Washington, D.C., in January 1932, the nation was in the grip of catastrophic, worsening depression. The downward spiral of the economy had been touched off by the collapse of the stock market in October 1929 and then continued because of deep flaws in the country's financial and industrial system.

Since the last major depression in the 1890s, Americans had enjoyed thirty years of rising prosperity. This prosperity was based on industrial progress abetted by government policies that encouraged business and overlooked

[18]Opotowsky, op. cit., p. 55.

many adverse societal impacts. Between 1900 and 1930 mass production techniques increased efficiency and output enormously. However, workers and farmers were not increasing their earnings fast enough to absorb the torrent of products spilling from the nation's prolific factories. The overextension of credit covered this growing problem until the collapse of the stock market imposed huge losses on rashly leveraged brokerage houses and banks. Panic set in. According to prevailing wisdom industry tried to maintain price levels, but lower sales led to layoffs of workers. Layoffs, in turn, led to increasing sales drops and further layoffs. Thus a downward spiral cruelly oppressed the economy. The result was the worst depression the nation had experienced.

By 1932 the value of stocks on the New York Stock Exchange was 11 percent of their 1929 value. The GNP fell from $104 billion to $41 billion during the same period. The wages of industrial workers fell by 60 percent. Farmers, who had not enjoyed prosperity prior to the depression era, saw income from their farms drop from $12 billion to $5.3 billion. Pretax corporate profits plummeted from $9.8 billion to $−3.0 billion. Auto sales dropped 80 percent and production fell from a high of 5.6 million cars in 1929 to only 1.4 million in 1932. Steel mills were operating at 20 percent of capacity.[19]

Government had done little to blunt the force of the depression as it worsened. President Herbert Hoover refused to stimulate the economy through federal intervention; he believed that doing so would threaten individual freedom and liberty. Most leading economists supported this laissez-faire view, and business leaders, overwhelmingly committed to the extreme ideology of social Darwinism, coldly lectured that the depression was essential, since it weeded out weaker firms. Hoover believed that if only confidence in business could be restored, the private enterprise system would again create prosperity. Several months after the stock market crash he said that the worst would be over in sixty days, and he kept up a stream of optimistic prognostications.

Believing that Americans would despair if he lost faith, Hoover tried to be a symbol of prosperity by dressing in black tie each evening for a complete seven-course dinner at the White House.[20] When Congress passed a $2 billion relief bill, he vetoed it and only permitted a $25 million authorization to feed starving farm animals on the condition that a bill to spend $120,000 to feed hungry people be shelved. Belatedly, however, Hoover realized the depths of the problem and sensed the need to use the powers of government to shore up the economy. His major programs—the Reconstruction Finance Corporation, which extended federal credit to banks, and the Federal Home Loan Bank Board, which aided people who faced foreclosure of home mortgages—were needed measures but insufficient to revive the economy. The Hoover administration was discredited, a source of parody. Urban shantytowns were called

---

[19]These figures are from George A. Steiner. *The Government's Role in Economic Life*. New York: McGraw-Hill, 1953, p. 156.

[20]William Manchester. *The Glory and the Dream*. Boston: Little, Brown and Company, 1973.

"Hoovervilles." The newspapers a hobo used to keep warm were "Hoover blankets."

Outside the White House human misery mounted. Over 15,000,000 workers, 23.6 percent of the work force, were unemployed and had little prospect of finding a job. In New York, men who had once been teachers, engineers, brokers, and millionaires lined up each morning at the Apple Growers' Association depot on Manhattan's Lower East Side. There they bought apples they polished and sold for a nickel on street corners. In Chicago, teachers had been paid in only five of the previous twelve months. Of 2,400 teachers in that city 1,000 were laid off, and 759 of the 1,400 remaining lost their homes.[21] In other states schools were closed for extended periods or open only several days a week. Most city school districts prohibited employment of wives on the basis of the assumption that a working wife deprived a male breadwinner of income.

In every city there were food lines of unemployed, homeless, and hungry men, women, and children. Millions of hoboes traveled the highways and railroads of the land, and millions in the cities lived by scavenging through garbage dumps and household refuse. In restaurants hungry diners ordered tea for a nickel and mixed the catsup on the counter with hot water to make a kind of tomato soup. Farmers fared no better than city folk. Prices for crops dropped precipitously to the point where the price of a wagonload of potatoes would buy no more than one pair of shoes. Thousands of farmers lost their farms and were destitute. In the midst of this nationwide hunger President Hoover made one of the great political gaffes in American history when he permitted himself to be photographed feeding his pet dog on the White House lawn.

Hard times undermined respect for the social contract. There was a wildness in the air. Mobs in Oklahoma City, Minneapolis, and St. Paul broke into grocery stores to steal food. In the Pacific Northwest men set forest fires so they could be employed to fight them. The wealthy began to fear the desperation of the poor, and there was an ominous rumbling of class violence. Some spoke openly of the need for revolution. In the country armed farmers patrolled their land to prevent foreclosure. In the cities where crowds of idle men collected, jealousy of wealth was a source of unity. In Times Square a Communist party rally attracted 35,000 listeners. When Congress reconvened briefly in December 1931, its members were met by a mob of 2,500 people chanting: "Feed the hungry, tax the rich! Feed the hungry, tax the rich."[22]

These were the prevailing, abject conditions when the hour struck for Huey Long on the national stage.

Senator Long

Huey's first day in the Senate was January 25, 1932. Senate tradition holds that new senators are escorted to the vice president's chair to take their oath by the

---

[21]Ibid., p. 47.
[22]Ibid., p. 64.

Huey Long raising his hand as he was sworn in on the floor of the U.S. Senate in 1932. (*Source: Courtesy Louisiana State Museum.*)

senior senator from their state. But Huey had fallen out with Louisiana's senior senator, Edwin Broussard, and angrily refused to walk with him. Another senator volunteered, and Huey walked in, carrying a lighted cigar in violation of Senate rules, slapping new acquaintances on the back and giving others a friendly elbow in the ribs. On his second day, in defiance of Senate tradition that freshman senators spend a long apprenticeship period of silent observation, he spoke up for the first time and was voluble thereafter.

After three days, however, Huey left Washington, D.C., and took the train back to Louisiana to reassert his dominance of state government. In fact, during his first 139 days in the Senate he spent 81 in Louisiana. Even though he held no official position, he convened and addressed the state legislature at will, determined the agendas for its committees, made all patronage appointments, and sat in the office of the compliant Governor Oscar Allen to conduct his business. Governor Allen was so supine in Huey's presence that he followed instructions unquestioningly. Huey's brother Earl Long once joked that "a leaf blew off a tree and through the window onto Oscar's desk one day, and Oscar signed it."[23]

Back in the Senate, Huey began trumpeting his solutions for the ills of depression. He advocated federal farm surplus controls, limiting the workweek

[23]Opotowsky, op. cit., p. 62.

to 30 hours, deficit spending, and lowered tariffs. But his central theme was the need to redistribute wealth. "I had come to the United States Senate with only one project in mind," he said, "which was that by every means of action and persuasion I might do something to spread the wealth of the land among all of the people."[24]

Huey rose in the Senate in March to blame the depression on maldistribution of wealth. "The country has been going toward communism ever since the wealth of this country began to get into the hands of a few people," he cried.[25] In April came a major address in which he called upon Congress to enact higher inheritance and income taxes before starving people were moved to revolution. The wealthy should not oppose him, he said. Of his ideas he said: "It is no campaign to soak the rich. It is a campaign to save the rich. It is a campaign the success of which they will wish for when it is too late."[26] And later that month Huey proposed a revenue bill amendment prohibiting any citizen from earning more than $1 million a year or from inheriting or receiving gifts of more than $5 million over a lifetime. When the measure got only a few votes, Huey attacked the other Democrats in the Senate for being afraid to anger the rich and insensitive to the needs of the poor and hungry. Dramatically, he resigned all his committee memberships, an unheard-of action.

In attacking the Democratic party he employed a familiar tactic. By pitting himself against a large target he assumed increasing stature. He offended party leadership, but destitute people around the country took notice of this new advocate of the poor in Washington, D.C. Soon he announced that there was no difference between Democrats and Republicans. Hooverism, he said, controlled the Senate, "spouting through two foghorns."[27] This was the same technique he had used to ridicule his political opponents in Louisiana.

In his first months in the Senate Huey proved nettlesome to the leadership, and his blustering speeches were crowd pleasers for tourists who jammed the galleries on days when he spoke. But that summer he executed a bold stroke that showed he was a political force to be reckoned with. In the Senate that year was Mrs. Hattie Caraway, widow of Senator Thaddeus Caraway, who had been charitably unopposed in a special election to fill her late husband's seat eight months before. She faced five opposing candidates in the summer of 1932 and no longer had the endorsement of the Arkansas Democratic party. No one gave her a chance for reelection to a full term. No one except Huey. Mrs. Caraway had been one of the few to vote for Huey's wealth-limiting amendment, and he decided to campaign for her. He went to Arkansas to stump for her, touring the state with a caravan of sound trucks.

At each stop he announced that he was in the state to "pull a lot of potbellied politicians off a little woman's neck."[28] Then he made a powerful appeal

---

[24]In Long, op cit., p. 290.
[25]In Williams, op. cit., p. 557.
[26]Ibid.
[27]Ibid., p. 563.
[28]Ibid., p. 588.

to redistribute wealth. "We have more food in this country . . . than we could eat up in two years if we never plowed another furrow or fattened another shoat—and yet people are hungry and starving." Why? Because rich misers had more money than they needed. In Congress it was Wall Street calling the tune. "They've got a set of Republican waiters on one side and a set of Democratic waiters on the other side, but no matter which set of waiters brings you the dish, the legislative grub is all prepared in the same Wall Street kitchen."[29] Only redistribution of wealth could save the country and voters should return Senator Caraway to Congress. She would support his plan. On election day she won in a landslide, and Huey Long was the reason. He became a stronger presence in national politics.

In the fall of 1932 he supported Franklin D. Roosevelt as the presidential candidate most amenable to his redistribution of wealth plan. He told Roosevelt to provide him with a special loudspeaker-equipped train in which he could campaign for the Democratic ticket all across the country. Jim Farley, Roosevelt's campaign manager, asked him to campaign more modestly and only in North and South Dakota, Nebraska, and Kansas. Huey did, and turnouts were astonishing wherever he spoke.

The Long Presence Grows

When the Senate convened in 1933, it considered and passed legislation in support of Roosevelt's New Deal programs. It acted against the backdrop of national emergency. After three years of decreasing economic activity, industry and commerce were moribund. The banking system was in crisis, high unemployment continued, a "Bonus Army" of 12,000 homeless veterans—the raw material of revolution—was encamped on the Capitol Mall, and millions watched to see if Roosevelt could do anything to defuse the situation.

Huey briefly supported Roosevelt but soon announced that Roosevelt was failing to carry out campaign promises to support Huey's wealth-sharing plan. He obstructed the passage of Roosevelt's emergency relief programs with paralyzing filibusters and unrelated tax-the-rich amendments. For nearly three weeks in January he commanded the floor to prevent passage of a banking reform bill. The Democratic leadership was unable to control him, and the Senate was reduced to inaction by his long tirades. Other senators found his impudence distasteful, but challenging him was dangerous. When, for example, Senator Alben Barkley of Kentucky rose to dress Long down, Huey's quick wit turned the tables. Huey said he had always hoped Barkley had a high opinion of him and would go to his grave regretting this was not so. He was reminded of a God-fearing farmer in Louisiana.

> One day this farmer was plowing and stopped at the end of a row to inspect his plow. As he was bending over it, a pet goat that he had trusted ran at him and gored

---

[29]Ibid., p. 589.

him mortally. His shrieks of agony brought his wife to the scene, and he cried out that he was dying. "But you never was afraid of dyin'," she said. "You're a religious man. You know you're going to Heaven. Why do you carry on this way about dyin'?" He answered: "Honey, I don't mind dyin', but I do hate to face my Maker on the horns of a vicious goat."[30]

In an editorial *The New York Times* inquired: "How long will the Senate lie down under his insults?"[31] Huey, however, was impervious to criticism in the Senate. He had shrewdly put himself in the national limelight with his grandstanding and planned to stay there.

In May he introduced three bills which constituted "the Long Plan" for redistribution of wealth. These bills would have levied a charge on all fortunes over $1 million, limited annual income to $1 million, and put a ceiling on inheritances and gifts of $5 million over a lifetime. Huey spoke on the Senate floor and on nationwide radio in favor of his plan, but it went down to defeat by a lopsided 14-50 floor vote.

Roosevelt tried to undermine Long. He gave instructions that federal patronage in Louisiana should go to anti-Longs. Democratic leaders in the Senate sponsored hearings into charges of corruption in the election of a Long crony, John Overton, to the Senate in 1932, even though evidence was too weak to take action. Several of Huey's political allies in Louisiana were indicted on tax evasion charges under a program of harassment ordered by Roosevelt. Huey responded by charging Postmaster General Jim Farley, Roosevelt's chief political adviser, with a variety of conflicts of interest, but the Senate refused to formally investigate them.

In the meantime, Huey continued to dominate state politics in Louisiana. He used special sessions of the state legislature to pass laws giving him near-dictatorial powers. Anti-Long legislators would receive notice of these sessions at their homes late the night before. The next morning he would present dozens of bills, assign them to committees, and then tell the committees to approve them without change. On the floor he would call for a vote before discussion could take place and secure passage from a blind-voting, pro-Long majority. One such bill, for example, removed the mayor of a town who had opposed Long. Venomous hatred grew among his opponents, many of whom were afraid to speak out. Said one foe: "If you were against him, God help you unless you were an extraordinary man."[32] But the people of Louisiana cheered him. The irony of his antidemocratic methods in championing the cause of the common people was lost on them. At one time Roosevelt considered sending federal troops to "restore Republican government" in Louisiana, but he never did.[33]

---

[30]Arthur Krock, memoir in Columbia University Oral History Project. Quoted in Williams, op. cit., p. 681.
[31]"The Impotent Senate," January 17, 1933, p. 18.
[32]Edward A. Haggerty, quoted in Williams, op. cit., p. 737.
[33]Brinkley, op. cit., pp. 79–80.

Share Our Wealth

In February 1934 Huey spoke on a nationwide radio hookup to announce a new movement, the Share Our Wealth Society, formed to redistribute fortunes and provide a comfortable life for all. Its slogan, derived from William Jennings Bryan's Cross of Gold speech, was "Every Man a King." He encouraged the formation of local chapters. Any two persons could form one, and there were no dues. He advanced a specific platform. The plan began with proposals to tax wealth:

• A capital tax would be imposed on all fortunes of over $1 million. This graduated tax would be 1 percent on the second million, 2 percent on the third, 4 percent on the fourth, 8 percent on the fifth, and so forth, finally becoming 100 percent on any fortune over $8 million. The levy would be imposed each year, so big fortunes would be continuously reduced.
• An income tax of 100 percent on yearly income above $1 million.
• Gift and inheritance taxes of 100 percent on amounts over $1 million annually and over $5 million in a lifetime.

Long calculated that these confiscatory taxes would raise a total of $90 billion in the first year. This money would then be divided among all Americans.

• Each family would get a "homestead" of $5,000, enough to buy a home, a car, and a radio.
• Each family would be guaranteed an annual income of $2,500.
• Those among the elderly earning less than $1,000 a year and possessing less than $10,000 in cash or property would receive a $30-a-month pension.
• The federal government would provide free college education.
• Veterans of World War I would receive a bonus of unspecified amount.[34]

In addition, the plan advocated a workweek of 30 hours to increase the demand for labor, a vacation of one month every year for workers, federal purchase of crop surpluses to balance supply and demand, and public works programs.

Fertile Ground for the Share Our Wealth Society

The winter of 1934 found the country still in the throes of bleak depression. Foreclosures on homes were running at nearly 1,000 a day. Impoverished couples postponed marriage. People who lacked warm clothing and fuel stayed in bed all day to keep warm. Trains ran with few cars. Mail deliveries were light. Paint peeled from houses and stores, giving cities a decaying appearance. In Pittsburgh the air was clean because factory smokestacks were idle. In New York Groucho Marx joked that "the pigeons started feeding the people in Cen-

---

[34]The plan is spelled out in the *Congressional Record*, 74th Cong., 1st sess., vol. 79, pp. 8040–8043. Details of the plan were changed over time.

tral Park.''[35] Despite Roosevelt's emergency relief programs over 8,000,000 workers remained unemployed. Over 3,000 banks had closed their doors, and Hoovervilles still dotted the urban landscape. Great windstorms blew through the northern prairies and Texas panhandle, removing topsoil and foreshadowing the end for many farmers.

It was a time when Americans were receptive to radical solutions. On the left, socialists advocated people's utopias. On the right, business leaders denounced Roosevelt for destroying capitalism with his ineffectual efforts to restore prosperity through government make-work programs. Today, it is easy to forget the tumult of that year, the fear that capitalism would not survive, the vicious hate that was affixed to Roosevelt, the jealousy of the hungry, and the self-consciousness of the rich about their wealth.

In this fertile soil of discontent the Share Our Wealth Society took hold. After a month there were 200,000 members, and by the end of the year there were 3,700,000. Huey had day and night shifts of secretaries working in five offices to send out pamphlets, tin buttons, and political literature to the membership. He even wrote a song; one verse was:

Every man a king,
Every man a king,
For you can be a millionaire.
There's something belonging to others.
There's enough for all people to share.
Be it sunny June or December, too.
In the wintertime or spring:
There'll be peace without end,
Every neighbor a friend,
With every man a king.

There was heated national discussion of Huey's plan. Some said it was socialistic. If government annually taxed away part of the assets of a company such as General Motors, after a few years it would come to own it.[36] Huey replied that his plan strengthened the capitalist system by fixing the problem of excessive concentration of wealth. He would simply tame the wealthy rather than do away with them. Others noted that the plan was impractical. How, for example, could great fortunes be broken up by capital levy and redistributed when they were based on assets such as factories or railroads which could not be dismantled?[37] Some were simply cynical: "The genius of Huey Long lies in his gift to exploit the misery and the confusion of the American people," said one critic.[38]

---

[35]Edward Robb Ellis. *A Nation in Torment.* New York: Coward-McCann, 1970, p. 239.

[36]Walter Lippmann, "Huey Proposes," *New Republic,* March 20, 1935, pp. 146–47.

[37]See, for example, Raymond Gram Swing, "The Menace of Huey Long," *The Nation,* January 23, 1935, p. 99 and George E. Sokolsky, "Huey Long," *The Atlantic,* November 1935, p. 527.

[38]Benjamin Stolberg, "Dr. Huey and Mr. Long," *The Nation,* September 25, 1935, p. 346.

The most perceptive analysts, however, saw the plan for what it really was—a grass roots political base. Huey intended to form a third-party movement to challenge FDR in the presidential election of 1936. The local Share Our Wealth chapters would be the nucleus of that movement. By 1935 he had confided to followers that he planned to form a third political party based on the Share Our Wealth platform. He did not believe he could win the presidency in 1936 and planned to select another candidate to run for the Share Our Wealth party. The Republicans would renominate Hoover, and the Democrats would renominate Roosevelt. Huey thought he could siphon enough votes away from Roosevelt to ensure the reelection of Hoover, who would be nominated once again by the Republicans. He did not believe Hoover could end the depression and calculated that after four years of Hoover's inadequate policies the country would still be in such distress that it would then turn to Huey Long, running for the Share Our Wealth party in 1940, as the leader to restore prosperity. This heartless ploy, permitting four years of national suffering to promote his presidential ambition, surprised no one who knew Long well.

By 1935 there were over 27,000 Share Our Wealth chapters around the country with a total membership of between 5 and 7 million people. Roosevelt was deeply distressed. A secret poll conducted by the Democratic National Committee showed that Huey would get 3 to 4 million votes if he decided to run for president—enough, in a close contest, to tip the balance in favor of the Republicans and deny FDR reelection.[39] His support was not just regional; the poll showed as much support in the North and West as in the South.

In July Roosevelt surprised Congress with a special tax bill designed to bring about a more equitable distribution of wealth. The bill sharply increased income taxes, inheritance taxes, and corporate taxes. The bill illustrated Roosevelt's need to shift leftward to co-opt some of Huey's fire. It was not, of course, enough to convince Huey to drop his attack on Roosevelt, and it did not diminish public infatuation with the Share Our Wealth Society.

LONG AND AMERICAN IDEOLOGY

Huey Long's Share Our Wealth program was popular because it appealed to values held dearly. Throughout American history two sets of fundamental values have coexisted. The first is *agrarian idealism,* which extols the ideal of a rural, agrarian nation of individual landowners operated on principles of egalitarianism, humanitarianism, and social justice. This set of values was represented in the earliest years of American history by Jeffersonian democracy.

The second set of deep values is *industrialism,* which is derived from the basic tenets of capitalism and equates progress with economic growth, accumulation of capital, and technological advance. According to this set of values, the human and environmental dislocations of industrial activity are to be en-

[39]James A. Farley. *Behind the Ballots.* New York: Harcourt, Brace & World, 1938, pp. 249–250.

dured because, all the while, greater social good is created. The purpose of government is to promote commerce. This set of values was present in our colonial era in the thought of Alexander Hamilton and the actions of the Federalists.

There is a built-in tension between these two value sets, and much of American history prior to the 1930s had been shaped by conflict between them: the decline of the Federalist party and the rise of Jeffersonian democracy early in the nineteenth century, the ascendancy of the Northern industrialists over the Southern planter class in 1865, the Republican party juggernaut turning aside the futile revolt of the Populists in the 1890s (but bending to the moderate reforms of the Progressives in the first years of the twentieth century).

Over time, as society has changed, the two value sets have been expressed in many different yet specific ways. In the 1930s, for example, the onset of economic depression discredited business leadership, and values such as humanitarianism and individualism—values at the core of the agrarian ideal—were reasserted as important. At this point in our nation's history it was too late to go back to being a nation of farmers, but the people-centered values of agrarian idealism were subtly reshaped to apply in the prevailing industrial context. In this manner, the spirit of Huey Long's attacks on centralized wealth and big business was profoundly within the tradition of agrarian idealism. Fundamentally, he represented the view that government should place priority on the welfare of commoners over plutocrats.

The Rise of Industrialism Challenges Agrarian Values

Though the United States, early in its history, may have corresponded to the ideal of an agrarian commonwealth composed of sturdy yeoman farmers, extremely favorable conditions for industry and commerce in the young country led to two centuries of sustained industrialization. It would be hard to underestimate how the fever to industrialize transformed our society in the years between the Civil War and the turn of the century. Statistics tell part of the story. There were only 9,021 miles of railroad track in 1850, but by 1900 there were 194,321. The population grew from over 23 million in 1850 to 73 million in 1900, more than tripling. Crude-steel production grew from 19,643 tons in 1867 to 10,188,329 in 1900. Coal production jumped from 27,974,000 tons in 1876 to 172,608,917 in 1900. The number of Western Union offices went from 2,250 in 1866 to 23,238 in 1900.[40]

As the use of steam power and the factory system encouraged the growth of cities, more and more people abandoned farm life. In 1850 only 15.3 percent of the population lived in the 236 then-existing cities of more than 2,500, but by 1900 39.7 percent lived in 1,737 such cities. In that year 14.1 million people

---

[40]These figures and others in this paragraph are from various editions of the *Statistical Abstract of the United States*.

lived in cities of over 10,000, but by 1930 over 27 million did.[41] The growth of corporations was equally rapid. Immediately after the Civil War no company had a billion dollars of capital, but there were 318 by 1904.[42] Huge monopolies developed in industries such as oil, cigarettes, hemp, and sugar. Financiers such as J. P. Morgan controlled the supply of capital and decisively influenced the path of commerce.

The coming of giant corporations and concentrated capital was profoundly threatening to many Americans. The individual property owner, a central figure in the agrarian ideal, became the employee of a large corporation. The small-shop owner was set upon by chain stores. Workers were used as interchangeable inputs in factories. The impersonality of remote managers offended folksy rural values. Urbanization aggregated workers, the raw material of the factory system, but brought with it slums, crime, and disease. City life also placed agrarian values under attack. The country person, once the exemplar of society, appeared to be a bumpkin or hick compared with the wealthy, progressive business leader in the city. Cities spread a culture of materialism. Fashion trends swept urban populations; ads in mass circulation newspapers and magazines spread new desires. The capitalist class flaunted its wealth by building outsized Victorian mansions. Still, agrarian values remained strong in American culture. The United States had embraced industrialism, but many still harbored the romantic agrarian ideal of yesteryear.

Agrarian Protest and the Progressive Movement

The unsettling, expansive social change of post–Civil War industrialization led to the rise of populism, a political protest movement that flourished in the 1890s. The Populist party represented the grievances of farmers in a few midwestern states, who had suffered from declining crop prices since the 1870s. These declines were largely the result of increased production made possible by new machinery and a concurrent transportation revolution which put American farmers in competition for the first time with farmers worldwide.

The farmers, however, blamed their troubles on the growth of industry. They accused distant capitalists, monopolists, and "plutocrats" of conspiring to control the economy through low agricultural prices, high freight charges on railroads, and continuation of the gold standard for currency, which brought about high interest rates, tight money, and growing farm debt. Populists advocated government ownership of railroads, direct election of senators, use of the initiative and referendum, and the breakup of large trusts. The farmers in the movement were joined in the 1890s by silver miners and some workers in urban areas, but their power base was too small to challenge successfully the

---

[41]Louis M. Hacker. *The World of Andrew Carnegie: 1865–1901*. Philadelphia: J. B. Lippincott Company, 1968, p. 315.
[42]Thomas C. Cochran and William Miller. *The Age of Enterprise*, rev. ed. New York: Harper & Row, 1961, p. 190.

dominant political coalition of conservative Republicans and Eastern industrialists.

The Populist movement did not die. After the turn of the century its appeal was transformed and broadened into the Progressive movement. The Progressive movement included not just farmers but also the middle-class, urban population. It was a movement of moral indignation that focused on using government regulation to correct the worst abuses of feverish industrial development. One chronicler of the period wrote:

> Everywhere that progressives looked they saw poverty, injustice, and political corruption in the midst of growing abundance and seemingly limitless opportunity. One percent of the nation's families owned seven eighths of its wealth and ten million Americans lived in abject circumstances.[43]

It is one of the great accomplishments of American democracy that the Progressive movement succeeded in peacefully wresting reform from the conservative establishment of that era, limiting monopoly, improving working conditions, and correcting social ills in the cities. But while the Progressives celebrated modest reforms in the early years of the century, the same remarkable scale of industrial growth which had fired reformist zeal in the first place continued unabated until halted by the depression of the 1930s.

This new growth ripened American society for a new round of reform inspired by Populist-Progressive values. The 194,321 miles of railroad track in 1900 grew to 260,570 in 1929.[44] The population nearly doubled, growing from 73,303,387 in 1900 to 137,008,435 in 1930. Iron and steel production rose from 13,789,000 tons in 1900 to 42,614,000 tons in 1929. This growth placed continuous pressure on remnants of rural values in society. The great prosperity of the 1920s put a gloss on the doctrines of industrialism and masked the numerous adversities of commercial growth.

Long Takes Up the Humanitarian Banner

Populist-Progressive themes resurfaced with the depression. Huey Long, who had ridden the discontent with industrial domination in Louisiana to power there, was now in the national limelight with his proposal to redistribute wealth, and he planned to ride nationwide populist sentiment into the White House. His speeches made clear that rich capitalists were the cause of the depression. And he put his ideas in simple language. "How many men ever went to a barbecue and would let one man take off the table what was intended for nine-tenths of the people to eat?" he once asked. "The only way you'll ever

---

[43]Louis B. Wright et al. *The Democratic Experience*. Chicago: Scott, Foresman and Company, 1963, p. 292.
[44]The figures in this paragraph are from various editions of the *Statistical Abstract of the United States*.

be able to feed the balance of the people is to make that man come back and bring back some of the grub he ain't got no business with!''[45]

He promised to use government for humanitarian ends—to make sure every person had money, individual dignity, and opportunity for betterment. The benedictions of progress would flow freely into every home; they would not be just for the rich.

THE ROAD NOT TAKEN

At the height of his power in Louisiana, Huey decided to attack Standard Oil once again. He never had forgiven the company for organizing the impeachment effort against him when, as governor, he had tried to impose a tax on each barrel of oil refined in the state. At a special session of the legislature in December 1934, Huey rammed the same tax measure through without any opportunity for debate. Anti-Long legislators and company lobbyists were unaware of the contents of the bill until it was too late.

Stung by the 5-cents-a-barrel tax, Standard Oil laid off 1,000 employees in January 1935 and announced that it might have to move its major refining plant to another state. Huey responded that the tax money was needed to finance university education and said that Louisiana might have to expropriate the plant and run it.

Huey had once again underestimated support for Standard Oil in the state but quickly compromised with the company when a storm gathered. The tax would be only 1 cent a barrel, and Standard Oil would recall its employees. In the meantime, some of these refinery workers had called a mass rally to oppose the tax. It was attended by a volatile mix of angry laid-off men and anti-Longs. In the middle of the meeting the compromise was announced, but the rally continued to cries that the rule of Long the dictator must be ended. The meeting resulted in the formation of the Square Deal Association, a group organized to end Huey's rule. Chapters were formed in many cities. Large numbers of gun-carrying Square Dealers twice confronted state police, but each time the situation was defused without violence. Later, a paramilitary group called the Minutemen was organized. Its members wore uniforms and talked of marching on the capitol in Baton Rouge to take over the government.

Now there was a bone-deep hatred of Huey among his Louisiana opponents. Cocktail party talk in fashionable residences speculated on whether he should be killed. Huey was never without a large retinue of police and personal bodyguards.

On September 8, 1935, Huey was in Baton Rouge for another special session of the legislature, where he introduced forty-two new bills that would further extend his power. One was designed to allow Huey to fine and jail federal officials who undertook actions for "political" purposes. Huey planned to use this measure to stop Roosevelt from harassing him in Louisiana. A second bill

---

[45]Ellis, op. cit., p. 404.

redrew the geographic boundaries of the thirteenth judicial district so that an old political enemy, Judge Benjamin Pavy, could not be reelected to the judgeship he had held for twenty-eight years.

At 9:20 that evening Huey was walking just ahead of five bodyguards down the main capitol corridor. From the recess behind a marble pillar a slim young man in a white linen suit emerged. He merged with the group and fired one shot at Huey with a small Belgian Browning 7.6-caliber automatic pistol held outstretched in one hand. Huey cried out and ran down the hall, a bloodstain spreading on the front of his white shirt about six inches above the belt line. Behind him the gunman, a twenty-nine-year-old physician named Carl Weiss, Jr., crumpled lifeless on the floor, his body jerking as Huey's bodyguards fired dozens of rounds at point-blank range. Legislators who had convened in nearby chambers to pass Huey's bills panicked at the gunfire and ran into the halls. In the governor's office the always loyal Oscar Allen hid under his desk.

Huey was taken to a nearby hospital with severe internal hemorrhaging from his wound. Responding to falling blood pressure, doctors performed exploratory surgery in the abdominal cavity. They sutured intestinal punctures and repaired visible damage, but he continued to deteriorate afterwards. The reason was soon discovered. Inexplicably, no preoperative catheterization of the urinary tract had been done to detect bleeding, and doctors had missed damage to the right kidney. Huey was too weak to withstand a second operation to remove his kidney and died on September 10, thirty hours after being wounded.

The assassin was identified as the son-in-law of Judge Benjamin Pavy, whose district Huey had been ready to gerrymander. Apparently Weiss acted alone, but he was surely inspirited by the malign undercurrents of that time. Thousands attended Weiss' funeral to show support for what he had done. But 100,000 mourners stood by as Huey was laid to rest in front of the state capitol building. The Louisiana State University band played Huey's composition, "Every Man a King," in a minor key as his dirge. At the funeral Reverend Gerald L. K. Smith said:

> The lives of great men do not end with the grave. . . . This place . . . marks only the burial ground of his body. His spirit shall never rest as long as hungry bodies cry for food, as long as lean human frames stand naked, as long as homeless wretches haunt this land of plenty. . . . [46]

The death of Huey Long removed a powerful political force from the national scene and foreclosed an alternative for the country. No other personality was in a position to challenge Roosevelt for leadership of the nation. There was a multitude of utopians with prescriptions for the economic disease of depression, but none had Huey's cunning, force of character, and national constituency. Only Huey, as demonstrated in his Share Our Wealth movement, knew exactly how to strike the populist chord at its most resonant among millions of Americans. And perhaps only Huey was ruthless enough to bend the suffering of those millions to his personal ambition. While worldwide depres-

---

[46]In Beals, op. cit., p. 407.

sion in the 1930s led to the rise of fascist dictatorships in Italy and Germany, in the United States an assassin's bullet ended speculation that Huey would similarly suppress democratic institutions. There was a sense of destiny about Huey, but his was the road not taken.

Questions

The story of Huey Long raises many questions. Foremost is: What would have happened if Long had lived? Another important question is: Do the deep, historical currents of public opinion that Long rode continue to exist? Is "Longism" lying in wait for another period of economic crisis? Does it continue to exist in the form of modern criticism of business in the Populist-Progressive mold? Can the whole episode of Long's life be explained by the "great man" theory of politics, or is it simply one example of the periodic resurfacing (albeit spectacularly) of a continuous force in American political culture? The reader is invited to ask whether any part of Long's agenda remains important today. For example, what level of income inequality is ethically justified? Did our society exceed it in the 1920s and 1930s? Does it exceed such a level today? Or, does contemporary economic growth continue to erode the freedom of individuals in society? Do the Populist-Progressive ideals still have enough support to challenge business interests? What would it take to activate them?

MILESTONES IN THE LIFE OF HUEY P. LONG

1893	Born on August 30 in Winn Parish, Louisiana
1906	Skips the seventh grade at the Winnfield school
1909	Wins a scholarship to Louisiana State University in a debating contest
1910	Drops out of high school in his senior year; takes a job selling cooking oil door-to-door
1911	Works at brief jobs in Houston and Memphis; attends divinity school at Oklahoma Baptist University
1912	Attends University of Oklahoma and then drops out to work at sales jobs
1913	Marries Rose McConnell; sells patent medicine in Louisiana
1914	Attends law classes at Tulane University in New Orleans
1915	Admitted to the Louisiana bar by special committee exam; sets up law practice in Winnfield
1918	Elected to Louisiana Railroad Commission as a Democrat
1923	Runs for governor at age thirty but loses election of 1924
1928	Elected governor of Louisiana at age thirty-five
1929	Louisiana state legislature votes on impeachment in March; stock market crash in October
1930	Elected U.S. senator, promising to stay in Louisiana until 1932 to complete his four-year term as governor
1932	Assumes Senate seat in January during depth of the Great Depression
1933	Obstructs passage of Roosevelt's relief measures in Congress
1934	Announces the Share Our Wealth Society on nationwide radio; lays groundwork for third-party challenge to FDR in presidential election of 1936
1935	Assassinated in state capitol building in Baton Rouge on September 8

DEREGULATION OF THE AIRLINE INDUSTRY

In the 1970s proponents of airline deregulation thought more competition would benefit consumers. Opponents said unregulated companies would engage in predatory behavior. There being a ground swell of support for less regulation, Congress passed the Airline Deregulation Act of 1978. It rapidly phased out federal controls. Not all regulation ended, only economic regulation. The airlines were still subject to strict flight safety rules and laws that applied to many industries, such as those regulating civil rights and environmental quality.

With deregulation big changes came rapidly, and the industry began a remarkable period of transformation not yet ended. This is the story of airline deregulation and its consequences. It is a story with an ending that not everyone likes.

DEVELOPMENT OF AIRLINE REGULATION

The airline industry in the United States developed in the 1920s but struggled to survive. Its major problem was safety. The rickety, unreliable planes used by early entrepreneurs often crashed, and the public felt air travel was dangerous. In the winter of 1921 an airliner ran into a crowd, slashing several people with its propeller and killing one. A short time later a flying boat killed five bathers on a beach. Then in the spring of 1922 came an especially gruesome accident. An Aeromarine Airways flying boat bound from Bimini broke its propeller and came down 40 miles from Miami in the Gulf Stream. The plane carried two businessmen and their wives plus a third woman. Seas were heavy, and the passengers struggled to bail out the cabin. After one day in the water a pontoon sprang a leak, and the plane turned upside down. As sharks circled, the two husbands and the pilot struggled to hold the women on top of the wreckage, but one by one they died and slipped away. On the second day the two male passengers succumbed to exhaustion and fell off. The pilot lashed himself to the wreckage with two ropes and after seeing nine ships go by was finally rescued by a tanker. In delirium he gradually recounted the 56-hour ordeal over the next few days, and newspapers fed details to a morbid audience.[1] This accident scared passengers and repelled investors in the financial community.

European governments directly subsidized fledgling airlines, but in America widespread belief in free enterprise and laissez-faire capitalism turned public opinion against subsidies. It was not until 1925, when Army pilots stopped flying airmail and private airlines were allowed to do so, that the government found a way to support the new industry. This was the first government intervention, and it was promotional. A year later, in response to public safety concerns, the Department of Commerce began setting safety standards for planes and pilots.

But accidents continued, and two crashes, among many, catalyzed demands for more regulation. In 1931 football legend Knute Rockne was killed in the crash of a Fokker biplane when wood rot caused its wings to break in midair. In 1935 a well-known senator, Bronson Cuttings of New Mexico, was killed when a TWA DC2 went down in Kansas. Why was the airline industry unable to raise safety standards and gain public confidence? One writer explains:

> The economic "laws" of minimizing losses while maximizing short-term gains had led to the incorporation of a speed-(or any other related new technology)-at-any-cost mentality. No single aircraft manufacturer or airline operator could afford to adopt costlier safety regulations without a guarantee that competitor compliance would follow; to have done so would have meant certain bankruptcy due to lowered profit margins. With no mechanism—state, market, or otherwise—to ensure a minimum level of safety, remedies awaited crises.[2]

What was needed were federal imposition of safety rules and competitive restraints on the industry. So in 1938 Congress passed the Civil Aeronautics Act and established a regulatory regimen that would last with little change for forty years.

The Civil Aeronautics Act of 1938

The Civil Aeronautics Act authorized extensive economic regulation of the airline industry and broadened safety standards. After some bureaucratic turmoil

---

[1]Associated Press, "Five Died at Sea in 56-Hour Drift on Disabled Plane," *The New York Times,* March 26, 1922, pp. 1–2.

[2]Vicki L. Golich, "Airline Deregulation: Economic Boom or Safety Bust?" *Transportation Quarterly,* May 1988, p. 163.

HOW THE AIRLINE INDUSTRY STARTED

The first air passenger service was by zeppelin and began in Germany in 1910. The first scheduled passenger airline anywhere was the St. Petersburg–Tampa Airboat Line in Florida, a short-lived venture which lasted for six months in 1914. But the airline industry first developed in Europe because of unique circumstances existing at the close of World War I. The armistice left a surplus of aircraft and skilled pilots who longed to continue flying. At the time the utility of air travel was especially great because railroads on the Continent had suffered war damage. So it was that in Great Britain, France, and Germany the airline industry began to flower.

The airliners of that day were often bombers converted to carry passengers in the bomb compartment. Yet this primitive equipment was combined with exceptional elegance in passenger service. An example was the French Farman F.60 Goliath, a twin-engine biplane made of wooden braces, wire, and cloth fabric covering the wings.

The pilot flew in an open-air cockpit, his scarf blowing in the wind, while twelve passengers enjoyed extravagant luxury in the enclosed fuselage.

They sat in upholstered wicker chairs next to cabin windows framed with fabric drapes. Each seat had a crystal bud vase containing flowers, and the walls were covered with lively floral wallpaper. This level of refinement was typical. A German competitor, Lufthansa, featured planes where passengers walked on Oriental rugs and ate in dining rooms at tables set with linen and crystal. Such ostentation was necessary to lure passengers away from the luxurious railway cars then in use in Europe. It may also have served to distract passengers from the discomforts of cabins that were unheated and uninsulated against the cacophony of moving air and piston engines outside.

Early airlines in the United States never had this European panache and flew passengers in small planes with Spartan cabins.

---

the act came to be administered by the Civil Aeronautics Board (CAB) and the Civil Aeronautics Authority (CAA).

The CAB had authority to regulate economic aspects of the industry and set safety standards for all airlines. It was an independent regulatory commission presided over by five commissioners appointed by the President for six-year terms with the consent of the Senate. This independent status, plus wording in the Civil Aeronautics Act making CAB findings "conclusive," gave the agency exceptional power beyond which the industry had little appeal. In later years the CAB was often criticized as dictatorial.

The CAB granted the right of an airline to operate, determined what cities it could serve, and approved its ticket prices. Once a fare was established, say between New York and Los Angeles, all airlines on the route had to comply, and no rebating was permitted. This shielded the industry from price competition. The CAB approved or disapproved mergers, acquisitions, and all agreements between companies, such as sharing baggage-handling facilities. Over the years the CAB applied a type of regulation typically used with public utilities and limited an airline's rate of return on investment to predetermined levels. This approach created an industry which provided efficient service, but profits were low.

The other agency created under the act, the CAA, was set up in the Department of Commerce and had less independence than the CAB. It was responsible for operating air traffic control systems and policing safety in the industry. It shared other safety-related functions with the much stronger CAB. After a shocking midair collision in 1956 between a TWA Constellation and a United DC7 over the Grand Canyon which killed 128 passengers, public sentiment again demanded stronger safety rules. So the Federal Aviation Act of 1958 created a new and more potent agency, the Federal Aviation Agency (FAA), to take over and broaden the safety functions of the CAA.

The Move toward Deregulation

After 1938 the airline industry grew rapidly. Between 1938 and 1978 the domestic routes flown by the six largest airlines increased from 26,770 miles to 246,474 miles; the number of passengers carried yearly increased from 1 million to 267 million.[3] Total assets of the industry in 1978 were $17 billion, and it employed 300,000.[4] Technological advances in aircraft provided the public with more comfort, speed, and range. As the industry grew, economies of scale held increases in air travel costs far below the general inflation rate. A series of interairline agreements sponsored by the CAB created an integrated air transport system in which passengers could check bags through on different airlines or exchange tickets with no cost penalty involved. In many ways the regulatory system set up in 1938 was highly successful.

Nevertheless, a push for deregulation began. The huge expansion of federal regulation in the 1960s and 1970s had led to general sentiment for regulatory reform in many industries. Influential academics and government economists argued that the airline industry, though it was being regulated as a public utility, did not show the underlying characteristics of monopoly. Rather, its airplanes were highly mobile assets which could be moved in response to competitive forces. If airlines were given free entry and exit in serving cities and allowed to compete on fares, consumers would benefit. The heavy hand of government was inefficient and unnecessary.

At the time this viewpoint was popular, conspicuous problems in the industry attracted attention. For one thing, the introduction of new fleets of wide-bodied planes in the 1970s had led to overcapacity. At a time when fuel costs were high, empty seats seemed a waste of money. The CAB was criticized for announcing a four-year moratorium on new routes which prevented smaller, low-cost competitors from challenging the dominance of major established airlines. Some CAB actions seemed to senselessly hinder competition. For example, "closed-door" restrictions prohibited planes from picking up passengers on intermediate stops. A Delta Airlines flight from Miami to Seattle which

---

[3]Melvin A. Brenner, James O. Leet, and Elihu Schott. *Airline Deregulation*. Westport, Conn.: Eno Foundation for Transportation, Inc., 1985, p. 5.
[4]*Ibid.*, p. 6.

made one stop in Denver would be prohibited from picking up passengers in Denver. This protected other carriers, such as Continental Airlines, which flew the Denver-Seattle route. Such rules made the CAB appear to coddle the airlines and deprive the public of the benefits of competition.

The Carter administration made airline deregulation a top priority, and Alfred E. Kahn, a deregulation advocate, was appointed in 1977 to head the CAB. Kahn immediately began to ease CAB restrictions on route entry and fare cutting.

The Airline Deregulation Act of 1978

When deregulatory legislation was introduced in Congress, it faced some opposition. In floor debate liberals such as Senator George McGovern (D–South Dakota) argued that deregulation would lead to cutthroat competition of the kind that historically leads to monopoly power. "Historians will recall that a century ago," said McGovern, "the stagecoach lines in the Western United States engaged in such economic warfare until, eventually, there was only one company, Overland Stage Line, left in the business. Consumers soon found this 'single carrier' provided miserable service at exorbitant rates."[5] He predicted predatory pricing, declining safety, and worsening service to small communities. In response, Senator Howard Cannon (D-Nevada) said: "If Senators believe that a free enterprise marketplace is an efficient allocator of resources, in plain English if they think it works, it is totally inconsistent to accept [Senator McGovern's] arguments."[6] And Senator Adlai E. Stevenson III (D-Illinois) thought that "more competition will mean more rational business decisions, more rather than fewer scheduled carriers, service to more communities, and improved financial health for the efficient carriers."[7]

Some major airlines opposed deregulation. Their underlying fear was that the industry, which typically earned a return on investment about half that of all U.S. industries combined, would be exposed to price and service competition that would lower revenues while nothing was done to reduce costs. In testimony before congressional committees William Casey, president of American Airlines, spoke against the application of "new and untested theoretical concepts," and Phillip E. Boucher, a vice president of TWA, argued against "dropping fares to levels producing predatory competitive action."[8] Airline unions also opposed deregulation because new, nonunion carriers were sure to enter the industry with lower wages. But most major trunk carriers favored deregulation, believing that competition, whatever its imperfections, was pref-

---

[5]Quoted in "Should Congress Enact Pending Legislation to Deregulate the U.S. Airline Industry?" *Congressional Digest,* June–July 1978, pp. 173–77.
[6]Ibid., p. 172.
[7]Ibid., p. 180.
[8]Ibid., p. 177 and p. 183.

erable to CAB regulation, which Richard J. Ferris, president of United Airlines, called "a bureaucratic apparatus approaching witchcraft."[9]

In the absence of united opposition by the industry the Airline Deregulation Act of 1978 passed by overwhelming margins: 83-9 in the Senate and 363-8 in the House.[10] Its major provisions were these.

• The economic powers of the CAB were gradually phased out over a seven-year period. In 1985 the agency was to be discontinued, its remaining powers transferred to other government agencies.

• In the meantime, the CAB was to place maximum reliance on competition. Procedures were to be simplified and speeded and restrictions eased. For example, "closed-door" rules were eliminated.

• The CAB was ordered to grant operating rights to any carrier to enter any route served only by one existing carrier.

• Under an "automatic market entry program" airlines could begin service on one new route each year between 1979 and 1981 without CAB approval. However, each airline was allowed to designate one of its existing routes as protected from new competition so other airlines could not enter. CAB authority over domestic routes would end in 1981.

• Small communities were protected from loss of service by a provision enabling the CAB to order an airline to provide continued service where such service was "essential." Otherwise, carriers could stop service to any city simply by notifying the CAB. Federal subsidies for carriers serving small communities would continue for ten years.

• Airline mergers and acquisitions were to be approved by the CAB, but the burden of proving anticompetitive impact was placed on opposing parties.

• Airlines were permitted, without CAB approval, to adjust their fares 50 percent below or 5 percent above fares as they stood in 1977. CAB regulation of domestic fares would end in 1983.

• Any long-term employee who lost work, suffered a wage cut, or was forced to relocate because of competitive forces brought about by deregulation was made eligible for compensation.

With passage of the Airline Deregulation Act the nation embarked on a great experiment with one of its major industries.

CHANGES IN THE AIRLINE INDUSTRY

The Airline Deregulation Act was, with minor exceptions, implemented as planned. The CAB moved quickly to open the industry to competitive forces. It awarded new routes freely, in some cases granting new entry to a dozen or more carriers at once. In January 1985, on schedule, the CAB permanently ceased operations. In the early years of deregulation change was rapid and tu-

[9]Ibid., p. 188.
[10]Pub. L. 95-504, 92 Stat. 1705 (1978).

multuous. Later, the shape of a new industry structure emerged, and some measure of stability was restored. Many consequences of deregulation were anticipated, but some were not.

Initially, a highly competitive atmosphere developed. The major airlines took advantage of free entry by moving in on each other's high-density, long-haul routes. TWA, for example, served thirty-eight U.S. cities in 1978, but by 1984 it had expanded service to sixty. Smaller in-state carriers, such as Air Florida and Pacific Southwest Airlines, entered interstate routes in competition with the majors. Local service airlines such as USAir, Ozark, and Republic, which had specialized in regional short-haul flights, expanded their route systems. New carriers appeared—Midway, New York Air, Muse Air, People Express, Jet America, Pacific East, and Hawaii Express. Former charter services such as Transamerica Airlines reorganized to become scheduled carriers. In 1978 there had been 36 interstate passenger carriers; by 1983 there were 123.[11]

The effects of this competitive whirlwind quickly showed. Competition created fare wars that lowered ticket prices. By 1983 over 75 percent of passengers traveled on discount fares compared with 25 percent prior to deregulation.[12] Between 1978 and 1983 the number of passengers increased 18 percent.[13] Many fliers were attracted by fare savings the Federal Trade Commission recently estimated to have averaged $11 billion per year, but much industry growth is the natural result of years of economic expansion after 1982.[14] Increased travel strained every aspect of the air transport system, causing delays and discomforts and raising concerns about safety. Although passenger traffic increased, the market share of the major trunk lines fell from 90.8 percent in 1978 to 80.5 percent in 1983 as new competitors gained entry into lucrative, high-traffic markets.[15]

After five years of competition the predictions of deregulation advocates were largely realized. Then the industry began to change again. Passenger travel continued to increase. By 1987 over 90 percent of fliers were traveling on discount fares, and the airlines were carrying 63 percent more passengers than in 1978.[16] Fares remained low. But the major carriers began to crush and absorb smaller competitors. Between 1983 and 1988 there were nineteen airline failures and twenty-six mergers and acquisitions by the largest carriers. As a result, by 1989 only 59 carriers of the 219 created since 1978 remained, and

---

[11]Figures are from a speech by Robert L. Crandall, president of American Airlines, at the Wings Club, September 1, 1984. Cited in Brenner et al., op. cit., p. 20. Not included in these figures are the approximately 200 commuter airlines that existed in 1983. They were a growing segment of the market but accounted for only about 1 percent of total passenger miles flown.

[12]Thomas Gale Moore, "U.S. Airline Deregulation: Its Effects on Passengers, Capital, and Labor," *Journal of Law and Economics,* April 1986, p. 9.

[13]*Moody's Transportation Manual.* New York: Moody's Investors Service, 1986, pp. a39–a41.

[14]Council of Economic Advisers. *Annual Report of the Council of Economic Advisors.* Washington, D.C.: U.S. Government Printing Office, February 1988, p. 199 and p. 203.

[15]Ibid., p. 18.

[16]"The Big Trouble with Air Travel," *Consumer Reports,* June 1988, p. 363.

the 8 largest had a 94 percent market share. More consolidation was predicted.[17] New airlines could no longer find financial backing, and no new national carriers had entered the industry for several years. By 1988 the major carriers had begun to restrict discount fares and raise regular fares. Service problems continued. A survey by *Consumer Reports* reported that 50 percent of passengers found air travel worse than prior to deregulation; only 20 percent thought it better.[18] Poor service, higher fares, and diminishing competition were unintended consequences of deregulation and seemed to bear out the warnings voiced by opponents in 1978.

COMPETITIVE STRATEGIES IN THE AIRLINE INDUSTRY

To understand how this situation developed, we look more closely at the competitive strategies used by the airlines after 1978. Competitive strategies are the specific actions companies take to achieve business goals. After deregulation airline companies were drawn by the logic of the environment to similar strategies, as follows.

Hub-and-Spoke Operations

Prior to deregulation the CAB pushed airlines to institute more nonstop service between cities because the public found it convenient. Between large city pairs such as New York and Chicago this was profitable, but traffic from smaller cities often did not justify nonstop flights. The airlines, therefore, made two or three stops before landing in a city such as Indianapolis, and passengers picked up in Dayton or Columbus added enough revenue to support a nonstop continuation flight from Indianapolis to Los Angeles. After deregulation, however, routes to these backup cities were no longer protected from competition by the CAB, and the airlines could no longer count on collecting enough passengers for profitable nonstops.

This situation led to the development of hub-and-spoke flight operations. Airlines acquired a large number of gates in close proximity at major airports. Then, rather than increasing nonstop flights between city pairs, they increased flights into these hub cities. With closely coordinated flight schedules they were able to transfer passengers from feeder routes and fill departing flights. The system is analogous to a bicycle wheel, with passengers traveling into and out of the hub airport on routes resembling radiating spokes.

Before deregulation a few airlines maintained small hubs, but their growth was limited by restricted route entry. By 1987 there were twenty-five large and medium-sized hub cities, and the route systems of all major carriers came to

---

[17]See, for example, *Airline Consolidation*. Washington, D.C.: Airline Economics, Inc., 1987, and Kenneth Labich, "How Airlines Will Look in the 1990s," *Fortune*, January 1, 1990.

[18]"The Big Trouble with Air Travel," op. cit., pp. 362–63.

focus on hubs. Delta, for example, had hubs in Atlanta, Dallas–Fort Worth, Salt Lake City, and Los Angeles.

There are many advantages to hubs. Foremost is a multiplier effect, through which many more city pairs receive service with little increase in route miles flown. This is illustrated in Figure 3-1, a hypothetical situation involving ten cities. In the top portion of the figure, nonstop flights serve five city pairs among these cities. But with the addition of a hub, shown at the bottom, thirty-five city pairs can be served (twenty-five by linkage of the five eastern and five western cities through the central hub and 10 more through interconnection of the five western cities and the five eastern cities through the hub).

The hub aggregates commuter traffic from small cities and feeds it into the route system, making it worthwhile to maintain small-community service. Flights are more frequent, and the traveler does not need to change airlines (indeed, passengers are locked into an efficient system of coordinated baggage

FIGURE 3-1
Route multiplication through a hub. (*Top*) Point-to-point service without hub; (*Bottom*) Service via hub connections. (*Source: Melvin A. Brenner, James O. Leet, and Elihu Schott. Airline Deregulation. Westport, Conn.: Eno Foundation for Transportation, Inc., 1985, p. 83.*)

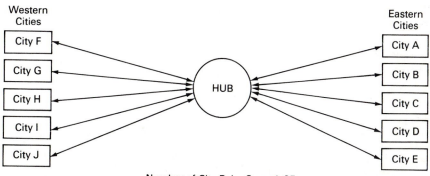

transfer, flight times, and gates in close proximity). When passengers are aggregated in hubs, airlines can fly larger planes, which have a more favorable ratio of cost to passenger revenue miles flown. Some disadvantages exist. The airlines schedule arrivals and departures at peak times, resulting in delays and congestion. And stops at hubs have increased travel time between 4 and 10 percent over pre-1978 averages, depending on the length of the trip.[19]

Hubs also have anticompetitive effects. The consolidation of hub systems by the major airlines has made it virtually impossible for new entries to compete in national markets. Hubs are essential for economies of scale in flight operations. With a properly functioning hub each spoke adds passengers to longer flights in larger aircraft. When fully loaded, these flights are highly profitable. For this reason even established airlines have difficulty penetrating markets in major hubs of competitors. The hub carrier can cross-subsidize spoke flights and engage in fare wars to drive out the interloper. Hence, in major hub cities one airline usually comes to dominate travel. In Minneapolis–St. Paul, for example, Northwest has a 78 percent market share. Delta has a market share of 77 percent in Salt Lake City. TWA has an 82 percent market share in St. Louis. The huge Chicago market is dominated by two airline hubs—United, with 50 percent, and American, with 30 percent.[20]

In addition, the investment in aircraft and airport equipment required to start a hub is prohibitive for new entries. And at key airports such as Chicago's O'Hare, gates and slots for flights are not available at any price because they are hoarded by the major airlines. Until significant new airport construction or facilities expansion takes place, the major airlines that have already locked up gate space and formed hub-and-spoke systems will have a decisive advantage over all challengers.

Frequent-Flier Programs

Frequent-flier programs are marketing promotions used to build brand loyalty among customers. They credit passengers with mileage traveled on the sponsoring airline. Additional credit or bonus points may be earned by flying first-class, leasing cars from specified rental agencies, staying at hotels affiliated with the airline, or flying on new routes promoted by the airline. When enough mileage is flown, the airlines give free trips to members of their frequent-flier clubs. In theory these free travelers occupy seats that would otherwise remain empty and bring in no revenue. In 1988 only 2 to 3 percent of passenger traffic was trips earned on mileage programs.

---

[19]Council of Economic Advisers, op. cit., p. 204.
[20]Figures are from Gisela Bolte and Lee Griggs, "The Sky Kings Rule the Routes," *Time,* May 15, 1989, p. 50; Judith Valente and Robert L. Rose, "Concern Heightens about the Airline Industry's March toward Near Domination by Only a Few Major Carriers," *Wall Street Journal,* March 10, 1989, p. A8; and Martha M. Hamilton, "The Hubbub over Airline Hubbing," *Washington Post National Weekly Edition,* February 13–19, 1989, p. 21. For an analysis of the anticompetitive aspects of hubs see Kirk Victor, "Hub Cap," *National Journal,* May 12, 1990.

The first frequent-flier program was started by American Airlines in 1981, but today all major airlines have them. In 1988 Delta introduced a triple-mileage plan, and other airlines followed to avoid losing passengers. The plans are primarily intended to attract business customers, who are a critical source of revenue. In 1986, business travelers were 32 percent of airline passengers, but because of their frequent trips and tendency to pay higher fares they accounted for 46 percent of airline fares and 68 percent of passenger revenues.[21] The loyalty of business travelers is also valuable because airline patronage is cyclical, and during periods of economic downturn business travel declines less than travel for pleasure. The airlines have been successful in getting about 18 million people signed up on one or more frequent-flier plans, including 72 percent of business travelers.[22]

Frequent fliers tend to take all trips, short and long, on the same airline to build mileage. Some fly out of their way or accept inconvenient schedules to patronize the same airline. Any airline without a frequent-flier program risks losing passengers to a competitor who has one. Even with a frequent-flier program, a new entry or smaller carrier is at a disadvantage competing with a major carrier that has an extensive route system. Frequent-flier plans also protect spoke flights from encroachment by smaller competitors. Business travelers would opt to fly all the time on the airline with which they could accumulate mileage fastest—the airline with the hub-and-spoke system. On occasion, airlines have offered mileage bonuses to meet new competition. Northwest Airlines, which holds a 65 percent market share in Detroit, increased mileage credits on Chicago-Detroit flights in a successful effort to fend off efforts by United and American to penetrate its Detroit hub.

Frequent-flier programs have worked well for the airlines but have raised ethical questions when free trips are awarded to employees whose companies have paid for their tickets. Airlines have steadfastly refused to report the names of free-trip winners to employers, citing an unacceptable paperwork burden. Indeed, the airlines have correctly assessed the attraction of the program. One survey of frequent-flier program members found that when benefits were left to employees, 62 percent thought mileage programs were important in choosing an airline, but when benefits accrued to the company, only 8 percent felt that way.[23]

In another survey 80 percent of corporate travel managers felt that frequent-flier programs increased corporate travel costs with higher fares, unnecessary air travel by employees, wasted employee time due to inconvenient flight schedules, and the use of more expensive rental cars and hotel rooms due to tie-ins with mileage programs. One observer of the plans notes that "in es-

---

[21]Frederick J. Stephenson and Richard J. Fox, "Corporate Attitudes toward Frequent-Flier Programs," *Transportation Journal,* fall 1987, p. 11.

[22]Michael Y. Hu, Rex S. Toh, and Stephen Strand, "Frequent-Flier Programs: Problems and Pitfalls," *Business Horizons,* July–August 1988, p. 53.

[23]Ibid., p. 54.

sence, there is a kickback built into the price of every $150-a-night hotel room and every full-fare airplane ticket. What we are witnessing is a massive, open and wildly successful campaign to corrupt the morals of the corporate class."[24] In 1986, it was estimated that companies wasted over $4 billion a year in travel costs because of frequent-flier incentives.[25] The Internal Revenue Service is interested in taxing frequent-flier awards, but since the airlines have refused to report winners to employers, the awards cannot be reported on W-2 forms.

In the late 1980s the airlines had so many mileage award winners that they tried to limit revenue loss by imposing restrictions on redemption, such as confining passengers on free tickets to a small percentage of seats. But frequent-flier plans are exceptionally successful marketing promotions and, in addition, a potent competitive weapon reinforcing the hub-and-spoke system.

Computerized Reservation Systems

Another strategic weapon that has been used to concentrate power in the hands of the largest airlines is the computerized reservation system, or CRS. The two largest—American's Sabre and United's Apollo—are leased by three-quarters of travel agents who sell airline tickets. Texas Air, Delta, Northwest, and TWA are struggling to catch up with their own systems. These systems list flight schedules and fares for all airlines but give a calculated advantage to the carrier that developed the system (for example, by giving more information about flights or making cross-booking to another airline a complicated procedure). They cost millions of dollars to develop and provide helpful features for travel agents such as menus, on-line help screens, and video images of hotels and travel spots. The systems are used, of course, by an airline's reservation agent.

There are four competitive advantages to having a CRS.

First, the CRS may earn money for the airline. Travel agencies pay to lease the systems, and a fee is charged each time they are used to make a reservation with an airline, hotel, or car rental agency.[26] This helps recover the millions of dollars in development costs needed to create and continuously update the system. In a good year the airlines may earn a return on investment of 8 percent in flight operations, but by one estimate they may earn up to 25 percent on a CRS.[27]

---

[24]Michael Kinsley, "Greed Gets Most Mileage Out of Airline Credits," *Wall Street Journal*, October 10, 1985.

[25]Stephenson and Fox, op. cit., pp. 14–15.

[26]Carolyn Phillips and Paulette Thomas, "Texas Air Asks Transportation Agency to Examine Rivals' Reservation Systems," *Wall Street Journal*, August 19, 1988. The fee for a booking was $1.85 in 1989.

[27]Richard Dalton, "Strategies from the Airlines," *Personal Computing*, March 1988, p. 83. A report by the Government Accounting Office estimated that booking charges are twice the cost of

Second, airlines use the CRS to practice "yield management." Through continuous updates of reservation activity, fares can be adjusted to maximize revenue on each flight. If, for example, a flight is being heavily booked, discount fares can be limited. But if a competitor has lowered fares or if the flight is lightly booked, seats can be heavily discounted. Fine-tuning of fares is so complex that it is not unusual for a big airline such as American to make over 100,000 adjustments in ticket prices each day. An airline with a CRS that uses yield management techniques has a tremendous advantage in securing high-load factors and getting the last marginal dollars from seats that otherwise might have flown empty. From the consumer's point of view, on the other hand, manipulation of fares with CRS data creates inequities. Passengers flying on the same plane, in the same class, often pay widely varying fares.

Third, the major airlines have used "code sharing" to incorporate smaller airlines into the feeder system at hub airports. In code sharing, the flights of smaller regional or commuter airlines are represented by the major carrier's designation. On the travel agent's video screen the turboprop flights of a commuter airline flying under an agreement with, say, American Airlines would be designated AA. In effect, the small airline becomes a feeder in the spoke system of the major airline. Code-sharing agreements, which usually include frequent-flier tie-ins, schedule coordination, cooperative baggage handling, and common airplane paint schemes, turn commuter airlines into satellites of the majors. Independent commuter airlines without code-sharing agreements find it hard to compete with code-sharing rivals.

The major carriers have code-sharing pacts with over fifty regional and commuter airlines. In some cases, the majors have purchased their junior partners. Continental Airlines, for example, acquired a formerly independent commuter line in Texas, Britt Airways, and changed its name to Continental Express. Its planes now feature the Continental logo, and new Continental pilots use the airline as a training ground. In 1987 Continental Express was providing 65 percent of connecting passengers at Continental Airline's hub in Houston.[28] Continental now owns four commuter airlines.[29] Not all major carriers, however, have purchased their commuter pawns, because the small companies are nonunion and the Airline Pilot's Association pacts of some big airlines would require equal pay for the commuter line's pilots. The pilot of a small turboprop might get a $100,000-a-year raise.

And fourth, with a CRS an airline can determine the exact amount of fares booked by travel agencies and offer incentives for heavy booking. Delta, for instance, offers "commission overrides" when agencies sell tickets over a target dollar amount. These are hefty amounts which the travel agency may pass

---

providing the service (see *Airline Competition: Impact of Computerized Reservation Systems,* GAO/RCED-86-74, May 9, 1986).

[28]David M. North, "Continental Upgrades Commuter Fleet with Purchase of ATR42 Aircraft," *Aviation Week & Space Technology,* October 16, 1987, p. 41.

[29]Robert L. Rose, "Major U.S. Airlines Rapidly Gain Control over Regional Lines," *Wall Street Journal,* February 17, 1988.

on to consumers as savings or share with its agents. Most agencies give commission overrides to agents as bonuses. Thus, travel agents are motivated to book passengers on Delta in preference to other airlines. Critics argue that these bonus systems operate to redirect the loyalty of the travel agent away from the consumer and to the airline providing the incentive. Smaller airlines, of course, have neither the CRS nor the volume of business needed to compete in this game. It is one more way that the major airlines have squeezed out frail competitors.

Discount Fares and Cost Cutting

Prior to deregulation in 1978, airline employees were well paid. Between 1970 and 1978 their wages doubled and benefit packages were generous. Rising labor costs were passed along to the public in higher ticket prices, and the average compensation in wages and benefits among employees of major airlines was well above the national average for all industries. Between 1979 and 1983, however, fourteen nonunion airlines entered the industry, and their labor cost advantage enabled them to press a strategy of undercutting the fares of established airlines.

People Express, for example, inaugurated Newark–Los Angeles service in 1984 with a regular coach fare of $149 and a discount fare of $119. At the time the lowest coach fare of any established trunk carrier was $433. People Express pilots were paid an average of $30,000 a year compared with the $104,000 average of TWA pilots. In addition, the nonunion entries were not burdened with restrictive work rules. At People Express pilots put in a 40-hour workweek. When not flying they did paperwork, sold tickets, and even handled baggage. At TWA, on the other hand, collective bargaining agreements restricted pilots to working an average of 50 hours a month.

The fare wars that resulted from the entry of nonunion airlines led established airlines to adopt a variety of strategies to cut labor costs, which averaged 35 percent of total operating costs and were the airline's largest cost component. Some moves were plucky. In 1983 Texas Air chairman Frank Lorenzo took his Continental Airlines subsidiary into Chapter 11, claiming that existing union wage agreements would soon lead to bankruptcy. Shortly, he reorganized the airline as a nonunion carrier with labor costs 30 percent below the industry average. Other moves were inventive. American Airlines avoided strikes by adopting two-tier wage structures which paid newly hired workers lower wages. For example, flight attendants hired after 1983 received a beginning salary of $972 a month and had a ceiling pay of $1,200 a month after five years. Those hired before 1983 started at $1,142 a month and peaked at $2,306 after twelve years. Their jobs were identical; only their salaries were different. Other airlines copied American, and by 1985 62 percent of wage settlements in the industry were two-tier pacts.[30] One side effect of two-tier wages was that they spurred expansion of the major airlines. As they grew, the more new employees they hired, the lower was their labor cost per passenger revenue mile.

The airlines also relied on more traditional strategies for lowering the cost of labor. Between 1980 and 1982, 41,000 airline employees, including 5,000 pilots, lost jobs.[31] For those remaining, airline managements demanded wage concessions and work rule changes. Sometimes this worked. When financier Carl Icahn took over TWA in 1985, he asked for and received across-the-board wage cuts of $30,000 from all pilots. When strikes did occur, management hired nonunion workers to replace strikers. Over the years this made unions reluctant to strike, and they adopted other tactics to resist concessions. For example, in 1986 Texas Air, led by the notoriously antiunion Frank Lorenzo, acquired Eastern Airlines. Eastern had a high wage structure, and Lorenzo demanded concessions. When the unions proved recalcitrant, Lorenzo in 1988 set up subsidiaries of Texas Air to buy some of Eastern Airlines' routes and transfer them to nonunion Continental Airlines (also owned by Texas Air). The unions responded by organizing a campaign in which machinists wrote letters to members of Congress stating that Eastern's planes were poorly maintained and a safety risk to the public. This led to an unusual FAA special inspection of Eastern's planes and a $256 million loss for the second quarter as cautious passengers booked away from Eastern flights. Lorenzo sued two unions, accusing them of an illegal conspiracy to depress Texas Air's stock price so they could acquire the company. The inspection concluded that the planes were safe, and Lorenzo dropped the lawsuit, but poor labor-management relations continued. When Lorenzo tried to pull out of Eastern's Kansas City hub and eliminate 4,000 jobs later in 1988, the unions sought and received a temporary injunction, arguing that he was finessing the transfer of jobs and routes to Texas Air's nonunion subsidiary, Continental Airlines. Early in 1989 strikes by Eastern's machinists and pilots forced Lorenzo to take Eastern into Chapter 11 reorganization proceedings in bankruptcy court.

The efforts of airlines to reduce labor costs in the first decade of deregulation were successful, but they left a bitter legacy. Management pressure to hold down labor costs continues unabated. Unions remain strong despite reverses, and as the majors consolidate market power, they may once again be pressured to pass higher wage costs along to passengers as in pre-1978 days.

---

[30]"Two-Tier Wages Systems Still on Rise, Reported in 11 Percent of Pacts," *Daily Labor Report*, Bureau of National Affairs, no. 31, February 14, 1986, p. B-2.

[31]Bureau of the Census. *Statistical Abstract of the United States: 1985*. Washington, D.C.: U.S. Government Printing Office, 1986, Table 1071. To date, the employee protection program (EPP) in the Airline Deregulation Act of 1978 has not been activated. The program withstood a challenge by the industry based on the inclusion of a now unconstitutional legislative veto provision in its language. In *Alaska Airlines* v. *Brock,* 55 LW 4396 (1987), the Supreme Court upheld the EPP provisions while invalidating the right of Congress to veto Department of Labor guidelines.

Mergers and Acquisitions

Since deregulation major airlines have rushed to form ever more extensive route systems. There are many competitive advantages to a larger route system, including, for instance, greater attraction to members of frequent-flier plans. As infirm airlines have faltered in recent years, acquisition of their aircraft, gates, airport slots, and routes has accelerated. Since 1985, twenty-six mergers and acquisitions have been completed. The eight largest airlines all expanded by digesting one or more former rivals.

In addition, these major airlines have code-sharing arrangements with over fifty commuter airlines, rendering these small fry only nominally independent. The new airline industry is not the laissez-faire industry dreamed of by deregulators. Rather, it is an oligopoly in which a small number of major airlines have enormous market power. A sizable number of small regional and commuter airlines remain independent of the major carriers, but they do so by occupying uncompetitive niches and serving thin markets.

How does this emergent oligopoly work? As shown in Table 3-1, the largest airline, American, has only 18.6 percent of the national market, and some of the other major carriers have less than 10 percent. But the locus of airline competition is at specific airports. And in many hub cities around the country there is little competition for the dominant carrier. To illustrate, in 1989 Northwest Airlines had an 11.5 percent national market share but an 87 percent market share in Memphis, more than ten times the share of its nearest rival, Delta. TWA, with an 8.8 percent national market share, seized an 82.3 percent market share in its St. Louis hub after acquiring its only regional competitor, Ozark Airlines. It charges a $59 regular one-way fare on the 259-mile trip to Chicago's Midway Airport. But from St. Louis to Indianapolis, a slightly shorter flight, the fare is $200. The difference is that TWA has competition from Southwest Airlines on the flight to Chicago and no competition going to Indianapolis.

Both the Department of Transportation (DOT) and the Department of Jus-

TABLE 3-1
LARGEST U.S. AIRLINES RANKED BY MARKET SHARE IN JANUARY 1989

American Airlines	18.6%
United Airlines	17.6%
Delta Airlines	15.0%
Northwest Airlines	11.5%
Continental Airlines*	9.8%
Trans World Airlines	8.8%
USAir Group	8.5%
Pan American Airlines	7.3%
Eastern Airlines*	2.9%

Source: Adapted from ''An Industry Poised for Expansion,'' *The New York Times*, February 20, 1990, p. C5.
*Owned by Continental Airlines Holdings, Inc. (formerly Texas Air Corporation).

tice have responsibility for ensuring fair competitive practices among the airlines. But both have taken an exceptionally optimistic position about postmerger competition in local markets; of twenty mergers submitted since 1985 all have been approved. The 1986 TWA proposal to acquire Ozark exemplifies how liberal DOT and Justice have been. Both TWA and Ozark had St. Louis hubs and they competed on thirty-three nonstop city-pair routes. On nineteen of these routes there was no other nonstop competition. Ozark and TWA also operated a total of forty-one other St. Louis routes on which they did not compete with each other. Despite the certain knowledge that TWA was absorbing its major local competitor the DOT approved this acquisition, stating it was reasonable to assume that a new entrant could form a hub in St. Louis and that this threat provided market discipline for TWA.[32]

Critics argue that such acquisitions lead to monopoly pricing when consumers have no reasonable alternatives. They use the TWA-Ozark merger as evidence. After the merger the number of direct routes served by only one St. Louis carrier jumped from sixty to eighty-five, the number served by two or more fell from sixty-four to thirty-six, and those served by four or more fell from fifteen to seven. In the two years following the merger average fares on the thirty-three routes where TWA and Ozark had been in competition rose 18.2 percent compared with 6 percent nationwide.[33] TWA claimed that it had been in a "long-running destructive price war" with Ozark and prices were so low that only one carrier could survive in St. Louis and only then by raising prices dramatically following a merger.[34] The TWA computerized reservation system, PARS, has 77 percent of the market in St. Louis and charges other airlines a fee of $1.84 for every passenger booked (keep in mind that the average profit of all airlines per enplaned passenger ranges between $1 and $2!). In addition, TWA has long-term leases giving it exclusive use of fifty-eight of the eighty-one gates at St. Louis's Lambert Airport, while no other airline has more than three. And clauses in the TWA leases give it a major say in any proposal to expand the airport. To date no expansion is planned. In response to criticism that TWA has the power to discourage competition, raise prices, and obstruct the entry of new airlines into the St. Louis market, Secretary of

[32]TWA-Ozark Acquisition Case, Department of Transportation Order No. 86-9-29 (September 12, 1986), pp. 2–3. In 1989 the Justice Department objected to two pending deals. American Airlines and Delta were forced to drop plans to merge their computerized reservation systems. And Eastern was opposed when it attempted to sell eight gates in Philadelphia, to USAir because the additional gates would give USAir twenty-three of the airport's forty-nine gates, increasing USAir's current regional dominance and blocking new competition in Philadelphia markets. Opposition by DOT and Justice led Eastern to sell the eight Philadelphia gates to Midway Airlines. See U.S. General Accounting Office, *Airline Competition: DOT and Justice Oversight of Eastern Air Lines' Bankruptcy,* Washington, D.C.: Government Printing Office, GAO/RCED-90-79, February 1990, p. 4.

[33]*Hearing before the Committee on Commerce, Science, and Transportation,* "Airline Concentration at Hub Airports," U.S. Senate, September 22, 1988, p. 47. Statement of Kenneth M. Mead, General Accounting Office.

[34]Ibid., p. 98. Testimony of Robert Cozzi, vice president for revenue management, Trans World Airlines.

Transportation James H. Burnley IV argued before a congressional committee that airline markets can function competitively even when highly concentrated because "entry into a new . . . market requires little more than the shuffling of equipment, in other words airplanes, and the leasing of gates at an airport."[35]

Other mergers, such as the 1985 Southwest-Muse union, have been approved under the "failing company" doctrine.[36] This doctrine holds that no anticompetitive problem exists when a failing competitor is rescued by merger. If bankruptcy had occurred, competition would have been eliminated in any case. Thus, approval of the merger does not lessen competition, it is argued.

Two actions have been suggested to counteract the anticompetitive effects of growing industry concentration. First, domestic routes could be thrown open to international carriers. These routes are now reserved for U.S. airlines, a commonplace form of protectionism around the world. But there is no question that allowing foreign carriers into the country would increase competition. Second, airport facilities could be expanded. If there were more gates available, for example, it would be easier for competitors to start new hubs in cities where one airline now has a lock on most of the gates.

ASSESSING INDUSTRY PERFORMANCE UNDER DEREGULATION

A full assessment of the airline industry under deregulation requires consideration of the impact of industry operation on the public. Several areas of public concern prior to deregulation were safety, service to small communities, and the quality of customer service in the industry. How has the industry performed in these areas? Here is an assessment. Also, the financial performance of the industry is discussed.

Safety

Under deregulation the safety record of the airlines is excellent. Early fears that cost cutting would increase the risk of accidents proved unfounded. Airline safety has been gradually improving since the 1920s, and the long-term trend continued after deregulation. The number of air deaths per billion passenger miles declined from 1.6 in 1979 to 0.7 in 1985 and 0.02 in 1986.[37] Fatalities declined for both major carriers and commuter airlines. The decline may not have been the *result* of deregulation and may even be less of a decline than would have occurred if regulation had continued.

In fact, deregulation may have raised risks in subtle ways. For instance,

[35]Ibid., p. 7. Testimony of James H. Burnley IV, Secretary, Department of Transportation.
[36]Other airlines which were in extreme financial peril when they merged were People Express, Frontier, PSA, AirCal, Western, and Ozark.
[37]Richard B. McKenzie and William F. Shughart II, "Deregulation's Impact on Air Safety: Separating Fact from Fiction," *Consumer's Research,* January 1988, p. 12.

THE OVERLAND STAGE EMPIRE

Those who fear the growing market power of large airlines find an instructive parallel in transportation history. From 1861 to 1866 the Overland Stage Line held a monopoly on stagecoach travel in the West. Ben Holladay, its owner, accumulated 3,145 miles of stage routes using predatory tactics to drive out smaller competitors.

One effective method was to enter a new market with a lowball coach fare and subsidize his efforts on the route with profits from monopoly service elsewhere until local competitors went bankrupt. A small stage line between Denver and Central City in Colorado, for example, was charging $6 per run. Holladay put a lavish new-model stagecoach, a Concord Coach with a leather interior, on the line and charged only $2. The competing line, run by the sheriff of Denver, soon folded, whereupon Holladay replaced the new Concord Coach with a more primitive stage and raised the fare to $12.

In 1864 he used the same pitiless stratagem on the Virginia City–Helena run. The existing stage line charged $25 and used Concord Coaches. Holladay entered the route charging only $2.50 per passenger. In two months the local line quit, so Holladay raised the price of a ticket to $37.50 and replaced his Concord Coaches with crude wagons.

Holladay's record as a monopolist is not heartening. He charged extortionate rates to shippers, raised passenger fares when there was a possibility of encountering hostile Indians, and once hired in a supervisory position a killer who murdered several other employees to improve the efficiency of his district. The latter was a landmark in the history of management by fear.

Holladay sold the Overland Stage Line to Wells, Fargo & Company in 1866 when he sensed that railroads were about to end the dominance of stage lines in transportation west of the Mississippi. He started the Oregon & California Railroad but lost it in the financial panic of 1873. In 1887 he died an alcoholic in Portland, Oregon.

hub-and-spoke systems have increased the number of short flights, and there are more takeoffs and landings than under the simpler pre-1978 route systems. Since takeoffs and landings are the moments of highest danger, the risk of accidents has increased. Also, pressure on costs and debt from acquisitions has caused the major airlines to postpone purchases of new aircraft. The average jetliner in 1988 was 12.5 years old as compared with less than 10 years old in 1978.[38] This is the oldest air fleet of any industrial nation.

Aging increases the danger of metal fatigue, as was dramatically illustrated when part of the fuselage of an Aloha Airlines Boeing 737 flew off during a flight in April 1988. A stewardess was killed, and several passengers were injured. This plane was fifteen years old and had made 89,680 island-hopping flights, pressurizing and depressurizing its thin aluminum skin in the corrosive tropical atmosphere. Because a new competitor, Mid Pacific Airlines, had emerged after deregulation to challenge Aloha and Hawaiian Airlines, Aloha was forced into cost-cutting measures. Included were lengthened 737 maintenance cycles and staff reduction to an average of seventeen maintenance

---

[38]Judith Valent, Roy J. Harris, Jr., and Laurie McGinley, ''Should Airlines Scrap Their Oldest Planes for Sake of Safety,'' *Wall Street Journal,* May 6, 1988.

workers per plane, ten less than the U.S. industry average of twenty-seven. Aloha denies that these factors made its plane unsafe that day, but the accident embodies in a nutshell the situation in the whole industry and raises fears.

Much has been made of a rising number of near-misses. But these are attributable in part to increased flights and to more accurate reporting procedures. Near midair collisions increased from 311 in 1982 to 839 in 1986, but 96 percent involved private planes.[39]

Overall, deregulation has made travel in general safer for the public. Cheaper fares have led to the substitution of flying for other forms of transportation. Air travel is notably safer than other forms of intercity transportation, particularly auto travel. Auto travel has an average fatality rate of 35.7 per billion miles traveled, or roughly 1,700 times the rate for air travel! Thus, it is argued, deregulation has saved lives.[40]

Service to Small Communities

Under CAB regulation service to small communities was usually unprofitable for trunk carriers. As an incentive to continue service, trunk carriers were allowed to cross-subsidize the cost of service to small markets by charging slightly higher fares on longer routes. Both trunks and commuter airlines were also given direct federal subsidies.

With deregulation it was feared that airlines would abandon small airports and with free entry shift their planes to higher density routes. Hence, the Airline Deregulation Act of 1978 set up an Essential Air Services program which permitted continued government subsidy of airlines flying to small communities.

After deregulation many large carriers pulled jet service from small communities, and they were replaced by commuter airlines flying turboprops. In most cases flights were more frequent, but fewer seats were available. Between 1978 and 1983, 106 airports, or 17 percent of airports with scheduled flights in 1978, lost service altogether, and 23 airports with no service in 1978 had new service.[41] But deregulation was only the indirect cause of abandonment. As commuter airlines replaced departing trunk carriers, they expanded, bought aircraft, and took on heavy debt burdens. Many were unable to meet interest payments during recessionary years between 1980 and 1982, and as they went bankrupt, some small communities were left without service. When United pulled out of Modesto, California, for example, it was followed by a succession of five commuter airlines, each of which discontinued service because of financial problems.

As time passed, however, flights from smaller cities were increasingly included as spokes in developing hub-and-spoke systems. Recent studies con-

---

[39]Sharon Walsh and Martha Hamilton, "FTC Hails Deregulation of Airlines," *Washington Post National Weekly Edition*, February 15–21, 1988, p. 23.

[40]Council of Economic Advisers, op. cit., p. 211.

[41]Clinton V. Oster, Jr., "Deregulation and Passenger Transportation to Small Communities," *Policy Studies Journal*, June 1987, p. 743.

clude that even though some cities have lost air service, the overall level of service to small communities remains strong.[42] In 1978, 350 communities received subsidized flights, but by 1990 Congress had cut the budget of the Essential Air Services program so that only 90 were still being subsidized. In most communities which have lost air service, however, the government ended subsidy because there were few travelers (sometimes only one or two a day) or cities within an hour's drive had an airport. In the 1990s most small towns with continued service have more frequent flights now than prior to deregulation, but they are served by smaller planes with less seating capacity. Fares are typically high.

Customer Service

In 1986 former Senator James Abourezk boarded a New York Air jetliner in Washington, D.C., at 4 p.m. for the commute to a United Nation's cocktail party in New York. The plane left the gate and then sat on the runway for three hours. Having missed the cocktail party, Abourezk demanded to deplane but was refused. Forced to fly to New York and catch the earliest flight back, he arrived home after 1:00 a.m. His anger led him to file a lawsuit against New York Air seeking $200,000 in damages for "false imprisonment" by the airline.[43] Unfortunately, after deregulation experiences such as Abourezk's became more frequent. As fares dropped and passenger bookings increased, the air transport system was increasingly overburdened. The result was delays, flight cancellations, lost baggage, and general service problems.

There are many reasons for service problems. Fundamentally, they result from competitive actions of the airlines under deregulation. For example, the primary cause of flight delays is traffic overload. Traffic overload arises from more flights and more passengers. Hub-and-spoke systems overload airport landing capacities by scheduling too many flights at peak times. It is not unusual for a carrier to schedule forty to fifty planes to arrive within an hour of each other at a hub. After a 45-minute delay for transfer of passengers, the planes will be scheduled to begin taking off at a rate of one a minute. At airports with competing hubs, airlines schedule flights for popular times and overload the system. It is a physical impossibility for fifteen planes to depart at 9:00 a.m. at any airport. In 1987 ground delays averaged about 2,000 hours each day, the equivalent of grounding 253 planes or roughly one major carrier.[44] Department of Transportation data indicates that each month between one-quarter and one-third of all flights are late.

---

[42]Ibid.; Mary Kihl, "The Impact of Deregulation on Passenger Transportation in Small Towns," *Transportation Quarterly,* April 1988; and Jerzy Jemiolo and Clinton V. Oster, Jr., "Regional Changes in Airline Service since Deregulation," *Transportation Quarterly,* October 1987.

[43]Stewart Powell, "The Late, Late Show," *U.S. News & World Report,* December 22, 1986.

[44]Robert L. Rose, "Widespread Delays Seen Plaguing Summer Air Travel," *Wall Street Journal,* June 28, 1988, p. 31.

After President Reagan fired striking air controllers in 1981, fewer controllers were available and traffic was slower. Many airports are operating beyond planned capacity, and the nation's last new airport, Dallas–Ft. Worth, was built in 1974. Many airports are planning expansions, but only one new airport (in Denver) will be built in the 1990s.

Efforts at cost control by airlines have also created service problems. Layoffs of ticket agents, baggage handlers, gate personnel, and flight attendants mean fewer helping hands for travelers. Airline spending on customer service dropped at the very time the number of passengers was increasing. The airlines have purchased newer seat configurations in jetliners to carry more passengers. Early Boeing 747s, for example, seated 331 passengers, but by the mid-1980s some had been refitted to hold over 450. Disruptions inherent in mergers and acquisitions have also accounted for some service problems. Overall, there is no question that airline service problems exist.

Government has done little to force improved passenger service. In late 1987 the Department of Transportation did require airlines to disclose on-time performance data. Other proposals to relieve congestion without reintroducing the hand of regulation exist. Economists have, for example, advocated setting a price for takeoff and landing slots at airports that reflects the costs of congestion. These slots could be bought and sold by airlines. The airlines would then charge more for tickets on peak-hour flights, and travelers who were willing to pay to leave at popular times could do so. Travelers with flexible schedules would save money by taking off-peak flights. This proposal overcomes a problem with the present system, where delayed travelers who pay the costs of congestion in loss of their time cannot signal the market that they are willing to pay a premium for on-time performance.[45]

Industry Profit and Loss Performance

The airline industry has a history of earnings volatility, and over the years its return on investment has been below the average for all industries. Airline financial reporting characteristically relies on operating profit figures to represent earnings. Each year between 1950 and 1978 (the year of deregulation) the industry earned an operating profit. But operating profit does not include interest payments on borrowed money, and when these payments are included, the industry is shown to have suffered a net operating loss in four years (1961, 1970, 1971, and 1975).

After deregulation a combination of factors—inflation, a large rise in jet fuel prices in 1979, fare wars, and economic recession—raised costs and weakened balance sheets. Between 1978 and 1984 long-term debt increased by 111 percent, while equity grew only 29 percent.[46] The impact was hardest on major

---

[45]Council of Economic Advisers, op. cit., p. 217.
[46]Brenner et al., op. cit., p. 51.

airlines, which suffered operating losses from 1980 through 1983. In 1984 the industry earned an operating profit, but heavy interest payments wiped out small operating profits in 1985 and 1986. In 1987 the industry once again achieved modest profitability and in 1988 earned record profits. But overall returns have been disappointing: a net profit margin of 1.6 percent between 1978 and 1988 compared with 4.6 percent for all U.S. manufacturing companies.[47] The smaller airline segment, on the other hand, recorded aggregate operating profits each year after deregulation. The reason is that while major airlines engaged in ruthless fare wars on high-density routes, the small regional and commuter airline were able to move into routes abandoned by the majors, routes better than those they had flown under the CAB system.

Not surprisingly, aggregate industry operating profit and loss results mask wide discrepancies in company performance. In 1984 and 1985, for example, the industry reached $2 billion in operating profits. But 60 percent of this, or $1.2 billion, was earned by just three companies (American, Delta, and Eastern).[48] Twelve other carriers reported losses, and twenty filed bankruptcy petitions. This diversity of company performance persists and is typical of both large and small airlines.

To the casual observer it might seem that the airlines should be doing well; after all, passenger traffic has soared. The problem for airlines of all sizes, however, has been that costs per passenger revenue mile have risen faster than revenues. Revenues have been depressed by fare wars. And even though fares and revenues began to rise in 1989 after industry consolidation and stabilization brought at least temporary respite from fare wars, a wave of mergers and acquisitions by the major carriers put huge amounts of long-term debt on balance sheets—so much, in fact, that between 1984 and 1988 long-term debt in the air transport industry doubled.[49] Companies such as Texas Air, with over $4 billion in debt, may eventually have to resort to renewed fare slashing to keep revenues up so they can make interest payments.

In the late 1980s the profit picture of the airline industry was in keeping with historical trends of low average return on investment and cyclical volatility. In the early 1990s industry structure appears to be stabilizing, but apparently this new stability has not altered the traditional ebb and flow of financial performance. As an oligopolistic market structure begins to emerge, it is not surprising that fares are inching up. The low fares of 1978 through 1987 were probably not sustainable. In the long run higher revenues will be necessary to buy replacements for aging aircraft, pay for noise control and safety equipment, fund a higher level of customer service, and pay for increases in jet fuel costs.

---

[47]Labich, op. cit., p. 51.
[48]Golich, op. cit., p. 174.
[49]Garland Chow, Richard D. Gritta, and Ronald Hockstein, "Airline Financing Policies in a Deregulated Environment," *Transportation Journal,* spring 1988. The figure on debt is derived from Marilyn M. McKellin, "Air Transport Industry," *Value Line Investment Survey.* New York: Value Line, Inc., July 1, 1988, pt. III, ed. 2, p. 251.

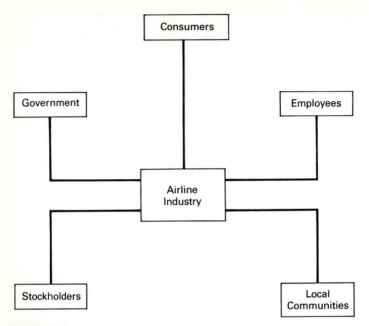

FIGURE 3-2
A map of major airline industry stakeholders.

AN OVERALL ASSESSMENT OF DEREGULATION

The results of deregulation must be assessed from the standpoint of important stakeholders of the airline industry. Stakeholders are groups, institutions, or individuals who have both an influence on the industry and a stake in its welfare.

Figure 3-2 is a map of the most important airline industry stakeholders. What follows is a brief comment on how each has fared under deregulation.

Government

Since the early days when the industry began carrying airmail, the government has had an important stake in developing and maintaining an efficient air transport system. The legacy of forty years of CAB regulation was a remarkably good system, and under deregulation, the system expanded to fly more passengers and cargo. The air transport system still functions well, but to the extent that problems have arisen in the era of deregulation, government may be partly responsible.

Former CAB head Alfred E. Kahn argues that the government is guilty of "gross derelictions" in doing its job.[50] The federal government has failed to provide an adequate number of air traffic controllers to manage the system. Local governments, in the absence of federal stimulus, have failed to expand airport capacity to handle growth in air travel; airports have failed to price

---

[50]Alfred E. Kahn, "I Would Do It Again," *Regulation*, no. 2, 1988, p. 26.

landing fees in a way that ensures on-time departures at peak hours; and Washington bureaucrats who approved mergers seem "to have no appreciation whatever of the dangers our antitrust laws were set up almost a century ago to forestall."[51]

Consumers

Extensive price discounting has made it possible for more people to fly. Passenger volume increased from 240 million in 1978 to 455 million in 1989 and keeps rising. There is no question that price competition has benefited millions of consumers. A 1990 DOT study concluded that since 1981 airfares have fallen 26 percent when adjusted for inflation.[52] This national trend, however, masks interesting countertrends. For example, in cities where there is less competition airfares have actually risen. The DOT study found that the average airfare at the eight most concentrated hub airports had not fallen. It was, in fact, 19 percent higher. Prices have also risen on shorter routes, although airline costs are higher for service to small cities, and lack of competition may be only partly to blame. One other trend should be noted. Most of the decrease in airfares took place prior to 1986, before the end of the great merger wave. And since 1988, prices have risen slightly. Service problems such as crowding, delays, longer flights through hubs, and lost baggage have nagged travelers, leading some to suggest that they are getting less for their lower fares. Overall, the picture for consumers is mixed. But the blame for problems may lie more with government inaction in building new airports than in deregulation itself.

Employees

Airline employees have suffered firings, wage cuts, work rule changes, dual wage structures, and union-busting activities. Deregulation has made labor more productive, but the price has been considerable trauma for many.

Local Communities

Larger communities have more frequent service through hubs. Most smaller communities continue to have service by commuter airlines, even where the majors have pulled out. The loss of service to small airports that was feared never materialized.

Stockholders

Despite depressed earnings in the early years of deregulation, stocks of the major airlines have slightly outperformed the New York Stock Exchange

---

[51]Ibid.
[52]Sam Fulwood III, "Deregulation Cut Air Fares, DOT Study Says," *Los Angeles Times*, February 15, 1990.

average.[53] The stocks of smaller or regional carriers performed even more strongly. For individual investors, however, much depended on specific companies invested in and share activity during acquisitions. As industry leaders consolidate their domination of markets in the 1990s, they may be able to increase fares and reward stockholders more.

Questions

The results of airline deregulation raise many questions. The preceding paragraphs offered a brief commentary on how deregulation has affected the welfare of industry stakeholders. What conclusion should be reached as a result? Is deregulation a net gain or net loss to public welfare? Alfred E. Kahn, one of the driving forces behind deregulation in 1978, says, "I would do it again. . . . I still assert with total conviction that it would be thoroughly irrational to contemplate going back to regulation as it was practiced between 1938 and 1978— a policy that thoroughly and systematically suppressed all price competition from the outset."[54] Others are not sanguine about the results. Hobart Rowen, economic writer for the *Washington Post,* wrote:

> Not everybody—especially its sponsors—wants to admit it, but the Airline Deregulation Act of 1978 has resulted in a highly concentrated, monopolistic industry.
>
> It not only triggered an era of lousy management/labor relations, but also the penny-pinching it sanctioned delayed the acquisition of new aircraft and forced "savings" that may have been a factor in a number of tragic accidents.[55]

The emerging oligopolistic structure of the industry raises many questions. Foremost is: Will further concentration of market power create abuses, and should antitrust laws be applied more restrictively?

The competitive strategies of the airlines raise ethical questions, including these: (1) Do frequent-flier plans encourage a subtle larceny among business travelers? (2) Are two-tier wage plans fundamentally unjust in unequally compensating individuals with identical jobs? (3) Does "yield management" violate commonsense notions of equality by selling seats on the same flight at differing prices? (4) Is it ethical to lower fares on one route to drive out a smaller competitor which cannot cross-subsidize the route by charging higher prices elsewhere?

Another area of concern is government. Should the federal government act to reregulate the airline industry in any way? Without reregulation, should actions be taken by government to improve the competitive environment of the industry?

---

[53]Moore, op. cit., p. 23.
[54]Kahn, op. cit., p. 26.
[55]"Deregulation Monopoly," *Washington Post National Weekly Edition,* March 27–April 2, 1989, p. 5.

FACTORY FARMING

For thousands of years domesticated animals for human consumption were raised on small farms. Memories of these farms inspire the idyllic stereotype of animal husbandry held by urbanites. In it, chickens strut in the barnyard, catch insects for food, and roost in nearby barns. Pigs wallow in mud and gorge on swill from the farmer's table. Cattle and sheep graze in verdant pastures.

Today, however, few food animals live on such farms. Consumer demand for poultry and livestock products is so great that animals must be processed in huge numbers. Chickens, for example, are raised in flocks of 100,000 within a single building, and some farms have as many as 3,000,000 at one time. Cattle and sheep fatten on densely populated feedlots in such numbers that their wastes create pollution problems for local watersheds. Pigs are fattened in serried cages over the concrete floors of warehouselike buildings. These operations resemble factories as much as farms—hence the nomenclature "factory farm."

As animal agriculture has adopted mass production techniques, it has exposed itself to critics who see a conflict between factory farming and animal welfare. They believe that state-of-the-art husbandry is cruel. Some believe that farm animals, like humans, have fundamental rights and that these rights are violated on factory farms. Farm owners, on the other hand, say that animals are more productive when happy and so are well kept. This debate raises unique ethical questions, questions which challenge the legitimacy of a major industry. Are modern farmers violating animals' rights and important social values? By reading what follows you may be able to answer this question.

POULTRY PRODUCTION

To illustrate how factory farming techniques affect the lives of captive animals we turn first to poultry. It was in poultry production, especially chicken rearing, that techniques of factory farming were first introduced, and it is here that they have reached their zenith.

Chickens are gallinaceous birds; that is, their species is part of the order Galliformes, which also includes turkeys, pheasants, grouse, and partridges. Galliformes are heavy-bodied, short-duration fliers that feed on insects and seeds, nest on the ground, and hatch precocial (self-caring) young. They are social birds which communicate with each other and establish complex hierarchies in flocks.

The earliest wild chickens, members of the species *Gallus gallus,* ran wild in the jungles of southeast Asia, where they were hunted for food. About 4,000 years ago they were domesticated by local civilizations, and in addition to being a source of food, they were used as religious sacrifices and for cockfighting. From the jungles of Asia the domesticated chicken, *Gallus domesticus,* spread across the globe. In Persia they were used in religious sacrifices, in ancient Greece they were used in the sport of cockfighting, and in imperial Rome prophets read the future in their entrails. Chickens were such objects of superstition to the Romans that generals in battle kept special flocks in the belief that their behavior could foretell victory or defeat. We can find humor in the image of hardened legionnaires crowding around the sacred flock in the hours before combat to seek portents. Roman legions left chickens behind as they marched, and this contributed to their geographic diffusion in ancient times.

In the United States chickens brought by European settlers were used as a food source. But the poultry industry was slow to develop. As late as the 1920s the largest chicken farm in the country had a flock of only 500 birds. Today the industry is highly specialized, with some farms in egg production and others raising broilers (or chickens that are slaughtered for meat; literally, chickens that can be broiled—or baked or fried). Prior to World War II farmers raised dual-purpose breeds as both egg producers and broilers.

For years the industry was labor-intensive. Typically, small flocks of chickens were raised in coops with large outdoor runs. In the 1940s there were over 2,000,000 farms selling eggs, and most of these also sold broilers.[1] In those days it took about 16 hours of labor to raise 100 chickens to slaughter weight, and the price of chicken was high compared with the price of beef and pork.[2] The average American ate only 17.5 pounds of chicken a year.[3]

Then two developments transformed the industry. First, scientific research resolved the mystery of vitamin requirements and made possible the invention of poultry feed containing vitamin D. Previously, attempts to raise chickens in

---

[1] William J. Stadelman, "The Egg Industry," in William J. Stadelman and Owen J. Cotterill, eds. *Egg Science and Technology.* Westport, Conn.: AVI Publishing Company, 1986, p. 7.
[2] Robert Sobel and David B. Sicilia. *The Entrepreneurs.* Boston: Houghton Mifflin, 1986, p. 79.
[3] "The Competition Gets Hotter as Meats Battle for Consumers," *Farmline,* March 1987, p. 3.

indoor cages were hindered by leg weakness and rickets due to lack of sunlight. With the advent of commercial feed containing vitamin D, however, chickens could be adapted to confinement in large batteries of tiered cages. Cage rearing had enormous laborsaving advantages. Second, government economic controls during World War II created a market favoring poultry consumption. Red meat was rationed during the war, but not poultry. Because of efficient cage rearing and greater consumer demand the price of chicken began to fall relative to that of beef and pork, and the bird became an everyday staple rather than a special meal for Sundays and holidays.

Since World War II the popularity of chicken has waxed with production efficiency. Today chicken production is so automated that a single worker can tend a flock of 100,000, and only 6 minutes of labor are needed to raise 100 broilers![4] Although average per capita consumption of eggs and red meats has remained about the same since the 1940s, consumption of poultry has increased over 400 percent to nearly 80 pounds per year.[5] This is a fabulous success story tarnished only by animal advocates who say that economic efficiency has a heartless dimension.

THE MODERN EGG FACTORY

How do the more than 5 billion chickens raised each year in the United States spend their days? What follows is a description of state-of-the-art confinement and husbandry techniques in modern egg factories.

Hatching the Chicks

The first step in producing eggs is breeding the biological machines that lay them. Most egg-laying hens, called layers, are specially bred strains of single-comb white leghorn chickens produced by a small number of breeding companies. Geneticists have used selective breeding to create desirable characteristics in layers. Over the years they have pushed back the age of sexual maturity, increased rates of egg laying, and reduced body size to cut feed consumption. In the 1940s, for instance, layers weighed about 4.5 pounds and produced about 130 eggs a year. Today the average layer weighs only 3.9 pounds but lays about 240 eggs a year. Genetic improvement has eliminated the tendency of leghorns to interrupt egg production during winter months. Selection for desirable traits such as productivity, shell toughness, and disease resistance continues. One problem is that selection for strains that lay more eggs results in more aggressive chickens. This is because more prolific hens are more dominant hens.

In hatcheries, eggs from breeding flocks are collected and cooled to about

---

[4]*Statistical Abstract of the United States 1988,* 108th edition, table no. 1090.
[5]"The Competition Gets Hotter as Meats Battle for Consumers," loc. cit.

60°F. They can be stored for 7 to 14 days without significant increases in hatching failures. In large hatcheries as many as 1,000,000 eggs a week are put into automated forced-air incubators for mass hatching. These machines keep the eggs at 98.6° to 100.4° and 50 to 60 percent humidity and rotate them at 45-degree angles six to eight times a day to duplicate the natural tumbling of a fussy nesting hen. They monitor and stabilize oxygen and carbon dioxide levels because small variations lead to reduced hatching rates. In a well-managed hatchery 96 percent of the eggs hatch. They open in 21 days when the chick breaks the shell by striking it repeatedly with a small egg tooth. Within 2 hours the chick is up and walking. Slow-hatching eggs are thrown away to avoid delaying production cycles. Unfortunately, they sometimes hatch in the trash.

Male chicks will never lay eggs and are of no further use to the commercial hatchery. Years ago they might have been raised as broilers, but today only big-bodied strains that convert feed to meaty breasts more efficiently make profitable broilers. So the young chicks are sorted by skilled "chick pullers," who examine their sex organs and separate males from females. Males are tossed into large garbage bags, where those on the bottom may suffocate before the bag is filled. Some hatcheries simply close the bags and suffocate the rest. Others gas the male chicks or use a 2-hp "chick/poult eliminator" manufactured by K. L. Products that grinds up living chicks at 3200 rpm. The machine is advertised as a "humane way of disposal of chicks," and the macerated remains can be recycled into animal feed or fertilizer.[6]

Since the egg industry is highly specialized, the female chicks are sent from the hatchery to a company that specializes in growing pullets, as immature laying hens are called. Before the chicks are shipped, however, the hatchery may perform other services for the grower. Most commonly, the chicks are debeaked. In this operation minimum-wage employees cut the tips of their beaks off in machines with hot, sharp blades. The purpose of debeaking is to reduce cannibalism and harmful pecking among chickens when they are later unnaturally crowded into cages. When broilers are being raised and males are not killed, they may have their wattles and combs removed in a process called dubbing. This is done so that males crowded together in cages will not recognize each other as well and be less inclined to aggress. Similarly, toes are clipped behind the claw to prevent damage from scratching and back ripping later on. Chicks may also be vaccinated or injected with antibiotics. Some die from shock or ineptitude in the administration of these procedures.

Caging the Flock

Hatchery chicks are sold to poultry houses for about $0.50 each. There they grow to sexual maturity and can begin egg production at 20 to 22 weeks of age. Poultry houses are plain, single-story buildings with gabled roofs. The typical house is 40 feet wide and as long as necessary to hold flocks of the desired

---

[6]"Product Showcase," *Poultry Digest*, August 1988, p. 378.

A row of cages in a modern henhouse. (*Source: Courtesy of Humane Farming Association, 1550 California Street, Suite 6, San Francisco, CA 94109. Used with permission.*)

size. The reason they are only 40 feet wide is that greater width requires expensive truss supports and increases construction costs. The need for economy in construction gives poultry buildings their characteristic long, low, narrow appearance.

Inside, the pullets are put in small side-by-side cages assembled in rows extending the length of the building. These cages may be stacked up to six levels high. In most egg-laying operations four to six fully grown layers are placed in a cage with the floor space of a record album. The birds cannot flap their wings and fly, are unable to run, and cannot move freely. Crowding stresses the hens and reduces their egg output, but it raises returns per cage, an important financial measure for poultry producers.

To illustrate, in cages with two white leghorn hens, each hen will lay an average of 267 eggs each year, and 5.7 percent of the flock will die. In cages with four hens, on the other hand, stressful crowding reduces egg output to an average of only 241 per hen each year and raises flock mortality to 15.7 percent.[7] But with four hens the total egg output per cage is 946, far exceeding the 534

[7]Carmen R. Parkhurst and George J. Mountney. *Poultry Meat and Egg Production*. New York: Van Nostrand Reinhold Company, 1988, p. 204.

eggs produced in cages with two hens. After subtracting costs from egg income the farmer will earn a significantly higher profit per cage from cages with four hens—or six! Some of the hens pay for this with lives valued at approximately $2.50 on the replacement pullet market.

Chicken Ethology

Ethology is the scientific study of animal behavior in habitats.[8] Each animal species has a repertoire of behaviors adopted to permit survival in an ecological niche. Early wild chickens in the jungles of southeast Asia, for example, timed egg laying to coincide with seasons of termite flight to avoid infested nests.[9] (These seasonal laying patterns have since been bred out of leghorn hens.) Descriptions of natural activity in domesticated or wild environments suggest that animals have needs. When basic needs are thwarted by intensive husbandry methods, animal productivity may be lower.

Ethograms (behavior maps) of domestic chickens delineate clear tendencies. They are social animals that live in flocks and establish dominance hierarchies called pecking orders. Chickens tend to break up into flocks of ten or so. For the first six weeks of life chicks play cooperatively, but then interactions become aggressive. Soon firm pecking orders are established in a series of individual challenges. Pecking with the beak is one way that chickens communicate dominance. The dominant bird in a flock can peck any other bird, and that bird will yield. Status in the pecking order is also communicated by sounds such as crowing or cackling, aggressive or passive postures, spacing, access to more or less desirable nesting sites, and activities such as running at or away from rivals. In mixed-sex flocks there are two pecking orders, one for cocks and one for hens, but the hen hierarchy is completely subordinate. All hens yield to even the lowest cock. This is a genetically predisposed trait essential for species survival because a cock will not mate with a dominating hen.

Pecking orders have survival value in many ways. Once dominance is established, fighting ceases and energy is used in socially productive ways. Stressful disputes are minimized. Dominant chickens benefit by getting access to better nesting sites and a wider selection of mates. Subordinate chickens still benefit by being part of a flock which lays claim to the resources of a territory. Outsiders who try to become members are unmercifully pecked. And various cries and calls by flock members alert the group to the presence of predators.

Chickens are omnivorous, eating plants, insects, and small animals such as lizards. Hens are secretive and often build hidden nests, preferably on the

---

[8]Edward O. Wilson. *Sociobiology: The New Synthesis*. Cambridge, Mass.: Harvard University Press, 1975, p. 584.

[9]R. Kilgour, "Management of Behaviour," in A. F. Fraser, ed., *Ethology of Farm Animals*. Amsterdam: Elsevier, 1985, p. 446.

ground. During the day chickens spread out to forage, but at dusk they reduce the spaces between them. At night they will often roost in trees.

This partial ethogram suggests that life in high-density cages frustrates natural behaviors. Studies suggest that layers cannot establish full pecking orders in densely packed wire cages. Instead, one hen tends to emerge as a despot dominating all others. But subordinate hens do not develop dominance relations with each other.[10] With less crowding, more complex pecking orders are formed.[11] Without a complete pecking order, individuals do not yield to threat displays, and physical attacks are frequent as birds compete over space, food, and water. In confinement, weaker hens have no way to escape by running and may be assaulted repeatedly until they die.

In addition to suffering from cannibalistic behavior, hens in crowded cages are unable to engage in a range of preferred foraging, grooming, nesting, brooding, and roosting behaviors. Critics of battery cages claim that this deprivation violates the right of an animal to satisfy needs through natural behaviors and imposes suffering.

THE MANAGEMENT OF LAYERS

In confinement houses *Gallus domesticus* is protected from predators and extremes of weather. But the crowning advantage of the cage layer system is that flocks are assembled in one place. It is an arena of rigid organization where human labor requirements are minimized. The cages are serviced by an array of automated equipment. Intricate piping delivers water, mechanical systems bring food, scrapers remove manure, and conveyor belts move eggs. Ventilators, heaters, and coolers whir overhead, conditioning the atmosphere. All the separate parts of this automated life support system can be controlled by timers and computer software. The egg factory is an efficient meshing of biological and mechanical parts.

Disease Prevention

Strict precautions are taken to maintain sanitary conditions in poultry houses, where unnaturally dense bird populations invite the wildfire spread of viral and bacterial illnesses. Although chicks are vaccinated and geneticists have bred layers resistant to major illnesses, indoor chickens are unable to gradually build resistance to a range of diseases as they do in nature. Because younger birds have the lowest disease resistance, workers on their daily rounds visit

[10]T. R. O'Keefe, H. B. Graves, and H. S. Siegel, "Social Organization in Caged Layers: The Peck Order Revisited," *Poultry Science*, July 1988, p. 1013.

[11]D. L. Cunningham, "Effects of Population Size and Cage Area on Agonistic Activity and Social Structure of White Leghorn Layers," *Poultry Science*, February 1988, p. 198, and K. E. Anderson, A. W. Adams, and J. V. Craig, "Behavioral Adaptation of Floor-Reared White Leghorn Pullets to Different Cage Densities and Cage Shapes during the Initial Settling-In Period," *Poultry Science*, January 1989, p. 70.

their buildings first and then move on to buildings with older birds as the day progresses. On the largest farms separate crews and equipment are used for each age cohort of birds to avoid the carrying of viruses and bacteria from house to house on boots or clothing.

Networks of water pipes extend to waterers in each cage. Mechanical devices called proportioners drip vaccines or antibiotics into the water supply as a precaution against contagious bacterial diseases. Critics of this practice believe that because the administration of antibiotics to huge poultry flocks is routine, several strains of salmonella are resistant to popular antibiotics. Therefore, when humans eat undercooked poultry tainted with salmonella, it is more difficult to treat the consequent infection.[12] Antibiotics are also sprayed in fine mists for the layers to breathe inside the confinement building. Mountainous accumulations of poultry manure in moist indoor atmospheres are a fertile breeding ground for mites, flies, and litter beetles. To combat this nuisance chemical pesticides are added to feed to make droppings toxic to vermin.

Because flocks can number in the millions, individual layers get no veterinary care. Dead and dying birds are culled daily and placed in piles. They may be delivered to a processing plant, ground up, and recycled in poultry feed, or they may be incinerated or buried nearby. Deaths are routine, and it is normal to lose 0.5 to 1.0 percent of caged flocks monthly. In a flock of 100,000 birds this is 500 to 1,000 per month; in a flock of 1,000,000 it is ten times these numbers.

Feed and Waste

Down on the factory farm, feed is not taken from a sack and tossed by the farmer's hand into the barnyard. It is delivered by trucks in 20-ton loads to storage silos and then carted to central hoppers in the confinement houses. Revolving augers in troughs shaped like rain gutters carry food from these hoppers down long lines of cages, metering portions. Feed is the largest expense in egg production and is formulated to provide precise nutritional requirements at each age. "The main objective of the poultry producer," notes one text, "is to achieve efficient economic conversion of feedstuffs into human food."[13] Most chicken feed is based on corn, and 20 percent of the American corn harvest each year goes to feed chickens.[14] Additives such as vitamins, minerals, and trace metals ensure a balanced diet. Beta-carotene is added to compensate for lack of sunlight so that egg yolks and skins will be yellow and appeal to consumers. Antibiotics such as penicillin are added because for reasons not fully understood they promote growth. Routinely, other drugs are added to feed as prophylactics to fight common diseases. Feed formulation is exacting; its goal is to provide over forty amino acids, vitamins, minerals, fibers, and additives in the amounts needed but for the lowest cost. Chickens used for different pur-

---

[12]Bruce Ingersoll, "U.S. Agencies Move at Last to Unscramble Mess They've Made of Combating Salmonella in Eggs," *Wall Street Journal,* January 9, 1990, p. A16.
[13]Parkhurst and Mountney, op. cit., p. 111.
[14]Ibid., p. 8.

poses may utilize specially designed formulations. Actively laying hens, for example, require more calcium, phosphorus, manganese, and vitamin D because these nutrients affect shell strength. These ingredients may be reduced for molting hens. Broilers need a higher fat content to put on weight.

Underneath the wire cages (some are made of plastic to avoid rust) manure falls into troughs in the concrete floor, where robot scrapers periodically push it out of the building. When the layers begin to produce eggs, the eggs roll down a chute under the cage to a conveyor belt which takes them out of the building to automated washing and sorting equipment. Heaters and air conditioners maintain a steady, comfortable climate. If birds are too cold, they eat more, and if they are too hot, mortality increases. Poultry houses need constant air exchange to dissipate ammonia fumes from the litter and lower humidity. Chickens, because of their unique physiology, secrete urine in solid form and must discard water through respiration. Humidity builds up rapidly and encourages disease organisms in the litter if it is not checked by ventilation.

Lighting

Since poultry houses are windowless, growers can manipulate flock behavior with artificial lighting. Sunlight stimulates chicken pituitary glands to release hormones that promote growth and egg formation. In spring, when days grow longer, chickens grow and lay eggs faster. Chickens in windowless poultry houses can, therefore, be tricked by artificial lighting regimens. Replacement pullets are illuminated only 10 hours a day to delay the onset of sexual maturity until their bodies are fully grown. Then their energy will not be expended producing smaller eggs. At maturity, however, layers are given unnaturally long days. The most common lighting regimen in layer houses is 23 hours of fairly dim light (25 to 40 watts per 1,000 birds) and 1 hour of complete darkness. The daily 1-hour blackout prevents panic and mass deaths among birds unaccustomed to darkness should a power failure occur. Dim lighting decreases activity in hens, reducing cannibalism and stress. Some producers use lighting programs that slightly increase the period of daily illumination to simulate perpetual spring. Longer orange-red wavelengths stimulate sexual maturation and may increase egg laying.[15]

Lighting is also used to manipulate chickens into molting. At about 12 months of age, chickens go through a 2- to 3-month cycle of feather loss and replacement called molting, during which egg production drops. During molting, the chicken's metabolism rechannels energy from egg production to feather replacement. Natural molting allows a period of rest for the reproductive system. Left alone, a flock of layers a year old will suffer substantial productivity declines as individual chickens start to molt. But layers in confinement house flocks can be forced into synchronized, shortened molts.

[15]N. G. Zimmermann, "Broiler Performance when Reared under Various Light Sources," *Journal of Poultry Science,* January 1988, p. 43.

When egg production in a flock begins to drop, forced molting is induced by plunging the chickens into darkness 16 hours a day and cutting off all feed (but not water) for 10 days. This shocks the hens' systems, and most go into molt. After 10 days the hens are returned to a lengthened lighting period and fed reduced amounts of low-protein feed. After 6 weeks the protein content is raised, and the flock starts a second egg-laying cycle. Forced molts cut natural molting time by as much as 50 percent, but they stress the birds; mortality is 5 to 25 percent of the flock.[16]

When the End Comes

After a forced molt the hen's second laying cycle is less productive than the first. Some flocks are kept through a second forced molt, but because replacement pullets are cheap—only $2.50—most laying hens are sold for slaughter at the end of their first year of laying, when they are 18 to 20 months old. The natural life span of a hen is 15 to 20 years, but the retired layer has market value only as a carcass to be ground up for pet food, chicken soup, and chicken dogs. Laying hens are not bred to be big-bodied like broilers, and their lives in crowded battery cages encourage flaws such as bruises, cuts, patches of discolored skin, and broken bones that lead U.S. Department of Agriculture (USDA) inspectors to downgrade a carcass.

At the appointed hour groups of laborers called "catching crews" are hired by the farmer to take the hens from their cages and put them into traveling pens. The chickens may not have been fed the day before, since the farmer gets no return on investment for feed at this point. The laborers grab the hens and stick them in cages on tractor-trailer trucks. The trucks usually have open sides, and so the hens are exposed to sun, rain, and the winds of highway speeds on the trip to a slaughter plant. On arrival, workers grab the chickens and slip their legs into U-shaped brackets hanging from an overhead conveyor line. Hanging upside down by the feet, the birds are suddenly freed of crowding and have the unaccustomed opportunity to flap their wings. They do. Soon, however, the belt dips them into a water tank, where they are stunned by a 5-second, 150-volt electrical charge.[17] Then the belt rises, workers or machines cut their necks, and they pass through a bleeding tunnel. As hearts continue to fibrillate, blood drips from severed arteries in their necks and is collected in tanks for recycling into fertilizer. As the conveyor rolls on, the carcasses are bathed in hot water to loosen feathers and pulled through defeathering machines with mechanical rubber fingers. Soon, the lifeless regiment is eviscerated, inspected, cut apart, processed, packaged, marketed, and found (unrecognizable) in a pet cat's bowl or your chicken soup.

Meanwhile, the silent, depopulated confinement house which was home to

---

[16]Humane Farming Association, "Scrambled Priorities: HFA Exposes Egg Industry Practices," *Watchdog,* spring 1989, p. 5.

[17]Neville G. Gregory and Lindsay J. Wilkins, "Effect of Slaughter Method on Bleeding Efficiency in Chickens," *Journal of Science in Food Agriculture,* vol. 47, p. 14.

the layers is scrubbed and disinfected to rid it of infection and pestilence before new birds take up residence. It will not be empty more than a day or two.

PRODUCTION OF OTHER FARM ANIMALS

Of all livestock species (excluding honeybees) chickens are best suited to mass production. They hatch on a highly predictable schedule, their numbers can be rapidly expanded, they adapt to close confinement in a small area, and they convert feed energy to food with great efficiency. Although other animals are less easily adapted to factory methods, the example of applied technology set by chicken growers is contagious. Swine and cattle are two illustrations.

Swine

Trends in hog rearing parallel those in chicken operations. About 80 percent of the nation's 95 million hogs are in close confinement systems. When a sow becomes pregnant, she is placed indoors in a tight farrowing pen which allows some freedom of movement. Lights are off most of the day in these windowless buildings to keep the sows quiet and reduce stress. Pregnant sows are fed only light rations once every 2 or 3 days to prevent weight gain from inactivity. After birth, piglets are rapidly weaned in 2 to 3 weeks. The sow is then returned to a breeding area, and the piglets are placed in small wire pens stacked two and three levels high. Automated lighting, feed, watering, and manure sys-

---

ELOQUENCE INSPIRED BY EFFICIENCY

Critics of factory farming say that a veil of innocence shields people from full awareness of the consequences of their meat-eating behavior to animals. If the reader is disheartened by the chicken's fate, a brief poetic interlude may be in order.

The following verse was written by W. R. Gorton, a pioneer factory farmer in the 1930s, when early poultry confinement systems were called battery brooders. Neither time nor lack of Shakespearean polish clouds the enthusiasm evident in this excerpt from his poem "The Battery Way."

The Battery Idea has come to stay,
It's better than the other way.
It raises chicks with half the trouble,
And brings in profits almost double.

The chicks have everything they need
And so grow with lightning speed,
The proper muscle, bone and feather
Are all developed right together.
They have no chance to pick up germs,
No noxious bugs—no poison worms—
You know they get the proper food
And that it's going to exclude
Those unknown hazards always found
When chicks are let run on the ground.
And, furthermore, you'll find their meat
Is toothsome, tender, firm and sweet.
They make the most delicious frys,
The most delightful chicken pies,
Discriminating people say,
"They're better, grown the Battery Way."[18]

[18]*Broilers: The Battery Way.* 10th ed. Quincy, Ill.: Elgee Publishing Company, 1945, p. 7. Gorton's enthusiasm is unbounded. In beginning the book he notes: "Rare indeed is the person, old or young, who has not had the desire to raise poultry" (p. 5).

tems maintain the indoor environment in these "growing" buildings. After 20 weeks the pigs weigh about 220 pounds and are ready for slaughter.

In less confining husbandry systems piglets are placed in buildings with crowded growing pens. To prevent a common vice called tail biting, their needlelike teeth are clipped and their tails are cut off at birth. For identification their ears are notched. And males must be castrated. Anesthetics are not used for these procedures. The pens become confining as the pigs grow to market weight. An observer describes one farmer's pens.

> A pen of pigs on Joe's farm is like one of those Chinese number puzzles that hold fifteen numbered squares in a rack big enough for sixteen numbers, and by sliding numbers into the empty slot, one is supposed to arrange things in order.
>
> Whichever pig is farthest from the feeder is the number farthest out of place. Hunger is the manipulative thumb. ... The pigs at the feeder are like stuck squares—they are hard to move away. With four pigs allocated to every feeder flap, the puzzle is never solved, the pigs are always in motion, in combat, and in a state of stress animal scientists would term "tolerable."[19]

Hog farmers face the same economic trends as broiler and egg producers. In 1950 there were over 2,000,000 farms selling an average of 31 hogs per year. But by 1980 the number of farms had dropped 80 percent, and the average number of hogs sold per year had risen to 300. Only 3 percent of the farms sold 40 percent of all hogs.[20] Small hog farmers are continuously squeezed out by large agribusinesses with access to capital for financing confinement operations.

Meat and Dairy Cattle

Most beef comes from cattle fattened in outdoor feedlots, which are huge fenced areas interlaced with concrete feeding troughs. Few beef growers use total confinement buildings with automated environmental controls, but this is a trend.

About one-third of veal, however, comes from confinement production. Veal growers buy calves only a few days old at auctions and chain them individually in "crates," or pens 22 inches wide and 58 inches long. The calves cannot turn, groom, or lie in a natural head-down position. The pens are too small to permit motion because if the calves exercised, their muscles would toughen and the veal would not be as tender as desired. Calf confinement buildings are kept dark to encourage inactivity and promote weight gain. Gourmets prize light-colored meat, so the calves are fed a liquid "replacer" that substitutes for mother's milk. The replacer is low in iron and limits the formation of myoglobin, an oxygen-carrying protein with a reddish pigment that gives a reddish tint to veal flesh. Lack of iron keeps the calves chronically anemic. The replacer also has no fiber, so their ruminant stomachs bloat, and they suffer from chronic diarrhea.

---

[19]Mark Kramer. *Three Farms: Making Milk, Meat, and Money from the American Soil.* Cambridge, Mass.: Harvard University Press, 1987, p. 139.
[20]"A Lean Hog Industry Faces Lean Times," *Farmline*, February 1986, p. 12.

THE ANTIVEAL CAMPAIGN

Beginning in 1987 the Humane Farming Association, a San Francisco–based group opposed to factory farming, ran one-page ads in *Time, Newsweek, Ms., Harper's,* and other magazines that pictured veal calves in cramped enclosures. To verify that these ads had an impact, one member wrote the following letter, which appeared in the fall 1988 issue of *Watchdog,* the group's publication.

Dear HFA,

The most extraordinary thing happened the other night. Though I care deeply about the abuse of farm animals, I'm never very comfortable telling my friends and co-workers about what they should or should not be eating.

Well, I was at a restaurant with three business associates. My heart sank as I looked at the menu. "Milk-fed" veal must have appeared in nearly ten different dishes. Sure enough, when the waiter came by the first person to order selected a veal dish. As I considered whether or not to say something, the gentleman to my right looked at the person who ordered the veal and said, "Excuse me, but I don't think you really want to order that." He then proceeded to inform everyone what they do to calves raised for veal. He said he learned about it from an "unforgettable" ad in *Time* magazine. Needless to say, *nobody* ordered veal after that. We all ended up ordering pasta and salad. The waiter, who was there for the entire conversation, even chimed in that he had seen the ad. He said several other customers had also "expressed concern" about veal dishes. I can't tell you how proud I am to be part of this campaign.

Linda Hamilton
Georgia

Antibiotic additives fight an uphill battle against disease in anemic calves deprived of the mother's milk, which would have conferred natural immunities. Calves are taken from their mothers because they would drink milk which otherwise could be marketed to consumers. To encourage consumption of their milky liquid diet, veal calves are given no water. They are fattened in 14 to 16 weeks to about 330 pounds and then sold. It is not cost-effective to keep them longer because at this point one in four has died, and mortality from intestinal and respiratory diseases increases rapidly.

New technology has reshaped the dairy industry, where cows now wear microchips instead of bells. Increasingly, cows are confined to holding barns with mechanized feeding and caretaking equipment. Twice a day they move to automated milking parlors, which are described by an observer:

Electronic sensors, automatic gates, automatic feeders, and vacuum-operated milking machines ensure a steady flow of cows and milk. About all the operator has to do is to wipe each cow's udder with disinfectant, apply suction cups to the cow's teats, and watch the machinery.[21]

Dairy farmers inject cows with recently synthesized bovine growth hormone, which speeds metabolism and raises milk yields 10 to 40 percent within

[21]Jim Mason and Peter Singer. *Animal Factories.* New York: Crown Publishers, Inc., 1980, p. 13.

days. They add a mixture of fatty acids known as isoacids to feed which tricks the cow's digestive system into more efficient conversion of feed to energy. And computerized feeding programs read tiny transducers on cow collars and then meter feed to match the milk production of individual cows. A system for 500 dairy cows costs $60,000. The net result of these technologies has been a huge increase in milk output. Between 1965 and 1985 the average milk output per cow grew from 8,300 pounds to 13,030 pounds. Simultaneously, the number of dairy farms fell by 70 percent as economic pressures related to confinement technology favored large, capital-intensive operations.[22]

The Spread of Mass Production

Confinement techniques have spread to other livestock industries. They are applied to turkeys, quail, geese, rabbits, sheep, mink, and other animals. To a greater or lesser degree all these industry sectors are marked by the twin trends of higher output per farm and fewer (but larger) producers.

Since 1940 the proportion of farm residents in the U.S. population has declined from about 30 percent to only 2 percent.[23] Despite this decline, technology has so unceasingly raised productivity and cut costs that this tiny percentage supplies plentiful food. Now 98 percent of Americans are freed to contribute to the economy in other occupations. In fact, because of efficiencies found in the largest confinement operations, 90 percent of livestock comes from only 30 percent of farmsteads.[24] Unceasingly, the march of capital-intensive agriculture is squeezing out small family farms and replacing them with huge factory farms.

Not surprisingly, trends toward mechanization and industry concentration are characteristic of slaughter plants too. Fewer and bigger plants handle a larger percentage of the animals slaughtered each year. To illustrate, in 1972 there were 522 poultry slaughter plants, but by 1982 only 375 plants remained, and 21 establishments accounted for almost 50 percent of shipped poultry.[25] To remain competitive slaughter plants have invested heavily in automated equipment. Practiced workers can kill about 66 chickens a minute on a manual line, but new mechanical killing machines dispatch 300, or 5 per second. Defeathering machines pluck 160 birds each minute, cutting machines slice 70 birds a minute into nine pieces for further processing, and deboning machines process 800 pieces of chicken a minute.

Slaughter operations for cattle and hogs have followed apace. Captive-bolt compressed-air stunners can be maneuvered by skilled employees to stun up

[22]Figures in this paragraph are from "Bovine Biotechnology," *Farmline*, May 1986, pp. 8–9.
[23]"Farm Depopulation Down to 2 Percent," *Farmline*, April 1988, p. 16.
[24]"What (Exactly) Is a Farm?" *Farmline*, March 1986, p. 4.
[25]Ziaul Z. Ahmed and Mark Sieling, "Two Decades of Productivity in Poultry Dressing and Processing," *Monthly Labor Review*, April 1987, p. 36.

to 6 animals per minute. After bleeding, huge machines tear apart the carcasses. The Best & Donovan Model 2900-90-02 Automatic Carcass Splitter, for instance, is advertised in slaughter plant industry publications as able to split 550 head per hour. It runs on a hydraulic system with pneumatic controls and requires no operator. Workers wield an array of power tools and specialized knives to further dismantle the body. Each day an average of 9 million animals are slaughtered.

As mechanization and efficiency have speeded processing lines, slaughter plants have become increasingly dangerous for employees. In 1988 the industry averaged 38.4 injuries per 100 workers, ten times the rate for all other manufacturing businesses.[26] A vice president of the United Food and Commercial Workers Union described conditions at a Nebraska slaughter plant for cattle.

> Workers stand in a sea of blood. . . . Nearly all workers stand on treacherously slippery floors covered with animal fat buildup, which provides a situation where workers slip frequently. . . . Lines of people stand side-by-side with approximately 48 inches of working space between them. Nearly all the workers wield razor-sharp knives and power tools. . . . Because of the breakneck chain speeds and close working conditions, workers frequently are accidentally stabbed by their neighbors.[27]

Plant operations are increasingly designed to accommodate the behavior tendencies of animals. Cattle and hogs about to be killed are kept in a crowded pen and then moved single file through a chute (usually a wooden tunnel) into the stunning area. But sometimes they balk at entering this chute, and its design must be carefully contemplated. Cattle will move up a ramp of 20 degrees, but hogs prefer only level entrances and will refuse to climb ramps over 10 degrees. An expert cautions that for both species "the level portion . . . must have a minimum length of one-half to one whole body length for low-speed kills, and two to three body lengths for high-speed kills."[28] If a chute looks like a dead end, animals will be reluctant to enter it, so the design should allow them to see 2 to $2\frac{1}{2}$ bodies ahead before entering a curve. Refusal to enter a confined space is a natural tendency of animals, but balking creates two problems. First, it slows down the assembly line. And second, if animals become too scared, they lower meat quality by releasing large amounts of adrenaline at the last minute or by crashing against each other or into the pen walls. Commotion leads to bruising and the rupture of tiny blood vessels, which allows blood to leak out into the meat, a condition known as "bloodsplash" in the industry. These are the main reasons why animals' behavior is accommodated so late in their lives.

---

[26]"Morrell: A Renewal?" *Meat & Poultry,* March 1989, p. 21.

[27]Colman McCarthy, "Slaughterhouses: Butchery for Animals, High Danger for Those Who Kill and Hack," *Los Angeles Times,* April 4, 1988.

[28]Temple Grandin, "Common Hog Chute Design Mistakes," *Meat & Poultry,* May 1987, p. 30.

THE ANIMAL PROTECTION MOVEMENT

Changes in animal production techniques have exposed animal agriculturalists to the wrath of groups formed to protect farm animals from cruelty and exploitation. The existence of these groups is unique to the modern era, and their agenda represents a radical departure from historical attitudes toward animals.

Historical Development of Attitudes toward Animals

To put the animal protection movement in perspective, it must be realized that deep concern with animal welfare is a recent eyeblink in time. For most of the 50,000,000 generations in human history our hunter-gatherer ancestors killed wild game to survive, and farming of domesticated animals was unknown. But after the last Ice Age the domestication of animals and plants wrought a radical change in the relationship of humans to nature. Scientists believe that the wolf was the first animal to be domesticated, and anthropologists have found traces of domestic wolves, the ancestors of the dog, in Asian settlements of 12,000 years ago.[29] Soon after came domestic sheep and goats. About 9,000 years ago cattle and pigs were domesticated, followed by horses, asses, camels, and water buffalo. These are all highly social species with behavior traits that accommodated early husbandry practices. Less adaptable species such as moose and gazelles were husbanded, but their genetically predisposed behaviors did not accommodate well. The last species to become domesticated were fowl and cats.

The pact between humans and animals was mutually rewarding. Humans got food and economic benefits. Domesticated animals gained an advantage in the Darwinian struggle for survival. They were no longer competitive with humans for food and received protection from predators and harsh weather. Domestication created a new biological niche, and population growth was rapid among species which occupied it. Selective breeding and intensive husbandry today herald a new stage of domestication in which farm animals are losing the ability to survive and reproduce without human intervention. Behaviors suited to existence in the wild and on the old-time farm, such as foraging skills and intersex social patterns for mating, are not crucial in sex-segregated confinement systems with automatic food delivery. Hence, cossetted animals with incomplete behavior repertoires survive and reproduce deficient offspring.

The cultivation of large herds of animals made possible greater division of labor in human economies by relieving some of the need to hunt for food. More energy could be put into the inventions, organizations, wars, and arts that transformed society. Domestication of animals was, indeed, a critical foundation for cultural building blocks such as urbanization, science, and industrial technology.

In the meantime, social attitudes formed which supported the dominance of

[29]James Serpell, *In the Company of Animals*. New York: Basil Blackwell, 1986, p. 4.

humans over animals. In Western civilization the tone was set in the biblical story of creation where God gave man "dominion over the fish of the sea, and over the fowl of the air, and over every living thing that moveth upon the earth."[30] In ancient Greece, Aristotle noted that animals existed to supply food and clothing for humans. In the Roman Empire animals were objects of instrumental value. Public cruelty in arena games pitting animals against each other and against humans was part of popular culture.

The rise of Christianity in Rome's waning days failed to temper inhumane attitudes. The New Testament contains no injunction against rude treatment to animals, and prominent theologians reinforced the idea that animals were created to serve the higher, human species. The Renaissance brought no surcease. Prevailing thought elevated the uniqueness and dignity of humans in contrast to the brutish and limited capacities of animals. The formidable philosopher Descartes wrote that humans were unique in nature because they had immortal souls, whereas animals were simply machines or automatons. Another major Enlightenment thinker, Immanuel Kant, similarly devalued animals. He wrote:

> . . .so far as animals are concerned, we have no direct duties. Animals are not self-conscious, and are there merely as a means to an end. That end is man.[31]

Prior to the modern era, rare dissenters advocated kindness, but usually for the reason that cruelty toward animals begot cruelty in the personality, which could poison human relations. For this reason the Pilgrims forbade mistreatment of animals. In the new American nation, meanwhile, settlers viewed the forests as dark, inhospitable places filled with ferocious predators and useless vermin. To extend the dominion of humans, the wilds needed taming and the animals needed killing.

Only since the 1960s have protective attitudes toward animals had enough moral force and political significance to spawn protest movements in the United States and Europe. The agricultural revolution over 10,000 years ago created a society predicated on the subjugation of nature. But after 1850, worldwide industrial growth brought menacing pollution problems. Now, views of the human-nature relationship are changing; the wisdom of our dominance and manipulation of the natural environment is challenged. And as the sanctity of nature as a value has been elevated, so has been the value of humane treatment of animals.

Still, except for a small contingent attentive to animal welfare, most people limit concern for animals to pets and endangered species in the wild. Protective feelings for other animals get screened out by common defense mechanisms. In some cases people focus on aspects of a species behavior which would be evil if found in humans. Rats, for example, are killed by poisons that cause lingering, painful deaths. They bite, their foraging destroys food and

---

[30]Gen. 1:28.
[31]*Lectures on Ethics*, trans. L. Infield. New York: Harper Torchbacks, 1963, pp. 239–40.

property, and they carry contagious diseases. Anthropomorphic projection allows the moral detachment necessary to kill them without anguish. Farmers who raise huge flocks in containment systems cannot form emotional bonds with individual animals; thus they escape inhibitions about slaughtering them. As one observer notes: "The animal becomes a mere cipher, a unit of production, abstracted out of existence in the pursuit of higher yields."[32] And consumers use euphemistic words to avoid the reality of their ultimate responsibility for slaughter. Processed chicken flesh is called Chicken McNuggets, slices of pig are pork chops in the United States and white steak in Israel, the muscle tissue of anemic calves is milk-fed veal, and slaughterhouses are hidden from view and called processing plants.

Current Attitudes in the Animal Protection Movement

There are three basic philosophies in the animal protection movement today. The first is the *animal welfare* philosophy, which has been defined as encompassing "the notions of the animal in physical and mental health; the animal in harmony with its environment; the animal's feelings; and the animal adapting without suffering."[33] Welfarists are not opposed to rearing animals for food and clothing. What matters is that the animals get humane treatment. They try to prevent physical abuses to individual animals such as those occurring when chicken-catching crews grab layers by the legs to put them in trucks and break leg bones in the process. And they seek to correct confinement practices that cause animals to suffer by thwarting instinctive behaviors.

The second philosophy is that of *animal rights,* and its adherents think that animals have moral rights. Moral rights are strong entitlements to dutiful treatment by others—in this case human beings. Rightists feel that the traditional, absolute dominion of humans over animals is an unfair exploitation. Because animals are living, sentient beings capable of suffering, their interests are entitled to equal consideration with human interests. In the words of a leading animal rightist, Peter Singer: "No matter what the nature of the being, the principle of equality requires that its suffering be counted equally with the like suffering . . . of any other being."[34] Thus, animals have the inalienable right to have their needs accommodated by human beings. Denial of this right is speciesism, or the prejudicial favoring of one species over another. Speciesism, according to Singer, is an evil akin to racism and sexism because it restricts moral rights to one species just as racism and sexism have restricted them to one race or sex.

Like welfarists, rightists condemn specific cruelties and confinement prac-

---

[32]Serpell, op. cit., p. 155.

[33]I. J. H. Duncan and M. S. Dawkins, "The Problem of Assessing 'Well-Being' and 'Suffering' in Farm Animals," in D. Smidt, ed. *Indicators Relevant to Farm Animal Welfare.* The Hague, Netherlands: Martinus Nijoff, 1983, p. 13.

[34]*Animal Liberation.* New York: Avon Books, 1975, p. 8.

tices. But, going further, they also reject the entire system of animal agriculture. They reject the utilitarian argument that raising food animals brings benefits to society greater than the harm of animal suffering. "I don't believe it is morally permissible to exploit weaker beings even if we derive benefits," says one rightist. "A right doesn't yield automatically because a stronger party might benefit."[35] The existence of rights, of course, always calls forth corresponding duties in others. Hence, another rightist argues: "We do not accept the contention . . . that the public demand for cheap food decrees that the cheapest possible methods of production must be adopted. . . . [S]ociety has the duty to see that undue suffering is not caused to animals and we cannot accept that duty should be set aside in order that food may be produced more cheaply."[36] Recently, a group of rights advocates chided McDonald's Corporation, the fast-food chain, for neglecting its duties toward farm animals. After pointing out that each year hundreds of millions of chickens and millions of cows and pigs were killed for processing into McDonald's food, they raised this challenge:

> We like McDonald's philosophy of "giving something back to the communities in which we do business." Could the company not "give something back" to the community of animals upon whom it depends for the very basics of its business?[37]

A third fraction of the animal protection movement holds a philosophy of *animal liberation*. Liberationists are a small, radical, fringe element which believes in taking "direct action" to free oppressed animals. They are uncompromising and secretive, because what they do is frequently illegal. One group, the Animal Liberation Front, recently raided two turkey farms in northern California, causing $12,000 in damage and freeing about 100 turkeys, which were taken to "safe homes." The group later broke into an egg operation in Delaware, taking 25 hens and leaving the message "Animal Auschwitz." Members of these groups frequently draw an analogy between Nazi death camps and factory farms. A publicist for the livestock industry responds: "It's an insult to victims of the Holocaust."[38]

The animal protection movement today is a protest movement in the mold of the consumer, civil rights, and environmental movements. It is composed of a loose collection of mostly small groups with diverse outlooks and objectives. Members are mostly nonagriculturalist urban dwellers. In addition to its anti–factory farming efforts the movement targets an array of abuses, including laboratory experiments, pound seizure laws, testing of drugs and cosmetics by companies, use of animal fur for clothing, mistreatment of animals by the en-

---

[35]These statements were made by Gary Francione, a law professor at the University of Pennsylvania who litigates animal rights cases, and are in a discussion moderated by Jack Hitt, "Just Like Us?" *Harper's Magazine*, August 1988, p. 45 and p. 47.

[36]M. W. Fox, "Philosophies and Ethics in Ethology," in A. F. Fraser, ed., op. cit., p. 27.

[37]"Shareholder Proposal" submitted to McDonald's Corporation by the American Society for the Prevention of Cruelty to Animals, November 29, 1988, p. 2.

[38]Quoted in Kevin Thompson, "Meat Is Murder?" *Meat & Poultry*, September 1987, p. 39.

tertainment industry, pit bull fighting and cockfighting, sport hunting, rattle-snake roundups, whaling and tuna fishing, and city horse carriage rides. In the United States most of the attention given to the movement has come in publicity about efforts to free animals in university laboratories. This is because most activists live in urban areas and universities make more convenient targets than more distant farms.[39]

The Anti–Factory Farming Movement

The anti–factory farming movement, a branch of the larger animal protection movement, was galvanized in the 1960s with the publication of a book. In 1964 a Humane Society member, Ruth Harrison, published an exposé of factory farming techniques in England. Her book, *Animal Machines*,[40] was serialized by *The Observer,* and the British populace became so irate that an official commission was appointed to study farm animal welfare. This commission, called the Brambell Committee, released an official report a year later which identified "Five Freedoms" of farm animals: freedom to turn around, to groom, to get up, to lie down, and to stretch limbs. The commission's work led to the passage of laws in European countries restricting intensive confinement practices. Today these basic freedoms are still a rallying point for opponents of confinement rearing.[41]

In the United States no event has had the triggering effect of Harrison's book, and the movement has progressed more slowly. There are, however, a variety of groups pressing for reform. Efforts by these groups to pass federal and state legislation have so far failed, in part because of opposition by powerful industry lobbies. But using publicity tools they press a reform agenda that would limit the use of factory farming methods. Their criticisms of these methods can be generalized to the following categories.

1 The mortality rate of animals in factory farms is too high. Laying hens have the highest preslaughter death rate, 53.2 percent, because male chicks are destroyed at the hatchery. Other preslaughter mortality rates are 8.1 percent for turkeys, 12.5 percent for cattle, 23 percent for swine, 25 percent for veal calves, 30 percent for sheep, and as high as 40 percent for rabbits.[42] These

---

[39]This, at any rate, is the belief of one expert on the movement. See Peter Singer, "Unkind to Animals," *New York Review of Books,* February 2, 1989, p. 37. See also Merritt Clifton, "Out of the Cage: The Movement in Transition," *The Animals' Agenda,* March 1990.

[40]London: Vincent Stuart, 1964.

[41]The American Society for the Prevention of Cruelty to Animals prepared a shareholder's proposal for McDonald's Corporation in which it requested the company to notify suppliers of chicken, eggs, and beef that it would only buy from operations according these "Five Freedoms" to their animals. The resolution was withdrawn before the 1989 annual meeting after negotiations with the company.

[42]These figures are from the U.S. Department of Agriculture and cited in Merritt Clifton, "Death before Slaughter," *The Animals' Agenda,* January/February 1989, p. 24. The figure for rabbits is from Jason Zweig, "Bunnyburgers," *Forbes,* March 20, 1989, p. 42.

deaths are higher than necessary. Animal rights groups wish, of course, to give farm animals the right to natural life spans.

2 Confinement techniques strain the ability of animals to adapt and deprive them of basic need satisfaction. Chickens crowded into battery cages are unable to form normal social orders. Veal calves taken from their mothers and chained in crates are deprived of maternal love. Pigs in metal cages cannot relieve their boredom and bite each other's tails.

3 Handling and transportation practices are cruel. Because they deal with animals in large numbers, farmers may become callous toward them. This leads to practices such as tossing late-hatching eggs from incubators into the trash, where they hatch later in garbage bins, and the chicks die. Rations for some animals, particularly chickens, are cut off a day or two in advance of slaughter because there is no return on the investment in feed. Animals raised in dark sheds are traumatized when they are suddenly loaded on trucks bound for the slaughterhouse. Each year "shipping stress" claims the lives of 416,000 pigs.[43]

4 Animal agriculture creates unnecessary risks for consumers by overusing chemicals. Pesticides and growth hormones added to feed may still be present in meat. Feeding regimes for additives suspected of being toxic to humans call for cessation of feeding for a period of time before slaughter, but farmers do not always comply. Some antibiotics are no longer effective against common infections because their use in animal feeds has generated resistant bacteria.

5 Livestock management techniques are cruel. Debeaking and dubbing chicks, cutting off piglets' tails to prevent tail biting, and castrating the males of various species are examples of painful insults necessitated only by the pathologies of social order that come from unnatural confinement. Hot-iron branding of cattle, forced molting of hens, and the early separation of calves from dams are other cruelties.

6 Some slaughter practices are inhumane. Shackling the feet of chickens and hanging them upside down before stunning is punishing to the birds. Even though federal legislation requires humane handling procedures, rough handling of cattle and hogs occurs.[44] The law requires feed and water to be available only if animals are held longer than 24 hours before slaughter. Rough treatment of balky animals and the use of electric prods should be further restricted.

7 In a hungry world animal flesh is an inefficient source of food protein. Livestock consume huge amounts of corn, oats, sorghum, barley, and soybeans in feeds, and most of the food energy therein is lost to consumers of meat, eggs, and milk. Only about 17 percent of the energy in grain fed to a

---

[43]Ibid., *Animals' Agenda*, p. 24.

[44]Two laws regulate slaughter practices: the Humane Slaughter Act of 1958, which requires livestock to be rendered insensible to pain by a single blow or shock, and the Humane Methods of Slaughter Act of 1978, which sets forth defined acceptable prestunning handling procedures. See A. B. Childers, "New Advances in Humane Slaughter of Meat Animals," *Journal of Food Protection,* August 1987, pp. 709–10.

dairy herd is subsequently recovered in milk, and the meat from beef cattle contains only 6 percent of the protein used to fatten them.[45] Similarly low conversion rates apply to layers, broilers, and pigs.

8 Powerful industry lobbies prevent reform. Government policy is influenced by the dairy, beef, lamb, and poultry industries and is biased in favor of large agribusinesses. Chemical and drug companies also support major agribusiness customers. In 1988 a group of twenty animal protection groups placed a referendum called the Humane Farming Initiative before Massachusetts voters. It would have required state officials to set standards of animal protection, banned suffocation of male chicks, and prohibited calf confinement in veal crates. National farm groups such as the Grange and the American Farm Bureau formed the Massachusetts Committee to Save the Farm Family and with support from agribusiness companies plus drug and chemical companies such as Monsanto, American Cyanamid, and Pfizer outspent animal protection groups by a 20-1 margin.[46] The referendum was portrayed as an effort to turn citizens into vegetarians and an impossible burden for small farmers. It got only 30 percent of the vote.

This is not a complete listing of complaints, since different issues arise for different livestock species.

Do Animals Suffer?

Animal rightists and critics of factory farming deplore cruelty. But animal husbandry is cruel only if it causes suffering. How do we know whether animals suffer or share other human emotions such as pain, pleasure, anger, and boredom? Is animal suffering a real condition, or is it an unscientific speculation?

In fact, science cannot define animal sentience in human terms, and those who argue that animals have feelings are said to be guilty of anthropomorphism, or the unscientific attribution of human traits to animals. But there is considerable research evidence that animals do experience something akin to suffering. Two strategies have been used to evaluate these animal feelings. The first is to study animal stress. Stress is a physiological process related to suffering in humans which can be measured in animals. Stress is an adaptive response which provides energy to adjust to a changing environment. Upon experiencing stress, an animal's sympathetic nervous system is activated, causing increased respiration and heart rate and releases of hormones from the adrenal cortex. These hormones promote the release of pituitary hormones and stored glucose, thus giving the animal more energy to cope with the stressor. In the short run these physiological changes are beneficial and facilitate coping, but if stress is prolonged, the health effects are bad.

[45]Mason and Singer, op. cit., p. 74.
[46]Mark Sommer, "Farm Animal Abuse Goes on the Ballot," *The Animals' Agenda,* February 1989, p. 27.

There is some evidence that confinement techniques increase stress in farm animals. Veal calves, for example, exhibit pronounced increases in adrenal cortex hormones in the blood when they are removed from their mothers and confined. After long-term confinement they show impaired ability to respond to these hormones, a sign of stress fatigue.[47] Male Holstein calves housed in pens 0.66 meter wide with grated floors had slower weight gains and more disease than calves in pens 1.36 meters wide with straw bedding. The researchers blamed higher stress caused by confinement in the smaller pens.[48] Some studies indicate that confinement does not raise stress; for example, one study found that chickens in cages had no greater physiological stress than chickens in open pens.[49] In another study sheep had less stress, as measured by corticosteroid production, from being chased by a dog or dipped in an insecticide tank than from simply being sheared. The reason was that shearing separated them from the flock, and since they are social animals, this was extremely stressful.[50] Farmers call for more research and argue that the jury is still out on the cruelty of confinement systems.

A second method of detecting animal suffering is to examine behavior. Confined animals sometimes exhibit abnormally aggressive, self-injurious, or stereotyped behavior. Pigs in dense populations bite each other's tails off. Confined veal calves sometimes bite themselves. In isolated, sterile, or confining environments farm animals develop repetitive behaviors called stereotypes. Cattle rub their horns off on walls, pigs chew constantly with empty mouths, and sheep pull the wool out of their coats. These behaviors, which do not occur in more natural settings, are caused by stress. If animals are studied outside of strict confinement, husbandry systems can be designed to reduce stress. Studies have shown, for instance, that pigs like to relieve themselves where there is a view. Thus, some pigpens have been designed with wire mesh openings in the concrete walls right at the point where floor slats open to allow manure to flow into a holding tank. The pigs come to enjoy a vista down the pens and eliminate. Their tendency is satisfied, and less labor is required for the farmer to clean the pens.

In the end it must also be recognized that animals suffer stress and cruel circumstances in the state of nature. They face disease, death by predation, starvation, and extremes of weather. In Hobbesian terms, life may be "nasty, brutish, and short." Individual animals may not suffer more in confinement than in the wilds. But the key question is: Do they suffer needlessly?

[47]Joy A. Mench and Ari van Tienhoven, "Farm Animal Welfare," *American Scientist,* November–December 1986, p. 600.

[48]L. J. Fisher, G. B. Peterson, S. E. Jones, and J. A. Shelford, "Two Housing Systems for Calves," *Journal of Dairy Science,* February 1985, pp. 368–73.

[49]Ibid., p. 600.

[50]Benjamin L. Hart. *The Behavior of Domestic Animals.* New York: W. H. Freeman and Company, 1985, p. 357.

IN DEFENSE OF FACTORY FARMING

"I like animals, but I like cheap meat more."[51] This statement, made by a farmer in defense of confinement systems, sums up the main case for factory farming. It is an efficient use of land, labor, and raw materials. Animal agriculturalists have created a bountiful, safe, and affordable food supply. In addition, shrinking farmlands and persistent worldwide grain shortages imply that without continuous advances in efficient husbandry, animal proteins will become a costly extravagance.

Another implication of the efficiency argument is that intensive husbandry is a response to market command. According to some farmers, consumers bear the ultimate blame for creating it. More animal welfare would unquestionably raise meat and poultry prices. In one study increases in square footage per animal on cattle feedlots led to estimated price increases for beef of 1.3 to 19 cents per pound; doubling of cage space for broilers led to an estimated increase in the price of chicken of 7 to 17 cents per pound.[52] Many agriculturalists believe that cost increases such as these are unacceptable to the public.

Total abolition of confinement systems is not a realistic goal, only an ideal, and some lack of realism is also found in animal rights arguments. Human beings have always killed animals for food, and today's production and slaughter techniques are perhaps more humane than those of past centuries. They may be far more humane than life in the wild. One defender of factory farming notes that "these animals are now protected from disease, predators, and the weather ... they do not suffer many of the vicissitudes which farm animals once faced."[53] And because of prolific reproduction in factory farms, billions of animals have been given the precious gift of life, even if that life is cramped and short. This argument annoys animal rightists, who say that there is no duty toward nonexistent beings to bring them to life. Rather, our duties are toward existing animals.

Animal agriculturalists refuse to concede that modern husbandry techniques are cruel. Rather, since so few people live on farms and work with animals now, "the climate is very fertile for suspicion and misunderstanding."[54] Old-time hands say they like animals. One admitted problem is that minimum-wage workers in automated confinement systems and state-of-the-art slaughter plants are not the compassionate farmhands of yesteryear. In one survey of slaughter plants to evaluate humane handling the author concluded that "some of the newer companies have a poorer attitude toward animals than some of

[51]W. F. Prickett, letter to the editor, *American Scientist,* March–April 1987, p. 118.

[52]James R. Simpson and Bernard E. Rollin, "Economic Consequences of Animal Rights Programs," *Journal of Business Ethics,* August 1984, p. 220 and p. 224.

[53]Richard McGuire, "Agriculture and Animal Rights," *Vital Speeches of the Day,* October 1, 1989, p. 767. McGuire is the state of New York commissioner for agriculture and markets.

[54]Ibid., p. 766.

the older firms" because "there are no true livestock people in their corporate offices."[55] He noted that:

> The two most horrible incidents of deliberate animal cruelty I have ever witnessed occurred in slaughter plants which had new, well designed facilities. One man got sadistic pleasure shooting the eyes out of cattle before he killed them. In the other plant, a man stabbed a meat hook deep into a live hog's shoulder and dragged it like a hay bale.[56]

There is great concern among animal agriculturalists about humane treatment; they say that animal rights groups exploit extreme examples of mistreatment to mislead the public. Throughout the 1980s farmers and agriculture school researchers have called for modification of confinement systems to meet basic behavior needs and for promulgation of conduct codes for farmers.[57] In defense of animal growers an agriculture school professor notes: "Most producers are as humane in their thinking and care of animals as are those people involved in the many activist organizations springing up around the United States.[58] But there is also the realization that a trade-off between animal welfare and the profit motive may occur. There is a temptation, for example, to increase the density of animal populations in confinement systems to raise revenues in relation to fixed capital requirements. In addition, the welfare of confined animals is often measured in terms of building or unit productivity instead of the health of individuals. In fact, when levels of disease are too low, it is a sign that confinement operations are operating at less than full efficiency. The industry is cognizant of these problems but argues that there is an unavoidable economic penalty for cruelty. Abused animals don't lay eggs, gain weight, and multiply, placing the cruel farmer at a disadvantage in the marketplace.

QUESTIONS THAT LIE AHEAD

Poultry and livestock industries face an increase in public criticism. The public has been naive about modern husbandry practices, but today it is being educated by increasingly organized and publicitywise animal advocates. If industry is complacent, it may face laws imposing costly animal welfare regulations. The most stringent farm animal protection law, the one used as a model by protest groups worldwide, is the New Animal Protection Law passed by the

---

[55]Temple Grandin, "Animal Abuse: Industry's Shame," *Meat & Poultry,* September 1987, pp. 45–46.

[56]Ibid., p. 45.

[57]See, for example, J. L. Albright, "Status of Animal Welfare Awareness of Producers and Direction of Animal Welfare Research in the Future, "*Journal of Dairy Science,* October 1983, pp. 2208–20; J. L. Albright, "Dairy Animal Welfare: Current and Needed Research," *Journal of Diary Science,* December 1987, pp. 2711–2731; Stanley E. Curtis, "Review," *Agriculture and Human Values,* summer 1984, pp. 41–42; and Parkhurst and Mountney, op. cit., pp. 94–95.

[58]Albright, op. cit., October 1983, p. 2208.

Swedish Parliament in 1989. It grants strong rights to animals and prohibits husbandry practices common to confinement farming. Its specific provisions include these:

• Domestic animals have the right to "a natural environment in which their natural behavior is safeguarded."
• Cattle must be allowed to graze.
• Hens may not be confined in battery cages.
• Sows cannot be tethered in pens, must have freedom of movement, and must be provided with straw and litter.
• New technology must be tested and shown to conform to animal needs before being applied in production flocks.
• The government may forbid genetic engineering and the use of growth hormones.
• Farmers may be fined and given prison terms of up to one year for violations of the law.

An earlier but less extensive law in England led to many welfare improvements, a more costly food supply, and regulatory shenanigans such as government inspectors hiding in observation vehicles with telescopes to spy on farmers tending livestock.

It will be a long time before strong farm animal protection laws can be enacted in the United States. But the prospect of such laws raises many questions. Among them are these:

• Are modern societies making rational use of domesticated animals?
• Is typical treatment of farm animals unacceptable?
• What reforms, if any, are called for?
• Do animals have rights? If so, what are they? What important duties do human beings have toward animals?
• Is the utilitarian argument for domestication more compelling than the animal rights position?
• Is there a common ground on which rights advocates and farmers may compromise?
• How much animal welfare is society willing to pay for?
• What should be the response of industry to growing criticism?
• Does factory farming have troublesome implications for the competitive structure in livestock industries?

THE THREAT OF GLOBAL WARMING

It is the year 2040 and earth's climate has changed. Temperatures average 8° warmer than those of 1990, with higher increases in the mid-latitudes, lower near the equator and the poles.[1] In the United States people no longer migrate to the Sunbelt. In fact, people are leaving Phoenix, Arizona, where temperatures hit 140° in the summer, and Dallas, Texas, where the temperature is over 100° for an average of 78 days each year. The Midwest has become a dry dust bowl; it no longer produces bountiful food crops. Warmer temperatures and melting polar ice have caused a 3-foot rise in the seas, flooding most of New Orleans. Foundations of oceanfront property in Miami are undermined by wave action. In Egypt 15 percent of farmland has been flooded, and 8 million displaced people have crowded into the cities. The most severe tropical storms on record bring catastrophic flooding in Bangladesh and southern India.

The business environment has changed dramatically for many industries. Electric utilities struggle with changing patterns of demand—less energy use in the winter for heating and more in the summer for cooling. Auto companies struggle to comply with new regulations that require unprecedented reductions in the emission of certain gases from automobile emissions. Oil companies in Alaska face extraordinary maintenance costs as the permafrost on which drilling rigs, roads, offices, and pipelines are built begins to thaw. Forest products firms with tree plantations in southern states are hurt by the dieback of longleaf pines, which cannot adjust to a warmer, drier climate. Maple sugaring in New England shifts northward as trees in its southern range die. But oppor-

[1]Note that all temperatures discussed in this case are represented in Fahrenheit degrees.

tunity is present along with catastrophe. The Great Lakes are ice-free most of the year, and commercial shipping booms. Millionaires are emerging in a new industry that started to dredge sand from the ocean and replenish beaches; contracts are $100 billion a year on the East Coast alone.

The situation described above is the result of a climatic change equivalent to the one that brought the earth out of the last ice age 18,000 years ago. At that time much of Europe and North America were covered by ice sheets up to 2 miles thick. This glaciation on a monumental scale was the result of mean global temperatures only 5° colder than today's. It took about 10,000 years for the ice sheets to recede, and the current climate has existed for about 8,000 years.

Civilization since the days of ancient Greece has developed in a steady climate never deviating more than 2° from the present global mean average temperature. Since 1850, however, mean average global temperatures have risen about 1°, and climatologists predict that temperatures will rise between 3° and 9° by the year 2070.[2] This will be the fastest change of this magnitude in recorded history. Instead of taking place over centuries it will take only about 60 years, a lightning-fast event in geologic time. And instead of resulting from natural causes such as a changed tilt of the earth's orbital axis, it will be the result of industrial pollution.

Since about 1850 massive amounts of coal, oil, natural gas, and wood have been used to fire industrial processes. Carbon dioxide (CO_2) released as a by-product from the combustion of fossil fuels and wood fiber has built up in the atmosphere in unnaturally large concentrations. The result is an unanticipated warming of the earth because higher concentrations of carbon dioxide and other trace gases trap more heat in the atmosphere. Current levels of anthropogenic, or human-generated, atmospheric gases already commit the earth to an increase of 1.3° to 3.6° in average global temperature in the next century. If carbon dioxide emissions are permitted to continue increasing at current rates, the temperature may rise as much as 9°.

This is the story of the global warming threat. It explains how the greenhouse effect works and why the earth is warming now. Major policy options for the United States and other countries are set forth, and key issues are raised for discussion.

HOW THE GREENHOUSE EFFECT WORKS

The term *greenhouse effect* refers to the atmospheric mechanism that insulates the earth's surface from the cold of space. The atmosphere acts to maintain a

---

[2]In early 1989 a study of temperatures in the United States between 1895 and 1987 showed no warming trend. However, global climate models predict no warming of the lower forty-eight states until about 1990. Larry B. Stammer, "No Major Warming Found in Studies of U.S. Climate," *Los Angeles Times,* January 26, 1989. Two other summary assessments of scientific opinion are Bette Hileman, "Global Warming," *Chemical and Engineering News,* March 13, 1989, pp. 24–38, and Richard A. Houghton and George M. Woodwell, "Global Climatic Change," *Scientific American,* April 1989, pp. 36–44.

delicate balance between energy gained by absorption of sunlight and energy lost when it is reradiated by the earth back into space. In retaining heat the molecules of the atmosphere are analogous to the glass in a common greenhouse where plants grow. Sunlight comes through the clear panes, and heat builds up inside. Actually, the analogy is flawed, since heat buildup in the greenhouse is due mainly to the blocking out of wind currents; the action of glass in blocking reradiated heat is trivial. The atmosphere, however, efficiently traps 85 percent of the heat radiated from the earth's surface. This planetary greenhouse is not caused by a barrier such as a pane of glass; it is created by a set of predictable interactions between radiant energy and atmospheric molecules. Here is how those interactions work.

Incoming Solar Radiation

The sun's radiation arrives at the edge of the thin atmospheric envelope surrounding the earth in energy waves. These waves are part of the *electromagnetic spectrum,* which is shown in Figure 5-1. Their length determines the amount of energy they carry, with shorter wavelengths having more energy than longer ones. Some solar radiation comes in very short, high-energy wavelengths of 0.01 to 0.4 micrometer.[3] This is called *ultraviolet radiation,* and its high energy makes it capable of disrupting chemical bonds in plants and animals. The emergence of life on earth in prehistoric times was delayed until a shield of ozone molecules was formed in the upper stratosphere approximately 30 miles high. These molecules absorb the energy in ultraviolet radiation so that it does not reach the planet's surface.

The bulk of solar radiation, however, arrives in wavelengths between 0.4 and 1.0 micrometer which overlap the spectrum of visible light. The characteristic blue of the sky results from the scattering of solar radiation in the 0.4- to 0.5-micrometer wavelengths when it hits small molecules in atmospheric gases. The eyes of humans and animals evolved to register solar radiation within the so-called visible-light range which is prevalent in the planetary environment. They convert different wavelengths of solar radiation into specific colors.

Incoming solar radiation, called *insolation* from a combination of the words "*in*coming *sol*ar radi*ation,*" is absorbed when wave particles of light collide with atmospheric molecules.[4] When collision occurs, energy in the light ruptures molecular bonds and moves electrons in the atoms into new orbitals; thus radiant energy in sunlight is converted to energy stored in these atoms. This conversion also causes a temperature rise in the upper atmosphere, where it occurs. The process is analogous to making a space on a bus bench by shoving aside the person sitting where you want to sit. The bumped person is still

---

[3]One micrometer equals one-millionth of a meter.

[4]A description of the precise nature of light is elusive. Light has some properties associated with waves, such as amplitude, wavelength, and velocity. It also has some properties associated with particles and has been described in terms of energy units called quanta.

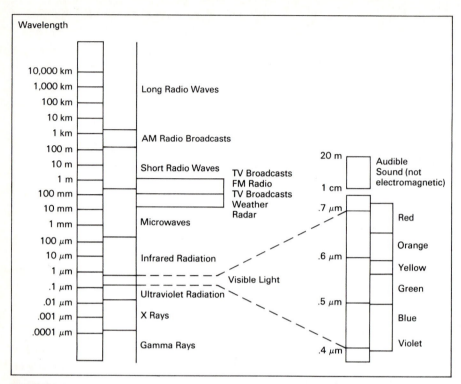

FIGURE 5-1
The electromagnetic spectrum. Ultraviolet radiation from the sun, visible light, and the infrared radiation given off by planet Earth are different wavelengths on the same spectrum. (*Source: By permission from Joe R. Eagleman,* Meteorology: The Atmosphere in Action, *D. Van Nostrand, copyright © 1990 by Litton Educational Publishing, Inc. Reprinted by permission of Wadsworth Publishing Co.*)

there but in an angry, more energetic, agitated mood. The atom with an *excited electron* is more likely to combine with other atoms in the atmosphere to form a molecular compound. When, for example, ultraviolet radiation strikes ozone molecules in the stratosphere, they are broken down into excited oxygen atoms which tend to seek out other oxygen atoms and molecular oxygen to form ozone once again.

The wavelengths of solar radiation that a molecule will absorb constitute its *absorption band.* Simply put, atmospheric molecules absorb wavelengths that carry an amount of energy roughly equal to that needed to excite an electron to higher energy levels. Molecular nitrogen and ozone in the atmosphere have strong absorption bands in the short wavelengths and block out insolation at wavelengths up to 0.3 micrometer. Beyond that, in the range of 0.3 to 0.5 micrometer, insolation is not absorbed before reaching the surface. Between 0.4 and 1.0 micrometer, the remaining range of the strongest insolation, water vapor in the air is strongly absorbent.

All told, the atmosphere absorbs 25 percent of insolation and reflects 5 percent back into space. Another 22 percent is absorbed or reflected by clouds. The earth's surface reflects about 3 percent back into space. Thus, only the remaining 45 percent of the sun's energy is absorbed by the surface.

Terrestrial Radiation

Solar energy absorbed by the earth's surface is retained as heat that is radiated back into the atmosphere. There is an important difference, however, between this outgoing *terrestrial radiation* and the incoming solar radiation. Radiation from the earth is given off in much longer wavelengths (see Figure 5-2). The

FIGURE 5-2
Structure of the atmosphere.

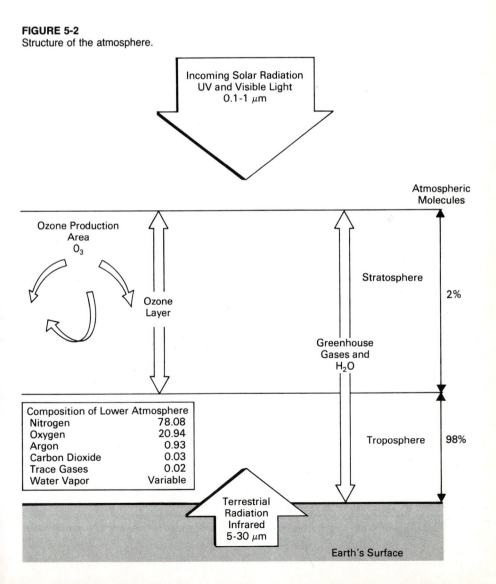

reason is that the wavelength radiated by a body is inversely proportional to the temperature of that body.[5] The mean surface temperature of the sun is 5,800°, so most of its energy is radiated in short wavelengths. The mean surface temperature of the earth, however, is a dramatically cooler 57°. So radiation from its surface is in much longer wavelengths—from 5 micrometers to 30 micrometers, with peak radiation between 8 and 18 micrometers. This is *infrared radiation.*

Because their absorption bands are closely matched to infrared wavelengths, gases in the atmosphere absorb terrestrial radiation more efficiently than insolation; almost 85 percent of radiant energy from the surface is absorbed or reflected back to earth by the atmosphere. This absorption of radiated energy from the earth constitutes the greenhouse effect. Infrared radiation is strongly absorbed between 0.5 and 7 micrometers and then upwards of 18 micrometers by water vapor. There is a "water window" between 7 and 18 micrometers through which outgoing radiation can escape. But it is partially closed in the wavelengths from 13 to 17 micrometers by atmospheric carbon dioxide. The growing concentrations of atmospheric carbon dioxide created by industrialization have increased the opacity of this window, causing more energy absorption and more heat retention in the atmosphere.

Even with more carbon dioxide in the atmosphere there still exists a window between 7 and 13 micrometers where up to 80 percent of terrestrial radiation escapes back to outer space. Disturbingly, this window is being dirtied by the buildup of trace gases with strong absorption bands in this range of the wavelength spectrum. These gases include methane, chlorofluorocarbons, nitrous oxide, and tropospheric ozone. Although the trace gases are small in quantity relative to the amount of carbon dioxide, because of their strong absorption bands in wavelengths which previously radiated into space freely, they constitute an important cause of global heat retention.

THE BUILDUP OF GREENHOUSE GASES IN THE ATMOSPHERE

The most important trace gases are those shown in Table 5-1. Of these, only the chlorofluorocarbons have no natural sources. Anthropogenic sources, however, are adding to airborne concentrations of all these gases. In addition to the gases listed in Table 5-1 there are about a dozen other trace gases produced entirely by industry that are building up in minuscule quantities in the atmosphere. These include, for example, the carbon tetrachloride used to clean electronic equipment and Halons used in fire extinguisher foams. Of all the trace gases carbon dioxide is present in the largest concentration and is clearly the biggest contributor to global warming. But even though concentrations of the other gases are minuscule, they absorb terrestrial radiation strongly. "These are

---

[5]This is Wein's law.

TABLE 5-1
GREENHOUSE GASES IN THE ATMOSPHERE

Name	Chemical composition	Pre-1850 atmospheric concentration, ppmv*	Current atmospheric concentration, ppmv	Annual emissions, metric tons per year	Estimated growth rate, % per year	Residence time in atmosphere % per year
Carbon dioxide	CO_2	275	348	23,000	0.4	0.5
Methane	CH_4	0.7	1.67	400–600	1	5–10
Nitrous oxide	N_2O	0.285	0.305	20	2	150
CFC-11	CCl_3F	0	0.00023	UK	5.1	100–110
CFC-12	CCl_2F_2	0	0.0041	UK	5.1	75
CFC-113	$C_2Cl_3F_3$	0	UK	UK	10	100
Tropospheric ozone	O_3	UK†	0.00013	NA‡	UK	0.1–0.3

*Parts per million by volume.
†Unknown.
‡Not applicable.
Note: Other greenhouse gases include carbon tetrachloride (CCl_4), methyl chloroform (CH_3CCl_3), Halon 1211 (CF_2CLBr), and Halon 1301 ($CBrF_3$).
Source: Pre-1850 column is from V. Ramanathan, "The Greenhouse Theory of Climate Change: A Test by an Inadvertent Global Experiment," *Science,* April 1988, p. 293.

the little guys," says one atmospheric scientist, "but they nickel and dime you to the point where they add up to 50 percent of the problem."[6]

Carbon Dioxide

Carbon dioxide occurs naturally as a trace gas; it is 0.034 percent of the atmosphere. It is produced by volcanoes, animal respiration, decomposition of dead plants or animals, and burning. Airborne carbon dioxide is absorbed by plants during photosynthesis, dissolved in the oceans, incorporated in animal tissues, and buried in organic matter in the soil. Without human intervention the carbon cycle would maintain a stable concentration of carbon dioxide in the air.

Much of the earth's carbon is found in our legacy of fossil fuels from prehistoric times. Coal is the remains of incompletely decayed plant material that grew in swamps during the Carboniferous period 345 to 280 million years ago. This organic material, containing huge amounts of carbon, was compressed for millions of years under sedimentary rock to form coal. Coal consists of carbon, water, and mineral impurities. When it is burned, the carbon atoms buried millions of years ago are released, and they combine with oxygen in the atmosphere and form carbon dioxide.

[6]Stephen Schneider, National Center for Atmospheric Research. Quoted by Michael D. Lemonick in "The Heat Is On," *Time,* October 19, 1987, p. 67.

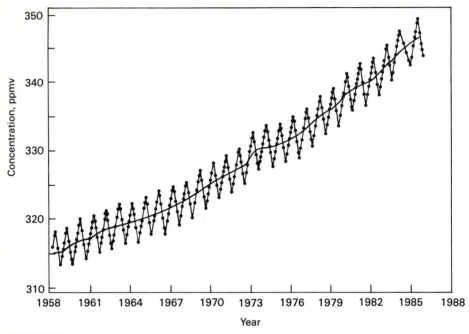

FIGURE 5-3
The rising concentration of CO_2 in the atmosphere (in parts per million by volume). Seasonal variations occur above and below the trend line because CO_2 is absorbed by plants during the summer growing season and released as fallen leaves decay in winter. (*Source: Charles Keeling, "Atmospheric CO_2 Concentration—Mauna Loa Observatory, Hawaii, 1958–85,"* U.S. Department of Energy Report NDP-001/R1. *Oak Ridge, Tenn.: Carbon Dioxide Information Center, 1986.*)

Oil and natural gas were formed by similar geologic processes, but they are different from coal in originating from the remains of organisms that lived in ancient seas, died, and sank to the bottom. Both oil and natural gas are called hydrocarbons because millions of years of pressure, heat, and bacterial action resulted in a molecular composition of almost entirely hydrogen and carbon atoms. Typically, crude oil is about 85 percent carbon and 15 percent hydrogen. Natural gas differs from oil by having a lighter density. A typical natural gas is 95 percent methane (CH_4) and contains more hydrogen than crude oil. As with coal, when oil and natural gas are burned, both release carbon dioxide into the atmosphere, but natural gas releases less.

Industrial activity since the nineteenth century has released so much carbon dioxide that natural *sinks,* or processes of storage or destruction in the environment, are unable to fully absorb it. In 1896 a Swedish chemist, Svante Arrhenius, first observed that the massive reinjection of stored carbon from coal burning might bring about climatic change.[7] He made a rough estimate

---

[7]*Philosophical Magazine,* vol. 41, 1896, p. 237.

that doubling atmospheric carbon dioxide would result in global warming of 9°, a remarkable estimate because it matches current predictions. But other scientists of that day thought that Arrhenius was wrong and that the oceans would absorb extra carbon dioxide emissions. Since then it has been shown that only about half of anthropogenic carbon dioxide is naturally absorbed.[8] The rest builds higher concentrations in the atmosphere. Major sources of fossil fuel combustion are cars, factories, and electric power plants. And the use of fossil fuels is increasing rapidly. Between 1950 and 1984 global carbon dioxide emissions from fossil fuels increased by 325 percent, and exponential growth continues.[9] This has led to a continuous rise in the concentration of carbon dioxide in the atmosphere. Figure 5-3 shows this rise in parts per million by volume, with seasonal fluctuations on either side of the exponential growth line. A recent Department of Energy report predicted a 38 percent rise in carbon dioxide emissions in the United States by the year 2010.[10] The increase in the rest of the world will be greater.

Carbon Dioxide Buildup and Forest Destruction

Plants absorb carbon dioxide during photosynthesis and store carbon in their tissues as they grow. For this reason forests are reservoirs of carbon. Deforestation releases carbon into the atmosphere in several ways. Burning rapidly releases carbon dioxide. Felled trees that are allowed to decompose release it more slowly. And forest areas cleared for agriculture expose soil, which contains the largest pool of carbon in the biosphere. Oxidation of carbon compounds in soil is a major source of atmospheric carbon dioxide.

In the nineteenth century there was extensive deforestation in the midlatitudes. The United States, Japan, Europe, and Russia stripped huge tracts of forest land for agriculture, timber, and fuel. In this country, for example, approximately 45 percent of forests existing in colonial days had been cleared by 1920. It has been estimated that the total release of carbon dioxide from worldwide nineteenth-century deforestation increased atmospheric concentrations by 40 ppm.[11]

Today, forest areas in the developed countries are stable. But extensive deforestation and degradation continue in tropical rain forests found within the borders of less developed countries. Tropical moist forests grow in the warm, precipitative climates prevailing in equatorial Africa, Asia, Central America, and South America. They occupy 7 percent of the earth's surface, or an area roughly equal to the continental United States, but cover only two-thirds of

[8]Stephen H. Schneider and Randi Londer. *The Coevolution of Climate and Life.* San Francisco: Sierra Club Books, 1984, p. 313.
[9]U.S. Senate, *Hearings before the Committee on Energy and Natural Resources,* "Greenhouse Effect and Global Climate Change," November 9–10, 1987, pp. 190–91. Testimony of Dr. James E. Hansen, atmospheric scientist.
[10]Bruce Ingersoll, "U.S. Conservation Urged to Stall Rise in Carbon Dioxide," *Wall Street Journal,* November 4, 1988.
[11]Schneider and Londer, op. cit., p. 312.

the area they occupied before the beginning of the industrial revolution. These complex repositories of plant and animal life are being cleared at the rate of about 31,000 square miles a year, with another 39,000 square miles of forest land degraded by commercial activity, road building, or settlement. Every minute, an average of 38 acres of tropical forest is completely cleared, an area equal to a good-sized college campus.[12]

The forests are cleared primarily by slash-and-burn techniques. In 1987 a satellite photo showed 6,803 fires in the southern Amazon rain forest of Brazil on a single day.[13] Scientists estimate that rain forest destruction releases as much carbon dioxide each year as combustion of all fossil fuels. And rain forest destruction hurts the environment in many other ways. Between 50 and 80 percent of the world's species live in rain forests, and 1 to 2 million, most as yet unknown to science, are threatened with extinction. If rain forest loss continues, it will cause the greatest mass extinction of species ever and will deprive the planet of its richest biological heritage. Imagine a library of 2 million original, but as yet unread, works of philosophy, science, literature, and poetry, burned before the books could even be cataloged. In addition, removal of the jungle leads to soil erosion and flooding. And where large swaths of jungle have been removed, such as in El Salvador, where 90 percent of the forested area has been cleared, the natural hydrologic cycle is disturbed and local weather patterns change.[14] One emotional observer of tropical deforestation uses these words to describe it:

> Visiting such areas it is hard to view without emotion the miles of devastated trees, of felled, broken and burned trunks, of branches, mud, and bark crisscrossed with tractor trails—especially when one realizes that in most cases nothing of comparable value will grow again on the area. Such sights are reminiscent of photographs of Hiroshima, and Brazil and Indonesia might be regarded as waging the equivalent of thermonuclear war upon their own territories.[15]

Methane

Methane (CH_4) is much less abundant than CO_2 in the atmosphere but is an important greenhouse gas because CH_4 molecules absorb 20 times more infrared radiation from the earth. Concentrations of methane have been increasing since accurate measurement began in the 1960s. On the basis of samples of

[12]The figures in this paragraph are taken from G. Tyler Miller, Jr. *Living in the Environment.* 5th ed. Belmont, Calif.: Wadsworth, 1988, pp. 277–78.

[13]"Hope for the Rain Forests," *Los Angeles Times,* November 28, 1988. In 1989 NASA released a photograph taken from the space shuttle Discovery showing a cloud of dense, white smoke covering 1 million square miles of Amazonian rain forest. Michael Rogers, "Weathermen of the Apocalypse," *Los Angeles Time Magazine,* May 21, 1989, p. 50.

[14]For more information see Catherine Caufield. *In the Rain-Forest.* New York: Knopf, 1985; Julie Sloan Denslow and Christine Padoch. *People of the Tropical Rain Forest.* Berkeley: University of California Press, 1988; Andrew W. Mitchell. *The Enchanted Canopy.* New York: Macmillan, 1986; and Ghillean T. Prance, ed. *Tropical Rain Forests and the World Atmosphere.* Boulder, Colo.: Westview Press, 1986.

[15]Nicholas Guppy, "Tropical Deforestation," *Foreign Affairs,* spring 1984, p. 943.

trapped air in ice cores, scientists believe that CH_4 concentrations are $2\frac{1}{2}$ times higher than at any time in the past 160,000 years.

The reason for rising CH_4 concentrations is not fully understood, but the largest anthropogenic sources are tied to industrial activity and food production. Most natural gas is over 95 percent methane, and both seepage of natural gas from the earth and its escape from production wells, pipelines, and storage facilities are sources of atmospheric concentrations. Another major source is *anaerobic bacteria,* primitive cells which developed before the earth had an oxygen-rich atmosphere and flourish in oxygen-poor environments. Such bacteria are found in the stomachs of ruminant animals, where they digest carbohydrates, giving off CO_2 and CH_4 as by-products. As cattle herds grow, so do methane emissions; one estimate is that worldwide 1.2 billion head of cattle produce 54.3 million metric tons of methane yearly.[16] Such bacteria flourish in stagnant water, and growth in acreage used for rice paddies makes them a source of increasing CH_4 emissions, up to 115 million tons a year in 1988.[17] Anaerobic bacteria are also found in the bodies of termites, where they digest the cellulose in wood and produce CH_4 as a by-product. Termite populations thrive in cleared forest areas and are skyrocketing in equatorial countries where rain forests are being burned.

When released, methane has an expected *residence time* of 5 to 10 years in the atmosphere before it undergoes a series of chemical reactions and is converted to CO_2. This natural cleansing process has slowed, however, because other pollutants increasingly compete with methane in the chemistry of the lower atmosphere. Notably, carbon monoxide (CO) from auto exhausts reacts with and destroys hydroxyl (HO), which is the major sink for methane in the troposphere. Methane emissions will continue to rise because they are tied to food production for a rising population, rain forest destruction, and natural gas production. Scientists warn that should the greenhouse effect lead to warming of the oceans, vast amounts of methane stored in continental slope sediments might become unstable and be released into the air.[18]

Nitrous Oxide

There are two major sources of nitrous oxide (N_2O), which is more commonly known as laughing gas. First, it is produced by soil bacteria that combine airborne nitrogen gas with hydrogen and oxygen to produce nitrogen compounds that plants can utilize. Since the amount of these nitrogen compounds in soil commonly limits food crop growth, nitrogen fertilizers are heavily used worldwide. These fertilizers speed the release of nitrous oxide into the atmosphere.

[16]Jerry E. Bishop, "New Culprit Is Indicted in Greenhouse Effect: Rising Methane Level," *Wall Street Journal,* October 24, 1988, p. A7.

[17]Ibid.

[18]Roger R. Revelle, "Methane Hydrates in Continental Slope Sediments and Increasing Atmospheric Carbon Dioxide," in National Research Council. *Changing Climate: Report of the Carbon Dioxide Assessment Committee.* Washington, D.C.: National Academy Press, 1983, pp. 257–60.

Second, nitrous oxide is a by-product of high-temperature combustion. When coal is burned in power plants or gasoline in autos, some nitrogen molecules in the air combine with oxygen to create nitrous oxide and other pollutants such as nitrogen dioxide. Each of these two sources accounts for about half of all nitrous oxide emissions. Other sources include human and animal waste and garbage dumps. Nitrous oxide is chemically inert, and its use in spray cans has grown since chlorofluorocarbon propellants were banned in 1978.

Nitrous oxide has been building slowly in the atmosphere. These are exceptionally stable molecules, with a lifetime of 150 years in the troposphere. They are strong absorbers of terrestrial radiation, and their recent buildup enhances the greenhouse effect. Over time, they rise into the stratosphere, where they are decomposed by ultraviolet rays. Like methane, nitrous oxide emissions are linked to population growth, food production, and industrial activity and are likely to continue rising.

Chlorofluorocarbons

Chlorofluorocarbons (CFCs) are compounds of chlorine, fluorine, and carbon invented in 1928 by a chemist in the Frigidaire division of General Motors who was experimenting to find a substitute for the flammable and poisonous substances then in use as coolants in refrigerators. The molecules he devised were excellent refrigerants: inexpensive to manufacture, nonflammable, and nonpoisonous. They were also exceptionally stable; that is, they did not react with oxygen or other chemicals in the troposphere.

The invention of CFCs made home refrigeration more practical and led to mass purchases of kitchen units for cooling food. CFCs are now used extensively in auto and building air conditioning. They also have a variety of industrial uses. Their inertness makes them ideal for cleaning semiconductor circuits and for blowing foams such as those used in fire extinguishers, insulation, and coffee cups. In the 1950s, CFCs began to be used in spray cans, where, again, they were ideal because they did not chemically react with toothpaste, whipped cream, oil, or other products. In 1978 the Food and Drug Administration and the Environmental Protection Agency banned CFC aerosols. By this time 75 percent of emissions were from these sprays.

As production of CFCs rose, so did their release into the atmosphere from industrial processes and leaky refrigeration units. Because they do not react with other substances, they are extraordinarily long-lived. CFC molecules float around in the lower atmosphere and, over many years, rise to the upper layers of the stratosphere, where their bonds are broken by ultraviolet radiation from the sun. There are numerous formulations of CFCs. The most common are CFC-ll, which has a longevity of over 100 years in the atmosphere; CFC-12, which lasts for 75 years; and CFC-113, which lasts for 100 years.[19]

---

[19]These letters and numbers are shorthand developed by Du Pont for CCl_3F, CCl_2F_2, and $C_2Cl_3F_3$. There are about a dozen other CFC formulations.

CFC molecules have strong absorption bands for infrared radiation emitted by the earth and have become important greenhouse gases. In fact, each CFC molecule is 20,000 times more absorbant of infrared radiation than a CO_2 molecule.[20] This makes them important contributors to the greenhouse effect.

CFCs pose a second threat to the environment. When CFC molecules drift between 12 and 30 miles up in the stratosphere, the collision with ultraviolet radiation from the sun frees chlorine atoms. Each newly freed chlorine atom serves as the catalyst in a chain reaction that destroys up to 100,000 ozone (O_3) molecules before it eventually drifts down to the lower atmosphere once again.[21] The destruction of stratospheric ozone permits more high-energy ultraviolet radiation to reach the earth's surface, where it breaks molecular bonds in living tissue and causes a higher incidence of skin cancers and crop damage. Destruction of stratospheric ozone is an alarming problem but is not a direct cause of global warming.[22]

At the height of CFC use in 1976 worldwide production was approximately 750 million pounds, about half of which was used in aerosol cans. When the United States banned the use of CFCs in aerosol cans, production dropped to a low of 600 million pounds in 1982 before rebounding to nearly 750 million pounds in 1986 because of increased industrial uses.[23] As production increased, so did atmospheric concentrations of CFCs, and studies showed that the protective ozone layer was being depleted. Since 1969 the ozone layer over the Northern Hemisphere has been depleted by 2.3 percent, and experiments have shown the existence of ozone "holes" over the polar regions.

Tropospheric Ozone

Tropospheric ozone (O_3) is chemically the same as the ozone in the upper stratosphere. While CFCs are destroying stratospheric ozone, tropospheric ozone has increased by 60 percent since measurements began early in the 1950s because it is produced in unnatural quantities by the photochemical processes characteristic of urban smog.[24] Some ozone is naturally created in the chemistry of the lower atmosphere, but the addition of more creates an elevated greenhouse effect, since ozone is an efficient absorber of terrestrial ra-

---

[20]U.S. House of Representatives, *Hearings before the Committee on Science, Space, and Technology,* "Stratospheric Ozone Depletion," March 10, 1987. Testimony of F. Sherwood Rowland, atmospheric chemist.

[21]Ibid., p. 9.

[22]For more information on the destruction of stratospheric ozone see John Gribbin. *The Hole in the Sky.* New York: Bantam Books, 1988, and F. Sherwood Roland. *Earth's Atmosphere in the Twenty-First Century.* Chapel Hill: University of North Carolina Press, 1987. Not everyone agrees with the Roland hypothesis about depletion of stratospheric ozone. A minority view among atmospheric scientists is that the ozone layer has the ability to quickly restore itself even if depletion caused by chlorofluorocarbons occurs. Erosion of ozone at the poles may be caused by the same electromagnetic disturbances from solar winds that cause the auroras.

[23]Thomas H. Maugh II and Larry B. Stammer, "Loss of Ozone Calls for Speedy Action, Experts Say," *Los Angeles Times,* March 21, 1988.

[24]Gordon J. MacDonald, "Scientific Basis for the Greenhouse Effect," *Journal of Policy Analysis and Management,* spring 1988, p. 435.

diation at lower levels. Even so, there is about nine times more ozone in the stratosphere than in the troposphere. Tropospheric ozone does absorb some cosmic radiation, but it cannot compensate for the ongoing ozone destruction at higher levels.

GREENHOUSE GASES AND CLIMATIC CHANGE

Climate is defined as a moving 30-year average of weather conditions. It is the result of complex interactions between factors such as the balance of solar heating and infrared cooling, terrain features, wind, ocean currents, and the evaporation and condensation of water. The source of energy for all weather patterns is sunlight, and enhancement of the greenhouse effect means that the net energy balance between incoming and outgoing radiation will be altered. Energy available to drive climatic processes will increase. Assuming an increase in the greenhouse effect paralleling the continued buildup of trace gases, it is possible to predict the following consequences:

• *Surface warming:* Global mean surface warming will occur in the range of 3° to 9° by the middle of the next century. Warming will be most pronounced in continental interiors, especially during the summer.

• *Ocean warming:* Ocean surfaces will absorb heat, and deep currents will take it to great depths. As the oceans warm, water molecules will expand and sea levels will rise, eroding beaches and flooding coastal cities.

• *More rain:* Warmer air and water will lead to greater evaporation, more clouds, and more precipitation in moist regions. Tropical storms will become more violent. The interiors of continents, however, will be drier.

• *Melting ice:* Polar ice and snow cover will begin to melt, further raising ocean levels. As ice, which is highly reflective, melts, the darker, exposed ground cover will absorb more of the sun's heat, contributing to further warming.

• *Biological changes:* As temperate zones shift farther toward the poles, plant and animal species will move with them. Warmer temperatures, more moisture, and growing seasons up to 40 days longer may make countries such as Canada and the Soviet Union more agriculturally productive. They will also have larger and more varied insect populations.

• *Extreme weather:* With more energy available to power the hydrologic cycle and other climatic mechanisms, the risk of floods, drought, heat waves, and typhoons will increase.

These climatic changes are predicted by mathematical models. The models currently in use, however, are not sophisticated enough to work out all the global interactions that will occur. There are many uncertainties, since climate is affected not only by atmospheric gases but also by the biosphere, oceans, clouds, glaciers, and the tilt of the earth's axis. There is considerable disagreement about how warming will change the interactions among these elements. For example, it is thought that global warming will cause more clouds to form.

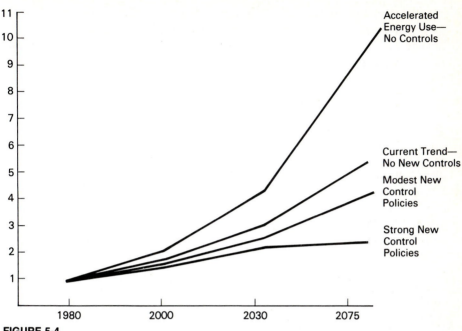

FIGURE 5-4
Four scenarios of global warming. Researchers at the World Resources Institute developed four scenarios representing alternative global responses to greenhouse gas buildup. A computer simulation determined the warming commitment for each scenario expressed as a temperature range. This graph depicts the midpoint temperature within these ranges, so warming might be as much as 50 percent higher or lower. (*Source: Adapted from Irving Mintzer, "Living in a Warmer World,"* Journal of Policy Analysis and Management, *spring 1988, pp. 552–54.*)

Clouds reflect solar energy back into space but also trap heat below. Among scientists there is disagreement about whether increased cloudiness will, on balance, increase or reduce warming. In addition, the climate models have a serious flaw—they are at present unable to account for about half the CO_2 released into the atmosphere since the industrial revolution began. Hence, even though scientists have formed a strong consensus that global warming is occurring, they cannot predict all its ramifications.[25] Humankind is conducting a vast, inadvertent experiment with earth's climate and the outcome is veiled.

STRATEGIC ALTERNATIVES

Further temperature rise is inevitable. Current global emissions of greenhouse

[25]The global warming hypothesis has not, of course, been proved in a strict sense. Accumulating evidence from research indicates that global warming is a real problem, but predictions must be made from incomplete, inexact data derived from atmospheric studies in which many experimental variables are uncontrolled, unknown, or both. Until atmospheric chemistry, weather patterns, and thermal transfer in oceans are fully understood, the global warming hypothesis must be

gases may already have committed the earth to a 1.3°–3.6° rise.[26] Figure 5-4 on page 115 shows how taking action to reduce greenhouse gas emissions might alter the magnitude of future warming. If no emission reductions occur, the rise could be as high as 9° after 2050. But if the nations of the world institute strict controls, it could be as low as 2°.

Expansive measures such as the following would be necessary.

Reduction of Fossil Fuel Combustion

The burning of coal, oil, and natural gas is responsible for 60 to 80 percent of planetary carbon dioxide emissions. One way to reduce dependence on fossil fuels is through improved efficiency and energy conservation. Since the 1973 oil shortage energy efficiency programs in the United States for buildings, appliances, and autos have cut energy consumption by one-third and reduced carbon emissions by 40 percent.[27] There is still much potential for more savings. For example, refrigerators in 80 million households use 25 percent of the nation's electricity, and a typical model uses 1,726 kilowatthours each year.[28] But new designs are available that, while being more expensive, reduce consumption by 90 percent. Relatively inefficient autos getting only 20 or 25 miles per gallon could be replaced by those getting 50 or more miles per gallon.

A second method of reducing CO_2 emissions is to develop ecologically safer, renewable energy sources. Hydroelectric, solar, geothermal, wind, and tidal energy generation does not emit CO_2. In 1988, however, these sources combined accounted for only 3 percent of energy consumption.[29] The massive investment of our society in fossil fuel energy generation precludes any rush to abandon oil, coal, and natural gas as primary fuels. Altering the mix of fossil fuels is more feasible in the short run. Coal emits the most CO_2 per unit of energy. Oil emits only 70 percent as much CO_2 as coal and natural gas only 50 percent as much. Both oil and natural gas cost more but may be widely substituted for coal.

A third option for reducing CO_2 emissions is to rely more on nuclear power. The nation's 98 nuclear power plants release virtually no CO_2 and produced 17 percent of the nation's energy in 1987. That figure will peak at 20 percent in the

accepted as a probability, not a certainty. Not all scientists accept the hypothesis. A summary of skeptical views is in Warren T. Brookes, "The Global Warming Panic," *Forbes*, December 25, 1989, pp. 96–102 and a layperson's commentary on the unreliable aspects of computer models of climatic change is Carolyn Lochhead, "Global Warming Forecasts May Be Built on Hot Air," *Insight*, April 16, 1990, pp. 14–18.

[26]U.S. House of Representatives, *Hearings before the Committee on Science, Space, and Technology*, "The National Climate Program Act and Global Climate Change," July 22, 1987, p. 151. Testimony of Dr. Irving Mintzer, World Resources Institute.

[27]"Summary of Global Warming Prevention Act of 1988," *Congressional Record*, October 6, 1988, p. S14935.

[28]Bill Green, "Policing on Global Warming and Ozone Depletion," *Environment*, April 1987, p. 5.

[29]U.S. Energy Information Administration, *Monthly Energy Review*, July 1988, p. 33.

early 1990s and then slowly decline as older nuclear plants are retired without replacement. Because of accidents at Three Mile Island and Chernobyl public opinion turned against nuclear power, and difficulties with radioactive waste and high operating expenses have further suppressed enthusiasm. In 1978, just before the failure of containment at Three Mile Island, there were 108 orders for new reactors. Since then, all have been canceled because of environmental and safety concerns and rising construction costs. Reactors built in the United States today would cost more per kilowatt of generating capacity than coal-powered plants, making them unattractive investments for utilities.

Elsewhere nuclear power has also been firmly rejected. Although several European countries rely heavily on nuclear power, most are unable to expand its use because of public opposition, and since Chernobyl, even Russia has shut down its program of reactor development. In the rest of the world new reactors have been built mainly in a few countries with authoritarian governments such as South Korea and Argentina. In industrializing third world countries, where carbon emissions are growing most rapidly, nuclear power is simply too expensive. Most third world countries are saddled with external debt and are unable to finance projects costing $1.5 to $2 billion and requiring foreign exchange payments of $200 to $300 million a year for 15 years.[30]

Global warming may, however, force reassessment of the nuclear power option. Would the risk of a few Chernobyls be warranted to forestall a 9° global warming? A new generation of reactor designs promises to be less expensive and inherently safer because these reactors do not require mechanical intervention to stop the fission process and dissipate heat if a malfunction occurs.[31] But the price of heavy reliance on nuclear power may be prohibitive. One study showed that to meet worldwide growth in energy demand between 1987 and 2025, roughly 8,000 new nuclear plants would be required. A new one would have to come on line every 1.6 days, and the cost would be $787 billion *per year* for 38 years![32]

Reduction of Other Trace Gas Emissions

With the remaining trace gases the most progress has been made in reducing chlorofluorocarbons. In 1989 an international agreement, called the Montreal Protocol, was reached with nations representing over two-thirds of CFC consumption, to halve CFC use by 1998.[33] A huge flaw in this agreement, however, was that while industrialized countries such as the United States and Ja-

---

[30]John Surrey, "Nuclear Power: An Option for the Third World?" *Energy Policy*, October 1988, p. 478.

[31]See Jack N. Barkenbus, "Prospects for Inherently Safe Reactors," *Energy Policy*, February 1988.

[32]Donella H. Meadows, "The Greenhouse: Down to Earth," *Los Angeles Times*, July 31, 1988.

[33]The final rule implementing this treaty, as published by the EPA, is "Protection of Stratospheric Ozone," 53 FR 30566 (August 12, 1988).

pan signed, rapidly developing countries such as Brazil, China, and South Korea did not. These countries, and smaller developing nations in the Third World, were churning out CFC-using autos, refrigerators, and air conditioners. Why, asked delegates from some Third World nations, should we cramp our industrial growth to protect fair-skinned Europeans in more developed nations from skin cancer? But in 1990 a revised Montreal Protocol was signed by 53 nations. Because of new evidence that the ozone layer was being destroyed faster than was previously believed, the new agreement called for a 100 percent phase-out of CFCs by the year 2000. This time, industrializing countries signed. One incentive was a $240 million fund set up by the United States and other advanced nations to help spread the technology for new CFC substitutes.

CFC manufacturers are experimenting with substitutes in which chlorine atoms are replaced by fluorine or hydrogen atoms to make the molecules less stable in the atmosphere.[34] Some substitutes are already available, such as Du Pont's HFC 134a, but they are two to five times as expensive and require higher pressure than is now feasible for auto air conditioners and small home refrigerators. Some other substitutes have turned out to be unacceptably toxic. By 1988 Du Pont, which made 25 percent of the world's CFCs, had agreed to phase the old compounds out of production by the year 2000, and major foam carton manufacturers were adopting substitutes. But unless better substitutes appear, large, powerful, CFC-dependent industries could be hurt. The air-conditioning industry, for example, had annual revenues of $12.9 billion in 1987 and employed 150,000.[35] Appliance costs will rise with the use of substitutes, and in the interim period when old CFCs are phased out, manufacturers may reap high profits from the shortening supply.

The other trace gases—methane, nitrous oxide, and tropospheric ozone—defy reduction. Minor sources of methane release such as natural gas pipeline leaks may be controlled by regulatory fines. But no methods exist to reduce emissions from cattle feedlots and rice paddies, which are proliferating to feed a hungry world. Efforts to reduce termite populations are not practical. Nitrous oxides may be reduced by burning less coal, since they are created in the combustion process. Both N_2O and tropospheric ozone may be reduced by stricter auto emissions controls, since both are promoted by the photochemical smog produced by chemical reactions with hydrocarbons in exhausts.

Protection of Tropical Rain Forests

The destruction of tropical rain forests both releases carbon into the atmosphere and reduces biomass absorption of carbon dioxide. About half of all

---

[34]See U.S. General Accounting Office, *Stratospheric Ozone: EPA's Safety Assessment of Substitutes for Ozone-Depleting Chemicals*, GAO/RCED-89-49, February 1989.

[35]Laurie Hays, "CFC Curb to Save Ozone Will Be Costly," *Wall Street Journal*, March 28, 1988.

tropical deforestation has occurred in Brazil, Indonesia, Colombia, and Mexico. The rest has come in thirty-eight other less developed countries, where it is caused by poverty, privileged landownership patterns, and high external debt.[36]

Rain forests are home to 150 to 200 million people, most of them poor. To survive, they tear apart the forests for wood to heat homes and cook food. They clear small plots of land for subsistence crops. In most Central and South American rain forest countries huge tracts of the best farming land are owned by a small number of wealthy families. In Costa Rica, for instance, 3 percent of landowners hold over half the farmland.[37] Similar figures hold for most African and Asian rain forest countries. As populations grow, the poor clear forests to create new farmland; they consume environmental quality to survive. Many countries started colonization programs which encourage the urban poor to settle in forested areas by giving them title to land that they clear. These programs are safety valves for social discontent and overcrowded slums.

The governments of rain forest countries strain under the burden of interest payments on the billions of dollars they have borrowed from foreign banks. In 1987, for example, Brazil had a foreign debt of $115 billion, Mexico $105 billion, and Venezuela $40 billion. These countries encourage logging, mining, and cattle-ranching companies to enter rain forest areas and convert natural resources to export earnings. In their politics, forests are assets that must be made to pay short-term dividends; long-range environmental benefits are of little interest where there is no economic surplus. Corrupt political regimes are often enslaved to the wealth of exploitative industries and unable to enforce weak forest protection statutes. In a few countries rain forests are perceived as hiding places for insurgents and destroyed for security reasons.

To protect rain forests the ills of poverty, population growth, debt, and political corruption must be mitigated. This will be a long process. In the meantime, environmental groups in the United States have proposed debt-for-nature swaps. These are financial transactions in which rain forest countries are forgiven a small part of their foreign debt in return for protecting a specific part of their forest land. In the first such swap in 1987, Conservation International bought $650,000 of Bolivia's debt from Citicorp Investment Bank. It suspended interest and principle collection when the Bolivian government set aside 3.7 million acres of protected forest in a lowland Amazonian region. Bolivia established a $250,000 fund for the management of this forest area. Several similar debt-for-nature swaps have been arranged. So far, though, the debt reductions and forest acreage involved are of minuscule proportion. They are an inspiration but hardly make a dent in debt or deforestation.

Rain forests are not renewable. Once plant, insect, and animal species are destroyed, evolutionary regeneration takes eons. But widespread replanting of trees is a strategy recommended by ecologists for recapturing excess carbon

---

[36]Miller, op. cit., p. 278.
[37]Tensie Whelan, "A Tree Falls in Central America," *The Amicus Journal,* p. 29.

FRONTIER DAYS IN THE AMAZON

One of the most environmentally destructive developmental policies ever undertaken was Brazil's Polonoroeste (Northwest Pole) program. It began in the early 1970s when the government sought to bolster its sagging, inflationary economy by moving the unemployed from festering urban slums into virgin rain forest lands to the north.

With a loan from the World Bank a 900-mile highway, BR 364, was constructed into the Amazon region. Using slogans such as "The Bold Ones March Westward," the government enticed settlers into the region and gave them title to rain forest land that they cleared for growing coffee and other cash crops. The settlers came. By the 1980s as many as 150,000 newcomers arrived each year.

They lived in towns with dirt streets and toiled in a climate where work was impossible under the midday sun. They faced disease-carrying black flies, giant stinging ants, venomous snakes, and bouts with malaria, but by 1988 they had burned 20 percent of the vast Amazonian jungle. As in the frontier days of the American West there was lawlessness. Disputes were sometimes settled in gun battles, as when Francisco Mendes Filho, an internationally known environmentalist, was murdered in 1989 at point-blank range with a 12-gauge shotgun by *pistoleiros* working for land-hungry cattle ranchers. Indians of the rain forest were sometimes massacred, but like their counterparts in the nineteenth-century American West, more died of exposure to settler-borne diseases such as measles. In 1950 an estimated 35,000 Indians lived in the Amazon, but by 1988 their number had dwindled to only 5,000.

Farmers were accompanied by gold miners, lumberjacks, and cattle ranchers. Miners carved muddy pits in the ground. The lumberjacks clear-cut vast tracts and shredded the felled canopy with chipping machines. Cattle ranchers built huge tracts by consolidating the farms of failed settlers and bribing distant bureaucrats in the resettlement agency. They poured fertilizer into the rain forest soil to grow grass and raised a type of cattle that produced tough beef suitable for sale only to dog food companies and fast-food chains such as McDonald's, Bob's, and Burger King. Affluent Americans who eat at these restaurant chains indirectly fuel the chain saws and bulldozers decimating Amazonian rain forests. Several years ago a consumer boycott of Burger King by the Rainforest Action Network forced Burger King to stop buying beef from rain forest countries.

Late in 1988 President Jose Sarney—under pressure from world opinion, the Brazilian press, and the World Bank—declared a temporary freeze on tax concessions for cattle, mining, and lumber interests in the Amazon. Early in 1989 he announced a new program named Our Nature, designed to slow forest degradation with a set of thirty-five decrees and proposed laws. It will be many years before the results of Our Nature can be judged.

from the atmosphere and reducing the cycle of drought and flooding common to deforested areas. Tree planting on a massive scale has been tried in China. In the 1970s, 2 million trees were planted around Beijing, lowering the average annual temperature by 2°.

Reduction of Population Growth

Exponential population growth represents a triumph of the human species but aggravates climatic warming. The world's population doubled from 500 million

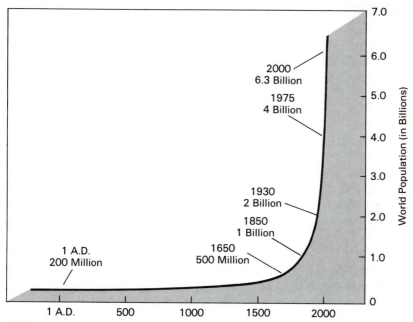

FIGURE 5-5
Population growth. (*Source: Paul R. Ehrlich and Anne H. Ehrlich, "The Population Explosion," The Amicus Journal, winter 1990, p. 25.*)

to 1.0 billion in the 200 years between 1650 and 1850, then doubled again to 2.0 billion in only 70 years. Within 40 years it had again doubled to 4.0 billion and, as shown in Figure 5-5, is expected to reach 6.3 billion by the year 2000.[38] Destruction of rain forest acreage and carbon dioxide emissions from fossil fuel combustion parallel population growth. Without programs of birth control the buildup of greenhouse gases cannot be decisively abated.

Population growth is not only a problem in less developed countries. The carbon dioxide burden of a lifetime in the developed nations is greater than in a poor country. According to population experts Paul and Anne Ehrlich:

> The birth of a baby in the United States imposes more than a hundred times the stress on the world's resources and environment as a birth in, say, Bangladesh. Babies from Bangladesh do not grow up to own automobiles and air conditioners or to eat grain-fed beef. Their life-styles do not require huge quantities of minerals and energy, nor do their activities seriously undermine the life-support capability of the entire earth.[39]

[38]For more information see Paul R. Ehrlich and Anne H. Ehrlich, "Population, Plenty, and Poverty, *National Geographic*, December 1988.
[39]Ibid., p. 918.

KEY ISSUES AND QUESTIONS

The draconian actions implied in the measures above may create social torment greater than the global warming they postpone. Painful choices will be made, and the great debates about these choices are now emerging.

One key issue is how to eliminate market imperfections in national economies which cause natural resources to be priced at less than their full value. The full value of a rain forest, for example, is greater than the current market value of the timber taken from it or the price of beef from cattle raised on cleared land to supply American fast-food chains. The prices of timber and beef do not include the eventual costs of lost species and future climatic change. Similarly, short-term profits from fossil fuel combustion may be dwarfed by the long-term costs of high carbon dioxide concentrations in the atmosphere. One study finds, for example, that the pollution costs of automobiles add up to about 80 cents more than the market price of each gallon of gasoline burned.[40] *Question:* What actions may be taken to incorporate the full environmental costs of industrial activity into the prices of goods and services?

A second key issue is how to maintain economic growth while limiting fossil fuel combustion. Even with strict conservation national economies in developed countries can continue to grow. But if coal and oil imports are denied to underdeveloped countries, many will be barred from further industrialization and full prosperity. In rain forest countries the poor are sometimes offended that rich Americans think of saving trees while millions live lives of deprivation. In the 1970s, Brazil even went so far as to declare a sovereign right to consume environmental quality without interference from other nations. More recently, China and India condemned some proposals made by environmentalists to limit carbon emissions as unfairly discriminating against the developing world. *Question:* Which policy options provide the best mix of insurance against climatic disaster while sustaining world economic development?

A third key issue is how to foster international cooperation. The causes of global warming transcend national borders; hence, effective remedial policies must be international in scope. Charles William Maynes, editor of *Foreign Policy* magazine, argues that a new "diplomacy of geo-ecology" must replace the old "diplomacy of geopolitics." "Nations," he says, "will have to break new ground in terms of strengthening relevant international institutions, restricting the traditional demands of the state and respecting new forms of international law."[41]

Progress toward international cooperation is tentative. Proposals have been advanced for an international law of the air which would assign pollution rights to each country and an international tax on fossil fuel use whose revenues would go toward protecting rain forests. Such ideas are important, but reach-

---

[40]Michael G. Renner, "Car Sick," *World Watch,* December 1988, p. 36.
[41]"To Save the Earth from Human Ruin, Enact New World Laws of Geo-Ecology," *Los Angeles Times,* September 4, 1988.

CONGRESS TAKES ON CLIMATIC CHANGE

In 1988 the first bill requiring comprehensive measures to reduce emissions of greenhouse gases was introduced. By 1990 there were fourteen bills under consideration. None have been enacted because of continuing scientific uncertainty about the need to impose billion-dollar expenditures. These measures are all lengthy. The Schneider bill, for example, is 200 pages. And they would be expensive. A strong policy measure could cost trillions of dollars.

The Global Environmental Protection Act, sponsored by Senator Robert Stafford (R-Vermont) and Senator Max Baucus (R-Montana) calls for a 35 percent reduction in CO_2 emissions by the year 2010.[42] It requires a 75 percent reduction in CO_2 emissions from autos and power plants by 2010, regulation of CO_2 emissions from home furnaces and water heaters, and new efficiency standards for air conditioners. Autos would also be subject to tough new emissions limits for hydrocarbons and oxides of nitrogen. CFCs are eliminated by the year 2000. Methane would be controlled by prohibition of releases at the wellhead and in refineries and by redesigning landfills to recapture some emissions. The act sets a national goal of 100 percent energy production from renewable sources by 2050.

The National Energy Policy Act, sponsored by Senator Timothy Wirth (D-Colorado), mandates a 20 percent reduction in CO_2 emissions by the year 2000.[43] It authorizes $450 million for research into clean energy technology and would establish joint government-industry energy conservation projects to cut energy use per unit of GNP by 2 to 4 percent annually between 1990 and 2005. The secretary of state is instructed to inventory tropical forests, set conservation goals, and act through international agencies to promote forest conservation. The act also appropriates $600 million for atmospheric research and $1.5 billion for international family planning services designed to reduce population growth.

The Global Warming Prevention Act, introduced by Representative Claudine Schneider (R-Rhode Island), stresses energy conservation and introduces economic incentives to cut fossil fuel consumption.[44] For example, the bill requires an average auto fuel economy of 45 miles per gallon by 1999. Tax rebates of up to $2,000 are given for purchasing fuel-efficient cars, and the gas-guzzler tax is raised. The act also authorizes federal funding for research into renewable energy, encourages greater of natural gas, and promotes urban tree planting programs. Several policy measures encourage family planning to reduce population growth.

In 1990 Rep. Fortney Stark (D-California) introfuced a bill that would impose a "carbon tax" on fossil fuels. Coal would be taxed at $15 a ton, petroleum at $3.25 a barrel, and natural gas at $0.40 per thousand cubic feet.

All these measures would require extraordinary expenditures. Early estimates of the cost of Rep. Stark's tax on fuels are $5 billion per year for the first five years.[45] Michael Boskin, chairman of the Council of Economic Adivsors has estimated that reducing greenhouse gases 20 percent by the year 2005 could cost a staggering $200 billion a year just in the United States.[46] Annual costs might be 5 percent of GNP, as compared to about 2 percent of GNP spent for all environmental programs combined right now.[47] Naturally, some benefits would accompany reductions in greenhouse gas emissions, including less urban smog, lower energy bills, and fewer respiratory illnesses. But most economists are skeptical of claims that benefits will match or exceed costs.

---

[42]S. 2663, *Congressional Record,* July 27, 1988, pp. S10112–29.
[43]S. 2667, *Congressional Record,* July 28, 1988, pp. S10282–308.
[44]*Congressional Record,* October 6, 1988, pp. E3263–65.
[45]Roger W. Gale, "A Carbon Tax Could Blacken Economy," *Wall Street Journal,* July 6, 1990.
[46]Bob Davis, "Bid to Slow Global Warming Could Cost U.S. $200 Billion a Year, Bush Aide Says," *Wall Street Journal,* April 16, 1990.
[47]Carolyn Lochhead, "The Alarming Price Tag on Greenhouse Legislation," *Insight,* April 16, 1990, p. 10.

ing and enforcing agreements will be hard. Environmental economist Lester Lave despairs of global cooperation.

> However much I might wish for concerted action among countries, I do not believe this is likely to occur. There are too many disparate interests, too much to be gained by cheating, too much suspicion of the motives of others, and too little control over all the relevant actors. Thus, reluctantly, I conclude that mitigation through adaptation must be our focus.[48]

Question: Are the nations of the world capable of meaningful international cooperation on the greenhouse problem?

Finally, policy choices raise ethical issues. Greenhouse gases that persist for over 100 years give the current generation stewardship over the climate that future generations will live with. *Question:* Does this generation have an ethical obligation to bear the cost of preventing global warming? And here is a second ethical issue. The United States now enjoys a high standard of living. It is uncontested that this affluence is built upon profligate destruction of forests, combustion of fossil fuel, and pollution of the atmosphere and land with toxic chemicals. *Question:* Is it fair for the United States to ask less developed nations to alter economic development paths in favor of strict environmental protection?

---

[48]In ''The Greenhouse Effect: What Government Actions Are Needed?'' *Journal of Policy Analysis and Management,* spring 1988, p. 468. For a different view see Kenneth W. Piddington, ''Sovereignty and the Environment,'' *Environment,* September 1989.

EARTH FIRST!
THE BATTLE FOR
OLD-GROWTH TIMBER

Throughout the twentieth century tension has persisted between two approaches to environmental protection. The first, *conservation,* grew as a movement during the presidency of Theodore Roosevelt. Adherents believe that resources such as minerals, timber, wildlife, and water should be harvested with restraint and in a responsible manner to satisfy human needs. The second, *preservation,* is founded in the philosophy of the American naturalist John Muir. Muir had a mystical reverence for nature and once stated that if there ever was a war between civilized man and wild beasts, "I would be tempted to sympathize with the bears."[1] He believed that vast expanses of pristine wilderness in North America should be sheltered from the selfish conquests of industrial civilization. Unlike conservationists, who asserted human dominance of nature, Muir believed humanity was but one part of an awesome natural intricacy and should respectfully live in harmony with nature rather than consume it.

Over the years, the conservation philosophy dominated. Its anthropocentric, or human-centered, view of nature harmonized with the urge to trade environmental quality for industrial growth. Government policy today is essentially conservationist. It permits corporations to harvest natural resources so long as ecological damage and pollution are minimized. But preservationist views persist, their adherents emboldened by extensive, continuing damage to the planet.

This is the story of one environmental group. It is, more fundamentally, the story of two competing ideologies of environmental protection.

---

[1]Quoted in Peter Borelli, "The Ecophilosophers," *The Amicus Journal,* spring 1988, p. 32.

IN THE FORESTS

We are drawn to the sounds of battle in the forests of the Pacific Northwest. There, the conflict between conservation and preservation has emerged from the dignity of scholarly pages into national forests, where environmentalists are challenging the right of logging companies to harvest timber from old-growth areas. In the environmental vanguard is a controversial group calling itself Earth First! (the exclamation point is intentional and symbolic of the group's emphatic determination).

In May 1983, in the Siskiyou National Forest of southern Oregon, a road crew started bulldozing a dirt road so that 150,000 acres of old trees in virgin forest could be logged. The timber harvest plan filed with the Department of Forestry called for clear-cutting large stands of trees. In a predawn foray Earth First! members blocked the road with logs. When these were removed, Dave Foreman, the group's founder, emerged from the trees and stood before a truckload of workers moving up the road. He was bumped by the truck and forced back. Accelerating, the truck ran up to him. He grabbed the bumper and was dragged down the road, suffering permanent damage to his knees. Foreman and forty-four others were arrested, but continuing blockades slowed construction until legal proceedings brought an injunction against the road.

In 1985, in the Sinkyone Wilderness of Mendocino County, California, the Georgia Pacific Lumber Company began to log ancient redwood trees up to 3,000 years old. An Earth First! cadre marched to the logging site with fifty soldiers trained for a week in tactics of civil disobedience. For several days the protesters slowed work by darting out in the area where trees were falling. As each runner was arrested, another dashed out. In the meantime, other environmentalists worked for an injunction against the logging. One morning eight demonstrators hugged the base of a large redwood called the Medicine Tree on sacred religious ground of the local Sinkyone Indians, holding hands, to prevent its dispatch by loggers. They were arrested. Others ran into the forest where the tree would fall, blowing air horns to announce their presence. In the meantime, another chain-saw operator felled a nearby redwood on top of a female demonstrator, breaking her collarbone. Work continued as sheriff's deputies arrested more people, some of whom were putting themselves between running chain saws and the trunk of the giant tree. Before the tree could be cut, however, an injunction came through. The Medicine Tree was saved.

Throughout the Pacific Northwest members of Earth First! attempt to raise the cost of logging by moving secretly through forests and driving long twentypenny nails into trees scheduled for harvesting. Trees which have been spiked tear up the chains on chain saws, and when the saw in a lumber mill hits a spike in a log, it may break and shatter. Earth First! members usually notify companies that trees in some areas are spiked, and the companies can use metal detectors to locate them.

But in 1987, George Alexander, a twenty-three-year-old worker in a Louisiana-Pacific Corporation sawmill in northern California, was seriously injured when a band saw 52 feet long and 12 inches wide hit an 11-inch spike in a log and exploded. The worker was wearing a hard hat and face shield, but a piece of shrapnel from the blade penetrated the face shield, slicing his jawbone and cutting his jugular vein. If not for the presence of several coworkers skilled in first aid, he might have bled to death. He required extensive reconstructive surgery. This is the only serious injury to date from spiking, but it motivated Louisiana-Pacific to offer a $20,000 reward for information leading to the arrest and conviction of tree spikers. Members of Earth First! denied responsibility.

These incidents are representative of a large number of others in an ongoing conflict between Earth First! and the forest products industry.

EARTH FIRST!

Earth First! was created in 1980 by Dave Foreman and four friends who shared disillusionment with the mainline environmental movement. Foreman, a lobbyist and regional coordinator with the Wilderness Society since 1972, was restive owing to that organization's growing bureaucracy and willingness to make political compromises at the expense of environmental quality.

The immediate focus of his ire was a decision by the U.S. Department of Agriculture to open 65 million acres of roadless wilderness to mining, logging, oil drilling, and tourism. This decision had been fought by environmentalists for many years. But in the end the Carter administration, the Wilderness Society, and other groups compromised with economic interests. In Foreman's view, grievous damage to forest ecosystems would follow.

Thus was born Earth First! It was to be, and is today, a militant group, uncompromising in its work to preserve wilderness and natural diversity. The philosophy of Earth First! spurns pragmatic compromise in the political process. The more traditional activities of environmental groups such as lobbying, letter writing, lawsuits, testimony at hearings, and research are not rejected. They are important but not sufficient to accomplish Earth First! goals. These require direct action, and a policy statement notes: "Either decide you can handle the militancy or find your environmental group elsewhere."[2] Earth First! is self-described as an "emotional, passionate, and angry" group with a "'hardass' militant style."[3]

Earth First! believes that all remaining wilderness should be protected from encroaching civilization. In addition, it advocates re-creation of vast wilds that have been damaged by human intervention. As Dave Foreman writes:

It is not enough to preserve the remaining roadless, undeveloped country. We must re-create wilderness in large regions: move out the cars and civilized people, dismantle the roads and dams, reclaim the plowed land and clearcuts, reintroduce extirpated species. While gasoline, asphalt, and concrete would be banned, indigenous peoples living a *traditional pre-European-contact* life-style could remain. . . . A large percentage of the United States should be returned to its natural condition.[4]

Although much attention is focused on wilderness areas, many Earth First! actions are directed toward environmental ills such as acid rain, the green-

---

[2]*Earth First!*—undated pamphlet distributed by Earth First!—p. 1.
[3]Ibid.
[4]In "A Modest Proposal for a Wilderness Preserve System," *Whole Earth Review,* winter 1986, p. 42.

house effect, ozone layer reduction, radioactive fallout, species endangerment, and pesticide spraying. Wherever external costs of industrial activity threaten nature, the mission of Earth First! is militant intervention.

The Organization of Earth First!

Earth First! has consciously avoided the use of a traditional, hierarchical organizational structure. Instead, it has adopted a free-form style. There are leaders but no formal leadership positions. Dave Foreman, who operates out of Tucson, is a founder and prominent figure, but he declines an official title. The operating units which constitute Earth First! are a half-dozen ongoing task forces and about seventy local groups in the United States and seven foreign countries. These groups are likened to the bands composing a hunter-gatherer tribe in Pleistocene civilization. A direct-action task force travels nationwide from its northern California base to support civil disobedience.

Earth First! has no constitution or charter. Its main adhesive is a newsletter, *Earth First! The Radical Environmental Journal,* published eight times each year on ancient European holidays that celebrate nature.[5] The newsletter is a forum for discussion and contains articles about activities of local groups. Intragroup communication is furthered at the annual Red River Rendezvous in July. New members are recruited there as well as at Earth First!-sponsored road shows featuring music and poetry.[6] These shows are appropriate because a central Earth First! belief is that appreciation of nature is best elevated through emotional right-brain stimulation rather than rational left-brain activities such as analysis and dialogue.

Earth First! claims to have 10,000 members, but the membership list of the newsletter is secret, and subscribers are welcomed under aliases. The membership is diverse and ranges "from animal rights vegetarians to wilderness hunting guides, from monkeywrenchers to careful followers of Gandhi, from rowdy backwoods buckaroos to thoughtful philosophers, from bitter misanthropes to true humanitarians."[7] The group supports its activities with newsletter subscriptions and sells cassettes, T-shirts, bumper stickers, and trinkets. In a small concession to tradition the Earth First! Foundation accepts tax-exempt contributions and makes grants for nonviolent environmental activities.[8]

The decentralized organization structure and loose management processes

---

[5]These are Brigid (February 2), Ecostar (March 20), Beltane (May 1), Litha (June 21), Lughnasadh (August 1), Mabon (September 23), Samhain (November 1), and Yule (December 21).

[6]See Daniel Conner, "Expressing Wilderness in Music," *Earth First! The Radical Environmental Journal,* August 1, 1988, pp. 26–27.

[7]*Earth First!,* loc. cit.

[8]In 1989 the Earth First! Foundation had an income of $50,131 and expended $50,334 on projects, leaving it with assets of $8,839. "Earth First! Foundation 1989 Treasurer's Report," *Earth First! The Radical Environmental Journal,* March 20, 1990, p. 23.

are one key to the attainment of Earth First! goals. There is little central authority. The exercise of strong centralized authority would alienate elements of the membership, especially in a group philosophically opposed to compromise. The absence of formal leadership positions is appropriate to a group in which some members are engaging in clandestine, illegal undertakings. Top officials cannot be held responsible for the behavior of members or local groups absent a formal chain of command.

The characteristic of Earth First! that most distinguishes it from mainline environmental groups is its belief in taking action outside the traditional political process. It departs the boundaries of democratic politics using two tactics: direct action and monkeywrenching.

Direct Action

In the lexicon of Earth First! direct action is nonviolent demonstration and protest. The first such action occurred in 1981, when a group atop the Glen Canyon Dam in Arizona rolled a 21-foot wide plastic ribbon over the side which depicted a wide crack in the concrete. Subsequently, many other actions have been undertaken. In Yellowstone National Park members in bear costumes blocked the bridge leading to a commercial development. Others have camped in the branches of old-growth Douglas firs and California redwoods to thwart loggers, occupied the offices of legislators in western states who have poor environmental records, sat in uranium mines, and chained themselves to tree crushers and logging road gates.

In the course of these and other actions hundreds have been arrested for trespass, unlawful assembly, and violation of court-ordered injunctions. Actions have, at times, been effective in slowing natural resource companies prior to injunctions or raising their operating costs.

Monkeywrenching

On the spectrum of civil disobedience, monkeywrenching is a degree beyond direct action. The term was adopted from a 1975 novel, *The Monkey Wrench Gang*.[9] In it author Edward Abbey, who became a cult figure among Earth First!ers, tells the story of four southwestern adventurers fighting polluters with sabotage. The gang burns billboards, yanks survey stakes, cuts wires on bulldozers in the dark of night, and blows up bridges to prevent coal trains from reaching a power plant. The spirit and tenor of the book are conveyed by the protagonist, George Hayduke: "I'd like to knock down some of them power lines they're stringing across the desert. And those new tin bridges up

---

[9]Edward Abbey. *The Monkey Wrench Gang*. New York: Avon Books, 1975. This book is now in its fifteenth printing. Abbey died in 1989.

Three Earth First! protesters, hands clasped, block construction of a logging road through the Siskiyou National Forest in southern Oregon. (*Source: Timothy Bullard.*)

by Hite. And the goddamned roadbuilding they're doing all over the canyon country. We could put in a good year just taking the fucking goddamned bulldozers apart."[10]

Inspired by Abbey's novel, Earth First! adopted a logo in which a Stone Age hammer is crossed by a monkey wrench. There followed a book edited by Dave Foreman entitled *Ecodefense: A Field Guide to Monkeywrenching.*[11] This book, now in a second edition, explains a wide range of "ecotage" tactics such as tree spiking. A "Standard Disclaimer" at the beginning notes that *Ecodefense* "is for entertainment purposes only." Five pages later, however, editor Foreman encourages readers to "go out and do something. Pay your rent for the privilege of living on this beautiful, blue-green, living Earth."[12] Monkeywrenching, he says, is not unethical. Practitioners should "remember

[10]Ibid., p. 64.

[11]Dave Foreman, ed. *Ecodefense: A Field Guide to Monkeywrenching.* Tucson, Ariz.: Ned Ludd Books, 1985. The second edition was published in 1987, and coeditor Bill Haywood joins Foreman.

[12]Ibid., p. 5.

AN *ECODEFENSE* SAMPLER

What follows is a sampling of the advice given to monkeywrenchers.

- The best type of hammer for tree spiking is a single-handed sledge hammer with a $2\frac{1}{2}$ to 3 pound head.
- To disguise spiking, glue a piece of bark over the entry hole or rub a brown felt marker over the nail's head.
- A twelve gauge shotgun firing 0-0 gauge shot is the best weapon for breaking insulators on overhead high voltage power lines.
- To flatten dirt bike tires pound many nails through plywood sheeting, place the board on a trail, and cover by sprinkling on dust or dirt.
- Mix Score hairdressing with HTH swimming pool cleaner in an envelope to create a gradual, heat-producing reaction that will in four or five minutes ignite gasoline poured on a billboard. Use this time delay to depart the scene.

- X-acto knives with blade style 23x are best for puncturing the sidewalls of off-road-vehicle tires.
- Granular sugar and Karo syrup in diesel or gasoline tanks does not disable heavy equipment. Dirt and sand in the oil reservoir are more crippling. Pour instant rice in the radiator.
- While browsing through fur coats in retail stores, you can slice the linings with a hidden razor blade.

These suggestions are typical of hundreds in the book. The chapters repeatedly emphasize steps to avoid hurting others. Eco-teurs are, for example, warned not to tamper with the fuel lines of airplanes used for pesticide spraying or engage in other "rapacious" activities because engine failure in flight could endanger lives. The last sixty pages of the book deal with "security precautions" such as losing pursuing vehicles.

that they are engaged in the most moral of all actions: protecting life, defending the Earth."[13]

Earth First! has not adopted monkeywrenching as an official policy and relegates it to individual initiative. It may be discussed at meetings. Then Earth First!ers, perhaps alone, perhaps in groups of two or three, go out and spike trees or burn billboards and keep the fact to themselves. The newsletter, however, carries a regular "Dear Ned Ludd" column about monkeywrenching and has taken a position of advocacy. It is alleged to be nonviolent because it is undertaken against inanimate objects for the purpose of increasing the costs of environmental exploitation for corporations.

It is hard to assess its impact. Earth First! claims that monkeywrenching enhances the bargaining positions of more conservative environmental groups. Corporations find the Sierra Club more reasonable in comparison. But the large, established environmental groups have disassociated themselves from Earth First! over monkeywrenching. Forest products companies are reluctant to publicize or discuss ecotage. Their security and maintenance costs have risen, and their production schedules have been disrupted. Cathy Baldwin, director of corporate communications at Willamette Industries, refers to Earth

---

[13]Ibid., p. 17.

First! as a "terrorist group,"[14] and following the incident in which a sawmill worker was seriously injured, Louisiana-Pacific condemned tree spiking as "terrorism."[15] Dave Foreman, on the other hand, argues that monkey-wrenching is simply defense of nature. "The terrorists," says Foreman, "are the ones cutting down thousand-year-old redwood trees to make picnic tables, and damming up wild free-flowing rivers."[16] Adds Foreman: "It's unfortunate this worker was injured and I wish him the best. But the real destruction and injury is being perpetrated by Louisiana-Pacific and the Forest Service in liquidating old growth forests."[17]

THE TRADITION OF CIVIL DISOBEDIENCE

Civil disobedience is intentional disobedience to government motivated by compliance with a higher authority. Citizens ordinarily have a duty to abide by the laws of their country. Theories of civil disobedience, however, provide grounds for breaking or resisting the law when it is unjust.

Over the years, political philosophers have allowed a role for civil disobedience in the just polity. This tradition begins with Socrates, who argued that there existed a higher law than the law of Athens. Every major political philosopher since that time has discussed the nature of a citizen's obligation to the government. At the risk of oversimplification, the discussion here is confined to only a few seminal thinkers.

The English philosopher John Locke argued that individuals, as part of God's creation, have natural rights to life, liberty, and property. To secure these rights, they join together and form governments, and the role of these governments is to establish fair laws and command allegiance from all. However, when governments become corrupt and violate their proper ends, their subjects may justly resist and disobey.[18] Locke had a lasting influence on American political theory in its formative stages. His views on civil disobedience are widely held today.

The conservative philosopher Edmund Burke made a powerful case against civil disobedience.[19] Burke argued that it was arrogance of the highest order for a person to claim that conscience invalidated a government policy or action. This was so because the art of government required a delicate balancing of competing interests. The achievement of a working government required

---

[14]Telephone interview, July 20, 1988.

[15]Steve Hart, "Tree-Spiking 'Terrorism' Blamed for Injuries," *The Press Democrat* (Santa Rosa, Calif.), May 15, 1987.

[16]Quoted in Dick Russell, "The Monkeywrenchers," *The Amicus Journal*, fall 1987, p. 30.

[17]Quoted in Dale Champion, "Tree Sabotage Claims Its First Bloody Victim," *San Francisco Chronicle*, May 15, 1987.

[18]For a fuller exposition of Locke's views, see *The Second Treatise of Civil Government*. Edited by Thomas P. Peardon. Indianapolis: Bobbs-Merrill, 1952, especially chaps. IX and XIX. This book was first published in 1690.

[19]See Burke's *Reflections on the Revolution in France*. New York: Doubleday, 1961. This essay was originally published in 1790.

considerable insight and experience not likely to be present in the average citizen. And a suitable balancing of interests might require compromises that from one or more vantage points in society appeared unjust. So, it was presumptuous for a citizen to declare a law invalid from an individual standpoint. In order for government to function, the laws must be obeyed by all. It follows that when citizens disagree with laws, they should seek to influence government and not unilaterally decide to disobey it.

An American philosopher and naturalist, Henry David Thoreau, wrote an essay, "Civil Disobedience," which was first published in 1849 and has since inspired generations of rebels.[20] Thoreau believed that the dictates of individual conscience were an "inner voice" that all people possessed. When, on rare occasions, a person's conscience came in conflict with the law, it was that person's duty to obey his or her inner voice, the voice of higher authority. When a conscientious objector deliberately chose to violate the law, that person must accept being jailed in consequence. The person's presence in jail would attract the attention of other moral individuals and bring reversal of the unjust government practice. Thoreau practiced his beliefs and once was jailed for refusing to pay a tax he felt was unfair. He was visited by Ralph Waldo Emerson, who asked: "What are you doing in there?" Thoreau replied: "What are you doing out there?"

The Influence of Gandhi

Thoreau's essay was intended to inspire abolitionists, but it was little read. Then, in 1900, it was rediscovered by a young law student at Oxford University named Mohandas K. Gandhi. Gandhi was greatly inspired by "Civil Disobedience," and through him it became the foundation of mass nonviolent protests that ended British rule in India. During years of struggle Gandhi continually renewed his inspiration by rereading "Civil Disobedience," and when jailed, he took a copy for study.

In his lifetime, Gandhi added to the theory of civil disobedience and refined tactics well suited for India. He coined the word *satyagraha* to describe the form of direct action he developed. It meant, literally, "holding on to the Truth" or "Truth-force."[21] Gandhi, like other civil disobedients, believed in the existence of a higher authority than government. This was the authority of God. And God was the ultimate Truth to which individuals should cleave. A satyagraha was a campaign in search of the truth launched in opposition to a law that violated God's Truth. The participant in such a campaign, called a

---

[20]Henry David Thoreau. *The Voriorum Civil Disobedience.* Edited by Walter Harding. New York: Twayne Publishers, 1967.

[21]Mohandas K. Gandhi. *Non-Violent Resistance.* Edited by B. Kumarappa. Ahmedabab, India: The Navijivan Trust, 1951, p. 3. For a discussion of Gandhi's satyagraha campaigns, see Joan V. Bondurant. *Conquest of Violence,* rev. ed., Berkeley, Calif.: University of California Press, 1965.

satyagrahi, was engaged in an uncompromising search for truth. The actions of a satyagrahi should be selfless and embody *ahimsa,* a term used by Gandhi to mean a combination of love and nonviolence. Truth was the goal in a satyagraha; ahimsa was the means.

Gandhi taught that civil disobedients were to regard the evil law as the enemy, not the individuals enforcing it. Authorities were not to be defeated or humiliated but converted to truth through the force of moral suasion. When nonviolent resistance was met with violence by police, it showed that the authority of the state rested on brutality. If participants in a satyagraha were arrested, that act would highlight the injustice of the law, and the jailing of many people would clog the enforcement machinery. If a satyagrahi suffered, the pain and hardship would demonstrate strength of conviction. Self-suffering would ultimately break down the emotional brutality of opponents by appealing to their moral sense.

For Gandhi, a satyagraha was a graduated series of steps. First came negotiation with the government. If that failed, then followers were prepared for direct action. They were pledged to nonviolence and purified by fasting for 24 hours. During nonviolent protest they were constantly to reexamine their motives and purge hatred for the enemy and violent impulses.

These tactics were powerful. Their use is illustrated in the noted Salt Satyagraha of 1930–31. In this action Gandhi challenged laws of the British colonial government setting up a monopoly in the production of salt. The laws forbade Indians to manufacture or sell salt. He petitioned the British viceroy to work for repeal of the Salt Laws, but when there was no satisfaction, he then announced that he would undertake nonviolent disobedience in which he intended no harm to any of the British.

Accompanied by a group of fewer than 100 trained satyagrahis, Gandhi marched 200 miles through India to the shore of the Indian Ocean, where he dug up sea salt and sold it in violation of the laws. He was immediately jailed, but thousands of supporters all over India rushed to the beaches to repeat his breach of the laws. Gandhi went on a hunger strike in prison to impose the self-suffering of the truth seeker. When his health declined, the British released him, but he returned to the beaches as soon as he was physically able, repeated his salt gathering, and was again jailed.

In the meantime, over two thousand followers made a nonviolent march on the Dharasana Salt Works, the government salt plant. The crowd approached the plant gate and extruded an organized column of demonstrators, who walked toward a police line barring the entrance. Immediately, dozens of police fell upon them with steel clubs, striking violent blows to deter the vanguard. An observer describes the scene:

Not one of the marchers even raised an arm to fend off the blows. They went down like ten-pins. From where I stood I heard the sickening whack of the clubs on unprotected skulls. The waiting crowd of marchers groaned and sucked in their breath in sympathetic pain at every blow. Those struck down fell sprawling, unconscious or writhing with fractured skulls or broken shoulders. . . . The survivors, without breaking ranks, silently and doggedly marched on until struck down.

They marched steadily, with heads up, without the encouragement of music or cheering or any possibility that they might escape serious injury or death. The police rushed out and methodically and mechanically beat down the second column. There was no fight, no struggle; the marchers simply walked forward until struck down.[22]

The brave satyagrahis marched for many hours but failed to occupy the Salt Works that night. During the Salt Satyagraha over 50,000 of Gandhi's followers had to be arrested. At times the sympathies of hardened civil police were so aroused that they refused to strike or punish the dissidents further. The British government, deprived of its moral prestige, suffered in world opinion. Ultimately, the British conceded their inability to enforce the Salt Laws and modified them to permit individuals to make salt.

Civil Disobedience and Martin Luther King

The influence of Thoreau and Gandhi pervaded the American civil rights movement. Martin Luther King first encountered the essay "Civil Disobedience" as a college freshman at Atlanta's Moorehouse College and was so absorbed that he read it three times. The profound influence of Thoreau and, later, of Gandhi on King was reflected in nonviolent campaigns of civil disobedience such as the Montgomery bus boycott and the campaign challenging segregation in Birmingham.

King adopted virtually the entire corpus of Gandhi's thinking. As a minister he was also heavily influenced by the black church, but he found compatibility between the teachings of Jesus and the concept of ahimsa in Gandhi's work. Like Gandhi, King believed in a higher moral order. In speeches a favorite observation was that "the arc of the moral universe may be long, but it bends toward justice," and in a sermon he remarked:

[God] has placed within the very structure of this universe certain absolute moral laws. We can neither defy them nor break them. If we disobey them, they will break us. The forces of evil may temporarily conquer truth, but truth will ultimately conquer its conqueror. Our God is able.[23]

Unlike Gandhi, King did not have numerical superiority in the American South, but he realized that violent opposition to white prejudice would be self-defeating. For strength he counted on the righteous suffering of nonviolent blacks who focused their attacks on a morally corrupt system of segregation rather than the fallible individuals who upheld it out of ignorance. He cautioned against both physical violence and inner violence of the spirit. Either

---

[22]Quoted in Louis Fischer. *The Life of Mahatma Gandhi.* New York: Harper & Brothers, 1950, p. 273.

[23]Martin Luther King, Jr. *Strength to Love.* New York: Harper & Row, 1963, pp. 128–29. Quoted in William D. Watley. *Roots of Resistance.* Valley Forge, Pa.: Judson Press, 1985, p. 21.

could corrode the love ethic of *agape* that was central to the movement. Agape was a New Testament concept commanding Christian love of others as part of God's creation rather than love of others for any objective quality they might have. White bigots were not the enemy; they only symbolized a greater evil. They were entitled to love, respect, and dignity as part of the human family. Violent action against whites could never lead to reconciliation.

King knew that negotiation and reconciliation would not take place without the moral force of civil disobedience, but he unfailingly presented points for negotiation to white officials and waited for their rejection before taking direct action. He wrote: "In any nonviolent campaign there are four basic steps: collection of the facts to determine whether injustices exist; negotiation; self-purification; and direct action."[24] The purpose of direct action was to develop a "creative tension" between the campaign for justice and the system of injustice so that reconciliation could occur. Nonviolent action did not create animosity between blacks and whites; rather, it released latent hostility into the open, where it could be dealt with. The acceptance of suffering without retaliation would eventually convert an opponent.

King lived by his beliefs. During his civil rights career, he was arrested a dozen times. His house was twice bombed, and he survived a vicious knifing. Despite hardship, he never urged violent retaliation. In 1968 he was felled at an Atlanta motel by a rifle bullet.

The American Tradition of Civil Disobedience

There is a long tradition of civil disobedience in this country beginning with the Boston Tea Party and running through the antislavery, labor, women's rights, civil rights, and antiwar movements. Today, in addition to Earth First!, antinuclear groups, sanctuary movement workers, and abortion clinic protesters use civil disobedience tactics.

Civil disobedience implies a certain contempt for the political process. The U.S. Constitution and state constitutions prescribe ground rules for changing laws. Citizens have the right to vote, to lobby, and to publish and speak freely. The act of civil disobedience expresses frustration about the inefficacy of these rights. If civil disobedients object to a major statutory enactment, they are implicitly expressing disdain for the majority will and the checks and balances between branches of government. On the other hand, the function of civil disobedience in American history has been to alert the majority to unjust government actions or imprudent laws. The audacity of opposition has often been balanced by a commitment to fine ideals. Civilly disobedient action frequently succeeds in changing public policy.

It would be fair to say that our political culture accepts many acts of non-

---

[24]Martin Luther King, "Letter from Birmingham Jail," in Curtis Crawford. *Civil Disobedience: A Casebook.* New York: Thomas Y. Crowell Company, 1973, p. 231.

violent civil disobedience as legitimate. A political necessity defense has even grown in civil law. Here are the elements of the defense. Civil disobedients who have been arrested may argue (1) that they acted to avoid imminent harm, (2) that no reasonable legal alternative was available, (3) that the harm created by the disobedient act was not disproportionate to the harm it sought to avoid, and, finally, (4) that the action taken could or did avert the harm.[25] If a jury agrees that all elements are satisfied, it can vindicate the acts of demonstrators. This defense has been used primarily by peace activists, who argue that their defiance of law is essential to avert nuclear war (but seldom is their defense successful). Jailed disobedients who use this legal ploy cast aside the time-honored tactic of suffering to underscore the point that an unjust system penalizes just people. On the other hand, it allows activists to bring their case before a jury and perhaps to set a precedent permitting actions that are currently illegal (not to mention publicizing their cause).

Civil disobedience is, at times, acceptable in American society. But are the actions of Earth First! in the same mold as the actions of colonists resisting British occupation or blacks resisting racist oppression? To assess this possibility, it is necessary to look closely at the underlying rationale used by Earth First! to justify its actions. What is the moral universe where are found rules of truth for the Earth First! tribe? To answer this question we look at recent trends in *ecophilosophy,* the philosophical contemplation of harmonious relationships between nature and humanity.

TRENDS IN ECOPHILOSOPHY

Ecophilosophy has intellectual roots in both the science of ecology and the old environmental movement. It derives basic ideas from the scientific study of ecosystems. And it draws inspiration from pioneering thinkers such as Ralph Waldo Emerson, Thoreau, Muir, Aldo Leopold, and Rachel Carson. Ecophilosophy is the study of humanity's relationship to nature. A special branch of ecophilosophy, environmental ethics, searches for the ethical implications of this relationship.

Throughout our history, philosophical discussions of nature accepted the superiority of humans over other species, the need for industry, and the utilitarian notion that benefits from responsible resource exploitation outweigh the costs of environmental damage. Pollution problems were relative to social benefits, not an absolute evil. These beliefs created a strong paradigm, or worldview, that dominated the thinking of mainstream environmentalists.

Then, in the early 1970s, a more radical form of thinking—"deep ecology"—emerged to challenge the dominant paradigm. The wellspring of deep ecology was a 1973 article by Arne Naess, a Norwegian philosopher and the

---

[25]See Steven M. Bauer and Peter J. Eckerstrom, "The State Made Me Do It: The Applicability of the Necessity Defense to Civil Disobedience," *Stanford Law Review,* May 1987, p. 1175. These criteria are applied, for example, in *United States* v. *Bailey,* 444 U.S. 394 (1980).

author of two books on Gandhi. Naess wrote that the mainstream environmental movement in the United States and elsewhere was "shallow" because it accepted the industrial-age worldview and busied itself trying to conserve natural resources and reduce pollution. These projects were worthy, but he said that their objective was to promote affluence and that we should reexamine our value systems. "There are," he wrote, "deeper concerns."[26]

For Naess these "deeper concerns" included the following: (1) The man-in-environment image should be rejected in favor of a relational, total-field image in which man is part of nature rather than dominating it. (2) Humans should reject anthropocentrism and replace it with the notion of biospheric egalitarianism. Every life form has an equal right to live and blossom. (3) Humanity must protect environmental diversity by coexisting and cooperating with nature and diverse cultures. (4) Exploitation and suppression of nature and class domination in human society should cease. (5) The fight against pollution and resource depletion should continue. (6) Profound human ignorance of biospheric relationships requires innovation to foster harmony with nature. (7) And there should be more local autonomy and decentralization in society, since once a local region has attained ecological equilibrium, it should not be threatened by influences from afar.[27] In a more recent defense of the deep ecology movement Naess gave this formulation of its tenets:

> (1) The well-being of nonhuman life on Earth has value in itself. This value is independent of any instrumental usefulness for limited human purposes. (2) Richness and diversity in life forms contribute to this value and is a further value in itself. (3) Humans have no right to interfere destructively with nonhuman life except for purposes of satisfying vital needs. (4) Present interference is excessive and detrimental. (5) Present policies must therefore be changed. (6) The necessary policy changes affect basic economic and ideological structures and will be the more drastic the longer it takes before significant change is started. The ideological change is mainly that of appreciating life quality . . . rather than enjoying a high standard of life. . . . (8) Those who subscribe to the foregoing points have an obligation directly or indirectly to try to implement necessary changes.[28]

The final point suggests the need for action by environmentalists, though it is vaguely worded.

Other developments also added momentum to the new ecophilosophy. James Lovelock, a chemist, developed the extraordinary Gaia hypothesis (named after the Greek earth goddess Ge), which holds that the earth itself is alive because "the Earth's living matter, air, oceans, and land surface form a complex system which can be seen as a single organism and which has the ca-

---

[26]Arne Naess, "The Shallow and the Deep, Long-Range Ecology Movement. A Summary," *Inquiry,* spring 1973, p. 95.

[27]Ibid., pp. 95–98.

[28]Arne Naess, "A Defense of the Deep Ecology Movement," *Environmental Ethics,* fall 1984, p. 266.

pacity to keep our planet a fit place for life.''[29] Lovelock described the earth's atmosphere and oceans as giant conveyors recycling chemical nutrients essential to life on the planet. They demonstrate how the living planet harmonizes biologic cycles and inorganic equilibriums. Gaia, the live earth, was seriously tormented by human industry. Lovelock stressed that Gaia had vital organs— expanses of tropical rain forests, the continental shelves, the wetlands—that might be essential to its ability to adjust to the impact of humanity. The activity of human beings should not disturb these regions; otherwise all life would be threatened.

There are many other strands of the new ecophilosophy. For example, the theory of bioregionalism suggests that political boundaries should coincide with natural boundaries within the ecosystem of a geographic region.[30] In West Germany, environmental activists coalesced around the principles of deep ecology to create a political party, the Green party. This party combined the interests of ecophilosophy with the strength of the peace movement in Eu-

---

HE LAID TREES TO REST

In May of 1984 Earth First! began a series of road blockades to prevent Willamette Industries from trucking out logs from the sale of old-growth timber on U.S. Forest Service land. Eventually over thirty peaceful protesters were arrested by Linn County, Oregon, sheriff's deputies. In a jury trial fifteen civil disobedients were forced to pay $13,500 in damages to the corporation.

That winter, as legal proceedings against Earth First! members moved through courts, heavy snows prevented logging. In January, the company was warned anonymously that uncut timber in the sale area had been spiked. But logging proceeded.

How do loggers feel about trees and spiking? A letter to the editor of the Sweet Home, Oregon, *New Era* on July 31, 1985, is poetic testimony.

After many happy years as a timber faller I have finally finished the most distasteful job of my whole career.

I am the timber faller that was chosen to end the misery of those trees the so-called environmentalists drive nails into. For those people to say they are trying to save those trees is an absurdity.

If all the people of this great country could have seen the misery of those great forest giants with their bleeding and festering sores inflicted from those nails.

And to think they had to stand there with their open wounds in the wind and cold all winter long before the loggers could get to them and end their misery and make some good use of them. I could just hear their sigh of relief when we finally laid them down and let them rest in peace.

Bill Sieg
24960 Crescent Hill Road
Sweet Home

---

[29]J. E. Lovelock. *Gaia: A New Look at Life on Earth*. New York: Oxford University Press, 1987, p. x. This book was first published in 1979.

[30]See Peter Berg, ed. *Reinhabiting a Separate Country*. San Francisco: Planet Drum Foundation, 1978.

rope, and despite some infighting, it has held a number of seats in the Bundestag throughout the 1980s.

There are clear ethical ramifications to the new ecophilosophy. First, if the human species exists as a coequal partner with other species, then these other species have rights, such as the right to life. Many environmental ethicists accuse *Homo sapiens* of the crime of speciesism, which is akin to the prejudicial dominance of racism and sexism. We must expand the circle of altruism from its current narrow focus on human relationships to encompass relationships with organic and inorganic elements of the ecosystem. A second implication of bioequality (the equal worth of humans and other species) is that plants, animals, and landscape features have intrinsic value. They are not to be valued by their utility to human civilization. Third, since nature is all-encompassing and its mystery transcends human understanding, it follows for some ecophilosophers that preserving nature represents the highest good. Right and wrong in human activity may be judged by consequences to nature. Natural laws have priority over statutory laws. A truth akin to Thoreau's "inner voice" is embodied in the biosphere. For those who ascribe near-religious sanctity to nature, pollution is analogous to sin. And finally, the good samaritan principle, a staple of civilized ethics, may require enlightened students of deep ecology to rally to the aid of Mother Nature in distress. This is precisely the motivation of Earth First! founder Dave Foreman, who, arguing metaphorically, said:

> You walk into your house, there's a gang of Hell's Angels raping your wife, your sister, and your old mother. You don't sit down and talk balance with them, you go out and get your twelve-gauge shotgun and come back in and blow them to hell.[31]

These ethical beliefs are the source of Earth First! activism. They justify direct action in the same way that beliefs in racial equality justified lunch counter sit-ins in the 1960s. The principles of deep ecology pose a radical challenge to the American system. They are fundamentally antibusiness because pollution and resource extraction are inevitable at some level in all industries. There is a certain atavistic message in these principles as well. The current stage of civilization is the most damaging to nature. Earth First! advocates turning back the clock by expanding wilderness and decreasing world population. This would lessen the burden on the planetary environment and is permissible in an ideology which places earth first.

---

[31]From an October 1981 speech quoted in Elizabeth Kaufmann, "Earth-Saving: Here Is a Gang of Real Environmentalists," *Audubon,* July 1982, p. 119. For more on Foreman's philosophy see *Defending the Earth: A Dialog between Murray Bookchin and Dave Foreman.* Edison, N.J.: South End Press, 1990, and Daniel B. Botkin et al., "Only Man's Presence Can Save Nature," *Harper's,* April 1990.

THE FOREST

The forest is a community of terrestrial plants and animals existing in equilibrium with its physical setting. It is distinguished from other floral ecosystems by its great height. In a mature forest the soaring vertical space between the canopy and the floor, a space occupied by successive layers of verdure, is a source of resplendence. The forest habitat creates a sheltered environment regulating sun, wind, and temperature and cradling a multitude of niches, the headquarters for competing species.

Human history begins in the forest. Sixty million years ago ground-dwelling mammals in tropical forests ascended to the trees. There they evolved into the primate ancestors of *Homo sapiens*. The arboreal environment favored the evolution of traits such as grasping hands, quick balance, binocular vision, and increased intelligence. These attributes later made possible the use of tools and the growth of human culture. During periods following ice age retractions primates emerged from trees to live on the African grasslands. There humanoid species learned to use fire and tools, developed forms of group cooperation, and began a process of cultural evolution distinct from simple biologic evolution.

The history of cultural evolution shows that humans have always had a marked dependence on the planet's vast forests. In early civilizations wood was used as fuel. As the agricultural era dawned 10,000 years ago, wood was used to build storehouses for food, shelter, and military stockades. The advent of agricultural civilization created two trends that continue today. First, it prompted a major population increase. Second, farmers began clearing forest land to grow the crops needed to feed a larger population. These two trends interacted; each quickened the other in a lockstep not yet ended.

As civilized colonies grew, organized warfare based on wood technology increased tree harvesting and further shrank forests. Homer recounts that Agamemnon launched 1,100 ships at the siege of Troy in 1100 B.C.[32] The ancient Romans similarly had a vast fleet of wooden hulls. Timber harvesting in Greece and Italy to construct these fleets was followed by erosion and overgrazing, and the forest land was never reclaimed.

The great European empires of the sixteenth to nineteenth centuries rested on huge fleets of wooden vessels. A ship of the line, such as Admiral Horatio Nelson's flagship H.M.S. *Victory,* commissioned in 1778, was over 200 feet long and 50 feet wide. The *Victory*, 226 feet long with three decks and carrying 102 cast-iron cannon, was hewed from elm and oak. Its fabrication required felling 2,500 trees, or roughly 60 acres of forest.[33] Making these ships permanently denuded Europe of much forest land. Wood was also essential to the industrial revolution. Although rapidly replaced as a fuel by coal, it was used,

---

[32]J. P. Kimmins. *Forest Ecology*. New York: Macmillan, 1987.
[33]A. B. C. Whipple. *Fighting Sail*. Alexandria, Va.: Time-Life Books, 1978, p. 17.

to illustrate, for mine timbers and factory construction. Industrial development caused mass deforestation.

The primary threat to forests today is demand for forest products and agricultural land due to explosive population growth. Between 1950 and 1985 world population nearly doubled, growing from 2.5 billion to 4.8 billion. As a result, since 1985 the world's forests have been vanishing at the rate of 18 to 20 million hectares a year, an area roughly the size of California.[34] World population is expected to continue increasing and to exceed 6 billion by the year 2000 and 8 billion by 2025. Such a population increase will place extreme pressure on governments to harvest remaining forest land.

Old-Growth Forests

In the Tertiary period of 50 million years ago the North American continent was almost entirely covered with an expanse of forest. In time, this ancient forest was divided by the upthrusts of mountain ranges—the Cascade and Sierra Nevada ranges and the Rockies—which forced moist westerly winds from the Pacific Ocean to rise and release precipitation.

In the Pacific Coast regions of California and the Pacific Northwest these mountains created ideal conditions for the growth of conifers. Winters and summers are mild, and there is a great deal of moisture. Conifer species growing in these areas of California, Oregon, and Washington attain great size and longevity. For example, the tallest tree and most important source of lumber east of the Rockies, the eastern white pine (*Pinus strobus*), averages about 100 feet in height. By contrast, the Douglas fir in the coastal ranges averages 200 feet in height in old-growth areas, and seven other species of hemlock, pine, and cedar average between 150 and 200 feet in height. The giant redwoods, of course, typically grow to 250 feet in height and may be as much as 40 feet wide.[35] Nineteenth-century northern California loggers used redwood stumps for dance floors on Saturday nights. Thus, nature created the conditions for western forests which, once discovered, brought on a "timber rush" that paralleled the frenzied search for gold.

The North American forests receded and advanced with four continental ice sheets, finally assuming their modern distribution at the end of a final glacial retreat 17,000 years ago. Thus, when the Pilgrims landed on Plymouth Rock, they discovered a continent dominated by wild, dense, seemingly endless forest. Confronted by the abundance of timber, the settlers, who brought with them European wood-based technology, proceeded to log the great eastern seaboard forests and clear vast acreage for farmland. By the 1850s much of the land east of the Mississippi had been cleared for agriculture. Then the demand for charcoal to stoke blast furnaces in defense plants during the

---

[34]Constance Holden, "The Global 2000 Report," in Charles H. Southwick, ed. *Global Ecology*. Sunderland, Mass.: Sinauer Associates, 1985, p. 12. See also Paul R. Ehrlich and Anne Ehrlich. *The Population Explosion*. New York: Simon and Schuster, 1990.
[35]Richard L. Williams. *The Loggers*. New York: Time-Life Books, 1976, pp. 24–27.

But few indeed, strong and free with eyes undimmed with care, have gone far enough with the trees to gain anything like a loving conception of their grandeur and signifi- cance as manifested in the harmonies of their distribution and varying aspects throughout the seasons, as they stand ar- rayed in their winter garb rejoicing in storms, putting forth their fresh leaves in the spring while steaming with resiny fragrance, re- ceiving the thunder-showers of summer, or reposing heavy-laden with ripe cones in the rich sungold of autumn. For knowledge of this kind one must dwell with the trees and grow with them, without any reference to time in the almanac sense.[36]

John Muir

Civil War sealed the fate of many remaining forest expanses in the East and South.

The lumber companies soon turned their attention to the north woods of Michigan, Minnesota, and Wisconsin. When prime timber areas were ex- hausted in these states, the industry moved west to the great western conifer forests of redwoods, firs, spruces, hemlocks, pines, and cedars. One admirer of these vast western forests saw them as inexhaustible: "California will for centuries have virgin forests, perhaps to the end of Time."[37] This was in 1858. Today, there are only remnants of the original timber expanses of yesteryear. To be precise, there are 7.5 million acres of old-growth forest in Oregon and Washington, less than 1 percent of the original heritage. Most of this historic timber is in national parks or designated Wilderness Areas. But about 3 million acres are open to commercial exploitation.[38]

Old-growth forests have matured over long periods without catastrophic disturbance in the environment. In the Pacific Northwest these forests require a minimum of 175 years to evolve, and many stands are 750 years old.[39] They are ancient, living museums, mirrors of the past. The conifers in an old-growth area in Oregon may have been quietly forming growth rings while Marco Polo traveled in Asia, Michelangelo painted the Sistine Chapel, and Napoleon rav- aged Europe.

The ecology of an old-growth forest is unique. Unlike newer forests, older ones combine the presence of dominant trees with many snags (dead trees still

[36]*The Mountains of California.* New York: The Century Company, 1898, pp. 139–40.

[37]Quoted in Ray Raphael. *Tree Talk.* Washington, D.C.: Island Press, 1981, p. 4; from "Rem- iniscences of Mendocino," *Hutchings California Magazine,* October 1858.

[38]John Benneth, "The Impact of Federal Wilderness on Timber," *High Lead,* July 1988, p. 8. Similar figures are found in Northwest Forest Resource Council. *Old Growth Timber.* Undated pamphlet. Overall, there were 850 million acres of forest on the continental United States when European settlers first arrived. By the 1920s only 138 million acres of virgin forest remained, and these are about what we retain today according to the estimates of Michael Williams in *Americans and Their Forests: A Historical Geography.* Cambridge, England: Cambridge University Press, 1989, pp. 3–4.

[39]Stephen Whitney. *Western Forests.* New York: Alfred A. Knopf, 1985, p. 39. See also David Kelly and Gary Braasch. *Secrets of the Old Growth Forest.* Salt Lake City: Peregrine Smith Books, 1988, and Elliott A. Norse. *Ancient Forests of the Pacific Northwest.* Washington, D.C.: Island Press, 1990.

standing) and fallen logs. This creates conditions favoring habitat diversity, complexity, and beauty. Snags provide a home for insects such as the giant carpenter ant (*Camponotus laevigatus*), which nests and stores eggs in decomposing wood pulp. The presence of these small insects makes snags a source of food for many small birds.

Rotting logs on the forest floor slowly release stored nutrients to the soil and create new ecological niches when they fall over streams. A large conifer that falls over a stream may remain intact and deflect its flow for 100 years, diverting water into slow-moving eddies and backchannels where insects can breed. Fish, in turn, are attracted to the depressions formed as water flows over fallen logs and to the presence of breeding insects. The towering rise of fully grown trees and the intricate disarray of life underneath the canopy stimulate the aesthetic instinct. One observer has noted: "In the primeval forest humans know the most authentic of wilderness emotions, the sense of the sublime."[40]

Logging and Forest Management

Old-growth forests are attractive to the forest products industry. Roughly 40 percent of the demand for wood products comes from new housing starts, and softwood growth such as fir, spruce, pine, and redwood is best suited for making the kind of lumber and plywood ideal for building construction. About half the nation's softwood timber is on government land, such as U.S. Forest Service land in Oregon, yet only about 20 percent of softwood production comes from government timber sales.[41]

Harvesting old growth on government land would have many advantages. It would be the easiest way to increase softwood production. It would avoid a steady annual loss from natural causes of several billion board feet of lumber—enough to build 300,000 houses. If the old-growth areas could be logged, forests could be made more economically productive through silviculture. This would mean more lumber for our children and grandchildren. Also, older trees with narrow growth rings produce high-quality, top-value boards. For example, old Sitka spruce (*Picea mariana*) with a tight grain is exceptionally resonant and ideal for the construction of guitars and pianos. It is much in demand by makers of musical instruments.

Once a virgin area is logged, however, two consequences ensue. First, under the National Forest Management Act of 1976, construction of logging roads eliminates the possibility of future designation as a wilderness preserve. If logging can be prevented by Earth First! or other groups, that land remains eligible for future designation as a Wilderness Area.

Second, the existing ecosystem is transformed. Logging companies usually clear-cut old-growth sites, knocking down every tree. In Oregon this has been the primary timber harvest method for over 100 years. Clear-cutting is contro-

---

[40]Holmes Rolston, "Values Deep in the Woods," *American Forests,* May/June 1988, p. 67.

[41]*Green Paper: Forest and Industry Facts.* Washington, D.C.: American Forest Institute, June 1982, p. 3.

versial, because it at first leaves scarred, barren landscapes. But it has advantages. It is cost-efficient for logging firms, which do not have to work around existing timber stands and can build shorter, easier logging roads. From an ecological standpoint clear-cutting approximates natural forest fires, which were unwisely suppressed by government policy until the 1970s. In addition, clear-cutting opens the area to modern techniques of forest management which rapidly regenerate timber.

When an old-growth area is clear-cut, the Forest Service or a wood products company will replant it, usually with two-year-old Douglas fir seedlings. Douglas firs (*Pseudotsuga menziesii*) are valued for their swift growth. They can be harvested thirty to fifty years after reseeding, much more quickly than other conifers. Douglas firs are shade-intolerant and require sunlight to achieve their full growth potential. When, therefore, an area is clear-cut, it is ideal for seeding with these fast-growing trees. If an old-growth forest is allowed to decay naturally, on the other hand, then as dominant Douglas firs die, new seedlings fail to take root in the shade of the forest floor and are replaced by more shade-tolerant species. In this way an old-growth forest of Douglas firs, if left alone, evolves into a spruce and hemlock forest.

The seeding of Douglas firs is analogous to planting a farm crop. The seedlings are selected from genetically strong varieties. The forest soil is prepared by plowing or fertilizing. Once planted, the trees are closely watched. Aerial spraying of pesticides and herbicides is common, as is the trapping of rabbits, gophers, and mountain beavers, which nibble the bark of saplings. Populations of deer and elk are reduced by permitting hunting. After ten or fifteen years a thinning crew removes some trees to prevent too much competition for sunlight and nutrients. The time for harvest and crop rotation is carefully calculated.

The forester's creation is less biologically diverse than was the old-growth forest. It is more fragile, more subject to imbalance, than what it replaces because there are fewer species. The white-headed woodpecker (*Picoides albolarvatus*), for example, nests in the snags common to old-growth areas and controls populations of boring beetles which can kill trees. In newly planted forests with no snags, beetle populations may soar, requiring foresters to apply pesticides. The economic rotation of the forest, which maximizes corporate return on investment, is much quicker than ecological rotation, which is the time the forest needs to recover its undefiled, primordial ecology. A forest continually used for tree crops does not support the same complexity of life as a wild forest.

Forest management is valuable for releasing and renewing wood resources that a fast-growing world population demands. There were roughly 1.4 million housing starts in the United States in 1989, and there is a growing overseas market for hardwood logs and manufactured wood products.[42] In fact, Forest

---

[42]U.S. Department of Commerce, *U.S. Industrial Outlook 1990.* Washington, D.C.: Government Printing Office, January 1990, p. 5-1.

Service timber-harvesting permits are geared to the demand for lumber suggested by economic forecasts.

The wood products industry is a mainstay of the economic base in Pacific Northwest states, employing over 100,000 workers, whose wages support local economies.[43] A major reduction in timber harvests would lead to additional losses in employment in an industry where employment has suffered already because of widespread mechanization of logging and milling. Since 1980 the forest products industry has invested over $5 billion in improving its facilities.[44] If present harvest levels of old-growth timber are not sustained, corporations may be unable to repay debt. Since the government owns 55 percent of timberland in the Pacific Northwest, forest products companies depend on government timber sales to augment timber harvesting on their own lands.

THE FIGHT OVER THE NORTHERN SPOTTED OWL HABITAT

By 1989 environmental groups had succeeded in blocking about one-third of U.S. Forest Service and Bureau of Land Management timber sales. This created a severe timber shortage. The centerpiece of their legal onslaught was a bid to get the U.S. Fish and Wildlife Service to list the northern spotted owl (*Strix occidentalis*) as a threatened or endangered species under authority of the Endangered Species Act of 1973. This would empower the Secretary of Interior to protect the owl's habitat. The spotted owl is a mottled brown raptor, 14 to 16 inches tall at maturity, that lives exclusively in old-growth areas, where it can prey on flying squirrels that live in dead logs on the forest floor. It is believed that the owls cannot survive in younger, reforested areas, which lack rotting logs that support prey species of small mammals and which do not yet have many of the old snags that they use for hunting perches. Each mated pair of owls requires 1,000 to 2,700 acres of old-growth hunting ground to survive. The U.S. Fish and Wildlife Service has estimated that there are only 2,000 breeding pairs of spotted owls and that 90 percent of these are on federally managed forest lands.[45] Environmentalists claim the owl is facing extinction and its message is like that of the canary in an old-time coal mine. If it shows signs of distress, the environment is in trouble.

In 1987 the Department of the Interior refused to list the spotted owl as endangered or threatened.[46] But in 1988 a federal district court ordered reconsideration, and in 1989 the agency reversed itself and issued a preliminary rul-

---

[43]Charles E. Keegan III and Paul E. Polzin, "Trends in the Wood and Peper Products Industry: Their Impact on the Pacific Northwest Economy," *Journal of Forestry,* November 1987, p. 34.

[44]*The Environmental Community Should Stop Mischaracterizing the Terms of the National Forest Management Debate.* Portland, Oreg.: Northwest Forest Association, 1988, p. 1.

[45]55 FR 26118 (July 26, 1990).

[46]*Federal Register,* "Finding on Northern Spotted Owl Petition," Vol. 52, December 23, 1987, p. 48552–54.

ing that listing the northern spotted owl was warranted.[47] After a year of hearings, this ruling became final in 1990.[48] Once a species is listed as threatened under the Endangered Species Act of 1973 it may not be collected, hunted, harassed, or harmed in any way. Federal agencies are required to act together to protect threatened species. Nowhere does the Endangered Species Act authorize flexibility to trade off species survival against human economic welfare.[49]

Environmentalists thought they had won a great victory. Since the owl had been classified as threatened, the U.S. Forest Service and the Bureau of Land Management would seemingly have to stop timber sales in old-growth sales and prohibit further destruction of the owl's habitat. However, only four days after the U.S. Fish and Wildlife Service put the spotted owl on the list of threatened species, the Bush Administration announced that federal agencies would continue timber sales while a cabinet-level task force met to recommend (1) changes in the Endangered Species Act and (2) a long-term timber management plant for federal lands that would balance the need to protect the owl with the needs of the Northwest timber industry. Environmentalists were irate. "The cloak is off George Bush," said a Wilderness Society leader, "I don't think there is any more pretending he is the Environment President."[50]

Timber interests were hopeful that logging could proceed. They argue that the species is not yet at the danger point, and its presence in old-growth forests is only a flimsy pretext for advancing the unreasonable antilogging agenda of environmentalists. The Northwest Forest Resource Council, a timber industry group, has estimated that protecting the owl over its full range would cost 28,000 workers their jobs and cost the federal government $1 billion in lost revenue from timber sales. The federal government shares up to 40 percent of this revenue with local counties where harvests occur, and those counties use it for roads, schools, and other public services. Thirty-five sawmills representing 2,500 jobs in the Pacific Northwest had closed by the summer of 1989 because of a "timber gap."

This gap the result of several factors. First, lawsuits had slowed timber sales. Second, private forests were overlogged during the boom in housing

[47]See *Northern Spotted Owl* v. *Hodel*, no. C88-573-Z, W.D. Wash., May 5, 1988, and "Proposed Threatened Status for the Northern Spotted Owl," *Federal Register,* vol. 54, June 23, 1989, pp. 26666–77.

[48]See *Federal Register,* "Endangered and Threatened Wildlife and Plants; Determination of Threatened Status for the Northern Spotted Owl, vol. 55, no. 123, June 26, 1990, p. 26114.

[49]This position, at any rate, was taken by the U.S. Supreme Court in the famous Snail Darter case, *Tennessee Valley Authority* v. *Hill,* 437 U.S. 174 (1978). The court held that the Endangered Species Act permitted no trade-off between economic benefits and species preservation. Reacting to this decision, Congress in 1978 set up a special cabinet-level Endangered Species Committee empowered to exempt federal projects from the provisions of the act even if a species would be made extinct. Exemption could be granted if (1) there is no reasonable and prudent alternative to the proposed action, (2) the benefits of the proposed action clearly outweigh the costs, and (3) the project is in the public interest. But no such action was ever taken by this committee.

[50]Quoted in Mark A. Stein, "Logging in Owl Country Will Proceed," *Los Angeles Times,* June 27, 1990, p. A21.

construction after World War II. They are now depleted, and replacement firs are mostly too immature to harvest. And third, Japanese companies were buying logs and shipping them overseas for milling. Since the Japanese yen had grown stronger and the dollar had weakened, Japanese companies outbid American sawmills for raw timber. Thus, laid-off mill workers in port towns such as North Bend, Oregon, watched from their porches as trucks carried logs to the docks for loading onto Japanese freighters. The Japanese buy logs rather than milled timber because finished boards from U.S. sawmills do not have the quality the Japanese demand, and most U.S. mills are unequipped to cut in the metric sizes used in Japanese construction.

Feelings are running high in logging communities. In Sweet Home, Oregon, a town dependent on the logging industry, workers have put bumper stickers on their pick-ups reading "SAVE A LOGGER/EAT AN OWL" and "I LIKE SPOTTED OWLS . . . FRIED." They and their families began sticking small, adhesive yellow dots on the money they spent to demonstrate the importance of their spending to the local economy. In Escalante, Utah, embittered sawmill workers whose jobs were threatened wear baseball caps reading "SUWA Sucks," in reference to the Southern Utah Wilderness Alliance, a group working for logging restrictions. Members of SUWA fear for their safety and receive their mail in plain envelopes.

Environmentalists, of course, argue that a priceless national heritage should not be sacrificed to prevent temporary structural readjustment in the forest products industry. All the while, Earth First!ers have continued to interrupt logging operations in the northwest woods. Acting as the environmentalists' light infantry, they spike trees, stand with arms linked on logging roads to block trucks, and picket U.S. Forest Service offices. One of the latter "actions" is described by an Earth First!er at the scene.

> Four of us were boosted onto the roof of the building, while two others chained themselves in front of the entrance. The remaining 120 people decorated the building with statements written in chalk and water soluble paint.
>
> Protesters scattered sawdust over the building entrances, symbolizing the ghosts of logged old growth trees back to haunt their murderers.
>
> They also spread cow pies, symbolic of destructive grazing on public lands . . . and rubbed the pies into the intakes of air conditioner units on the roof. This forced Freddie [Earth First! slang for forest rangers] to shut down his artificial air and swelter in 80 degree heat. . . . "WOLVES AND GRIZZLIES FOR A GREATER NORTH CASCADES" bumperstickers were placed on police cars.[51]

[51]Mitch Feedman, "26 Arrested in Washington Demo," *Earth First! The Radical Environmental Journal,* Lughnasadh ed. August 1, 1988, p. 1. In the afternoon twenty-six demonstrators were arrested and taken to jail, where they held a one-day hunger strike while fifty sympathizers picketed outside. Ultimately, they were released on $50 bail, and charges were dropped.

QUESTIONS

In order to choose sides in the battle for the forests, it is necessary to answer certain questions. First, do new insights into natural ecology imply a need to change our ethics? Second, does civil disobedience based on the higher law of ecology command respect? When does the need to stop environmental damage outweigh the need to obey the law? Third, do the ends adopted by Earth First! justify the full range of direct-action tactics the group employs? How much old-growth forest should be preserved for future generations and how much consumed to make new homes? And finally, should the spotted owl be protected even if severe economic hardship is created in the Northwest?

THE FIGHT FOR THE ROAD DISPATCHER'S JOB

In 1986 the United States Supreme Court issued a landmark ruling on affirmative action. In it, the majority held that an employer could give preference to women when making promotions. This confirmed the right of employers around the country to use gender as one consideration in personnel decisions, a common practice. The ruling in *Paul E. Johnson* v. *Transportation Agency, Santa Clara County, California* was hailed by feminists as a victory for women and derided by conservatives as unfair to men.[1] On the surface this is the story of a man and woman in competition for a road dispatch position. On a deeper level the events recounted here were the pretext for a clash of contending legal theories about civil rights. On both levels there were winners and losers.

THE PROTAGONISTS

Our story begins with the two individuals who would have an indelible impact on each other's lives, Diane Joyce and Paul Johnson.

Diane Joyce

Diane Joyce was born in 1938 as Diane Dolman into a blue-collar family on the South Side of Chicago. Her father was a tool-and-die maker, and her mother worked at a nearby Walgreen's Drug Store handling returned goods. She grew

[1]No. 85-1129; 107 S.Ct. 1442 (1987); 55 LW 4379; 35 FEP 725.

up in the same Chicago neighborhood and excelled in school, skipping a grade in grammar school and achieving academic honors in high school. An important formative influence in her life was her father's union activism. He filed many union grievances, and Joyce notes that in the family they "used to say that he got a foreman fired every two years."[2] Once he came home bloodied from duty on a union picket line, and this taught Joyce a lesson: "I learned from him that there's always a price to pay."[3]

At eighteen she married Donald Joyce, an apprentice tool-and-die maker at the plant where her father worked. In the first year of their marriage she attended the University of Illinois with the intent of becoming an architectural engineer, but a counselor told her that respectable women did not aspire to engineering and diverted her to courses in theater arts and social studies. Though she did not know it at the time, the counselor was a harbinger of chauvinistic male attitudes that would challenge her aspirations again and again. She dropped out of the university after one year and applied for a trainee's job in computer programming at IBM. She scored in the highest group on an aptitude test, but the personnel department told her the jobs were only for men. She became a housewife.

When a recession hit in 1958, her husband was furloughed for nine months, and Diane went to work at the Triner Scale Company in Chicago as an account clerk. She liked the job, but when Donald again found work as a machinist, he insisted that she quit. She refused. He soon consulted a lawyer and began to threaten divorce, but eventually he relented, since the family needed cash. After Diane had worked eleven years at Triner, Donald died of liver cancer, leaving her with four children (including one retarded daughter who would always need support) to raise on her own.

After the funeral Joyce decided to come to California, and in 1970, at the age of thirty-three, she moved with all four children to a small town near San Francisco. She got a low-paying clerical job with the Santa Clara County Department of Education. After a year, she learned of a senior account clerk position with the Roads Division of the Department of Transportation paying $50 a month more than she was then earning. She applied. Because the job had recently been reduced in pay, no men applied, and she was chosen from sixteen women applicants. Joyce worked at this job and in 1974 applied for a promotion to the position of road dispatcher. She was rejected as not qualified because she did not have the requisite four years' experience working on county roads. Thus, in 1975 she applied for a position as a county road maintenance worker. She had the third highest score among eighty-seven applicants and was one of ten applicants hired.

Joyce was the first woman ever to hold that job classification and was subjected to ostracism, humiliation, and harassment. She found vulgar graffiti on

---

[2]In Susan Faludi, "Diane Joyce," *Ms,* January 1988, p. 65.
[3]Ibid.

Diane Joyce. (*Source: Mickey Pfleger/Time Magazine.*)

the sides of her truck. The road crew foreman refused to permit her to detour to a ladies' room. In order to get the county coveralls worn by the men, she had to file a union grievance. The men threw darts at union notices she put on the bulletin board. Sometimes hostility was frank and open. In a meeting one day a coworker gained the nodding approval of others by storming: "I hate the day you came here. We don't want you here. Why don't you go away?"[4] But at least one man disagreed. Douglas Jurden, a maintenance worker on the road crew, married Joyce. Of the ceremony Joyce says: "I told the justice of the peace, no vows, none of this me obeying him. I'll promise only to be his wife."[5]

During her five years on the road crew Joyce sometimes filled in as one of the two road crew dispatchers. Over that time she accumulated about three months of dispatch experience, and when a retirement left the position vacant, she applied for it. So did Paul Johnson.

[4]Ibid., p. 90.
[5]Ibid.

Paul Johnson

Paul Johnson is a strong, physically powerful man. He grew up as one of five boys on a rented 180-acre farm. His father died during the depression years of the 1930s, and his mother valiantly struggled to keep the farm going by doing physical labor in the fields, but ultimately it failed. He struck out on his own into a lifetime of blue-collar work. His first job was laying pipeline in Kansas. Then he worked for a time on oil rigs in Texas. After marrying and settling down he worked for seventeen years with a cement company, where he was a dispatcher for seven years and a supervisor for another eight years.

When the cement firm went bankrupt in 1967, Johnson came to work for Santa Clara County as a Road Yard Clerk II. He processed purchase orders and requisitioned asphalt and mix. It was not a job with great potential for advancement. In 1974 he applied for the single road dispatcher position but came in second. In 1977 the county downgraded his clerk's job, so he applied for the position of road maintenance worker, the same job classification held by Joyce. He got it and for two years worked cleaning culverts, picking up trash from grassy median strips, patching potholes, and shoveling detritus from roadside ditches. When one of the road dispatchers retired in September 1979, Johnson was asked to fill in on a temporary basis. He was fifty-five years old and hoped to work at the job until retirement at age sixty-five.

MEN AND WOMEN AT WORK

The coming battle for promotion to the dispatcher's position was to be a microcosm of clashing social forces in the larger society. American society is marked by traditional sex role distinctions. Sex roles are specific, shared expectations about how men and women will behave and relate to each other. From birth, children are socialized into male and female roles, and, as one feminist sociologist has written, "pink and blue blankets are only the symbolic tip of the socialization iceberg."[6] Male socialization trains boys for independence, aggression, competitiveness, emotional control, and logical thinking. Female socialization, on the other hand, emphasizes dependence on men, deference to their wishes, emotional expressiveness, and nurturant behavior. Although the traditional gender role stereotypes have been under pressure in our society, they persist. The traditional sex role socialization process was untouched by feminist assault in the 1930s and 1940s, when Paul Johnson and Diane Joyce were growing up.

Male dominance is part of the structure and functioning of the workplace. It is reflected in many ways. There is a persistent salary gap in which men earn more than women in similar job categories and in overall wages. In 1987, for example, the median weekly earnings of women were only 70 percent of those

---

[6]Jean Lipman-Blumen. *Gender Roles and Power*. Englewood Cliffs, N.J.: Prentice-Hall, 1984, p. 54.

Paul Johnson. (*Source: Matthew McVay/SABA.*)

of men.[7] Many women are segregated in traditionally female occupations such as nursing, teaching in elementary and secondary schools, and service positions such as bank teller or telephone operator. In mixed-gender occupations women may face sexual harassment and sexist discrimination. In these and many other ways the employment structure reflects male dominance.

The blue-collar workplace inhabited by Paul Johnson and Diane Joyce is a world especially dominated by masculine values. In the traditional working-class family the husband is the breadwinner and supports his wife and children. There is a division of household labor in which the wife does household chores and child rearing. It is preferable for the wife not to work, but if family finances are weak, she may typically take a low-income service job to supplement her husband's paycheck. Such work is a necessity, not the self-fulfillment of a career woman. A working-class husband may feel that his ad-

[7]"Women Narrowing Salary Gap with Men, Study Says," *Los Angeles Times,* February 2, 1988.

equacy as a provider has been called into question if his wife works; he may find her new independence threatening. For these reasons, he may not support his wife's working outside the home.[8]

Blue-collar work has been one of the most sex-segregated occupational categories. In 1979, when the dispatcher position became vacant, there were 13.2 million skilled craft workers, but only 836,000, or 6.3 percent, were women.[9] Women who occupied these positions ventured into a world structured by male tradition and values. Men reacted to the entry of women in these positions by placing them in comfortable, known female roles, that is, mother, wife, or daughter. Interaction based on these role expectations, even if blue-collar women resisted, typically led to patterns of male dominance rather than gender equality. For many working-class men the place of a woman is in the home, and her presence at work hints that a male provider has been displaced from a job.

Blue-collar men see their identity and self-worth as affirmed in their muscular strength, skill in using specialized tools and machinery, and knowledge of workplace etiquette. They share a common male bonding that excludes women. The assumptions of male work culture are revealed in these comments by a journeyman electrician who was required to train a woman who would become his peer.

> Ginny hasn't been up here long enough for me to make a good judgment. But I have strong feelings that a woman doesn't belong in all fields of a man's world. My experience so far with Ginny has been that she has done some good work and that she's smart, but she lacks the common sense that the average man has about how to go about doing things.[10]

The presence of a woman in the workplace may be threatening for a number of reasons. If attractive, women may inject sexual tension into work and incite jealousy or other uncomfortable feelings. If competent, they contradict bedrock assumptions of male workers about their strength and superiority. If they come in large numbers, men fear they will devalue the status of the occupation; male-dominated job categories traditionally pay more. And if women demand equality or fail to show feminine deference, they challenge the sex role assumptions cherished by working-class men.

To protect their masculine culture traditional workingmen often fail to nurture women coworkers. Lack of support takes a variety of forms. Physical intimidation is common, and, indeed, Diane Joyce believes that one day a male

[8]Lipman-Blumen, op. cit., p. 119.

[9]*Statistical Abstract of the United States*, 102d ed. Washington, D.C.: U.S. Government Printing Office, 1981, p. 401.

[10]Anthony Astrachan. *How Men Feel: Their Response to Women's Demands for Equality and Power*. New York: Anchor Press, 1986, p. 84. For more on the gap between the ideal of sexual equality and the reality of work group norms see Sylvia A. Law, "'Girls Can't Be Plumbers'—Affirmative Action for Women in Construction: Beyond Goals and Quotas," *Harvard Civil Rights-Civil Liberties Law Review*, Vol. 24, 1986, pp. 45–77.

road worker tried to purposely hit her with a forklift. There is reluctance to impart technical knowledge about machinery and equipment, as occurred when Joyce tried to master a bobtail truck. Obscene language is used by blue-collar men to affirm their masculinity. Sexual jokes about women affirm male dominance. In these and other ways men can sabotage the developing competence of a woman at work. Diane Joyce was a woman who clashed with the male juggernaut and kept fighting.

THE SELECTION PROCESS

In December 1979 the Transportation Agency announced that the position of road dispatcher was vacant and invited applications. Johnson, who by then had been working in the position for three months, applied. So did eleven others, including Diane Joyce. The position required four years of experience in dispatch or road maintenance work and familiarity with county roads and maintenance procedures. Of the twelve applicants nine, including Johnson and Joyce, were deemed as having met these requirements.

The selection process was conducted according to Merit System Rules derived from the Santa Clara County Charter. The first step was a fifteen-minute oral test on job duties conducted by a two-person board on which applicants had to score 70 or above. Johnson tied for second with a score of 75. Joyce came in third with a score of 72.5 (which was rounded off to 73). In all, seven applicants scored over 70, and the board rated them all as "well qualified." According to county personnel policies, all candidates scoring over 70 were to be considered equally qualified at this point.

The next step was an interview before a panel of three agency supervisors. Joyce was dismayed to learn the names of these panel members, for she had had significant differences with two of them in the past. One was her first road maintenance supervisor, who had refused to supply her with county-issue coveralls. The second supervisor had differed with Joyce over the implementation of safety policy in her role as chair of the Roads Operations Safety Committee. He had once referred to her as a "rebel-rousing, skirt-wearing person."[11] After interviewing all seven candidates the panel unanimously ranked Paul Johnson first for promotion to the road dispatcher position; Diane Joyce was ranked third. This recommendation was sent to Ron Shields, director of the Road Maintenance Division. Shields was empowered to select any of the seven applicants, considering their records and the recommendations of the panel of supervisors. He picked Paul Johnson. Prior to the formal announcement, a rumor arose that Johnson had the job. When Diane Joyce heard it, she grew angry and telephoned the County Affirmative Action Office.

This selection procedure invites criticism for its inherent bias against women. The stated job requirements limit the flow of female applicants be-

---

[11]Tr. 153, 55 LW 4381, note 5.

cause they include extensive experience in road work, where there are few women. The panel of interviewers was composed of men who had demonstrated bias against Joyce and other women.[12]

THE COUNTY AFFIRMATIVE ACTION PLAN

Almost two years before, in 1978, the Santa Clara County Transportation Agency had adopted a voluntary Affirmative Action Plan. The objective of the plan was to increase the number of minority, female, and handicapped persons in job classifications where they were underrepresented.

The long-term goal of the plan was to build a work force whose composition matched the proportion of women and minorities in the area labor force. At the time, women were 36.4 percent of the area labor market but were only 22.4 percent of the Transportation Agency's employees.[13] In furtherance of the plan the agency calculated the percentage of women in specific job categories. Women made up 76 percent of office and clerical workers, indicating that most of the agency's women employees had traditionally female jobs. In other job categories women were scarce. They were only 7.1 percent of officials and administrators, 8.6 percent of professionals, 9.7 percent of technicians, and 22 percent of service and maintenance workers. The road dispatcher position fell into the skilled craft worker category, and it was here that the agency performed most poorly. Of 238 skilled craft positions, not one was held by a woman. The plan took note of the fact that there were no female skilled craft workers. While not acknowledging that this was the result of past discrimination, it admitted that in the past women had not been motivated to acquire training for these positions because only "limited opportunities" existed.[14]

To remedy imbalances the plan required the "hiring, training and promotion of . . . women throughout the Agency in all major job classifications where they are underrepresented."[15] It required that annual short-term goals for hiring women be established. These goals were not to become rigid quotas but were to be reasonable targets that took into consideration factors such as "turnover, layoffs, lateral transfers, new job openings, retirements and availability of minorities, women and handicapped persons in the area work force who possess the desired qualifications or potential for placement."[16] The plan firmly stated that "'goals' established for each Division should not be construed as 'quotas' that must be met."[17] At the time Diane Joyce telephoned the

---

[12]The selection process is attacked by Dorothy P. Moore and Marsha Hass in "When Affirmative Action Cloaks Management Bias in Selection and Promotion Decisions," *Academy of Management Executive,* February 1990, pp. 84–90.

[13]These labor force percentages are from *Johnson* v. *Transportation Agency,* op. cit., 55 LW 4380–81.

[14]Ibid., p. 4381.

[15]Ibid., p. 4384.

[16]Ibid.

[17]Ibid., p. 4385.

County Affirmative Action Office (June 1980), the Transportation Agency was still in the process of determining annual goals. None were specified at the time.

THE TABLES TURN

The County Affirmative Action Office, after receiving Diane Joyce's call, contacted the affirmative action coordinator within the Transportation Agency. The coordinator, in turn, recommended to the agency's director, James Graebner, that Joyce be promoted to road dispatcher rather than Johnson. Graebner walked to the roads operations office and asked Ron Shields if the rumor that he intended to promote Johnson was correct. Shields said yes, it was. According to witnesses, Graebner then asked, "What's wrong with the woman?" Shields replied, "I hate her."[18] Graebner decided to reverse the decision and give Joyce the promotion. On the certification form required by the county he evaluated Joyce this way: "Well qualified by virtue of 18 years of past clerical experience including $3\frac{1}{2}$ years at West Yard plus almost 5 years as a [road maintenance worker]." Of Johnson he wrote: "Well qualified applicant; two years of [road maintenance worker] experience plus 11 years of Road Yard Clerk. Has had previous outside Dispatch experience but that was 13 years ago."[19] Later, in district court, he testified:

> I tried to look at the whole picture, the combination of her qualifications and Mr. Johnson's qualifications, their test scores, their expertise, their background, affirmative action matters, things like that. ... I believe it was a combination of all those.[20]

When Paul Johnson heard the news, he was furious and "felt like tearing something up."[21] Johnson asked for a meeting with affirmative action officers to explain the decision. He later described the meeting this way:

> The affirmative action man walks in and he's this big black guy. He can't tell me anything. He brings in this minority who can barely speak English. I was so mad. I told them, "You haven't heard the last of me."[22]

Shortly thereafter Johnson hired a lawyer and brought a civil suit against the Transportation Agency in the District Court for the Northern District of California. The legal battle would last for six years as the case rose to the Supreme Court of the United States.

THE LEGAL BATTLE BEGINS

In district court, Johnson claimed that unfair employment discrimination had deprived him of a promotion because of his sex. His argument was that Title

[18]Faludi, op. cit., p. 91.
[19]*Johnson* v. *Transportation Agency,* op. cit., p. 4382.
[20]Ibid.
[21]Faludi, loc. cit.
[22]Ibid., p. 92.

VII of the Civil Rights Act of 1964 prohibited sex discrimination; hence, it prohibited the promotion of a less qualified woman in his place. Lawyers for Santa Clara County defended by arguing that the promotion of Joyce was justified by compliance with the County Affirmative Action Plan.

Title VII of the Civil Rights Act of 1964

The Civil Rights Act of 1964 was passed to prohibit discrimination in many areas of American life, including education, public accommodations and facilities, federally funded programs, and, of course, employment.[23]

Title VII is the section of the act that covers employment activities. It prohibits discrimination on the grounds of race, color, religion, national origin, and sex. The legislative history of the Civil Rights Act reveals that its supporters in Congress originally did not intend to include sex as a classification for which employment discrimination was prohibited. But in a prankish effort to reduce support for the entire Civil Rights Act, southerners in the House of Representatives amended it by adding sex to the other types of discrimination which were to be curbed by Title VII. This effort backfired, however, when women's employment rights proved less controversial than expected, and the entire bill passed. So sex discrimination became invalid, and its prevention was the purpose of the Transportation Agency's Affirmative Action Plan.

This is the exact wording of Section 703(a) of Title VII.

> It shall be an unlawful employment practice for any employer—
> (1) to fail or refuse to hire or to discharge any individual, or otherwise to discriminate against any individual with respect to his compensation, terms, conditions, or privileges of employment, because of such individual's race, color, religion, sex, or national origin; or
> (2) to limit, segregate, or classify his employees or applicants for employment in any way which would deprive or tend to deprive any individual of employment opportunities or otherwise adversely affect his status as an employee, because of such individual's race, color, religion, sex, or national origin.[24]

Affirmative action is mentioned only once in Title VII, in Section 706(g), where federal courts are empowered to "order such affirmative action as may be appropriate" in instances where employers are engaging in intentional discrimination.[25] Affirmative action by a court may include the reinstatement or hiring of employees, provision for back pay, and "any other equitable relief as the court deems appropriate."

The uneasy coexistence of Sections 703(a) and 706(g) is verified by a long trail of litigation. Section 703(a) requires that there be *no discrimination* by an employer against anyone in the protected classifications. Yet Section 706(g)

---

[23]Pub. L. 88-352; 78 Stat. 241; 42 U.S.C. Sections 1971, 1975a–d., 2000a *et seq.*
[24]42 U.S.C. Section 2000e-2(a).
[25]42 U.S.C. Section 2000e-5(g).

permits an employer to *give preference* to such persons. There is a logical tension between these two mandates. What did Congress intend?

When Title VII was being debated in 1964, congressional opponents charged that it would require employers who had discriminated in the past to lay off white, male workers and hire minorities and women in their place. To avoid the chaos and political opposition inherent in such a requirement, supporters introduced an amendment stating that an employer was not required to grant preferential treatment to any protected minority or female because an imbalance existed in the current work force.[26] Unfortunately, this amendment failed to make the law clear enough to avoid future litigation. Although employers were not *required* to give blacks or women preferential treatment, were they *permitted* to do so? In light of Section 703(a)'s strict prohibition of employment decisions based on race or gender, under what circumstances, if any, could an employer adopt a voluntary affirmative action program? After the passage of Title VII in 1964 the answers to these questions remained unclear for many years. Then, in 1979, the Supreme Court's ruling in the case of Brian Weber, a white steelworker, provided many answers and established important guidelines.

United Steelworkers of America v. Brian F. Weber

Brian Weber worked at a Kaiser Aluminum & Chemical Corporation plant in Louisiana, where he applied for a craft training program designed to teach production workers new skills and enable them to fill better-paying jobs. In the past, Kaiser had discriminated against blacks, and a severe imbalance in favor of whites prevailed in its work force. Blacks constituted 39 percent of the local population but only 1.83 percent (5 out of 273) of the skilled craft workers, an especially pronounced imbalance. To remedy the situation Kaiser and the steelworkers union agreed on an affirmative action plan, which was written into a collective bargaining agreement. The goal of the plan was to attain a 39 percent black skilled craft work force, and to help achieve it, 50 percent of the positions in craft training programs were reserved for blacks.

When Brian Weber applied for craft training, admission to the program was by seniority, but there were two seniority lists—one for whites and one for blacks. Weber's name was added to the white list. There were thirteen positions in the training program, and they were filled by choosing alternately from the seniority lists, beginning with the black list. One black was chosen, then one white, and so forth until seven blacks and six whites were picked. The result of this imaginative procedure, however, was that the last black selected had less job seniority than three whites not selected, including Weber. Weber quickly realized that he had missed admission because he was white and brought a "reverse discrimination" suit, claiming that Title VII prohibited discrimination based on race. In doing so he raised the question of whether an

---

[26]Section 703 (j), 42 U.S.C. Section 2000e-2(j).

employer could voluntarily adopt an affirmative action plan and give preferential treatment based on race.

In a 5-2 decision the Supreme Court ruled against Weber. In the majority opinion Justice Brennan argued that Congress did not intend to prohibit employers from adopting race-conscious affirmative action plans and that, indeed, such plans epitomized the "spirit" of Title VII. Without preferential treatment for blacks, Brennan argued, the elimination of discriminatory barriers would be too slow.

In addition, there were special features of the Kaiser affirmative action plan that made it permissible to the Court majority. First, its purpose was "to break down old patterns of racial segregation and hierarchy." Second, the plan did not "unnecessarily trammel the interests of white employees," since it did not "require the discharge of white workers and their replacement with new black hires." Third, the plan did not "create an absolute bar to the advancement of white employees." Half those admitted were white. And fourth, the plan was "a temporary measure."[27] Once racial imbalance was corrected, it would lapse. These four features were criteria by which other voluntary affirmative action plans (such as the Transportation Agency plan) could be judged.

The majority opinion in the *Weber* case was met with strong dissent. Chief Justice Warren Burger dissented, stating that the Court's decision was wholly at odds with the explicit language of Title VII prohibiting discrimination against any individual based on race. He called Title VII "a statute of extraordinary clarity" and accused the majority of unwarranted judicial activism which changed its meaning.[28] Justice Rehnquist agreed. "Quite simply," he wrote, "Kaiser's racially discriminatory admission quota is flatly prohibited by the plain language of Title VII."[29] Rehnquist reviewed floor debate over Title VII in the Senate, a traditional method of the courts when interpreting the meaning of a statute. He noted that leading sponsors of the bill agreed that the bill prohibited *all* discrimination, including that resulting from the use of racial quotas. Rehnquist concluded that the majority had introduced "into Title VII a tolerance for the very evil that the law was intended to eradicate. ..."[30] Despite the clear perspective of these dissents, however, Burger and Rehnquist made no converts. Brian Weber failed to get into the training program because he was white. He did, however, make an appearance on the *Tonight* show with Johnny Carson.

The *Johnson* Case at Trial

In 1981 Paul Johnson's case was given a two-day trial in San Francisco. Johnson advanced the argument that he had been discriminated against because of his sex in violation of Title VII. Deputy County Attorney Steven

[27]47 LW 4852.
[28]47 LW 4857.
[29]47 LW 4863.
[30]47 LW 4867.

Woodside defended the case for the Transportation Agency by arguing that seven candidates met the minimum qualifications and any could have been chosen. Woodside said the selection of Joyce was justified by the existence of the Affirmative Action Plan.

During testimony by individuals from the Transportation Agency the details of the selection process were laid out. After considering work records and examination board results, District Court Judge William A. Ingram ruled in favor of Paul Johnson. He held that "based upon the examination results and the departmental interview [Mr. Johnson] was more qualified for the position of Road Dispatcher than Diane Joyce," that "but for [Mr. Johnson's] sex, male, he would have been promoted to the position of Road Dispatcher," and that "but for Diane Joyce's sex, female, she would not have been appointed to the position. . . ."[31] The testimony of James Graebner, director of the Transportation Agency, was of particular importance in supporting this conclusion. For example:

Q: How did you happen to become involved in this particular promotional opportunity?

A: I . . . became aware that there was a difference of opinion between specifically the Road Operations people [Mr. Shields] and the Affirmative Action Director [Mr. Morton] as to the desirability of certain of the individuals to be promoted. . . . Mr. Shields felt that Mr. Johnson should be appointed to that position.

Q: Mr. Morton felt that Diane Joyce should be appointed?

A: Mr. Morton was less interested in the particular individual; he felt that this was an opportunity for us to take a step toward meeting our affirmative action goals and because there was only one person on the [eligibility] list who was one of the protected groups, he felt that this afforded us an opportunity to meet those goals through the appointment of that member of a protected group.[32]

Also, the county was not vindicated in its selection of Joyce because it had an Affirmative Action Plan. Judge Ingram ruled that the plan did not meet the criteria in the *Weber* case. The agency had failed to prove that the work force imbalance in favor of men was due to past discrimination. And since the plan contained no specific statement about its duration and no cutoff date, it failed to meet the *Weber* test of being "a temporary measure." Judge Ingram also remarked that because of these shortcomings the plan became an "absolute bar" to Johnson's advancement, which was a third failure under the *Weber* test.

Paul Johnson was given retroactive promotion to the dispatcher position with back pay, and the Transportation Agency was ordered to end its practice of gender discrimination. When the ruling was issued in 1982, Paul Johnson

---

[31] Tr. 4a, 12a, and 13a, 55 LW 4392.
[32] Tr. 16–18, 55 LW 4392.

was put into the dispatcher position while the agency appealed the decision. Diane Joyce was assigned to a new, temporary dispatcher position pending the outcome.

The Court of Appeals Reverses

Two years later, on December 4, 1984, the United States Court of Appeals for the Ninth Circuit reversed the decision of the lower court.[33] Writing for the 2-1 majority, Circuit Judge Fletcher said: "We conclude that the district court misapprehended the requirements for a bona fide affirmative action plan."[34] He wrote that although the plan contained no express statement limiting its duration, it nowhere stated that it was intended to be permanent. This, together with the plan's emphasis on attainment of a balanced work force rather than perpetuation of strict quotas, made the plan "sufficiently temporary" to pass the *Weber* guideline. In addition, statistics showing only a small number of women in traditionally male jobs within the Transportation Agency implied past discrimination and endowed the plan with a remedial purpose as required by *Weber*. Finally, although Johnson would be denied a promotion, the plan did not require the exclusion of all men from promotions. A single case did not constitute an absolute bar to male advancement. In other words, Johnson would lose the promotion, but he and other men could be promoted to other positions.

When the decision came down, Paul Johnson was deeply disturbed. He believed that the job had been rightfully his and that Diane Joyce had taken it from him. The publicity surrounding his defeat injured his pride, and he soon took early retirement. He and his wife, Betty, moved to the small town of Sequim in northern Washington, where, financed by her income as a bank teller, he persevered with the case by appealing to the U.S. Supreme Court.

Diane Joyce, though pleased with the decision, was uncertain of the eventual outcome in the Supreme Court. Moreover, the years of legal battle with Paul Johnson had become a strain to her marriage. When a job as road foreman with the county opened up, she applied. This proved to be the final straw for her husband, who also coveted the foreman's job but found it humiliating to compete for it against his wife. She did not get the promotion, despite being ranked first in the selection process. A fifth-ranked man was given the position. And her marriage ended early in 1985 when her husband walked out.

LAST STEP: THE SUPREME COURT

In order to have a case considered by the U.S. Supreme Court the appealing party must file a "petition of certiorari." The nine justices meet at weekly con-

---

[33]*Paul E. Johnson* v. *Transportation Agency, Santa Clara County, California,* 748 F.2d 1308 (1984); *modified* 770 F.2d 752 (1985).
[34]770 F.2d 752.

ferences to consider these petitions, and, as has been the custom since 1925, if four justices wish to hear a case, the petition is approved. These weekly conferences are attended only by the justices, and discussions are confidential. It is not known, therefore, why at least four members of the Supreme Court voted to accept the *Johnson* case. But on December 31, 1985, the Court announced that certiorari had been granted.

The Court was not required by law to hear the case. Sometimes the Court takes a case when the justices believe that precedent from a previous Supreme Court decision has been misapplied, and some may have felt that the circuit court misinterpreted *Weber*. On other occasions the Court agrees to hear a case when lower-court decisions on the same legal issue are in conflict. But the *Johnson* decision was not contrary to other recent decisions. A guess is that the Court accepted the case because voluntary affirmative action plans involved an unsettled area of law. Some of the activist justices may have wanted to extend and solidify the *Weber* decision. Conservatives surely saw an opportunity to overthrow *Weber*.

Oral Argument

The case then went to oral argument. Oral argument on cases is held in the imposing courtroom of the Supreme Court building in Washington, D.C., with its 30-foot tall Ionic columns and magnificent inlaid ceiling. There, at 10:00 a.m. on the morning of November 18, 1986, the marshal of the Court stood and said, "All rise." All nine justices entered the room and seated themselves behind their long, curved, wooden bench to hear lawyers argue both sides of the case. Each side would have one-half hour to present ideas and respond to questions from the bench. The marshal then intoned the ritual wording which marks the beginning of each session.

> Oyez, oyez, oyez. The Honorable, the Chief Justice and the Associate Justices of the Supreme Court of the United States. All persons having business before this honorable Court are admonished to draw nigh and give their attention, for the Court is now sitting. God save the United States and this honorable Court.

A female attorney, Constance Brooks of Denver, Colorado, presented the case for Johnson. She stressed that but for his gender, Paul Johnson would have been promoted to dispatcher. She made the point that the Transportation Agency's affirmative action plan did not meet the guidelines set forth in *Weber*. She asserted that the scarcity or absence of women in traditionally male jobs at the agency was not the result of intentional, past discrimination. Rather, women simply did not want and apply for such jobs. Since there was no past misdeed to remedy, the affirmative action plan did not meet the guideline set forth in *Weber* that suggested a voluntary plan was only legitimate if it redressed past discrimination. "Good intentions are not enough," said

The members of the *Johnson* Court are listed here in the order of their appointment. Their ages at the time of the decision are given in parentheses.

William J. Brennan (81), a lifelong Democrat, was appointed in 1956 by President Dwight D. Eisenhower. Some thought it was an effort to get liberal votes in an election year. Brennan's liberal judicial philosophy is typified by the majority opinion in the *Weber* case, which he authored, and by his dissent in favor of racial quotas in *Regents of the University of California* v. *Bakke*.[35] He favors strong affirmative action.

Byron R. White (70) is a 1938 All-American college football player who played several years for the Pittsburgh Steelers and the Detroit Lions in the National Football League. He graduated from Yale Law School and developed a friendship with John F. Kennedy which led to his appointment to the Court in 1962. He is generally regarded as a conservative, but he has sometimes voted with the liberal wing of the Court on civil rights issues.

Thurgood Marshall (79) is the great-grandson of a slave. For many years he was counsel for the National Association for the Advancement of Colored People and argued civil rights cases before the Supreme Court, including the famous *Brown* v. *Board of Education* school desegregation case.[36] He was appointed in 1967 by President Lyndon Johnson and confirmed by the Senate despite strong resistance from southerners. Marshall is a steady liberal and protector of minority rights.

Harry A. Blackmun (79) is a former law school professor and federal appeals court judge who was appointed by President Richard Nixon in 1970. Initially, Blackmun voted very conservatively. But by the time the *Johnson* case came before the Court, he was not as predictable and frequently voted with his more liberal colleagues on civil rights issues. He was best remembered for his majority opinion in *Roe* v. *Wade* in 1973, in which he invalidated state anti-abortion laws on the basis of the Fourteenth Amendment's protection of a woman's right to privacy.[37]

Lewis F. Powell (80) is a former president of the American Bar Association and trial lawyer who had no previous judicial position before being appointed to the Supreme Court by President Nixon in 1971. Powell was known for legal conservatism at the time of his appointment, but he has become a moderate. In civil rights and affirmative action cases he is a swing vote, sometimes siding with conservatives and other times with liberals.

William H. Rehnquist (62) was appointed by President Nixon in 1971. He had been an attorney in Phoenix who was active in the Republican party and had briefly held a post in the Department of Justice. Because Rehnquist is a consistent conservative, he was appointed chief justice in 1986 by President Reagan, who was attempting to shift the Court to the right. His blistering dissent in the *Weber* case typifies his resolute opposition to affirmative action.

John Paul Stevens (67) is a former law professor and appeals court judge appointed by President Gerald Ford in 1975. He is not easily characterized as a liberal or conservative, and court observers note his unpredictability. In affirmative action cases his views are erratic. He usually writes separate concurring or dissenting opinions.

Sandra Day O'Connor (57) was a classmate of Chief Justice Rehnquist's at Stanford Law School. After graduation in 1952 she was unable to get a job with any law firm because of discrimination against women in the legal profession. She formed a private law practice in Arizona and was later appointed to the Arizona Court of Appeals. In 1981 she was appointed by President Reagan and became the first woman member of the Supreme Court. In doing this he was fulfilling a presidential campaign promise. O'Connor has generally evidenced a conservative judicial philosophy but has sided with the liberal wing of the Court in several affirmative action cases.

Antonin Scalia (51) is the newest and youngest member of the high court. He had been appointed in 1986 just prior to the start of the Court's term by President Reagan, who supported Scalia's belief in judicial restraint. Scalia is the first Italian-American in the Court's history. He is a former law professor and federal appeals court judge. At the time the *Johnson* case came before the Court, Scalia had no record of opinions on civil rights cases, but he was known to be an outspoken conservative in the mold of Chief Justice Rehnquist.

[35]438 U.S. 265 (1978).
[36]349 U.S. 294 (1954).
[37]93 S.Ct. 705.

Brooks, who noted that the absence of women in craft positions stemmed not from sexist discrimination but from "societal norms."[38]

Justice O'Connor expressed skepticism about Brooks's line of reasoning and pointed out that of the 238 skilled craft positions not one was held by a woman. She suggested that this statistical zero was sufficient evidence of gender discrimination and asked rhetorically: "And you think that is not enough?"[39] Brooks replied: "In this case no."[40] She again emphasized that the disparity was created by the attitudes of women rather than by male discrimination.

Justice Stevens asked Brooks if, in the absence of past discrimination, Title VII required that all promotions be made solely on merit. "Yes, Your Honor," replied Brooks.[41]

Steven Woodside, county attorney for Santa Clara County, presented the other side. He argued that the Transportation Agency's plan was valid and met all the guidelines suggested in *Weber*. He insisted that the promotion goals in the plan were modest and did not absolutely bar the advancement of men. The plan, he stated, was implemented to remedy statistical disparities which "might" have been caused by sexist discrimination in the past.

Justice Scalia questioned Woodside closely. He asked whether it was realistic to expect as many women as men to want to work on a road crew and whether it was reasonable to conclude that male predominance in such jobs was the result of discrimination. Woodside responded that "human experience supports the view that women want to fill such jobs."[42] Scalia rejoined: "In this country?"

Justice Scalia remarked that Diane Joyce would not have gotten the promotion to dispatcher had it not been for the affirmative action plan. "She did not get it because she was better qualified."[43] Woodside replied that Joyce was one of the top applicants and that the selection process did not automatically require her promotion.

After the end of the one-hour session the justices retired to their chambers. That Friday morning, November 21, they met in conference to discuss the *Johnson* case and to assign one justice the task of writing the majority opinion. The discussions in such conferences are secret, and so parties to the litigation had to wait four months for the formal, written decision.

The Decision

On March 25, 1987, the opinion came out. It was 6-3 for the Transportation Agency; Diane Joyce finally had the dispatcher position.

[38]"Arguments before the Court: Employment Discrimination," 55 LW 3345.
[39]55 LW 3347.
[40]55 LW 3347.
[41]55 LW 3347.
[42]55 LW 3345.
[43]55 LW 3347.

The two liberals, Brennan and Marshall, were joined in the majority opinion by the Court's two moderates, Blackmun and Powell, and by the unpredictable Stevens, who wrote an additional concurring opinion. One of the four conservatives, Justice O'Connor, wrote a separate, concurring opinion. But three dissented: Justice White with an opinion and Justice Scalia with an opinion in which Justice Rehnquist joined. Altogether, then, there were five separate opinions on the *Johnson* case.

Justice Brennan delivered the opinion of the Court majority. In it he assessed the Transportation Agency's Affirmative Action Plan using the *Weber* guidelines and found that the plan fell within permissible limits. On the central question of whether statistical imbalance in the work force justified affirmative action for women, even if no past discrimination was proved, Brennan wrote:

> Given the obvious imbalance in the Skilled Craft category, and given the Agency's commitment to eliminating such imbalances, it was plainly not unreasonable for the Agency to determine that it was appropriate to consider as one factor the sex of Ms. Joyce in making its decision. The promotion of Joyce thus satisfies the first requirement enunciated in *Weber*, since it was undertaken to further an affirmative action plan designed to eliminate Agency work force imbalances in traditionally segregated job categories.[44]

Brennan also determined that the plan met the second and third criteria in *Weber* because it "had not unnecessarily trammeled the rights of male employees or created an absolute bar to their advancement."[45] It did not establish quotas for females or automatically exclude men from consideration. In any case, Johnson had "no legitimate firmly rooted expectation" of getting the job, and he still retained his employment at his old salary and could be promoted in the future.

To establish that the plan was a "temporary measure," the final *Weber* guideline, Brennan observed that it was "intended to *attain* a balanced work force, not to maintain one."[46]

In concluding, Brennan sanctioned the plan. "Such a plan," he wrote, "is fully consistent with Title VII, for it embodies the contribution that voluntary employer action can make in eliminating the vestiges of discrimination in the workplace."[47]

The majority opinion broke no new legal ground. It affirmed and echoed the opinion of the Ninth Circuit, adding little to it.

In his concurring opinion, Justice Stevens wrote that even though he did not believe that the original intent of Title VII was to permit benign discrimination, he would respect established precedent. "There is an undoubted public interest," he wrote, "in 'stability and orderly development of the law.' "[48]

---

[44]55 LW 4385.
[45]55 LW 4385.
[46]55 LW 4386.
[47]55 LW 4386.
[48]55 LW 4387, quoting Justice Cardozo at 427 U.S. 190 (1976).

In her concurring opinion, Justice O'Connor agreed that the affirmative action plan met the guidelines in *Weber*. She scolded the Court majority, however, for being vague about the kind of statistical work force imbalance that would justify remedial action by an employer. She suggested that job categories should be compared not with the number of women in the general population but, rather, with the number of women qualified for those jobs.

The dissenters echoed the clarion call of Justice Rehnquist's dissent in the *Weber* case. Justice White wrote a short paragraph which concluded simply: "I would overrule *Weber* and reverse the judgment below."[49] Justice Scalia, however, wrote a lengthy jeremiad. Prefatory to his detailed and at times poetic rebuttal of the majority opinion was this statement:

> The Court today completes the process of converting [Section 703(a) of Title VII] from a guarantee that race or sex will *not* be the basis for employment determinations, to a guarantee that it often *will*. Ever so subtly, without even alluding to the last obstacles preserved by earlier opinions that we now push out of our path, we effectively replace the goal of a discrimination-free society with the quite incompatible goal of proportionate representation by race and by sex in the workplace.[50]

Scalia drove on. The plan could not remedy past sex discrimination because there had been no sex discrimination.

> It is absurd to think that the nation-wide failure of road maintenance crews, for example, to achieve the Agency's ambition of 36.4% female representation is attributable primarily, if even substantially, to systematic exclusion of women eager to shoulder pick and shovel. It is a "traditionally segregated job category" *not* in the *Weber* sense, but in the sense that, because of longstanding social attitudes, it has not been regarded *by women themselves* as desirable .work.[51]

He concluded that Paul Johnson would have been appointed if the affirmative action coordinator had not intervened on behalf of Diane Joyce. The trial court had made a finding of fact that Johnson was better qualified than Joyce, and this finding should have been binding on appeal. Joyce had been appointed solely because she was female on the basis of an affirmative action plan that was invalid because it was not intended to redress past discrimination. The result of the precedent set by the Court in *Johnson,* warned Scalia, would be to OK the social engineering of work forces all over the country to make them match the percentages of minorities and women in the local labor markets. An employer who did not engineer a work force risked a Title VII suit whenever an imbalance existed. Now, reverse discrimination not only would be permitted but also would be required.

All told, it was a powerful dissent. It undoubtedly weakened the force of Brennan's majority opinion. Media commentators and legal scholars gave it considerable attention, and it provided a platform for continued opposition to

[49]55 LW 4391.
[50]55 LW 4391.
[51]55 LW 4394.

affirmative action. Was it prophetic? Only time will tell. As former Chief Justice Charles Evans Hughes noted: "A dissent in a court of last resort is an appeal to the brooding spirit of the law, to the intelligence of a future day, when a later decision may possibly correct the error into which the dissenting judge believes the court to have been betrayed."[52]

Reaction to the Decision

The *Johnson* decision expanded the definition of permissible affirmative action. Before *Johnson* the precise nature of a valid affirmative action program was not always clear. After *Johnson* several elements of such programs, previously of clouded legality, became clearly permissible. First, employers could consider gender as one element in promotions in addition to minority status. Second, affirmative action could legitimately be used not only to correct past discrimination but also to correct a manifest imbalance in a work force even where no past discrimination was proved. And third, the voluntary affirmative action plans of public employers were now sanctioned in addition to the plans of private employers.

The initial rush of legal scholarship was generally critical of Justice Brennan's reasoning. His opinion was criticized for extending the Court's record of fuzzy affirmative action holdings and failing to specify concrete guidelines for employers.[53] It was said that he extended *Weber* inappropriately to an employer not guilty of past discrimination.[54] And it was said that the holding would lead to "erosion of the meritocracy principle."[55]

Women's groups and feminists were winners in the decision. Although the decision did not validate the promotion of unqualified women, it gave employers the right to consider their sex as a "plus factor" in promotions. Men had less chance of successfully claiming reverse discrimination under Title VII as a result of *Johnson*. In fact, 1987 was a year of important Supreme Court victories for women. In January the Court had upheld a California law granting women workers four months of unpaid maternity leave and the right to return to their jobs.[56] In May the Court prohibited Rotary International from enforcing a policy that excluded women from membership in local Rotary Clubs.[57]

The business community generally supported the *Johnson* outcome. In the weeks that followed, the Business Roundtable, the Chamber of Commerce,

[52]In *The Supreme Court of the United States*. New York: Columbia University Press, 1928, p. 68.

[53]Marianne Malouf, "*Johnson v. Transportation Agency, Santa Clara County, California*," *St. Mary's Law Journal*, fall 1987, p. 469.

[54]Thomas J. Lonzo, "*Johnson v Transportation Agency:* Are We All Equal?" *Creighton Law Review*, vol. 21, no. 1, 1987–1988, p. 356.

[55]Robert Belton, "Reflections on Affirmative Action after *Paradise* and *Johnson*," *Harvard Civil Rights–Civil Liberties Law Review*, winter 1988, p. 129.

[56]*California Federal Savings and Loan Association* v. *Guerra*, 55 LW 4077 (1987).

[57]*Board of Directors of Rotary International* v. *Rotary Club of Duarte*, 55 LW 4606 (1987).

and the National Association of Manufacturers were joined by large companies such as General Electric, Du Pont, and Philip Morris in issuing statements of approval. Corporations generally favor numerical hiring goals for classifications protected by Title VII. This approach is in keeping with the quantitative, measurable approach to management systems favored by most large companies. When, in 1985, the Justice Department proposed deleting numerical hiring goals and timetables for federal contractors, a survey of 104 large corporations found 99 opposed.[58] In addition to sanctioning statistical procedures in affirmative action plans, the *Johnson* decision protected companies from reverse discrimination suits by white males.

Two months after the decision a nationwide Gallup poll showed marked public disapproval. Overall, only 29 percent approved of the *Johnson* decision, and 63 percent disapproved of it (8 percent had no opinion). Among women, only 32 percent approved, just slightly more than the 26 percent of men who approved.[59] This is not surprising; it continues a trend in which public opinion polls have shown low approval for affirmative action since it first became a policy issue in the 1960s.

The Court's Decision Comes Home

Immediately after the Court's decision Diane Joyce was besieged by the press and congratulated by supporters in women's groups. "I'm very proud," she told a *Time* reporter. "I've waited a long time for this."[60] To a *Newsweek* reporter she remarked: "There was never any doubt in my mind that I was going to bury the sucker."[61]

After the excitement subsided, however, many of her male coworkers made their hostility known. On the day following the decision friends sent her red and white carnations, which she placed on her desk in a container next to her dispatcher's microphone. The next day they were missing, and a road foreman announced that he had kicked them across the yard. She retrieved the bouquet from a garbage bin. She has faced taunting by male road workers on a daily basis since the Supreme Court ruling. Today she is building a house on a plot of land near Salinas and has applied for the position of assistant road district superintendent in nearby Monterey County.[62]

"I'm shocked and disappointed," said Johnson upon learning of the Court's ruling. "A ruling like this will cause prejudice in people who have never been prejudiced before."[63] Today Johnson lives quietly in retirement, playing golf

---

[58]Joe Davidson and Linda M. Watkins, "Quotas in Hiring Are Anathema to President Despite Minority Gains," *Wall Street Journal,* October 24, 1985.

[59]"Majority Opposes Supreme Court Ruling in Affirmative Action Case," *Gallup Report,* no. 260, May 1987, pp. 18–19.

[60]Richard Stengel, "Balancing Act," *Time,* April 6, 1987, p. 18.

[61]Aric Press, "A Woman's Day in Court," *Newsweek,* April 6, 1987, p. 58.

[62]Faludi, op. cit., p. 92.

[63]Stengel, loc. cit.

EDITORIAL OPINION ABOUT *JOHNSON*

What follows are the briefest of excerpts from newspaper editorials written about the *Johnson* decision in the week following its release. First is a sampling of favorable editorials.

- The Supreme Court majority, like the majority of Americans, faces in the right direction.

  The Baltimore Sun

- Affirmative action . . . is a rocky road to a good goal that must be maneuvered as carefully as a minefield. The Supreme Court is doing just that.

  The Honolulu Advertiser

- It's the proper course to be taking.

  The Sacramento Bee

- But over the years enough women have been excluded from jobs because of another, unspoken formula—"No women need apply"—that affirmative action is called for.

  The Christian Science Monitor

- Once again the court is making the law serve justice.

  Los Angeles Times

- No one has ever claimed the process is without pain, but affirmative action is also healing wounds that have torn this country for far too long.

  St. Petersburg Times

- White males can now be sure that they will have to compete more fully for employment and advancement.

  The Plain Dealer

Not all press opinion was positive. There were some disparaging words.

- . . . the Supreme Court delivered a bruising blow to the U.S. Constitution's paramount contribution to Western values—the concept of inviolable individual rights.

  The San Diego Union

- This is possibly the worst civil-rights decision since the court upheld the constitutionality of Jim Crow laws in *Plessy* v. *Ferguson* in 1896.

  The Arizona Republic

- The U.S. Supreme Court's 6-3 decision in a so-called sex discrimination case last week is abominable and atrocious.

  The Union Leader

- The court not only believes in reverse discrimination, it believes in reversing discrimination that never was.

  The Indianapolis Star

- On March 25, 1987, the U.S. Supreme Court struck the final blow on the near-dead body of the Civil Rights Act of 1964, hacking to death the provision that forbids hiring and promoting workers by race and sex.

  The Atlanta Constitution

- [T]he U.S. Supreme Court Wednesday expanded its determination to prove that two wrongs can make a right.

  The Hutchinson News

- More women and minority workers will be unfairly burdened by the "affirmative action" stigma at a time when many are making it on their own.

  Wall Street Journal

and cribbage with his wife, Betty. He believes that affirmative action programs allow less qualified women to victimize innocent men. Several months after the decision he sent an "Open Letter to the White Males of America" to newspapers. In it he advises:

You are now the only unprotected group in this country. . . . You can work and strive all your lives to provide for your family and their futures, but if one of the . . . "Protected Groups" is interested in this same promotion, even though they may not be as qualified, you will not stand a ghost of a chance, for the Supreme Court of the

United States of America has just ruled that the White Male is to be the SCAPE-GOAT for all the past discrimination in our history. . . . Well, fellow men, I believe it is time for us to object to OUR suppression.[64]

SOME QUESTIONS RAISED BY THE CASE

The Supreme Court, at a rarefied level, interpreted a federal statute, and it cost Paul Johnson a promotion and rendered him "empty." Was this a fair outcome? Do you believe that the case and the disturbance in the lives of Johnson and Joyce could have been avoided by a fairer selection procedure? If so, what would it be? To whom would you have given the promotion? What would have been the consequences in American society if the Court had ruled in favor of Johnson, and what legal reasoning could the Court have used to do so? Do you agree with the Court's decision in this case? Has the Court made a mistake in its interpretation of the wording of Title VII?

HONESTY TESTING

You apply for a job as a bank teller. After initial screening by the bank's personnel department you and other applicants are asked to sit at a conference table and complete a test booklet containing 100 multiple-choice questions such as these:

- How often do you blush?
- What percentage of employees take more than $1 a week from their employers?
- How frequently in recent years have you simply thought about stealing money without actually doing it?
- Do you do things you that you believe are bad?
- Have you ever cheated in school?
- How much in cash and merchandise did you steal from your last employer?
- Do you buy books or magazines that feature stories of successful criminal acts?

Welcome to the world of paper-and-pencil honesty tests. If your answers match the profile of an honest person, you will pass. If not, you will be labeled a potential miscreant. You won't get the job. And since few companies reveal honesty test scores to job applicants, you won't know why you were screened out.

THE PROBLEM OF EMPLOYEE THEFT

Each day an army of thieves relentlessly attacks the productive assets of U.S. companies. Employee theft, defined broadly, is any dishonest use of resources that lowers efficiency. It includes not only theft of cash, merchandise, office supplies, and workplace equipment but also more subtle larcenies such as theft of productive time, purposely inferior work or work diminished by alcohol and illegal drug use, abuse of sick leave or benefits, expense account exaggeration, vandalism, and industrial espionage. Violent behaviors such as fighting and arson also drain resources.

The cost of employee theft is hard to measure, but it is a huge problem. Recent estimates of the total cost of workplace theft in America are as high as $40 billion a year.[1] In the retailing industry alone employee theft losses may be $10 billion a year, and a recent survey of just 115 retailers revealed losses of $1.5 billion.[2] The Drug Enforcement Administration estimates that employees in drugstores and pharmaceutical companies annually steal 500,000 to 1,000,000 dosage units of controlled drugs.[3] And employee theft is implicated in 30 percent of business failures nationwide.[4]

Theft is not confined to a small percentage of employees. A survey of 9,175 employees in forty-seven retail department stores, general hospitals, and electronics manufacturing firms found that every year roughly one-third stole property. Over two-thirds of the workers were involved in production deviance (that is, time theft, sick leave abuse, slow or sloppy work, and work under the influence of alcohol or drugs).[5] Much of this theft was infrequent or trivial, and only a small percentage of workers admitted major theft. In the retail sector, for example, only 2 percent of employees admitted taking store merchandise more often than once every three months.

Serious thieves fit an objective profile. They are younger, usually under thirty years old, with most in the sixteen-to-twenty-five bracket. They are overwhelmingly male, and the majority are unmarried. They like to work alone when they steal. Most are full-time employees. They tend to express greater dissatisfaction with their work. And most steal merchandise. A study of 453 employees caught stealing showed that 60 percent stole merchandise and only 22 percent stole cash.[6]

Causes of Employee Theft

Why do employees steal? While there are many reasons for theft, three are of greatest importance. They are (1) the need to satisfy pathological emotional

---

[1]U.S. House of Representatives, *Hearings before the Committee on Education and Labor,* "Polygraph Testing in the Private Workforce," March 5–April 30, 1987, p. 205. Testimony of Ty Kelly, National Association of Chain Drug Stores.

[2]"Lie Detector Ban Impacts Retail Hiring," *Chain Store Age Executive,* October 1988, p. 198.

[3]U.S. House of Representatives, loc. cit.

[4]Donald W. Caudill, "How to Recognize and Deter Employee Theft," *Personnel Administrator,* July 1988, p. 86.

[5]John P. Clark and Richard C. Hollinger. *Theft by Employees in Work Organizations: Executive Summary.* Washington, D.C.: Department of Justice, 1983, pp. 12–16.

[6]"Stealing at Work," *Wall Street Journal,* November 11, 1986.

drives, (2) the presence of permissive work cultures, and (3) a state of financial exigency.

First, some theft is the result of personality disorganization in employees with obsessive, aggressive drives. These drives are dysfunctional because the harmful consequences of stealing usually far outweigh material gains. Why, then, do such persons steal? According to Karl Menninger, a psychiatrist, stealing has hidden significance for the pathological personality. In his words:

> Stealing is the taking of something belonging to another, but it is almost never done for the purpose of acquiring the thing taken. More frequently, perhaps, stealing is a symbolic method of attempting to obtain the love which one feels—often correctly— that he has been deprived of. [S]tealing is essentially a destructive act; taking unto ourselves and for our own use that which was once a belonging or a part of some other person is destructive in a double sense: it adds to one's self the object taken, and at the same time symbolically robs, strips, mutilates, or destroys a part of another person.[7]

Second, an underground work culture may permit employee theft. Sometimes, social norms take root that encourage minor forms of larceny as an informal reward system. One study of dockworkers, for example, found work group norms permitting theft of consumer goods and foodstuffs as the workers unloaded cargo holds. Their pilferage was seen as a "morally justified addition to wages" because they felt exploited in their jobs.[8] The work gangs defined the limits of acceptable theft and permitted stealing an amount of cargo roughly equal to the wages for each job. This was known in their lexicon as "working the value of the boat." Social norms further defined which property could be stolen. It was all right to steal from insured cargo, but the taking of personal property from passengers and crew was regarded as despicable. The work gangs exercised powerful social control. When, for example, one dockworker became too greedy, his car was broken into, and the stolen merchandise disappeared. It was widely known that his workmates did it. This study also noted that cargo theft was an important route to peer acceptance among these dockworkers.

A similar study found work group norms permitting theft among blue-collar workers in a midwestern television plant. These workers distinguished between company property, personal property, and property of uncertain ownership. The last category included low-cost objects the company could "afford" to lose, broken parts, tools used by an individual for many years, and special items such as a fan built from scrap parts on which a worker had painted his name. Social norms permitted stealing property of uncertain ownership. One worker said: "I don't like the word taken. It's not like I was steal-

---

[7]Karl Menninger. *The Vital Balance*. New York: Penguin Books, 1963, p. 235.

[8]Gerald Mars, "Dock Pilferage: A Case Study in Occupational Theft," in Paul Rock and Mary McIntosh, eds. *Deviance and Social Control*. London: Tavistock Institute, 1974, p. 224.

ing these screws. They're not worth anything."[9] There were two general guidelines for poaching: (1) property should only be taken for personal use, and (2) only small amounts of property should be taken to avoid a company crackdown on the ongoing system of poaching.

Third, employees steal because they need money. They may have gambling debts, monthly payments, or drug habits. When clerks in a southwestern convenience store chain were asked "Why do some employees steal from the convenience stores?" the number one reason was "financial need."[10] (The other reasons were, in order: low wages, no fear of apprehension, revenge against employer or company, for fun or thrill seeking, peer pressure, habit, to buy alcohol or drugs, dishonesty, and greed.)

Controlling Theft by Employees

Companies have several means of combating internal theft. They may be used separately or, more commonly, in combination.

First, some companies rely on strong security measures to control losses. They monitor workers with closed-circuit television cameras, post security guards, have unannounced inspections of lunch boxes and briefcases on randomly chosen days, hire undercover detectives, and invest in physical barriers such as locks, alarms, and fences. One disadvantage of draconian security measures is that they breed employee resentment. If carried too far, they send the message that workers are not trusted. In addition, determined employee thieves can generally foil security measures.

A second antitheft approach is to institute policies and controls. Some companies have written policies that define forms of theft and make penalties clear. A policy of prosecuting employees caught stealing is a strong deterrent. Training programs for first-level supervisors make them aware of ways to stop theft. A variety of simple controls such as inventories and independent audits make theft more visible. Requiring that invoices, shipping tickets, and purchase orders be cosigned reduces the opportunity to divert supplies to personal use. Keeping carbon copies of deposit records will deter embezzlers. Of course, thieves also circumvent policies. A shoe manufacturer, for example, fought theft with a shipping procedure that included documenting the number of shoe boxes in each shipment. Customers soon complained, however, that although they were receiving the proper number of shoe boxes in each parcel, some of the boxes contained no shoes!

A third approach to reducing theft loss is to weed out potential thieves in

---

[9]Donald M. N. Horning, "Blue Collar Theft: Conceptions of Property, Attitudes toward Pilfering, and Work Group Norms in a Modern Industrial Plant," in Erwin O. Smigel and H. Laurence Ross, eds. *Crimes against Bureaucracy.* New York: Van Nostrand Reinhold, 1970, p. 56.

[10]William Terris and John Jones, "Psychological Factors Related to Employees' Theft in the Convenience Store Industry," *Psychological Reports,* December 1982, p. 1225.

the hiring process. There are a number of preemployment screening methods used to detect applicants with records of dishonesty, but most have significant drawbacks. Application forms require the listing of past employers, who can be contacted for reference checks. But it is common for dishonest employees who are fired to strike a bargain to give back stolen property in return for the promise of a good (or at least neutral) reference in the future. Companies today are also reluctant to give negative references because of the fear of lawsuits. And, of course, most employee theft is undetected and cannot be discovered by reference checks. Background investigations by detectives can uncover past criminal records and signs of dishonesty, but they are prohibitively expensive for screening even a small number of applicants.

Trained interviewers in the personnel department may ask probing questions about dishonesty, using a technique called structured integrity interviewing in which answers to specific, probing questions are scored on a rating scale. Applicants are asked, for example, to describe past job situations in which they were particularly honest or dishonest. Other questions reveal how the applicant would respond to hypothetical situations wherein, for example, they discover a coworker stealing or face the opportunity to steal without much chance of being caught.[11] This is only an experimental approach now. Experience suggests that interviewers have trouble evaluating the veracity of job candidates. Also, pointed questions such as "Which drugs have you tried?" or "How much money did you steal from your previous employer?" are presumptuous in a conversation and create a strained atmosphere.

Because of the shortcomings of these screening methods many companies over the years came to rely heavily on preemployment polygraph tests to force admissions of past criminal convictions, illegal drug use, and prior undetected theft. In a polygraph, or "lie detector," test job applicants are questioned by a trained examiner while a machine records changes in pulse, respiration, and electrical conductivity of the skin that may result from emotional arousal. Tests can take up to three hours. Polygraph tests, however, have been attacked by labor unions and employee groups. The tests themselves are discomfiting; the cords and wires invade personal space, and questions about drug use, theft, and criminal activity intrude into solitary thoughts and emotions. Also, the tests are often inaccurate.[12] Congress passed the Employee Polygraph Protection Act in 1988, banning most preemployment polygraph screening and threatening a civil penalty of up to $10,000 per violation.[13] Exemptions are made in the law for security firms, drug manufacturers, nuclear

---

[11]John W. Jones and William Terris. *Employee Selection: Alternatives to Pre-Employment Polygraph.* Park Ridge, Ill.: London House Press, 1989, p. 6.

[12]For an overview of research on polygraph accuracy, see Julius Denenberg, "The Polygraph: Modern Wizardry Unmasked," *Defense Counsel Journal,* July 1988; Michael Tiner and Daniel J. O'Grady, "Lie Detectors in Employment," *Harvard Civil Rights–Civil Liberties Law Review,* winter 1988; and Office of Technology Assessment. *Scientific Validity of Polygraph Testing.* Washington, D.C.: Government Printing Office, 1983.

[13]Pub. L. 100-347, June 27, 1988; 29 U.S.C. 2001–2009.

facilities, and some employees of defense contractors. But after 1988, preemployment polygraph screening ended in most industries which relied upon it.

With this avenue closed many firms have turned to paper-and-pencil honesty tests. Shortly after the law was passed Michael Cartigiano, the corporate security director at Crazy Eddie's, a chain of consumer electronics stores, said: "I have nothing else. That's what's going to take the place of the poly. There's no doubt about it."[14] Other companies, such as Adolph Coors Co., also switched from polygraph tests to paper-and-pencil tests, and the market for honesty tests soared. At $7 to $15, depending on the quantity purchased, they are far less expensive than polygraph tests, which cost between $50 and $125. They remain legal in all states.[15]

No reliable statistics about honesty testing are available. A review of the tests in 1985 identified two dozen tests.[16] Recent claims of leading honesty test marketers imply widespread industry use. The Stanton Corporation claims to sell over 1,000,000 tests a year; London House claims 3,500 corporate clients; and Reid Psychological Systems claims over 2,000 corporate clients. In 1988 the Bureau of National Affairs reported that 7 percent of companies surveyed tested for honesty.[17]

HOW HONESTY TESTS WORK

Paper-and-pencil honesty tests are psychological tests. They are based on the theory that thieves think differently than honest employees, that the differences can be measured, and that theft-prone attitudes are predictive of future stealing. The typical test asks 60 to 100 multiple-choice questions, and the responses reveal the test taker's attitudes related to theft on a number of dimensions. Here are some of the major areas of inquiry on honesty tests.

Beliefs about the extent of honesty are of interest because those who steal tend to project their attitudes and see more dishonesty in the world than those who do not steal. Typical questions designed to elicit perceptions of the amount of honesty in society are "What percentage of people take more than $1.00 per week from their employer?" "How many taxpayers cheat on their

---

[14]"Lie Detector Ban Impacts Retail Hiring," op. cit., p. 200.

[15]A legal challenge to honesty testing was mounted in Minnesota in 1981, relying on a state law which banned "any test purporting to test honesty." The Supreme Court of Minnesota, however, allowed employers to continue using paper-and-pencil honesty tests by ruling that the state law prohibited only "tests and procedures which purport to measure physiological changes in the subject." *Minnesota* v. *Century Camera, Inc.,* 309 N.W.2d 735. Courts generally have been more permissive with invasive tests where public safety is at stake. See Anne E. Libbin, Susan R. Mendelsohn, and Dennis P. Duffy, "The Right to Privacy in the Workplace, Part 5: Employee Medical and Honesty Testing," *Personnel,* November 1988, pp. 38–48. And employers may wish to use honesty tests to avoid negligent-hiring lawsuits, which are currently on the rise. See Leigh Gaines, "Hiring Right, Hiring Honest," *Security,* May 1988, pp. 42–45.

[16]Paul R. Sackett and Michael M. Harris, "Honesty Testing for Personnel Selection: A Review and Critique," in H. John Bernardin and David A. Bownas. *Personality Assessment in Organizations,* New York: Praeger, 1985, p. 240.

[17]"Pre-Employment Tests: Most Firms Now Require Them," *Wall Street Journal,* July 5, 1988.

returns?'' and ''How many judges can be bribed?'' Responses that indicate high numbers of dishonest employees, taxpayers, and judges fit the attitudinal profile of a thief.

Attitudes about punishment for theft are important because the thief is more tolerant than the honest person. Examples of questions here are ''Should a person be fired if caught stealing $5.00?'' and ''Have you ever been so entertained by the cleverness of a crook that you hoped he would get away with it?''

Thieves often think obsessively about stealing, and some questions are designed to find this out. For example: ''Have you ever thought about taking company merchandise without actually taking any?'' or ''In your most recent job were you able to figure out ways a dishonest person could take merchandise without paying for it?'' or ''Did you ever think about committing a burglary?'' ''Yes'' answers to these and similar questions indicate a mind ruminating about theft and would be graded unfavorably.

Knowledge of employee theft is more likely among dishonest employees. Typical questions in this category are ''Do you know for certain that some of your friends steal from their employer?'' and ''Have you ever been told, by a fellow employee, how to cheat the company?'' ''Yes'' answers here are indicative of familiarity with theft in past jobs.

Thieves tend to rationalize about theft, and responses to statements such as the following shed light on this dimension of the test taker's attitudes toward theft. ''An employer who pays people poorly has it coming to him when employees steal.'' ''Stealing from an employer is different from stealing from friends.'' ''Dishonesty is OK as long as you are truthful.'' Agreement with these statements puts one under suspicion of rationalizing theft.

Most tests also require an assessment of personal honesty with questions such as these: ''Compared to other people, how honest are you?'' ''Do you do things you consider to be bad?'' ''Have you ever been disgusted with yourself because you did something dishonest?'' As a follow-up, some tests ask for admissions of past theft. ''Did you write a check knowing there was not enough money in the bank more than three times?'' ''The total amount of money (that did not belong to me) that I have taken from jobs would be about: (a) can't remember, (b) none, (c) $1, (d) $25, (e) $50, (f) $100, (g) $300, (h) $600, (i) $1,000, (j) $5,000 or more.''

In addition to questions measuring attitudes toward honesty, other scales may be embedded in the tests. On the theory that violence-prone employees are greater risks for dishonest behavior, some tests measure tendencies to be combative with questions such as these. ''How often have you been provoked into a fist fight?'' ''How often have you thought of hitting a person who really deserved it?'' ''How many people regularly get into fist fights and brawls?'' Other scales ferret out alcohol and drug abuse with questions such as ''How many people use marijuana daily?'' and ''How often do you drink alcoholic beverages?''

To catch workers who try to fake honest attitudes, the tests include questions that tempt people to make socially desirable answers that are transparently false. Questions on these so-called "lie scales" include, for example, "Have you ever told a lie?" Since everyone has lied sometime, any test taker answering "No" would be assumed to be faking goodness. Similarly: "Have you occasionally had ideas and thoughts that you would not like other people to know about?" "Do you sometimes enjoy listening to gossip?" "Do you ever worry about what other people think of you?" "Did you ever cheat in school?" The presumption is that a "No" answer to any of these questions is phony. A series of deceptive answers to similar questions scattered throughout the test would unmask fakers.

WHAT, EXACTLY, IS HONESTY?

Honesty tests which purport to measure attitudes toward stealing raise the question of what causes honest or dishonest behavior. Psychology has long debated the question of whether behavior is determined by intrapsychic factors or by external factors in the situations people find themselves in. If honesty is an inner trait, honest people will not steal even in situations where the opportunity is present, and dishonest people will try to steal in any situation. If, on the other hand, honesty is determined by workplace situations, then everyone will steal when the opportunity is present. Clearly these are extreme positions, and research in the field of psychology shows that ethical behavior is motivated by a mixture of internal disposition and situational incentives.[18]

Clever experiments show that certain situations bring out larcenous behavior. Lost-letter studies are an example. In one study researchers dropped addressed envelopes with postage on the street, and all were picked up by passersby within minutes. Some contained only a letter with a trivial message on a single sheet of paper, and 85 percent of these were mailed. Others contained a lead disk exactly the size and thickness of a 50-cent piece. Only 54 percent of these were mailed. The researchers concluded that "a sharp decline in the reliability of the public sets in under the effects of suggestion of financial gain."[19] In another study women pretended to leave coins in telephone booths in crowded public areas. When the women dressed attractively, the coins were returned 87 percent of the time, but when they dressed unattractively, they got the coins back only 64 percent of the time.[20] And in a third study customers in convenience stores bought 30-cent local newspapers with a $1 bill and, feigning absentmindedness, walked away from the cash register at a slow pace. In this situation 16 percent of the store cashiers made no effort to return the proper change. The relatively high percentage of honest responses was thought to be due to the face-to-face contact that had been made in buying the newspaper and to the close physical proximity of the victim.[21] Both of these conditions are believed to reduce theft, which is easier when the victim is anonymous or far away or is a large corporation.

Such studies make it clear that even though the attitudes toward theft revealed in honesty tests may predispose persons to crime, they are only part of the cause. Other incentives may exist in the workplace situation that encourage or discourage crime.

[18]See, for example, Hugh Hartenshorne and Mark A. May. *Studies in Deceit: Book One, General Methods and Results.* New York: Macmillan, 1928, and Kenneth S. Bowers, "Situationalism in Psychology: An Analysis and a Critique," *Psychological Review,* September 1973.

[19]Curtis B. Merrit and Richard G. Fowler, "The Pecuniary Honesty of the Public at Large," *Journal of Abnormal and Social Psychology,* vol. 43, 1948, p. 93.

[20]R. Sroufe, A. Chaikin, R. Cook, and V. Freeman, "The Effects of Physical Attractiveness on Honesty: A Socially Desirable Response," *Personality and Social Psychology Bulletin,* vol. 3, 1977.

[21]Thomas Gabor, Jody Strean, Gurnam Singh, and David Varis, "Public Deviance: An Experimental Study," *Canadian Journal of Criminology,* January 1986, p. 26.

WHAT THE TESTS REVEAL

When job applicants return tests, their answers can be scored in a variety of ways. Test booklets may be sent to the test vendor for scoring, or answers may be called in on a toll-free line (in some cases this can be done 24 hours a day and answers entered by using the keyboard of a Touch-tone telephone). Large test users may use IBM-compatible software which evaluates test answers and stores a running data base.

In scoring, the answers of job candidates are compared with the answers of a larger population of test takers which has been used to establish norms. To give one example, let's suppose that a woman named Sarah applying for a bank teller position has taken the *Bank Personnel Selection Inventory—Version 3,* marketed by London House Inc. This test is designed to screen out banking job applicants who are dishonest, use illegal drugs, or are violence-prone. Sarah has completed the 122 multiple-choice questions, and her answers are scored on three separate scales—honesty, drug avoidance, and nonviolence. The results are recorded in a "Confidential Report" which has a percentage score on each scale. If Sarah scored 75 percent on the honesty scale, for instance, it would mean that three-fourths of other applicants for banking jobs gave less honest answers. She scored in the top 25 percent.

In addition, the "Confidential Report" contains "significant behavioral indicators," which are statements of attitudes revealed by test answers. A positive indicator derived from Sarah's responses might read: "Believes the average person can be completely honest on the job." A negative indicator would be: "Is more likely than average to call in sick when not really ill." Later, an interviewer could probe these areas when talking to Sarah.

Did Sarah pass the test? The bank's personnel department would use it as part of a screening process and weigh the results along with other tests, qualifications, work experience, and interview impressions. Hiring needs would be another important factor. If vacancies existed and there were few applicants, the bank might accept lower scores on the test. But Sarah probably passed, since most employers set the passing score between 25 and 75 percent.[22]

VALIDITY OF HONESTY TESTS

In order to be valid, paper-and-pencil honesty tests should be able to predict future honesty on the job. Can they? In 1985 two researchers, Paul R. Sackett and Michael M. Harris, reviewed forty-one studies designed to assess the validity of honesty tests. They found that five different methods had been used: (l) comparing honesty test results with polygraph results, (2) comparing honesty test results with admissions of theft made on separate questionnaires, (3) comparing theft rates in stores before and after the introduction of honesty tests in hiring, (4) comparing the scores of prisoners with those of college stu-

[22]Sackett and Harris, op. cit., p. 271.

dents, and (5) comparing honesty test scores at the time of hiring with subsequent on-the-job behavior.

Sackett and Harris gave these studies mixed reviews. They rejected all polygraph comparisons, noting that "a criterion that is seriously questioned in the scientific community cannot serve as the basis for meaningful evaluation of ... honesty tests."[23] They criticized studies relying on admissions of past behavior because people tend to underconfess, even when admissions are anonymous. And studies comparing prisoners with college students were suspect because they were based on the assumption that convicts would try to "fake good" to enhance their chances of parole. In fact, some may have reasoned that faking would jeopardize parole. Other studies were criticized for technical reasons, such as small numbers tested or uncontrolled variables which might have influenced results. While recognizing that much of the research was blemished, Sackett and Harris concluded on a positive note. "What stands out," they wrote, "is the consistency of positive findings across tests and across validity strategies."[24] Indeed, virtually all the studies showed positive correlations between low honesty test scores and a larcenous life.

Recent studies continue to suggest that honesty tests are able to measure attitudes predictive of theft. One five-year study of employees in a chain of seventy-seven home improvement stores, for example, showed that testing reduced both inventory loss and employee firings related to theft, drug abuse, and fighting.[25] For the first three years of this study no honesty tests were used by the company to screen job applicants. Then, over the following two years, a version of the London House Inc. *Personnel Selection Inventory* was given to 1,600 job applicants. Of these, 900 passed and were hired. Subsequently, the number of employees terminated for theft was halved, terminations for drug abuse fell by more than 80 percent, and annual inventory shrinkage losses fell from 3.75 percent to 2.45 percent.

Another study, that of a chain of 145 convenience stores in Canada, showed that there was a "strong predictive relationship" between the score of an applicant for the position of store manager on Reid Psychological System's *Reid Report* and subsequent levels of inventory loss due to theft in the store.[26] The convenience store industry has notoriously difficult employee theft problems because stores are open long hours and cashiers are often alone on the premises. In this study the managers of stores that experienced large inventory

---

[23]Ibid., p. 268. For examples of polygraph comparison studies see Philip Ash, "Predicting Dishonesty with the Reid Report," *Polygraph,* June 1985, and Philip Ash, "Screening Employment Applicants for Attitudes toward Theft," *Journal of Applied Psychology,* April 1971.

[24]Ibid. But see Robert W. Moore, "Unmasking Thieves: From Polygraph to paper," *Journal of Managerial Psychology,* vol. 3, no. 1, 1988, pp. 17–21, for a classroom survey that fails to support the construct validity of honesty tests.

[25]Thomas S. Brown, John W. Jones, William Terris, and Brian D. Steffy, "The Impact of Pre-Employment Integrity Testing on Employee Turnover and Inventory Shrinkage Losses," *Journal of Business and Psychology,* winter 1987.

[26]John Kemp. *Relationship of the REID REPORT to Inventory and Turnover among Convenience Store Managers.* RPS Research Memorandum Number 12. Chicago: Reid Psychological Systems, February 1988, p. 1.

shrinkage losses had lower passing scores on the *Reid Report* than managers of stores with low losses.

These and other studies show that honesty tests are good predictors of future theft on the job for aggregates of workers. But how valid are they for individuals? James Walls, executive vice president of the Stanton Corporation, claims that the *Stanton Survey* is 88 percent reliable.[27] Ryan A. Kuhn, president of Reid Psychological Systems, asserts that the *Reid Report* has a "correct classification rate of 85 percent or more."[28] There are two possible errors in classifying job applicants. A "false positive" is a score predicting that an honest person will be a thief if hired. A "false negative" is a prediction that a dishonest test taker will be an honest employee. How many people are erroneously put into these categories?

No published studies give reliable information about "false positives," or honest people falsely predicted to be thieves. In practice these applicants are not hired because they show a dishonest attitude profile on their test scores. It is a certainty that some applicants who would never steal fail honesty tests. In some validation experiments employees are hired without regard to their test scores. But most employee thieves are never caught. This means that a worker who failed an honesty test, was hired, and was never caught stealing might nonetheless be a thief. It could never be proved that such a worker was a "false positive." Thus, accurately counting "false positives" is a futile task.

An estimate of the number of "false negatives," or thieves who pass honesty tests, may be made from studies of employees who have taken the tests and later are caught stealing. In one such study 3,700 grocery store chain employees took a preemployment honesty test and were hired irrespective of their scores.[29] Subsequently, 91 were fired for stealing. Looking back at the test results, it was discovered that 82 percent of these thieves had failed the test. But 18 percent of them were "false negatives"; they had passed the test and were not labeled as future crooks (therefore, they were mislabeled). If a similar percentage of honest people are labeled dishonest, it means that roughly 18 out of every 100 job applicants are wrongly branded as potential thieves. Robin Inwald, a psychologist, explains why even this figure is probably low:

> Since most agencies do not want to take chances with individuals who are predicted to fail on a computer printout (no matter how invalid such a prediction may be), many good applicants may be incorrectly screened out. For example, if a test screen sought all marginal applicants (perhaps 50 percent of a candidate group and 5% of those would actually turn out to be dishonest or to perform poorly on the job), no one will be suspicious. As long as all 50% are screened out, the 45% who were screened out incorrectly will never be able to prove themselves.[30]

[27]Christine Gorman, "Honestly, Can We Trust You?" *Time,* January 23, 1989, p. 44.
[28]"Putting Honesty to the Test," *Wall Street Journal,* Letters to the Editor, January 19, 1989.
[29]Thomas S. Brown and Dennis S. Joy. *The Predictive Validity of the Personnel Selection Inventory in the Grocery Store Industry.* Research Abstract No. 48. Park Ridge, Ill.: London House Press, 1985, p. 1.
[30]"How to Evaluate Psychological/Honesty Tests," *Personnel Journal,* May 1988, p. 44.

Overall, the literature supporting the validity of honesty tests is questionable. Few studies have been published in respected, refereed, and independent journals. And virtually all of these published studies are authored by employees or consultants of the psychological testing companies that market honesty tests. Most studies, including some cited here, are published only by the companies that market the tests. While the studies may be well-designed and well-executed (in fact, many have severe methodological shortcomings), there is a clear conflict of interest in their authorship by those who have a financial stake in the outcome. In addition, there have been no studies in reputable journals to support the claim that violent behavior can be predicted by any paper-and-pencil test on the market today.

EVALUATING HONESTY TESTING

The workplace is often the site of conflict between employers and employees. There is a historic tension between the employer's drive to maximize effi-

---

WHAT HONESTY TESTS REVEAL ABOUT OUR SOCIETY

Honesty test scores and admissions are a window into public morality. Over the years scores on the Stanton test have declined. Early in the 1960s about 11 percent of test takers were rejected as "high risk." Today almost 25 percent are so labeled.[31] Years of experience with the Reid test have revealed that applicants for certain job titles are more likely to show high integrity. About 70 percent of applicants for salesclerk positions get the "recommended" rating compared with 62 percent for warehouse clerks and only 8 percent for buyers.[32]

A random survey of 10,000 applicants for a variety of private-sector jobs who took the Reid test in 1988 showed the following rates of admissions.[33]

- Admits to one or more shouting matches at work in last two years   53.2%
- Admits to one or more fistfights or shoving matches in last two years   24.6%

- Admits to taking goods or merchandise from employer in last five years   16.9%
- Admits to taking money from employer in last five years   4.9%
- Admits that drugs or alcohol affected their job performance or caused missed work   3.6%
- Admits to weekly spending of money for illegal drugs   16.3%

When 10,723 persons applying for work at a national convenience store chain took the Lousig-Nont questionnaire in 1988, some tallies were these:

- 1,142 said they drank too much; 902 confessed thinking about shoplifting
- 777 admitted shoplifting an average of $33 in merchandise
- 39 said they used cocaine
- 290 admitted stealing an average of $233 from previous employers
- 37 admitted selling amphetamines[34]

[31]Ed Bean, "More Firms Use 'Attitude Tests' to Keep Thieves off the Payroll," *Wall Street Journal*, February 27, 1987.
[32]"Athlete's Foot Steps on Theft," *Chain Store Age Executive*, July 1987, p. 106.
[33]David W. Arnold. *Behavioral Correlates with the REID REPORT Inventory*. RPS Research Memorandum Number 21. Chicago: Reid Psychological Systems, January 30, 1989, p. 2.
[34]Mariann Caprino, "Bosses Ask: How Honest Are You?" *Los Angeles Times*, May 8, 1989.

ciency by standardizing work and the worker's need to retain individuality and fulfill basic human needs. Paper-and-pencil honesty tests lead to disputes along these lines. The question is, Do they further the employer's property rights at the expense of workers' rights to privacy and fair treatment?

Honesty Testing and Privacy Rights

In 1890 the future Supreme Court Justice Louis Brandeis and a coauthor suggested a definition of privacy which has the virtue of great brevity. It was, they wrote, "the right to be let alone."[35] Many years later, Alan Westin, a scholar in the field of employee rights, made a useful elaboration on this definition. Privacy, wrote Professor Westin, is "the claim of individuals, groups or institutions to determine for themselves when, how and to what extent information about them is communicated to others."[36] And recently, Professor David W. Ewing, another employee rights expert, defined privacy expectations to include "freedom from having to take tests that are unreasonable."[37]

Does honesty testing cross reasonable boundaries of privacy? Taking an honesty test requires giving specific information about inner attitudes and past behavior to others, who are usually strangers. This information ranges from ho-hum disclosures about procrastination to sensitive revelations about blushing, guilt feelings, and happiness which reside in one's emotional core. The persistent questioning about honesty on these tests would insult most job applicants and embarrass most interviewers if done face-to-face. However, even though questions deal with sensitive subjects, none have ever been found to be in violation of federal or state privacy laws, and no adverse impact on minorities has ever been found.[38]

The would-be employee is forced to take honesty tests because of a huge power imbalance existing between employers and job applicants. Applicants have no choice unless the employer makes the test optional, a course of action that would obviously defeat its purpose. Some evidence suggests that honesty tests are not seen as intrusive by job applicants. In 1988 a group of 1,800 applicants who took the honesty section of the *Reid Report* were asked "How much did you accept or resent answering the questions in this section?" The answers showed that 92 percent found the test acceptable, while only 8 percent resented it to some degree.[39] And the majority of those who expressed

[35]Samuel D. Warren and Louis D. Brandeis, "The Right to Privacy," *Harvard Law Review*, vol. 4, 1890, p. 193.

[36]*Privacy and Freedom*. New York: Atheneum, 1967, p. 39.

[37] "Sunlight in the Salt Mines," in Bette Ann Stead, ed. *Privacy and Rights in the Work Place: Managing the Issues*. Houston: University of Houston, College of Business Administration, 1988, p. 1.

[38]Kurt H. Decker, "Honesty Tests—A New Form of Polygraph?" *Hofstra Labor Law Journal*, fall 1986, p. 145.

[39]David W. Arnold. *Applicants' Reactions to Completing the Reid Report*. RPS Research Memorandum Number 19, Chicago: Reid Psychological Systems, December 1, 1988, p. 2.

resentment had received failing scores. This research, like much other honesty-testing research, was conducted by the company selling the test.

The fact that people will simply admit past theft on a preemployment test has surprised many. Why would a crook admit to being a crook? Why do applicants confess in answer to test booklet questions such as "How much have you stolen from your employer in the past year?" One reason given by those in the honesty-testing industry is that test takers believe in the potency of psychology. They sense the trap for fakers within the test and feel vulnerable. They are convinced that they have been stripped of the power to withhold information. And the power to withhold personal information is the essence of the privacy right.

Honesty Testing and the Rights of Employers

Employers have the right to protect their assets and to control crime in the workplace. In addition, competitive pressures are an incentive to hire the most productive employees. It has been estimated that the cost in lost productivity of mishiring and then terminating an employee ranges from $5,000 for an unskilled worker to $75,000 for a manager.[40] The cost is that much higher if the employee was a thief. If honesty testing weeds out potential misfits, it has utilitarian value.

Suppose, for example, that a department store chain annually hires 500 employees at an average salary of $15,000 each. Each year 10 percent, or 50, of these new employees are terminated for theft, drug abuse, and fighting. An honesty-testing program could be introduced which would, conservatively, screen out half, or 25, of the counterproductive employees. In addition, the tests would screen out some proficient thieves who would steal but never be caught. If even a low figure of $5,000 is used for the productivity loss caused by the termination of each thief, the loss of property, and wasted training expenses, the cost of 50 annual terminations is $250,000. By introducing honesty tests into the hiring process, the company will within a year cut this figure in half to $125,000. Subtracting the $5,000 cost of the testing program results in a net gain of $120,000 annually for the company.

In addition, a number of studies predict that inventory shrinkage loss would begin to fall as fewer undetected, long-term thieves took up residence in the employee population.[41] A department store chain with an inventory of $100,000,000 and an annual shrinkage rate of 1 percent endures a cost of $1,000,000. If this rate could be cut 10 percent by honesty testing, the savings would amount to $100,000 a year. Adding this figure to the $120,000 a year in

---

[40]Brian Dumaine, "The New Art of Hiring Smart," *Fortune*, August 17, 1987, p. 78.

[41]See, for example, William Terris and John Jones, "Psychological Factors Related to Employees' Theft in the Convenience Store Industry," *Psychological Reports*, December 1982, and Thomas S. Brown, John W. Jones, and William Terris. *Reducing Employee Turnover and Shrinkage Losses in the Home Improvement Industry: A Five Year Time Series Analysis.* Park Ridge, Ill.: London House Press, 1985.

productivity savings means that the company would save $220,000 as a result of its $5,000 investment. Savings of this magnitude are attractive in a competitive environment. Managers who are overly dainty about offending a job applicant's "right to be let alone" may pay a high price. What price should be placed on the inviolate personality?

A final consideration from the employer's point of view is that in some industries, such as home service industries, an honest workforce is essential to repeat business. An example is pest control. Here is how a security consultant for Orkin Pest Control argued the necessity of honesty testing in congressional hearings.

Each month Orkin Pest Control sends thousands of technicians into more than one and one half million private residences in 43 states. The almost unlimited access provided our employees could result in direct threats to the health and well being of our customers, their families, and guests by employees with criminal motives. Each time Orkin technicians are granted access to private residences our customers place their trust in our company's judgment as to the character of these employees. An average citizen who would not consider allowing strangers access to their home are willing to do so if that stranger identifies himself or herself as an Orkin employee. . . . We recognize that our responsibility, both morally and legally, is to continue to utilize the best methods available to protect our customers. . . . Orkin spends over $1 million a year to screen each potential employee to determine whether any such applicants

---

THE STORY OF DAVID BURKE

David Burke was employed by USAir as a terminal worker for fifteen years. Probably, he had been stealing a long time before he was finally caught. Three times he was investigated for theft of company funds, but no charges were brought against him. In 1985 he was investigated by the Rochester, New York, police for auto theft and narcotics sales, but no charges were filed. In 1986 he transferred to Los Angeles International Airport and in November 1987 was arrested and subsequently fired when a hidden ceiling camera recorded him stealing $69 from in-flight liquor sales money.

After being fired, Burke returned to the USAir offices several times to plead for leniency with Ray Thompson, the office manager who had fired him. He made no headway. On December 7, Burke boarded USAir's Flight 1771 bound for San Francisco. Another passenger was Ray Thompson. Halfway through the flight, when the British Aerospace commuter jet was 22,000 feet over Paso Robles, Burke emptied six chambers of a Smith and Wesson .44 magnum revolver inside the plane. It crashed in a pasture, killing all forty-three passengers. He had used an employee pass to reach the boarding area through USAir office corridors and avoided metal detectors in the terminal which might have been set off by the gun. Coworkers later remarked that Burke had never showed violent tendencies or any outward anger over being fired. In the wreckage of the plane, investigators found an airsickness bag on which this note was written in Burke's hand.

Hi, Ray. I think it's sort of ironical that we end up like this. I asked for some leniency for my family, remember. Well I got none. And you'll get none.

Would a paper-and-pencil honesty test have screened out David Burke when he was a job applicant back in 1973?

have ever been involved in criminal activity or exhibit character traits that would create a security risk to our customers.[42]

Daily, a horde of exterminators, appliance repairers, movers, interior decorators, and other home service workers invades the nation's homes. Their employers have a legitimate duty to determine their honesty. Hotel chains must protect guests from thieves on the staff. Effective security measures often require a small sacrifice of liberty—for example, in luggage searches made by airlines.

Honesty Testing as Part of a Trend

Honesty tests are only one kind of psychometric test that employers give to employees. Other tests have been designed to assess intelligence, personality, emotional health, work ethics, leadership ability, reaction to stress, safety consciousness, and specific aptitudes such as mechanical ability or abstract reasoning skill. These tests, like honesty tests, raise issues of fair treatment and privacy. The validity of many of them is not yet convincingly proved. And questions may be equally audacious. Some personality tests, for instance, ask questions such as "Do you worry about sexual matters?" and "Do you wish you could relive your life?" to discover the presence of anxiety or obsessive-compulsive tendencies.

Psychologists can devise new tests. Today industrial psychology is capable of measuring attitudes toward labor unions, and a test to predict union-joining tendencies of workers is possible.[43] A number of companies assess job candidates by analyzing their handwriting, a procedure acknowledged to have no proven validity but used nonetheless.

QUESTIONS RAISED BY HONESTY TESTS

Honesty testing raises many questions for ethically sensitive people. Among them are these.

First, on the basis of what you have read, are you willing to grant validity to paper-and-pencil honesty tests? In other words, do you believe that they measure honesty and can predict future thievery?

Second, an ethical guideline derived from canons of justice is that discrimination in the workplace should be based on impartial criteria equally applied. Do honesty tests comply with this guideline?

Third, are honesty tests too intrusive?

Fourth, does the problem of employee theft justify requiring job candidates to pass preemployment honesty tests?

And fifth, if you believe that honesty tests are permissible and necessary in some or all industries, can you explain how they should be used? In particular, how should passing grades be established and what should be done with the information the tests reveal?

---

[42]U.S. House of Representatives, op. cit., p. 94–95. Testimony of Nester Macho.

[43]Terry L. Leap, G. Stephen Taylor, William H. Hendrix, and Zhu Z. Wei, "The NLRB and Pre-Employment Screening," *Labor Law Journal,* April 1988, p. 218.

THE SATURDAY-NIGHT-SPECIAL CASE: *KELLEY* v. *R. G. INDUSTRIES*

Olen J. Kelley was the grocery manager at a Safeway in Silver Spring, Maryland. On March 21, 1981, he arose in the early morning hours and prepared for a busy Saturday at the store.

As he showered and ate breakfast, other Safeway employees were already arriving for their shift. As usual, they parked in the lot and were admitted one by one upon presenting themselves at a locked entrance. At 6:30 a.m., a female employee presented herself for admission, and two men suddenly appeared, grabbed her, and forced their way in. The intruders, one armed with a .38-caliber revolver, went around the store herding employees into the meat cooler.

The men questioned their captives about cars driven by management personnel who had the combination to the store's safe. What did they look like? When Olen Kelley drove into the parking lot and came to the door at 6:40 a.m., the robbers recognized his car and greeted him with demands to open the safe. He did and then lay on the floor as instructed while they wildly scattered the contents of the safe across the office floor and on top of him. Finding only a small amount of money, they demanded that Kelley open a locked compartment within the safe. He tried but could not.

The men were impatient and angry. Kelley felt a fist hit the top of his head. Then, the man with the gun pointed it at Kelley and fired at close range. The bullet entered his shoulder and exited his armpit, reentered his side, and came back out at the base of his ribs. He had four bullet holes, spent five days in the hospital, and missed forty-two days of work.

Following the robbery, Kelley and the other employees identified one of the robbers from police mug shots. The police apprehended the suspect at his home and found the robbery weapon, a .38-caliber revolver, Model RG-38S, designed by a West German firm, Roehm Gesellschaft, and marketed through a U.S. subsidiary called R. G. Industries.

This is the story of Olen Kelley, the revolver used to shoot him, and his extraordinary lawsuit against the company that made it. It is told against the backdrop of a society with a long-standing, violent gun culture.

AMERICA'S GUN CULTURE

People such as Olen Kelley are random victims in a country awash in guns. And the current popularity of guns is rooted in historical circumstances which have nurtured a special gun culture, or a set of traditions and values about the role of guns which is transmitted across generations.

In seventeenth-century Europe gun ownership was a sign of class status; only aristocrats had them. Farmers and members of the working class could not afford to own a gun. Monarchs who raised private armies to enforce their rule feared the insurrectionist potential of peasant hordes armed with muskets. The pilgrims who settled on North American shores were, however, in urgent need of firearms to defend their precarious foothold in the New World. Hunting game was critical to survival in their marginal agrarian society. Firearms were also necessary to defend settlements against marauding Indians, who murdered significant numbers of men, women, and children. Virtually every settler family was armed.

To defend against Indians, local farmers gathered with their guns at the signal of ringing church bells. This custom evolved into the organization of more formal colonial militias, which played an important role in the fighting of the Revolutionary War. When the war broke out, the Continental Army lacked a military tradition, but its soldiers were skilled with firearms as a result of defending their settlements and hunting. The British redcoats soon learned respect for their tactics and marksmanship.

The British also learned to fear the rifle used by the colonists. It was a firearm better adapted to the New World than the muskets of the British. When the original settlers arrived in America, the huge-bore, flintlock muskets used in Europe proved too heavy for wide-ranging hunting and inaccurate at distances over 60 yards. Colonial gunsmiths developed a new rifle that came to be known first as the Pennsylvania rifle and later as the Kentucky rifle. It was lighter and more easily carried over rugged wilderness terrain. It was also longer-barreled and had spiral grooves in the barrel to impart spin to the bullet. These features meant greater accuracy and a higher muzzle velocity so that smaller bullets could deliver as much energy on impact as the heavier shot fired by European muskets. The Pennsylvania rifle was accurate with a man-size target at up to 150 yards. This early adaptation of the gun to changing circumstances was the first of many in American history.

After the defeat of the British it became a tenet of American political theory that armed citizen-farmers, organized into militias, were a bulwark against tyranny. This belief is the underlying rationale for the Second Amendment to the Constitution, which reads: "A well-regulated militia being necessary to the security of a free state, the right of the people to keep and bear arms shall not be infringed." The universal ownership of weapons also symbolized one more break with the class structure of European society. These beliefs were the early foundations of America's gun culture. Their persistence is chiefly responsible for the continued failure of gun control advocates over the years to pass stringent firearms regulations.

Guns on the Western Frontier

As adventurers moved westward across the Mississippi, the gun was once again adapted for new uses. On the plains and deserts of the West the Kentucky rifle had shortcomings. It was a single-shot rifle, and by the time it could be reloaded, a herd of buffalo might stampede or an Apache shoot six arrows. Also, its bore was too small to hold the charges and bullets necessary to penetrate thick buffalo hides at a time when buffalo hunting was becoming a popular national sport. So, a generation of new rifles was created, including the .50-caliber Sharps rifle and repeating-action Winchesters and Remingtons of varying calibers.

The revolver was another landmark innovation in firearms technology that appeared as an adaptation to conditions of the western frontier. Samuel Colt, an inventor, produced the first revolver in the 1830s. It weighed almost 5 pounds, had a complicated mechanism, and was expensive. Few were sold, and Colt's company went bankrupt in 1842. Some of his revolvers, however, found their way into the hands of Texas Rangers, who gave them a prominent reputation. Demand grew, and before long Colt was back in business. He refined his weapon and produced many models, the most famous being the .45-caliber, single-action frontier revolver with a $7\frac{1}{2}$-inch barrel. This gun was light, suited to the needs of horseback riders, and with six shots, it was a tremendous advance in firepower. The Colt .45 became a fixture in American society. The revolver that shot Olen Kelley was a descendant.

In the frontier society of the West the gun was commonplace, a tool for ranchers and cowhands. As in the case of earlier colonists in the East, guns were needed to manage affairs in a hostile environment. They became, for example, a symbol of authority in a scattered population where no formal system of justice had yet taken root. It is not surprising that the cultural values of the old West reinforced proficiency with firearms and added new content to the American gun culture.

Guns in the Settled Areas

As the frontier moved westward, the growing urban populations of the East and Midwest remained armed. The practical necessity of firearm ownership felt by colonists and pioneers faded. In its place appeared widespread gun ownership based on tradition, myth, and symbolic necessity.

This tradition of gun ownership was especially strong in the South. A condition of surrender at Appomattox was that southern troops be allowed to keep their guns. The thousands of armed soldiers returning home were responsible for widespread violence in the years following the war, and although gun crimes soared in every section after its end, the South was most violent. Owning guns had always been a white prerogative, but after the war former slaves acquired guns as a symbol of emancipation. This created a lethal mixture resulting in hundreds of shootings of both whites and freedmen.

In the northern cities firearm ownership was widespread. There were three main forces encouraging it. First, mass production and technological innovation had brought down the price of handguns. In the 1840s Samuel Colt's original six-shooters cost the then tremendous sum of $35. But over fifty years later, in 1896, Sears Roebuck & Co. was advertising six different Colts, including the original .45-caliber army double-action revolver, for less than $14.[1] And Colts were high-quality, high-price handguns. Other handguns of that era sold for less than a dollar at newsstands, tobacco shops, hardware stores, or department stores. On New York's East Side, revolvers were sold on pushcarts.[2] These were the Saturday Night Specials of their day, and they gave the common man cheap access to a handgun. Many were designed to fit into pockets—for example, the $1.75 Vest Pocket Self Cocker offered by Sears Roebuck in its 1902 catalog.[3] Second, the gun culture of the western frontier was purveyed to the eastern city dweller in Wild West Shows, immensely popular dime novels about gunfighters, and sharpshooting competitions sponsored by gun manufacturers. Third, there was a real fear of urban crime. Explosive growth and waves of immigrants brought racial and ethnic tensions, poverty, and insecurity. To defend their homes, urban dwellers bought cheap pistols. And they often carried them in public because few states or cities banned the carrying of concealed weapons before the turn of the century.

Growth of the Small-Arms Manufacturing Industry

Small-arms manufacturing is not a major industry compared with giants such as steel and autos. In peacetime its production has never been more than a fraction of 1 percent of all industrial output. But it has been exceptionally innovative in production technology, and its underlying logic has served to stimulate civilian gun consumption.

---

[1]Fred C. Israel, ed. *1897 Sears Roebuck Catalogue*. New York: Chelsea House Publishers, 1968, p. 572.

[2]Lee Kennett and James LaVerne Anderson. *The Gun in America: The Origins of a National Dilemma*. Westport, Conn.: Greenwood Press, 1975, p. 175.

[3]*The 1902 Edition of the Sears, Roebuck Catalogue*. New York: Bounty Books, 1986, p. 318.

In colonial days rifles and pistols were custom-made by gunsmiths. By the early 1800s, however, small-arms manufacture had moved from a skilled craft to a mass production industry. The companies that made pistols and rifles in the last century usually located in the Connecticut River Valley. There were reasons for this. Foremost was the presence of the river. It provided transportation and water power to run machinery. In addition, the valley was close to large iron deposits, skilled workers lived in the region, and many small companies which could make parts as subcontractors sprang up nearby.[4] Today, because of these historical advantages, the small-arms industry is still concentrated in the Connecticut River Valley.

In the nineteenth century the small-arms industry pioneered critical innovations in industrial technology. It was the first industry to produce interchangeable parts. By the 1880s parts machined in gun factories could be put into a bin and reassembled at random into working guns. This was an amazing feat in an age when no other industry had moved from custom fabrication of parts to genuine mass production. Parts interchangeability came first in the small-arms industry because it pioneered machine tools and the use of precision measurement in the machining process. These innovations spread to other industries and spurred American economic development. The small-arms industry of the late nineteenth century was akin to the aerospace industry in the middle of the twentieth century in spinning off productivity advances useful in other industries.

Small-arms manufacturers, whether of handguns or rifles, have repeatedly faced the same underlying problems over the years. A fundamental characteristic of the industry is high overhead costs. Gun makers must make a heavy investment in machinery and pay high wages for skilled craft workers. Such high fixed costs make large production runs a necessity, but markets have been volatile. During wartime the industry has made heavy investments in production facilities only to see demand drop suddenly in peacetime and the government become a competitor by selling surplus weapons on the civilian market. Gun makers have tried to stabilize demand by seeking out foreign markets and encouraging domestic consumption.

The high costs of producing rifles and handguns, together with the volatility of the military market, have been the undoing of hundreds of gun makers over the years. Surviving companies have found it much in their interest to promote the market for guns among hunters, collectors, target shooters, and homeowners buying defensive weapons. As historians Lee Kennett and James Anderson note: "Early oriented toward volume production, and hence mass consumption, the industry placed a gun within the reach of every American and urged him to buy it—without any discernible qualm of conscience."[5]

---

[4]Felicia Johnson Deyrup. *Arms Makers of the Connecticut River Valley*. Menasha, Wis.: George Banta Publishing Company, 1948, pp. 43–45.

[5]Kennett and Anderson, op. cit., p. 107.

Early Efforts at Gun Control

After the turn of the century Progressive reformers focused on the ills of widespread handgun ownership. Gun advocates retorted that it was a traditional right and a benediction, since an armed citizenry could rise against government tyranny as in the Revolutionary War era. A few states and cities passed laws restricting the carrying of concealed weapons, but in most cases they were not zealously enforced. Criminal excess in the 1920s finally opened the door to federal regulation of firearms. Gangsters such as Al Capone, Clyde Barrow, Ma Barker, and Pretty Boy Floyd made conspicuous use of sawed-off shotguns and Thompson submachine guns, guns that the public saw as having no legitimate use for self-defense or sport. In 1934, Congress passed the National Firearms Act to restrict the sale of these malevolent weapons. It was followed in 1938 by the Federal Firearms Act, which required licensing and record keeping by gun dealers who sold across state lines. This legislation did nothing to curb the public's appetite for firearms and amounted to an exceptionally lax national gun control policy.

Guns in Modern American Society

After World War II, the United States, with its passive regulation of private firearms, was the only existing mass market for surplus weapons. By default, the country was flooded after 1945 with inexpensive rifles, pistols, and ammunition. In the 1950s, surplus NATO weapons were also sold in our domestic market. The most famous of these is the Italian Carcano rifle purchased for $12.95 by Lee Harvey Oswald and used to assassinate President Kennedy.

The strongest market for handguns in the postwar years has been among citizens who fear crime. As urban crime has risen so have gun sales. In the 1960s the violent aspect of easy firearm availability was shown in the assassinations of Martin Luther King, Jr., President Kennedy, and his brother Robert F. Kennedy. These public murders of the prominent created a climate of public opinion in which Congress was able to pass the Gun Control Act of 1968.[6] This legislation tightened federal controls over interstate gun sales, prohibited the importation of cheap handguns and surplus military weapons, and prohibited convicted felons and drug addicts from purchasing firearms. To prevent the wholehearted opposition of gun advocates such as the National Rifle Association, there were numerous compromises in the act, and nothing in it prevented most Americans who wanted a gun from getting one.[7] There has been no major federal gun control legislation since. In 1989 President George Bush responded to public concern about the increased private ownership of semiau-

---

[6]Originally Title IV of the Omnibus Crime Control and Safe Streets Act of 1968, 18 U.S.C. Sec. 921 *et seq.* Reenacted as a separate title before its effective date, Pub. L. 90-618, 82 *Stat.* 1213.

[7]When the Gun Control Act of 1968 was voted on in the House of Representatives, 118 members of Congress voted against it. A roll call analysis shows that virtually all these negative votes were from members from the South and West.

tomatic assault rifles by banning the importation of forty-three models of foreign manufacturers.[8] In 1990 Congress was considering a bill that would require a seven- to eight-day waiting period for gun buyers.[9]

Although the Vietnamese War and a domestic crime wave buoyed the small-arms industry in the 1960s and 1970s, forces in the domestic market in the 1980s depressed demand. Hard times for blue-collar workers and farmers mean fewer purchases by these groups, which are the mainstay of the domestic gun market. The growth of urban areas has shrunk the space available for hunting. Tighter gun control laws in states and cities have meant longer waiting periods for gun buyers and discouraged consumption. Younger consumers do not seem as interested in buying guns as their elders. Additionally, quality guns last fifty years or more, and sales of 55 million handguns and 200 million rifles in the past twenty years have saturated the market.[10] Falling demand has caused large retailers such as J. C. Penney and Target Stores to phase out gun sales.

As in other industries, foreign competition has hurt too. Foreign firms, such as Italy's Beretta, have encroached upon the military market in the 1980s, winning an increasing number of large military and police contracts. These foreign competitors pay lower wages and are more innovative with new polymers in gun construction. Their costs are lower too because they do not pay the skyrocketing product liability insurance premiums of American manufacturers.

As might be expected, falling gun sales are causing hard times for gun makers. Between 1982 and 1987 the pretax profits of revolver manufacturer Smith & Wesson dropped 41 percent.[11] This has been typical of the profit picture of other manufacturers. Between 1981 and 1984 the dollar value of gun sales for all manufacturers dropped 35 percent.[12] Rifle production fell 50 percent between 1975 and 1985 and pistol production 25 percent.[13] In the mid-1980s most firms had to lay off workers, and several have been unable to make ends meet, including U.S. Repeating Arms, which sought Chapter 11 protection in 1986.

In the turbulent environment of the 1980s some companies sought to diversify into new markets. Others invested in computerized production facilities and pursued innovation with plastics in gun construction. Famous names such as Colt, Remington, and Smith & Wesson were absorbed into conglomerates.

---

[8]Paul M. Barrett, "Permanent Ban Set on Semiautomatic Rifle Imports," *Wall Street Journal,* July 10, 1989. Earlier, Colt Firearms suspended the sale of its Model AR-15, a semiautomatic version of the M-16 military rifle. But other domestic manufacturers increased production of comparable rifles to take advantage of continued consumer demand. The NRA vigorously opposed the Bush administration ban.

[9]This was the proposed Brady Handgun Violence Prevention Act of 1990.

[10]Resa W. King, "U.S. Gunmakers: The Casualties Pile Up," *Business Week,* May 19, 1986, p. 74.

[11]Goeff Lewis, "A Raider's New World," *Business Week,* June 15, 1987, p. 49.

[12]King, op. cit.

[13]James Brooke, "Sales Decline Jolts Connecticut Gun Makers," *The New York Times,* July 9, 1985.

These were trying times for gun manufacturers. In addition to economic difficulties, they faced stepped-up attacks by gun control advocates, who focused on the dangers of handguns in society.

IS THE HANDGUN A SOCIAL PROBLEM?

Handguns are dangerous products. Their function is to propel accurately a high-speed lead projectile capable of incapacitating a person by inflicting gruesome injury to tissues.

Because of loose firearm registration procedures throughout the United States, no accurate estimate of the total number of guns owned is possible, but there may be as many as 309 million. In 1989 seventy million Americans owned guns, and 61 percent of gun owners owned a handgun. Handgun ownership has been rising. In 1985, 49 percent of gun owners owned a handgun and in 1972 only 36 percent.[14] Since 1900 there have been more Americans killed by handgun homicides than total military casualties in all wars throughout our history. In 1985 there were 17,545 homicides in the United States; in 10,296 of them the weapon used was a firearm, and 7,548, or 73 percent, of the firearms used were handguns.[15] Handguns, therefore, were responsible for nearly three-quarters of firearm homicides, even though they constitute only about one-quarter of firearms owned in the United States.[16] Handguns are also involved in the majority of the roughly 3,000 fatal home firearm accidents and 10,500 firearm suicides that occur each year.[17] It has been estimated that over $500 million is spent annually in hospital care for handgun wounds.[18]

Pro-gun groups argue that widespread gun ownership is not the underlying cause of this carnage. Rather, it is a general climate of violence in our culture. If guns were not available, people would use substitute weapons such as knives and clubs to kill each other. Banning all guns, or only handguns, would simply give criminals an advantage over honest citizens. In the words of Neal Knox of the National Rifle Association:

> Any form of restrictive law aimed against guns is misguided, misdirected, a misappropriation of public funds, and a futile effort to reduce crime.

---

[14]The 1989 figures are from a *Time*/CNN poll reported in Richard Lacayo, "Under Fire," *Time*, January 29, 1990, p. 21. Older figures are from "Handgun Control: Public Continues to Favor Stringent Curbs on Handguns," *The Gallup Report*, no. 248, May 1986, pp. 18–19.

[15]Federal Bureau of Investigation. *Uniform Crime Reports*. Washington, D.C.: Department of Justice, 1985, p. 10. This compares with only 5 handgun deaths in Canada, 8 in Britain, and 46 in Japan in the same year; see George J. Church, "The Other Arms Race," *Time*, February 6, 1989, p. 20.

[16]Stephen P. Teret and Garen J. Wintemute, "Handgun Injuries: The Epidemiologic Evidence for Assessing Legal Responsibility," *Hamline Law Review*, July 1983, p. 345.

[17]Robert Berkley Harper, "Controlling and Regulating Handguns—A Way to Save Black Lives," *Black Law Journal*, winter 1986, p. 229.

[18]Ibid., p. 230.

Gun laws fail because they do not address the issue. The issue is not possession of firearms, but misuse of firearms. We cannot expect criminals to abide by gun laws, when they have already shown a disregard for law and order by their criminal activity.[19]

Polls show, however, that the public favors stricter gun control. A 1988 Gallup poll showed that 67 percent favored registration of all firearms, 84 percent favored licensing anyone who carries a gun outside the home, and 91 percent favored a national law requiring a seven-day waiting period before a handgun could be purchased.[20] A 1989 *Time*/Yankelovich poll found 67 percent agreeing that "existing laws make it too easy for people to buy guns," 23 percent agreeing that the laws were "about right," and only 5 percent agreeing that they were "too difficult."[21]

Advocates of gun control assert that the large number of handgun fatalities could be reduced by disarming the populace. If guns were not easily available, they could not be used in violent incidents. A source of particular ire, then, is manufacturers who mass-produce cheap handguns—Saturday Night Specials—and market them to scared homeowners and predatory criminals.

What Is a Saturday Night Special?

The Saturday Night Special is an inexpensive handgun often used by criminals that is widely believed to have no legitimate purpose. The term is said to have originated in Detroit to refer to guns that were bought in neighboring Ohio, a state with more permissive laws regulating gun sales, and frequently involved in weekend crimes back in Detroit. Manufacturers of these guns are accused of imposing a cost on society paid by crime victims.

There is disagreement about exactly what kind of gun qualifies as a Saturday Night Special. Generally, the term refers to a low-priced, low-quality, small-caliber handgun with a short barrel that makes it attractive to criminals who value concealment. There have been attempts to be objective in defining which guns are Saturday Night Specials. In 1974, for example, the Bureau of Alcohol, Tobacco and Firearms (BATF) set up three basic criteria for these guns: (1) a retail price under $50, (2) use of low-tensile-strength alloys in construction to minimize production cost, and (3) a barrel length of three inches or less.[22] Several cities and states have laws which define the Saturday Night Special in objective fashion in order to ban its sale. Minnesota, for example, prohibits the sale of handguns with alloys which cannot pass laboratory tests

---

[19]Testimony in "Handgun Control Legislation." *Hearings before the Subcommittee on Criminal Law of the Committee on the Judiciary,* U.S. Senate, May 4, 1982, p. 33.

[20]"Gun Control," *The Gallup Report,* no. 280, January 1989, p. 26.

[21]Laurence I. Barrett, "Have Weapons, Will Shoot," *Time,* February 27, 1989, p. 22.

[22]Bureau of Alcohol, Tobacco and Firearms. *Project Identification: A Study of Handguns Used in Crime.* Washington, D. C.: Department of Treasury, 1974, pp. 6–7.

THE REVOLVER

The revolver is a handgun with a round cylinder in which a number of chambers (frequently, but not always, six) for cartridges are bored. These chambers are mechanically rotated by the firing mechanism and brought into line with the barrel for discharge. The revolver was invented by Samuel Colt in the 1830s. It was said that he had the creative inspiration for it on an ocean journey when he was seventeen years old and stood watching the ship's wheel turn and lock into position one evening.

The cylinder on a revolver may rotate clockwise, as on Colts, or counterclockwise, as on Smith & Wessons. This difference has led to a number of accidental suicides among cheating Russian roulette players who looked to see which chamber was loaded but failed to anticipate the direction of its movement into firing position.

Revolvers fire bullets, or lead missiles sometimes hardened by the addition of tin or antimony. The caliber of a handgun is determined by measuring from side to side in the bore hole of its barrel. Hence, the diameter of the bore hole in the Model RG-38S that shot Olen Kelley was .38 of an inch, and this was the size of the lead bullet the gun fired. The bullet weighed 158 grains. A bullet is propelled out the barrel by gases escaping when the charge in the copper cartridge burns rapidly. A Model RG-38S with a 4-inch barrel imparts a muzzle velocity of 725 feet per second.[23]

The velocity of the bullet when it leaves the barrel is determined mainly by the size of the charge in the cartridge and the length of the barrel. With longer barrels, bullets have a higher velocity because they are propelled longer by the charge gases. Sacrificing barrel length to enhance concealability results in a steep reduction in muzzle velocity. And foot-pounds of energy in the bullet vary with the square of velocity. Revolvers do not fire the big cartridges used in high-powered rifles because they function best when small and light, and there is not enough metal in the cylinder walls to contain hot rifle loads. The charge in a .38-Special cartridge, for example, is only about one-tenth that of some charges used by hunters in their rifles. Hence, the muzzle velocity, useful range, and potential energy of its bullet are less. As it is sometimes euphemistically put, its "stopping power" is less than that of a powerful rifle.

The severity of a wound produced by a handgun is determined by the amount of kinetic energy lost by the bullet in human tissue. A lead bullet of the kind fired by the Model RG-38S is soft and may flatten, thereby increasing its diameter and presenting a larger surface area to slow its passage through the body. A high-powered rifle bullet with a full metal jacket might have much greater velocity but pass through the body, leaving only a narrow wound track, losing little energy, and paradoxically hurting the victim less. A mushrooming lead bullet of the kind used by civilian hunters would cause the most gruesome wounds. International agreements prevent the military from using this type of ammunition. But if handguns were somehow banned, criminals might wind up arming themselves with hunting rifles and using this kind of ammunition. An extremely high velocity, large projectile creates what is called a temporary cavity in which adjacent tissue is hurled away from the wound track, and powerful shock waves capable of breaking bones and pulverizing organs spread out in a 6-inch radius from the path of the bullet.

The revolver is more maneuverable than a rifle or shotgun and is suited for close-in fighting. But it sacrifices accuracy because even a slight wrist movement can move the muzzle through a wide arc, and separation of the sights is short.

[23]Vincent J. M. DiMaio. *Gunshot Wounds.* New York: Elsevier, 1985, p. 98.

of pressure, temperature, and density.[24] But despite such laws there is no widespread general agreement about precise attributes.

Critics argue that there is no legitimate sport or hunting use for Saturday Night Specials. The length of a handgun's barrel is an important determinant of accuracy. Handguns with barrels of 2 or 3 inches are not reliable for target shooting or hunting. Because of this incapacity the primary appeal of these guns is to violent criminals who want to hide them. Handguns do not serve the public well as defensive weapons, since a handgun is six times more likely to be used against an acquaintance than to repel a criminal, and persons who resist criminals armed with handguns are eight times more likely to be killed than those who do not resist.[25]

Defenders of the guns argue that they do have legitimate uses. The most likely crime victims today are the urban poor, especially those exposed to the violent subcultures of city neighborhoods like Harlem and suburban communities like East Los Angeles. If cheap handguns were not available, many poor families would be unable to own a defensive weapon to deter crime. Hikers and hunters also carry inexpensive "trail guns" to plink at tin cans, signal for help in case of emergencies, shoot small game for food, or fend off wild animals.

Handguns are demonstrably useful to honest persons as defensive weapons. In a five-year period handguns were used by someone in defense against another person in 4 percent of U.S. households, or roughly 645,000 times a year. A study of robbery victims between 1979 and 1985 showed that when victims resisted with a gun, only 30 percent of robberies succeeded, and only 17 percent of victims were injured. But when victims remained passive, 88 percent of robberies were successful, and 25 percent of the victims were injured.[26] A survey of prison inmates in 1983 found that a majority of felons would avoid an armed victim, would not burglarize a house when the owners were home because of the fear of being shot, and worried more about meeting an armed victim when committing a crime than about running into the police.[27] These findings imply that widespread gun ownership is an important deterrent to crime.

In addition, criminals are not attracted to Saturday Night Specials. A survey of almost 2,000 violent felons in eleven state prisons showed that the hand-

[24]Paula D. McClain, "Prohibiting the 'Saturday Night Special': A Feasible Policy Option?" in Don B. Kates, Jr., ed. *Firearms and Violence: Issues of Public Policy*. Cambridge, Mass.: Ballinger, 1984, p. 203. See also Philip Cook, "The 'Saturday Night Special': An Assessment of Alternative Definitions from a Policy Perspective," *Journal of Criminal Law and Criminology*, winter 1981.

[25] "Handguns and Products Liability," *Harvard Law Review*, June 1984, p. 1914.

[26]These figures are cited in David P. Kopel, "Rowan Case and the Need to Bear Arms," *Wall Street Journal*, June 24, 1988.

[27]James D. Wright and Peter H. Rossi. *The Armed Criminal in America: A Survey of Incarcerated Felons*. Washington, D.C.: U.S. Department of Justice, 1985, p. 27. See also James D. Wright, Peter H. Rossi, and Kathleen Daly. *Under the Gun*. New York: Aldine, 1983, "Does Private Weaponry Deter Crime?" pp. 183–189.

guns they carried were predominantly large-caliber, high-quality, accurate, and relatively expensive.[28] Criminals had almost no preference for guns with the characteristics of Saturday Night Specials.

In sum, Saturday Night Specials are controversial. And so are the companies that make them. What follows is a closer look at the company that made the .38-Special revolver used in the Safeway robbery.

Roehm Gesellschaft

Roehm Gesellschaft is a family-owned machine tool business headquartered in Sontheim, West Germany, and run by three brothers. The company got into the gun business opportunistically when it began making blank-firing starter pistols shortly after World War II. In the mid-1950s, the brothers were approached by American importers, who suggested that the little blank pistols be configured for live ammunition and sold in the United States. The brothers complied and soon began shipping thousands of small-caliber, inexpensive revolvers to a Miami importer, who resold them to pawnbrokers, hardware stores, and gun shops across the continent.

These handguns were of low quality. An early 1960s model, the Roehm 10, was a .22-caliber revolver with a 2.5-inch barrel; it weighed 12 ounces and retailed for $14.95. In performance tests sponsored by the BATF the gun misfired 371 times in 2,100 trigger pulls and failed a safety test by firing when dropped.[29]

In the 1960s the domestic market for handguns grew rapidly, fed by increasing crime, civil insurrection, and the shootings of prominent political and civil rights figures. Americans sensed the embrace of a violent society and armed themselves in defense. Roehm Gesellschaft's business grew, and it produced new models. The most popular Roehm gun was the RG 14, the gun that would years later be purchased by John Hinckley for $39.95 and used to shoot President Ronald Reagan on March 29, 1981. There was also the Model RG-38S, used to shoot Olen Kelley just nine days prior to Hinckley's attack.

Soon, however, the prospering firearms importer faced a threat. Late in the 1960s public sentiment favored stricter gun control laws, and Congress passed the Gun Control Act of 1968. This law included a provision making it illegal to import cheap handguns with no sporting use. When the BATF established criteria defining guns which did not meet minimum import standards, Roehm Gesellschaft's most popular models did not qualify for importation. But the company exploited a loophole in the law to get around the import ban. Since Congress had failed to prohibit the domestic assembly of handguns from imported parts, Roehm Gesellschaft set up an assembly plant in Miami named R. G. Industries, Inc. The new plant was a subsidiary wholly owned by the three

[28]Ibid., *The Armed Criminal in America: A Survey of Incarcerated Felons*, pp. 31–34.
[29]Joseph Albright and Henry Eason, "Saul Eig Sold Americans the Gun-Toters Model T," in *The Snub-Nosed Killers*. Washington, D.C.: Cox Newspapers, 1981, p. 16.

Roehm brothers. The company machined the parts for various models in West Germany, put them in a box, and then shipped them to the Miami plant, where they were assembled.

Florida challenged the Roehm brothers' gambit by passing a law to prohibit the assembly of handguns from imported parts. But the brothers mounted a legal challenge that culminated when the Florida Supreme Court struck down the statute, calling it unconstitutional because it legislated in an area of foreign commerce preempted by Congress.[30] The company continued to assemble inexpensive revolvers in growing numbers. Over the years, R. G. Industries made about twenty models, all revolvers. These were mostly cheap, solid-frame revolvers, but some, including the Model RG-38S, were of better quality. The fully assembled Model RG-38S was imported from Germany between 1977 and 1986 because it met BATF standards.

Although R. G. Industries began importing some higher-quality handguns, over time it was tagged with the reputation of being a manufacturer of Saturday Night Specials. In 1977, for example, a study of crime guns seized in nine cities found that revolvers assembled by R. G. Industries ranked third in popularity with criminals, behind those made by Smith & Wesson and Colt. R. G. Industries' guns were used in 8.8 percent of crimes.[31] The author of this study, Steven Brill, decided to learn more about R. G. Industries but found his phone calls and inquiries unanswered. So he went to Miami, walked up to the plant alone, and presented himself as a vacationing New Yorker who had recently inherited a sporting goods business from his father-in-law. He said the store had never carried handguns, but he was thinking about selling them. He was given a tour of the plant, and his conversation with the company's head of sales was printed in a subsequent *Harper's* article. Brill was told that the company had sold 190,000 Model RG-14 .22-caliber revolvers the previous year. The salesperson added:

An entry in the *Shooter's Bible* describing the RG .38 "special." (*Source: Courtesy Stoeger Publishing Company.*)

MODEL RG 38S

A versatile 38 Special in two sizes with single and double action. Windage adjustable rear sight and swingout cylinder with spring ejector.

SPECIFICATIONS
Caliber: 38 Special
Capacity: 6 shots
Barrel length: 3″ and 4″
Overall length: 8¹/₄″ and 9¹/₄″
Weight: 32 oz. and 34 oz.
Action: Single and double
Sights: Windage adjustable rear sight
Finish: Blue
Price: $125.55 (plastic grips)
    135.00 (wood grips)

[30]*R. G. Industries, Inc.,* v. *Askew.* 276 So.2d 1 (1973).
[31]Steven Brill. *Firearm Abuse: A Research and Policy Report.* Washington, D.C.: Police Foundation, 1977.

If your store is anywhere near a ghetto area, these ought to sell real well. This is most assuredly a ghetto gun. . . . This sells real well, but, between you and me, it's such a piece of crap I'd be afraid to fire the thing.[32]

Two years later a team of investigative reporters from Cox Newspapers did an analysis of over 14,000 guns used in street crimes in eighteen large cities during a nine-month period in 1979. The team discovered that one of every seven guns was a Roehm revolver, and one of every twelve was the RG-14. This made the RG-14 the leading "crime gun" in America on a chart drawn up to illustrate the fifteen weapons most often seized by police.[33]

OLEN KELLEY SUES R. G. INDUSTRIES

In the eleven years he had worked for Safeway, Olen Kelley had been robbed five times by armed men before he was shot. He was a long-suffering victim of handgun crime. He and his wife filed a lawsuit against Roehm Gesellschaft and R. G. Industries in a federal district court.

This lawsuit was a tort action. A tort is a wrongful act that causes harm. It is a breach of the duty a person or company has to act reasonably toward other people. Olen Kelley believed, in this case, that R. G. Industries had breached a recognizable legal duty to prevent criminal use of its product.

When a tort is committed, those injured are entitled to damages. It would be up to a jury to decide how much money, if any, Kelley was entitled to if Roehm Gesellschaft was found to have acted wrongly in making the gun. Whether or not a company is guilty of a tort is determined by the application of standards found in common law, the body of law which has accumulated over centuries in court cases (as opposed to statutory law, based on legislation). In this case, Kelley and his attorneys relied on the broad area of common law known as products liability.

Specifically, they advanced two legal theories, both found in the subcategory of products liability law known as strict liability. Unlike the bulk of products liability law, which requires that some negligent action on the part of the manufacturer be proved, strict liability holds manufacturers liable for producing products with inherent dangers, even when they make them with the utmost care. First, they advanced the theory that Roehm Gesellschaft had committed a wrongful act because the manufacturing or marketing of handguns is an "abnormally dangerous activity." Second, they argued that the gun manufacturer was strictly liable because handguns are "abnormally dangerous products."

These were unusual arguments. Ordinarily, those injured by products claimed they were defective. In this case, however, the gun that shot Kelley had worked exactly as intended. Roehm Gesellschaft filed a motion asking the

---

[32]Steven Brill, "The Traffic (Legal and Illegal) in Guns," *Harper's*, September 1977, p. 40.

[33]Joseph Albright, " 'Snubbies': The Handguns Criminals Prefer," in *The Snub-Nosed Killers*, op. cit., p. 4.

court to dismiss the case immediately because the revolver was not defective and because the company was not responsible for the criminal acts of the gunman who shot Kelley. The federal court, finding no controlling precedents for these legal issues in Maryland common law, asked the Maryland Court of Appeals, a state court, to assess Kelley's legal arguments.

After oral arguments by both sides before a panel of seven judges, the Maryland court phrased three questions of law to be answered in response to the request of the federal court. These questions were as follows:

(1) Is the manufacturer or marketer of a handgun, in general, liable under any strict liability theory to a person injured as a result of the criminal use of its product?
(2) Is the manufacturer or marketer of a particular category of small, cheap handguns, sometimes referred to as "Saturday Night Specials," and regularly used in criminal activity, strictly liable to a person injured by such handgun during the course of a crime?
(3) Does the Roehm Revolver Handgun Model RG-38S, serial number 0152662, fall within the category referred to in question 2?[34]

The Court's Answer to Question 1

In answering question 1, the Maryland court, in an opinion written by Judge J. Eldridge, addressed the two theories of strict liability advanced by Kelley.

First, Kelley argued that Roehm Gesellschaft should be liable because the manufacturing or marketing of handguns is an "abnormally dangerous activity." In making this argument, Kelley relied on Sections 519 and 520 of the second edition of the *Restatement of the Law of Torts,* a summary compilation of tort law put together over many years by a committee of legal experts.

Section 519 states: "One who carries on an abnormally dangerous activity is subject to liability for harm to the person, land or chattels of another resulting from the activity, although he has exercised the utmost care to prevent the harm."[35] Section 520 then sets forth six factors to be considered by the court in determining whether an activity, in this case the manufacturing of handguns, is "abnormally dangerous." These criteria are as follows:

(a) the existence of a high degree of risk of harm to individual health and safety;
(b) the likelihood that harm will be great, i.e. serious bodily harm or death;
(c) the inability to eliminate risk of harm by exercising reasonable care;
(d) the extent to which the activity is uncommon or out of the ordinary;
(e) the inappropriateness of the activity to the place where it is carried on and;
(f) the extent to which the value to the community is outweighed by its dangerous attributes.[36]

---

[34]*Kelley* v. *R. G. Industries, Inc.,* 497 A.2d 1143 (Md. 1985) at 1145.
[35]*Restatement of the Law of Torts,* 2d. ed. Washington, D.C.: American Law Institute Publishers, vol. 3, 1965, p. 34.
[36]Ibid., p. 36.

Kelley's theory was that statistical evidence of the harm caused by handguns made them so risky that manufacturers and marketers were guilty of a wrongful act for putting them into the public's hands.

The court, however, rejected this argument without analysis of the six factors on the narrow grounds that the activity in question was the *manufacturing* of handguns, not their *use*. The manufacturing or marketing of handguns was not, in itself, an "abnormally dangerous activity," even if subsequent criminal use of handguns posed a risk to society. This legal theory, then, was rejected.

Kelley's second contention was that a handgun is an "abnormally dangerous product" for which the manufacturer or marketer should be strictly liable under Section 402A of the *Restatement*. Section 402A imposes liability for damages on anyone who sells a product in defective condition that is unreasonably dangerous to the consumer, where the product reaches the consumer without substantial change and causes the consumer injury, even though the

---

THE SLINGSHOT CASES

Two cases with instructive parallels to the legal questions raised in the *Kelley* case involved slingshots. They have been frequently mentioned in handgun liability briefs.

In the first case a ten-year-old San Diego boy went to a 7-11 Market and bought a slingshot. He used it to fire a projectile that injured the eye of a little girl he was playing with. The girl, through her guardian, alleged that the manufacturer and marketer of the slingshot were negligent in selling it to children because there was an unreasonable risk of harm to others.

In the second case, an eleven-year-old boy in Detroit purchased a slingshot for 10 cents at a discount store and gave it to a twelve-year-old friend. At the park, where the boys were shooting projectiles at frogs, one called to the other to look up into a tree while he shot at a bird. But while the boy was looking up, the projectile hit his eye and blinded him. The parents of the blinded boy sued the manufacturer and distributors for failure to exercise due care in marketing slingshots directly to children.

How would you decide these cases?

The courts decided the slingshot cases differently, illustrating the flexibility of common-law standards. In the first case, *Bojorquez* v. *House of Toys,* the California Supreme Court dismissed the complaint, saying that slingshots were designed for sale to youngsters and that if the court found the businesses guilty for being in this market, it would amount to a judicial ban on the sale of toy slingshots. Also, the danger of slingshots was so generally well known that sellers did not have to add a warning of potential risk.[37]

In the second case, *Moning* v. *Alfono,* the Michigan Supreme Court held that the ricochet of a slingshot pellet into a bystander's eye was a "recognizable risk of harm" arising from the sale of slingshots to children and a "normal consequence" of the conduct of the businesses being sued. A reasonable toy manufacturer and retailer must keep in mind the inevitable carelessness and immaturity of children. Thus, a manufacturer could be held negligent for making a slingshot to be sold to children.[38]

[37]62 C.A.3d 930 at 933 (1976).
[38]254 N.W.2d 759 (1977).

seller has exercised all possible care in the manufacture and distribution of the product.[39]

In making this argument, Kelley did not allege that the handgun which shot him operated in a defective manner. Rather, he suggested that the gun was defective by virtue of the fact that the risks posed to society by the misuse of handguns outweighed any benefits. Hence, the Model RG-38S that wounded him was a defective product.

The court rejected this argument also, stating that "Kelley confuses a product's *normal function,* which may very well be dangerous, with a defect in a product's design or construction."[40] For the handgun to be defective, there would have to be a malfunction caused by a weak or poorly designed part. This was not the case. The court refused to apply a risk/utility test, as is often done in design defect cases, on the again narrow grounds that a defect did not exist in the traditional sense. Judge Eldridge wrote that:

> . . .the risk/utility test is inapplicable to the present situation. This standard is only applied when something goes wrong with a product . . . in the case of a handgun which injured a person in whose direction it was fired, the product worked precisely as intended.[41]

In sum, both of Kelley's arguments were novel and proved unacceptable as legal theories. Had they been accepted, it would have set a precedent imposing liability on manufacturers of other dangerous products. Companies that made matches and knives could have been liable for injuries caused by their products. Manufacturers of automatic bank teller machines might have been liable for injuries to customers who were robbed while using them. These products, like handguns, pose risks to society even when they are not defective. If criminal use was legally a product defect, there would be no limit to lawsuits, since almost any product may be used for criminal purposes.

The Court's Answer to Question 2

Thus far, the court had held that handgun manufacturers were not, in general, liable for the criminal misuse of their products. But what about manufacturers of the dangerous subcategory of handguns known as Saturday Night Specials? Could they be held strictly liable? Judge Eldridge's answer to this question would startle the legal community. His answer was yes. And he created a new limited area of strict liability.

Judge Eldridge began his construction of a new theory of products liability by noting that even though common law is based on precedent, it is not static. It is dynamic. In order to provide fair solutions to the problems of society, common law must keep pace with social change; it should be, he wrote, "sub-

---

[39]*Restatement of the Law of Torts,* op. cit., vol. 2, pp. 347–48.
[40]*Kelley,* at 1148.
[41]*Kelley,* at 1149.

ject to judicial modification in light of modern circumstances or increased knowledge.''[42] Furthermore, this change in the common law should be in keeping with public policy. Judge Eldridge noted that the Maryland Assembly had passed a law in 1972 regulating the carrying and transportation of handguns. The law limited the right of Marylanders to wear and carry handguns but excepted police, hunters, and people at home. Since the legislature, then, found some handgun use legitimate, the judge stated that absolute liability against handgun manufacturers would be contrary to Maryland public policy. But, said the judge, a limited category of guns, Saturday Night Specials, was not sanctioned by the law.

> Saturday Night Specials are largely unfit for any of the recognized legitimate uses sanctioned by the Maryland gun control legislation. They are too inaccurate, unreliable and poorly made for use by law enforcement personnel, sportsmen, homeowners or businessmen. . . . The chief ''value'' a Saturday Night Special handgun has is in criminal activity, because of its easy concealability and low price. Obviously, the use of a handgun in the commission of a crime is not a ''legitimate'' use justified by State policy.[43]

Judge Eldridge also pointed out that federal handgun policy, as set forth in the Gun Control Act of 1968, forbade the importation of cheap handguns that could not meet BATF testing requirements. Since these requirements were established to keep out foreign-made Saturday Night Specials, the judge concluded that there was a federal policy against such handguns. Hence, both the Maryland Assembly and Congress had made laws permitting some handgun use while recognizing that ''there is a handgun species, i.e., the so-called Saturday Night Special, which is considered to have little or no legitimate purpose in today's society.''[44]

The manufacturer of a Saturday Night Special, continued the judge, should know that its chief use will be in crime. Since the manufacturer has chosen to place a product in society that will be misused by criminals, the manufacturer is more at fault than innocent victims who are shot. Therefore, he reasoned, if existing common-law theories of strict liability were not sufficient to place fault on Saturday-Night-Special manufacturers, then the law should adapt to the need of society to prevent violent crime and recognize a new area of strict liability based on public policy. Hence, the court created new law to bring about the end that Judge Eldridge felt was important.

The Court's Answer to Question 3

Still remaining was the question of whether the gun used to shoot Olen Kelley was a Saturday Night Special. If it was, Roehm Gesellschaft could, under

---

[42]*Kelley*, at 1151.
[43]*Kelley*, at 1158.
[44]*Kelley*, at 1158.

Judge Eldridge's new common-law theory, be held liable to pay Kelley damages for his injury. If it was not, Kelley would lose the case, and it would remain for future plaintiffs to prove they had been shot by Saturday Night Specials.

After discussing the characteristics of the Model RG-38S in question, Judge Eldridge wrote that the gun had a short ($3\frac{1}{2}$-inch) barrel, recently sold for a modest $55 if in excellent condition ($35 in good condition), would not meet BATF standards for importation, and had been made by a company "called the nation's major producer of Saturday Night Specials."[45] These indications showed that the gun was under suspicion, but its nature was a question of fact for a jury to decide, not a question of law for Judge Eldridge to decide. He would go no further.

The End of the Case

The effect of Judge Eldridge's opinion was to send the case of *Kelley* v. *R. G. Industries* back to federal district court for jury trial. However, attorneys for R. G. Industries prepared a pretrial motion to dismiss, arguing that R. G. Industries had been denied due process of law and that, therefore, the Maryland Appeals Court decision was unconstitutional. This was so, they argued, because Judge Eldridge penned his new theory without holding a hearing in which R. G. Industries could challenge the facts upon which he based his opinion.

This motion was never entered, because one of Kelley's attorneys, Howard L. Siegel, suddenly offered to dismiss the case with prejudice, meaning that the case could not be filed again. He noted that by this time the Roehm brothers had removed the assets of R. G. Industries to Germany, where they would be hard to reach.[46] The reasons why R. G. Industries went out of business have never been made public. Probably, falling demand for handguns in the mid-1980s made the assembly plant marginal. And a growing number of lawsuits such as Kelley's may have scared the owners. To date, however, they have not suffered an adverse final judgment or paid a penny in damages to a handgun injury plaintiff.

Other attorneys familiar with the case believe that three other (unstated) reasons may have had more to do with the offer to end the case. First, the motion alleging unconstitutionality was formidable. Second, the handgun in question, because of its large caliber, quality, and $3\frac{1}{2}$-inch barrel, did not fit neatly into any definition of a Saturday Night Special. And finally, if the case was not pursued further, Judge Eldridge's ruling, which permitted the imposition of liability on manufacturers of certain handguns, would stand

---

[45]*Kelley,* at 1161.
[46]Telephone interview with Howard L. Siegel, attorney-at-law, Rockville, Maryland, June 28, 1988.

unchallenged.[47] According to Olen Kelley, he had not been pursuing the case for money anyway. Rather, his goal had been to make cheap stickup guns less available. So ending the case here accorded with his goals and the goals of sympathetic gun control groups.

Reaction to the Kelley Case

The *Kelley* decision left handgun manufacturers unclear about their potential liability for criminal use of some product lines in Maryland (which was the only state where the precedent applied). Gun control advocates praised the decision. Pro-gun groups began trying to overturn it. There were three main axes of controversy over the *Kelley* case.

First, *Kelley* raised the subject of judicial activism. Courts have traditionally deferred to the legislative and executive branches of government in making new law in controversial areas. Judges are reluctant to make law in advance of democratically elected representatives, who are responsive to constituencies and better able to hammer out delicate compromises among fractious pressure groups. Gun control is a highly emotional, complex, political issue, and the *Kelley* court established a precedent that could effect a virtual ban on handguns by creating an expensive, perhaps uninsurable liability for manufacturers. However, there is a tradition of judicial activism being appropriate when, at times, legislatures are inactive. An example of such an occasion is the Supreme Court's school desegregation decision in 1954.[48] Was *Kelley* an appropriate occasion for judicial activism?

A small number of legal scholars defended the decision. One, for example, wrote that *Kelley* was a proper use of judicial power that "frustrated the gun lobby's attempt to thwart the democratic process."[49] The Maryland legislature was free to overturn the decision if it was unpopular, so the power of the court was checked. Another averred that *Kelley*'s activist thrust was "in keeping with the 'grand style' of judicial decisionmaking."[50]

Other observers were not so enamored. Richard Gardner, an attorney with the National Rifle Association, called the decision "a new low in judicial activism."[51] Many agreed. They reasoned that since neither Congress nor the Maryland Assembly had specifically banned the sale of Saturday Night Specials, this amounted to a policy choice by elected representatives who thought these guns had some merit.

---

[47]Telephone interview with Richard Gardner, assistant general counsel, National Rifle Association, Washington, D.C., June 28, 1988.

[48]*Brown* v. *Board of Education of Topeka, Kansas,* 349 U.S. 294 (1954).

[49]Patrick S. Davies, "Saturday Night Specials: A 'Special' Exemption in Strict Liability Law," *Notre Dame Law Review,* vol. 61, 1986, p. 491.

[50]Susan M. Stevens, "*Kelley* v. *R.G. Industries:* When Hard Cases Make Good Law," *Maryland Law Review,* winter 1987, p. 494.

[51]Telephone interview with Richard Gardner, assistant general counsel, National Rifle Association, Washington, D.C., June 28, 1988.

Second, the decision raised questions about current trends in tort law. Before the 1960s, American tort law was a simple system of corrective justice that compensated victims for injuries that resulted from wicked conduct. It was principally a set of rules to resolve disputes between two parties. Since the 1960s, however, tort law has been turned into a vehicle for broad social reform. This is why the doctrine of strict liability has been developed. It imposes liability without necessarily finding corporate conduct immoral, negligent, or blameworthy. With the advent of strict liability, tort law was used not only for the straightforward purpose of resolving disputes between parties but also for the indirect purpose of making corporations which sell unusually dangerous products the insurers of risk. Courts began to approve huge damage awards for consumers injured by asbestos, intrauterine devices, toxic chemicals, vaccines, and power machinery. Companies, in theory, placed a surcharge in their prices to cover the cost of compensating consumers for these injuries and were given an incentive to innovate safer product designs. In practice, many have questioned the ability of business to bear the added financial burdens of huge damage awards.

The *Kelley* decision promised to impose the tort system's penchant for social engineering on handgun manufacturers. Would this be desirable? There were differences of opinion. One legal scholar wrote:

> This development is innovative and in keeping with the traditional role of the common-law court. The court played a risk-allocation role, not a legislative one, in the *Kelley* decision. The immediate effect of this risk-allocation role will be to place the cost of a Saturday Night Special's use on those who benefit from that use. The long-term effect of this decision may well be a better system of handgun distribution.[52]

Another was reluctant to rest the heavy hand of tort damages on yet another industry.

> "If the *Kelley* reasoning prevails, the courts will then impose on the handgun industry a crushing economic burden that Congress and the state legislatures have indicated is unacceptable to the democratically elected elements of the polity."[53]

A third dimension of the *Kelley* controversy was the issue of fairness. Traditionally, tort law placed moral opprobrium on corporations which acted negligently and caused injury. But legal theories of strict liability relaxed the notion of the morally wrongful act in causing injury. Now a company didn't have to do anything blameworthy; it simply had to be in a position to spread the cost of injury among consumers. With handguns, though, criminals as third parties stood between manufacturers and injured consumers. It seemed to violate general standards of justice to impose the costs of criminal actions on law-abiding manufacturers. A law professor argued: "to the extent that it relieves crimi-

---

[52]Stevens, op. cit., p. 499.
[53]David Dana, "Tort Law: Handgun Manufacturer Liability," *Harvard Journal of Law and Public Policy*, vol. 9, no. 3, 1986, p. 768–69.

nals from civil liability in favor of imposing liability upon a lawful business, the *Kelley* decision serves to distort general notions of justice and fairness while creating the impression that the judiciary considers itself unable to punish adequately the perpetrators of criminal acts."[54]

Did R. G. Industries *cause* Kelley's gunshot wound? In legal terminology, was the action of the robber who pulled the trigger a "superseding cause" which broke the chain of causation that Kelley's attorneys tried to construct? Or was the criminal act so foreseeable that the simple manufacture of a handgun began a chain of causation inevitably leading to violent injury?[55]

Signs of Rejection Appear

The *Kelley* precedent was soon rejected by other courts.[56] In *Armijo* v. *Ex Cam, Inc.*, for example, a New Mexico court declined to adopt the *Kelley* precedent, using these words:

> This Court finds it unnecessary to engage in any lengthy discussion of the *Kelley* doctrine. To recognize such a cause of action in New Mexico would require an abrogation of the common law in a way bordering on judicial legislation. . . . Furthermore, creation of such a doctrine is extremely problematic insofar as *which* manufacturers would be held liable. All firearms are capable of being used for criminal activity. Merely to impose liability upon the manufacturers of the cheapest types of handguns will not avoid that basic fact. Instead, claims against gun manufacturers will have the anomalous result that only persons shot with cheap guns will be able to recover, while those shot with expensive guns, admitted by the *Kelley* court to be more accurate and therefore deadlier, would take nothing.[57]

In May 1988, the *Kelley* opinion came into the limelight in Maryland when the assembly passed a gun control law to ban Saturday Night Specials. The law established a state commission to decide which handguns are appropriate for legitimate uses and to set standards prohibiting all others. Pro-gun lobbies such as the National Rifle Association strongly opposed this bill, and in order to reduce political opposition, its supporters included a provision that voided the *Kelley* decision by banning the civil liability of handgun manufacturers. Kelley and his attorneys believe that this trade-off, the price for passage of the bill, was warranted. In 1988 the NRA succeeded in placing a referendum before Maryland voters to repeal the Saturday-Night-Special ban, but it failed to pass, and the law remains in effect.

---

[54]Michael A. Knoerzer, "Maryland Court of Appeals Takes Shot in the Dark at Saturday Night Specials," *St. John's Law Review,* vol. 60, 1986, p. 564.

[55]In a similar case, *Martin* v. *Harrington and Richardson,* 743 F.2d 1200 (7th Cir. 1984), the court ruled that the criminal misuse of a handgun was a superseding cause that was not foreseeable by the manufacturer and broke the causal chain.

[56]Some of the cases which specifically rejected the *Kelley* theory of strict liability include *Delahanty* v. *Hinckley,* nos. 82-409 and 82-490 *slip op.* (D.C.D.C., Dec. 9, 1986); *Caveny* v. *Raven Arms Co.,* 665 F.Supp 530 (S.D.Ohio 1987); and *Brady* v. *Hinckley,* Civil Action 82-549 (D.C.D.C., 1988).

[57]*Armijo* v. *Ex Cam, Inc.,* 656 F.Supp. 771 (D.N.M. 1987), at 775.

POSTSCRIPT

Today Olen Kelley continues to work as a grocery manager at a different Safeway store. He was disappointed when his case was dropped, but he avidly follows the continuing legal battle against Saturday Night Specials. Local television crews keep track of him, and when gun control is in the news, he continues to speak out because "it feels good to do what I am trying to do."[58] He is proud that attorneys for James Brady, who was shot with President Reagan, have called upon his counsel for advice. He would like to meet Jim Brady and his gun control activist wife, Sarah, someday.

The suspect arrested by police shortly after the holdup was charged with armed robbery, unlawful imprisonment, attempted murder, and handgun law violations. The maximum sentence for all violations was sixty years, but he was sentenced to serve only sixteen years and wound up in a prison near Kelley's house. He refused to name his accomplice, who was never found.

Although R. G. Industries was dismantled, other firms continue to make Saturday Night Specials. They have no legal responsibility toward victims of handgun crime.

QUESTIONS

The *Kelley* case raises many questions. Among the most important are these:

1 Are deaths and criminal problems with handguns primarily the result of violent aspects of American culture or the result of liberal firearms availability?

2 Are current gun control laws sufficient? If not, how do you favor changing them?

3 Are there handguns which have no legitimate use and ought not to be marketed? What are their characteristics?

4 Are any handguns so "inherently dangerous" that manufacturers commit a tort, or wrongful act, under the law when they make them? Do the risks they pose to society outweigh possible benefits? Do you agree with Judge Eldridge's decisions in the *Kelley* case? Should Olen Kelley have pursued the case to a jury trial?

5 Is current products liability law adequate to bring about a just result in handgun cases? Should it be reformed or reinterpreted by an activist judge?

6 What are the social responsibilities of handgun makers?

---

[58]Telephone interview with Olen J. Kelley, June 28, 1988.

SELLING TOBACCO

Marlboro cigarettes were first marketed by Philip Morris in the 1920s. They were aimed at women; advertisements said they were "Mild as May," and they had rose-colored tips so that lipstick wouldn't show. But women did not smoke much in those days, and the brand failed.

Then, in the 1950s, research began to suggest that smoking had pernicious health effects. To allay fears, filtered cigarettes such as R. J. Reynolds's Winston were developed; the implication was that they were safer. Philip Morris sought to market a new filtered brand to compete with R. J. Reynolds, but it needed to overcome the effeminate image that filters carried for many men. So when the Marlboro name was revived for the new cigarette, it was marketed with an ultramasculine theme. Early ads prepared by the Leo Burnett agency featured deep-sea fishermen, police officers, car mechanics, and a cowboy. The models were older, tough-looking men. Some had tattoos, which were calculated to imply an adventurous, romantic past life. The smokes also came in a "rugged" flip-top box, a major packaging innovation.

Marlboros were profitable, but a threat in the marketing environment soon appeared. In 1957 a ranking in *Reader's Digest* showed Marlboros to be among the brands highest in tar and nicotine. To allay health fears in customers, Philip Morris requested a change in the Marlboro ads, so the Burnett agency created what became known as the "settleback" campaign. It featured pictorial ads showing the Marlboro cowboy in tranquil, picturesque scenes designed to reassure smokers. TV commercials featured calf roping and broncobusting in Marlboro Country and were accompanied by theme music from a western film, *The Magnificent Seven*. The cowboy theme defined the brand image so successfully that other occupations never returned.

In the 1960s Marlboro sales jumped, especially among younger smokers age eighteen to thirty-four. Analysts said that the ads fit the era. For an anxious nation beset by radical social movements and the Vietnamese war, the cowboy harked back to simpler times and traditional values. For teenagers, the rugged Marlboro man exemplified independence; his lone image carried the right touch of rebelliousness.

The success of the Marlboro brand catapulted Philip Morris from a scrawny also-ran with 9 percent of the cigarette market in the 1950s to industry leadership with a 38 percent market share in 1988. By 1976 Marlboro was the nation's leading brand. In 1988 its market share was 25 percent, far ahead of the 11 percent share of second-place Winston, and no other brand had more than 7.5 percent. Today, Marlboro is the largest selling packaged-goods product in the world, with sales of $6.1 billion a year—more than the sales of all but seventy companies on the *Fortune* 500 industrials list. If the Marlboro brand alone was a company, it would have higher sales than Northrop, General Mills, Colgate-Palmolive, and Litton Industries. Ironically, Marlboros remain true to their origin as a woman's cigarette. The company does not advertise the fact, but more women than men smoke the brand. And it is a runaway best-seller among teenagers. A recent survey of smokers in grades 6, 9, and 12 in four Los Angeles school districts found that 56 percent smoked the Marlboro brand; only 5 percent smoked Camels, the next highest brand.[1]

Tobacco contains a powerful, addictive drug, and by historical accident, it came to be widely used before its health dangers were fully understood. It sustains a massive industry whose financial sinews wind deeply into the world economy. All the same, tobacco products are vilified by the surgeon general, the medical community, and citizen lobbies. Their hope is that advertising and promotional practices exemplified by the Marlboro theme ads can be restricted or banned.

This is the story of tobacco, those who use it, those who make a living from it, and those who would destroy it.

SMOKING IN AMERICA: AN UPDATE

About 55 million Americans, 30.4 percent of the adult population, smoke. Among men, smoking has declined from a high of over 50 percent in 1955 to about 34 percent in 1985. Among women, smoking has declined more slowly, from a high of 31 percent in 1974 to 28 percent in 1985.[2]

---

[1]William J. McCarthy and Ellen R. Gritz, "Madison Avenue as the Pied Piper: Cigarette Advertising and Teenage Smoking," in U.S. House of Representatives, *Hearings before the Committee on Energy and Commerce,* "Tobacco Advertising," 100th Cong., 1st Sess., July 27, 1987, p. 95.

[2]Michael C. Fiore et al., "Trends in Cigarette Smoking in the United States: The Changing Influence of Gender and Race," *Journal of the American Medical Association,* January 6, 1989, p. 51. In May 1989 a Gallup poll found that only 27 percent of Americans said they had smoked during the last week; see "Cigarette Smoking at 45-Year Low," *The Gallup Report,* no. 286, July 1989, p. 23.

A steady decline in the number of smokers is the predominant trend, but the drop is more pronounced in some demographic categories. Smoking is becoming predominantly a pastime of the less educated. There are fewer smokers at all educational levels, but the decline is five times faster among college graduates than among those with only a high school education. In 1985, only 18 percent of college graduates smoked, compared with 34 percent of high school graduates.[3] Smoking rates are highest for blacks. Over 35 percent smoke, and black men, at 41 percent, have the highest percentage of any racial group. Smoking, however, does not seem to be entirely a minority phenomenon; Asians and Hispanics have lower rates than whites.[4]

Each year about 1.5 million smokers quit, and 390,000 die of illnesses related to smoking, while 1.1 million people, almost all of them teenagers, start. New recruits are insufficient to prevent thinning of the ranks. But the industry does plenty of advertising to ensure consumer awareness of its products.

THE ROLE OF ADVERTISING

Advertising is a way of communicating information about products and services to consumers. It is ubiquitous in American society, where it is a larger part, in absolute dollars and percentage, of the gross national product than in any other country.[5] In traditional economic theory advertising is viewed favorably as contributing to market efficiency by bringing together buyer and seller.

But it has critics. Some economists argue that big companies use it to establish brand preferences and then drive out smaller competitors, leading to the growth of oligopoly, or domination of the market by a few large firms.[6] In the 1950s, John Kenneth Galbraith attacked advertising as a manipulative force driving consumers to excessive, wasteful consumption and encouraging shallow materialism.[7]

---

[3]John P. Pierce et al., "Trends in Cigarette Smoking in the United States: Educational Differences Are Increasing," *Journal of the American Medical Association,* January 6, 1989, p. 59.

[4]Luis G. Escobedo and Patrick L. Remington, "Birth Cohort Analysis of Prevalence of Cigarette Smoking among Hispanics in the United States," *Journal of the American Medical Association,* January 6, 1989, p. 67. There is also a negative relationship between smoking and income. Those in low-income households smoke more. Peat Marwick & Co., "An Analysis of the Regressivity of Excise Taxes," in U.S. House of Representatives, *Hearings before the Committee on Ways and Means,* "Revenue Increase Options," 100th Cong., 1st Sess., July 7–15, 1987, p. 717.

[5]Robert B. Ekelund, Jr., and David S. Saurman. *Advertising and the Market Process.* San Francisco: Pacific Research Institute for Public Policy, 1988, p. 7.

[6]Nicholas Kaldon, "The Economic Aspects of Advertising," *Review of Economic Studies,* vol. 18, 1950–51, p. 13.

[7]See, for example, John Kenneth Galbraith. *The Affluent Society.* Boston: Houghton Mifflin Company, 1958. Galbraith was joined by another social critic, Vance Packard in *The Hidden Persuaders.* New York: D. McKay Co., 1957.

Two basic types of advertising are *informational* advertising and *persuasive* advertising. Both are used by the tobacco industry. Informational advertising focuses on facts. R. J. Reynolds, for instance, advertises its Now brand with a large matrix comparing tar and nicotine levels in Now boxes, packs, 100s, and menthols with levels in American Tobacco Co.'s competing Carlton brand.[8] (Both, incidentally, claim to be lowest in tar and nicotine.)

Although all advertising is intended to persuade, persuasive advertising is characterized by heavy reliance on emotional appeals. Thus, Lorillard's Newport brand is advertised as "Alive With Pleasure" and features snapshots of young couples without descriptive text. Reynolds's Magna brand is shown in front of lightning on a blue background. This kind of emotional, nonlogical advertising is found in oligopolistic consumer products industries, such as the tobacco industry, with similar products and parallel pricing policies. It is used to build brand loyalty and market share and has the effect of keeping new entrants out of the market if they cannot afford the huge advertising cost necessary to launch a new brand. A second purpose of persuasive advertising is, of course, to attract new customers. In the tobacco industry this purpose is not openly acknowledged.

Persuasive advertising often involves the selling of life-styles. It is usually inefficient to advertise to the public as if it were an undifferentiated mass. But methods of targeting specific groups of consumers have changed over the years. It used to be assumed that consumer buying was determined by demographic characteristics such as age, sex, income, education, and occupation. So products were pitched to demographic segments of the population. But in the late 1960s market researchers developed a new approach to segmenting called psychographics. Psychographics is based on the assumption that people buy products to fulfill inner needs. The population can be divided into groups of people with different needs, and products are pitched to them. One illustrative psychographic approach is called VALS (for "values and life-styles").[9] It divides consumers into five groups.

1 *Belongers* are traditionalists and conservatives. They believe in community spirit, family values, and the status quo. They have been described as Archie Bunker types. Telephone company ads that depict long-distance calling as a means of maintaining family ties are directed at fulfilling their needs for companionship.

---

[8]"R. J. Reynolds" refers to the R. J. Reynolds Tobacco Co., which is a unit of RJR-Nabisco.
[9]The VALS categories presented here are simplified. For more information see Arnold Mitchell. *The Nine American Life-styles*. New York: Warner Books, 1984; William Meyers. *The Image Makers: Power and Persuasion on Madison Avenue*. New York: Times Books, 1984, chap, 1; or Berkeley Rice, "The Selling of Life-styles," *Psychology Today,* March 1988. VALS is only one of a number of psychographic typologies. For a discussion of some others see Eric Clark. *The Want Makers*. New York: Viking Books, 1989, chap. 5.

2 *Emulators* are younger people, mainly adolescents and teenagers, who feel insecure and are searching for identity and adult status. They want to fit in and will buy products that promise social acceptance. They were the targets of Dr. Pepper's "Be a Pepper" campaign, which associated the soft drink with friendship and group approval. They are only 12 percent of the population but an obvious target for cigarette companies.

3 *Achievers* are materialistic and consume expensive, quality brands to demonstrate high status. They have a drive to "make it" and often are the first to buy trendy products such as VCRs and cellular phones. They see everyday products as symbols of success. Ralph Lauren capitalized on their inner needs by sewing polo players on otherwise ordinary shirts and charging a premium price.

4 *Socially conscious* consumers are modern "flower children" who seek inner peace and want to protect the environment. They want uncomplicated products of high quality. They believe in simplicity and honesty and are offended by exaggerated ad appeals. They tend to smoke low-tar and -nicotine cigarettes.

5 *Survivors* struggle to exist on low incomes. They include minimum-wage earners, welfare recipients, and retirees living on social security. They spend little for luxuries or premium brands. Few ads are directed entirely at them.

People in all these categories are targeted by advertisers who endow brands with "life-style" themes that trigger inner drives. Ads imply that cigarettes are a path to subjective need fulfillment, not simply objects of utility. The physical differences between brands are trivial, but their life-style themes may be worlds apart. Note the difference between Liggett's "Chesterfield People" ads, which pictured mature adult smokers with successful lives, and R. J. Reynolds's Camel ads featuring a cartoonlike Camel labeled a "smooth character."

One VALS category, emulators, is of special interest to cigarette marketers. Emulators are only about 12 percent of the population, but most are adolescents. Virtually all smokers initiate the habit between the ages of nine and sixteen, so ads appealing to the needs of emulators encourage new smokers. There is a strong vulnerability to life-style advertising during this stage of psychological development. In adolescence a discrepancy develops between the real self and an idealized self that the person wishes to become. The gap between the awkward, shallow, and socially inept real self and the mature, accomplished, popular idealized self creates anxiety. So, the young person seeks ways of achieving the idealized self. Images of the idealized self are found in cigarette ads, which have themes of adventure, independence, social acceptance, physical beauty, mastery, and maturity. Teenagers who smoke have different personalities than those who do not. They have stronger tendencies to rebelliousness, impulsiveness, and risk taking, and they develop aspirations to grow up sooner.[10] The need to express these personality traits can be met by using certain cigarette brands.

THE STORY OF TOBACCO

The tobacco plant is an herb of the nightshade family (family Solanaceae) native to the Americas. It synthesizes an alkaloid compound in its leaves called nicotine as a natural deterrent for leaf-boring insects.[11] Nicotine, a mild natural insecticide in the plant, has pronounced physiological effects when ingested by humans. In the body it affects the nervous system and promotes the release of hormones. It is a stimulant, releasing adrenaline. Just 7 seconds after a smoker puffs on a cigarette, nicotine reaches the brain, where it becomes a psychoactive drug. Nicotine alters mood and subjective states of feeling. It improves concentration and memory by causing secretion of the hormone vasopressin and by direct attachment to receptors in areas of the brain linked to memory formation. It reduces pain and anxiety. Nicotine carried to the brain in the bloodstream also promotes the production of endorphins, opiatelike chemicals that are associated with pleasure and euphoria. Tobacco users become dependent on moods created by nicotine. Nicotine itself is not a clear health hazard. It is not a carcinogen. Other constituents of tobacco smoke are thought to be the most deadly culprits in tobacco-related illness.[12]

Cigarette manufacturers today understand the action of nicotine and know that the cigarette is simply a delivery system for the drug. The high-temperature combustion of tobacco in a burning tip releases nicotine in an aerosol form which is rapidly absorbed in the lungs. Here is how one Philip Morris employee described a cigarette:

> The cigarette should be conceived not as a product but as a package. The product is nicotine. The cigarette is but one of the many package layers. There is the carton, which contains the pack, which contains the cigarette, which contains the smoke.

[10]McCarthy and Gritz, op. cit., p. 74. See also David G. Altman, Michael D. Slater, Cheryl L. Albright, and Nathan Maccoby, "How an Unhealthy Product Is Sold: Cigarette Advertising in Magazines, 1960–1985," *Journal of Communication,* autumn 1987, pp. 95–106.

[11]*Nicotine* is named for Jean Nicot, a French ambassador to Portugal. In 1560 Nicot sent tobacco plant seeds to the Queen of France, and the tobacco leaves were used as medicine. The remedy was named *nicotiane.*

[12]A standard-size cigarette produces about 500 milligrams of smoke for inhalation by the smoker. About 80 percent of this smoke is composed of carbon monoxide, water, nitrogen, and oxygen. The other 20 percent is composed of about 4,000 constituents lumped together as "tars." These include substances such as ammonia, cyanide, formaldehyde, benzo[a]pyrene, and radioactive compounds. Forty-three of these substances are carcinogens, but they are present only in minute quantities down in the nanogram range, which equates to one one-thousandth of a billionth of a gram. A gram is about the weight of a paper clip. Daily breathing of urban air may expose a person to more of some of these carcinogens than are present in the smoke of a pack of cigarettes. The presence of forty-three known carcinogens, however, explains why smoking is linked not only to lung cancer but also to cancers in many different sites such as the bladder, pancreas, kidney, stomach, and uterus.

The smoke is the final package. The smoker must strip off all these package layers to get to that which he seeks. . . . Think of the cigarette pack as a storage container for a day's supply of nicotine. . . . Think of a puff of smoke as the vehicle of nicotine. . . . Smoke is beyond question the most optimized vehicle of nicotine and the cigarette the most optimized dispenser of smoke.[13]

For centuries tobacco was chewed, snuffed, and smoked in North and South American societies, but it was unknown in Europe. Recreational use among natives was widespread, and tobacco also had religious significance. In some tribes, novice shamans put wads of tobacco in their rectums, where the absorbed nicotine would shock their nervous systems, causing paralysis and loss of color vision. If the holy man lived, and there was some doubt, he returned to full capacity convinced of having taken a journey into the netherworld of dark spirits.

When Christopher Columbus and other early adventurers made contact with these civilizations, they returned to Europe with leaves and seeds. At first, tobacco was used as medicine. But by the early 1600s recreational smoking predominated. With smoking came antismoking sentiment. King James I of England tried to discourage smoking by his subjects and in a published tract called it "a custome Lothsome to the eye, hatefull to the Nose, harmefull to the braine, daungerous to the Lungs, and the blacke stinking fume thereof, neerest resembling the horrible Stigian smoke of the pit that is bottomeless."[14] Some countries criminalized tobacco use; in fact, smoking carried a death penalty in Turkey, Russia, and China during the late sixteenth century.

In early America, colonists in Virginia obtained tobacco seeds from Spanish

---

[13]U.S. House of Representatives, *Hearings before the Committee on Energy and Commerce,* "Health Consequences of Smoking: Nicotine Addiction," July 29, 1988, p. 4. Quoted in the testimony of Jack E. Henningfield, U.S. Department of Health and Human Services. Diana D. Bransfield, a researcher at the Memorial Sloan-Kettering Cancer Center in New York, offers these country-and-western song lyrics as testimony to the power of nicotine ("Chain-Chewin'," *Journal of the American Medical Association,* January 6, 1989, p. 45).

In a bar in Kentucky, I chain smoked one night
And met me a lady who felt might right;
But she said, "Sir, I don't kiss a smokin' chimney.
Lay down those smokes before you have me."

I told 'er, "Ma'am, you're seein' a pack-a-day man;
I don't promise to quit but I'll do what I can.
If you don't mind me chewin' while I give you a kiss,
I'll use nicotine gum to get my fix."

So now I'm a chain-chewin' on nicotine gum;
I'm chew-chew-chewin' til my jaws are numb.
I'm a chain-chewin' on nicotine gum,
I'm chew-chew-chewin' to get me some.

Before long she was hooked on my chewin' love;
She needed love after lovin' and lovin' after love;
But it wasn't my kisses that made her hum,
It was the nicotine in my chewin' gum.

[14]From his *Counterblaste to Tobacco,* published in 1604. Quoted in Joseph C. Robert. *The Story of Tobacco in America.* 3d. ed. Chapel Hill: University of North Carolina Press, 1967, p. 6.

traders and raised the leaf for export. Soon the crop became a mainstay of the colonial economy. The institution of slavery entrenched itself as tobacco plantations sought cheap African laborers. After independence, slavery was protected in the new Constitution in part because the economic importance of tobacco gave southerners leverage at the 1787 Philadelphia convention.[15]

Until the 1860s smoking was confined mostly to southern states, although there was a small, but steady, market in big cities such as New York. Cigarettes were seen as effete and sold in tiny quantities mainly to dudes and dandies in the cities. But during the Civil War, Union troops adopted the habit in occupied southern territory, where they chewed and smoked tobacco to fight boredom and stress.[16] Returning north after the war, these veterans created a national demand for tobacco. At first the consumer market developed slowly. In the late 1860s cigarettes were still largely a novelty, and production was low. Skilled hand rollers could make only about 2,500 cigarettes a day, but the invention of an automatic rolling machine in the late 1860s that could make over 200 per minute made mass production possible. (A state-of-the-art machine in the 1990s makes 7,800 cigarettes per minute; some plants make 450,000 million per day, and total industry output in 1988 was 555 billion.)

Mass production was soon matched by a mass market as entrepreneurs such as James B. Duke, founder of the American Tobacco Company, learned new advertising techniques to attract customers. In the 1880s, for example, Duke erected a billboard in Atlanta showing a beautiful actress smoking his cigarettes—a first. Later, he enclosed pictures of famous actresses and athletes in cigarette packs.[17] Smoking never enjoyed unanimous approval in those days, though. Mark Twain called it a "filthy habit." And Duke, throughout his life, had to fend off recurrent attacks by anticigarette leagues, ministers, and club women. At its high point in 1901 the Anti-Cigarette League, with chapters throughout the country, claimed 300,000 members. Between 1893 and 1909 its efforts succeeded in getting fourteen states to ban the sale, possession, advertising, or use of cigarettes. But in the century following the Civil War, cigarettes nonetheless became socially acceptable, in part because of pervasive advertising. One by one, the state laws were repealed.

---

[15]Article I, section 2, paragraph 3 of the U.S. Constitution originally permitted counting each slave as three-fifths of a person for the apportionment of seats in the House of Representatives. This language was rendered obsolete by the Thirteenth Amendment, which abolished slavery. Article I, section 9, paragraph 1 forbade Congress from prohibiting the importation of slaves prior to 1808. This provision, of course, became obsolete after that year.

[16]Tobacco use spread with troops after nineteenth-century wars all over the world. British soldiers, for example, were introduced to cigarettes during the Crimean War, from 1853 to 1856. Twentieth-century wars also expanded its use. In World War I, for example, the U.S. military command thought that cigarettes were essential to army morale. At home, patriotic citizens collected money and donations of cigarettes for Over There.

[17]For more discussion of Duke's activities and the growth of the modern cigarette industry see Maurice Corina. *Trust in Tobacco.* New York: St. Martin's Press, 1975; Patrick G. Porter, "Origins of the American Tobacco Company," *Business History Review,* spring 1969; or John K. Winkler. *Tobacco Tycoon: The Story of James Buchanan Duke.* New York: Random House, 1942.

Cigarette ads grew more sophisticated after 1900 and relied on themes appropriate to their time. At the turn of the century, when Turkish tobacco had a cachet of desirability among smokers, R. J. Reynolds's Camels were advertised as a "Turkish and Domestic Blend." Liggett & Myers followed suit by advertising its Chesterfields as "a balanced blend of the finest aromatic Turkish tobacco and the choicest of several American varieties." In the late 1920s companies began to market to women. Liggett & Myers was one of the first, with a print ad showing a man and woman sitting on a cliff near the ocean. When the man lighted a cigarette, the woman said: "Blow some [smoke] my way." The slogan "Reach for a Lucky instead of a sweet" was used in the 1930s to sell Lucky Strikes to female weight watchers. Lorillard responded by recommending that smokers "Eat a chocolate. Light an Old Gold. And enjoy both! Two fine and healthful treats!" In the depression years Philip Morris adopted its catchy "Call for Philip Morris" slogan featuring the inimitable voice of Johnny Roventini, a page at the Hotel New York. These ads played on depression-era fantasies of high living. During World War II cigarettes went to war. Chesterfield quoted bomber pilots, who said: "You want steady nerves when you're flying Uncle Sam's bombers across the Ocean." American Tobacco began marketing Lucky Strike cigarettes in red, white, and blue packages proclaiming "Lucky Strike Green has gone to war!" The implication was that the green dye was needed for soldiers' uniforms, but actually marketing research showed that women did not like the dark-green packs, and the colors had been changed to lure female smokers.

In response to budding worries in the late 1940s over health dangers, tobacco companies made subtle health claims. "More doctors smoke Camels," said one ad. "Just what the doctor ordered," said an L&M ad. The text of a Philip Morris ad said "medical authorities" found that "when smokers changed to Philip Morris, every case of irritation of nose or throat—due to smoking—either cleared up completely, or definitely improved." A 1950s ad for Kents stated that "no medical evidence or scientific endorsement has proven any other cigarette to be superior to Kent."

A GRIM MARKETING ENVIRONMENT FOR THE TOBACCO COMPANIES

By the early 1960s, the majority of American men smoked (and 34 percent of women). But in 1964 the U.S. surgeon general released an analysis of medical research that warned of a strong association between cigarette smoking and lung cancer.[18] It stated that death rates for male smokers were 170 percent those for male nonsmokers and that mortality increased with the number of cigarettes smoked and the number of years a person smoked. This report was

---

[18]U.S. Department of Health, Education, and Welfare. *Smoking and Health: Report of the Advisory Committee to the Surgeon General of the Public Health Service*. Washington, D.C.: U.S. Government Printing Office, 1964.

This ad associates cigarette smoking with masculinity, adulthood, athletic activity, and peer-group acceptance. (*Source: Stacey Pleasant/McGraw-Hill photo.*)

a decisive blow to the industry, putting it on the defensive. In 1979 the surgeon general released a second report, this one a 1,200-page compendium of evidence accumulated in the fifteen years since the first report. It indicted smoking as the primary cause of lung cancer, chronic bronchitis, and emphysema. Smoking was linked to heart disease, pregnancy disorders, and other cancers. This report ended long-term growth in U.S. tobacco sales and brought about a declining market (see Table 10-1).

The environment for marketing tobacco products grew increasingly unfavorable. In 1965, Congress acted to require health warnings on cigarette packs, and in 1971, it prohibited cigarette ads on radio and television. Over the next decade, the health warnings on cigarette packages were strengthened, and medical research on the ill effects of smoking accumulated. In 1985, Congress acted to require a rotating series of stronger warning labels on snuff and banned snuff advertising on television and radio. The surgeon general called for a "smoke-free society by the year 2000," the armed services restricted smoking, and the Government Services Administration restricted smoking in government office buildings. In a Gallup poll, 62 percent of tobacco users and 85 percent of abstainers disapproved of smoking in the presence of others.[19] Late in 1986 a special review of the medical literature by a select committee of

---

[19]Anastasia Toufexis, "A Cloudy Forecast for Smokers," *Time*, April 7, 1986.

TABLE 10-1
DOMESTIC CIGARETTE SALES   (Billions of Cigarettes)

Year	Total sales
1963	516.5
1964	505.0
1965	521.1
1966	529.9
1967	535.8
1968	540.3
1969	527.9
1970	534.2
1971	547.2
1972	561.7
1973	584.7
1974	594.5
1975	603.2
1976	609.9
1977	612.6
1978	615.3
1979	621.8
1980	628.2
1981	636.5
1982	632.5
1983	603.6
1985	599.3
1986	586.4
1987	556.0
1988	569.7

the National Academy of Sciences concluded that "passive smoking," or the exposure of nonsmokers to tobacco smoke, increased the risk of lung cancer in nonsmokers by as much as 30 percent and heightened risks for other ailments. This report fueled the increasing militancy of nonsmokers.

In 1990 smoking was banned on virtually all domestic airline flights. By this time forty-one states had restrictions on public smoking, and nine states, seventy cities, and thousands of companies restricted workplace smoking. A survey of 283 companies in 1988 found that 6 percent would not hire a smoker.[20] State and federal excise taxes had increased to an average of 34 cents per pack.

An additional burden to the industry has been 240 lawsuits by consumers who claimed injury to their health from tobacco products. Manufacturers had deflected such suits in the 1950s and 1960s, but in the 1980s new suits took advantage of changes in products liability law which made it easier for con-

[20]This was a study conducted by the Administrative Management Society. Milo Geyelin, "The Job Is Yours—Unless You Smoke," *Wall Street Journal,* April 21, 1989.

sumers to sue manufacturers of dangerous products. The tobacco companies defend themselves with two main arguments. First, they emphasize ambiguities in the scientific research that links smoking with cancer, convincing juries that this research does not show smoking to be an absolute cause of cancer. Second, they argue that smokers have adequate notice of the health dangers of smoking from warning labels on cigarette packs and are well educated by the flood of information about smoking in the media. Therefore, they contend that smokers voluntarily accept the risks of smoking. The use of these two defensive arguments puts the companies in the position of maintaining that smoking is not dangerous while simultaneously asserting that smokers are adequately warned that it is dangerous.[21] But in using these arguments the tobacco firms had never lost a case. Then, in 1988, a plaintiff finally prevailed in the *Cipollone* case.

THE *CIPOLLONE* CASE

Rose DeFrancesco began to smoke in 1942 at age sixteen, when she was still in high school. The impressionable teenager saw stars smoking in films and magazines and started because it was "cool, glamorous and grown-up."[22] She bought unfiltered Chesterfield cigarettes at the corner sweetshop and soon began to smoke one and one-half packs a day. In those days ads described benefits of smoking such as relaxation or weight control and featured endorsements by doctors.[23] One Chesterfield ad described her brand as "mild" and "just what the doctor ordered." Another promised that "Nose, Throat, and Accessory Organs [are] not Adversely Affected by Smoking Chesterfields." Actor Jack Webb (*Dragnet*) said in a third ad that he smoked two packs a day because: "Chesterfield is best for you."

She married Antonio Cipollone in 1947 and became pregnant. Her husband, a nonsmoker, began what would be an enduring crusade to convince her to quit. During her pregnancy she tried to stop but failed. During labor her doctor gave her a pack of cigarettes, and she smoked them all. In 1955, Rose Cipollone changed her brand to L&M cigarettes. Ads for L&Ms suggested that they were safer because they had filters, and she believed that filters would remove harmful substances in the smoke. In 1968, she switched to Virginia Slims because, she later said, they were slim and glamorous, and ads associated them with attractive, liberated women.

At this time she developed a persistent cough and worried about research linking smoking to lung cancer. Her husband placed articles on the dangers of smoking before her. She continued to smoke, relying on tobacco industry

---

[21]"Plaintiffs' Conduct as a Defense to Claims Against Cigarette Manufacturers," *Harvard Law Review*, November 1985.

[22]*Cipollone v. Liggett Group, Inc., Philip Morris, Incorporated, and Loew's Theatres, Inc.*, Civil Action No. 83-2864, D.C.N.J., April 21, 1988; *Current Opinions*, 3.5 TPLR 2.109.

[23]John E. Calfee, "The Ghost of Cigarette Advertising Past," *Regulation*, November/December 1986, p. 37.

statements denying that cigarettes caused cancer and believing that "tobacco companies wouldn't do anything that was really going to kill you."[24] In the 1970s Mrs. Cipollone switched to brands with lower tar and nicotine—Parliament and True—swayed by advertising that implied they were safer.

In 1981 she was diagnosed as having lung cancer, and in 1982 her right lung was removed. Her doctor told her to quit, but she continued to smoke in secret. In 1983 she learned that the cancer had spread and death was near. She died in October 1984, but not before bringing a lawsuit against the Liggett Group, which manufactured Chesterfield and L&M; Philip Morris, which made Parliament and Virginia Slims; and Lorillard Inc., which made True. After her death, the suit was carried on by her husband, Antonio.

Rose Cipollone brought a 14-count product liability complaint against the tobacco companies. In legal terms she alleged strict liability, negligence, and breach of warranty. Her theory was that the companies had produced unsafe products whose risks outweighed their benefits and then purposely advertised them in a way that would render health warnings ineffective. In addition, she argued that cigarettes were so addictive that health warnings on the packs were meaningless. The cigarette firms had also neglected their responsibility to warn smokers of health risks prior to 1966, when the federal warning labels became mandatory.

At first, the cigarette companies argued that the warning labels required on packages and ads since 1966 protected them from Rose Cipollone's arguments. In requiring these warning labels, they said, Congress intended to protect cigarette manufacturers from economic ruin in lawsuits such as this. In 1984 a federal district court dismissed this argument, stating that Rose Cipollone was entitled to her day in court to argue that the warnings were insufficient and ineffective.[25] This was a landmark ruling at the time, but on appeal it was partly reversed. A federal appeals court said that Liggett, Philip Morris, and Lorillard were shielded from illness claims based on smoking after 1966 because they had used warning labels since 1966.[26] But the case could go to trial if Cipollone argued that the companies acted wrongfully *before* 1966. Her attorneys elected to proceed.

The trial started in a New Jersey courtroom in 1987 and lasted five months. In closing arguments one of Rose Cipollone's attorneys summed up her case, saying that the tobacco companies had engaged in an "evil-minded conspiracy . . . that callously and with no remorse, sacrificed the lives of their loyal customers."[27] He cited subpoenaed cigarette industry memos and documents showing awareness of smoking's dangers prior to 1966 and stated that the industry had a legal and ethical duty to warn smokers. Liggett had breached an

---

[24]*Current Opinions*, op. cit., p. 2.109.

[25]*Cipollone* v. *Liggett Group, et al.*, 593 F.Supp. 1146, D.C.N.J. (1984).

[26]*Cipollone* v. *Liggett Group, et al.*, 789 F.2d 181 (3d Cir. 1986), *cert. denied*, 107 S.Ct. 907 (1987).

[27]Myron Levin, "Final Arguments Given in Smoking-Death Trial," *Los Angeles Times*, June 7, 1988, p. 16.

implied warranty before 1966 with advertising that said its products were safe. Various Chesterfield ads were introduced as evidence. After 1966, her attorney argued, she was addicted to nicotine and could not stop smoking, even when warning labels appeared.

Then tobacco industry lawyers made their closing arguments. They began by saying that of four pathologists asked to diagnose Rose Cipollone's lung tumor, three concluded that it was an atypical carcinoid, a tumor not associated with smoking in medical literature. Only one said it was a small-cell carcinoma, a common tumor in smokers. Therefore, the tumor was not shown to be caused by smoking. They went on to portray Rose Cipollone as an intelligent, well-informed woman who was aware of literature that said smoking was risky but who enjoyed it and continued anyway. Over 1.5 million smokers stop every year, so addiction is not present. She could have stopped in the fifteen years after warnings appeared on packs and ads if she had wanted to.

In June 1988 the six-member jury reached a verdict. It awarded $400,000 to the estate of Rose Cipollone, holding that Liggett was aware of the dangers of smoking before 1966 and should have done more to warn smokers. Moreover, the company had breached an implied warranty of safety in its pre-1966 ads, which the jury found misleading. A cigarette company had lost for the first time! However, the jury found Liggett, Philip Morris, and Lorillard innocent of a conspiracy to mislead the public before 1966. And, in a finding of comparative fault, it held that Rose Cipollone was 80 percent responsible for her death and Liggett only 20 percent.

The decision underlined the ethical responsibility of manufacturers to warn consumers of foreseeable risks. And it ended the era of tobacco company invulnerability. But in many ways, the tobacco industry was pleased by the outcome. The $400,000 award was costly, but it paled against the $2,000,000 that Cipollone's lawyers had put into the case over five years. The relatively small sum discouraged lawyers representing other smokers. Because cigarette firms throw a phalanx of skilled lawyers at every case, the litigation is very expensive. One litigation analyst estimated that Liggett spent $50,000,000 on the *Cipollone* case, or twenty-five times the amount spent by the plaintiff.[28] Smokers' lawyers are entrepreneurs; they take cases hoping to make money from their percentage of a final award.

In January 1990 a federal appeals court overturned the $400,000 award and ordered a new trial because the lower court's judge barred the jury from considering arguments that cigarettes were simply "unreasonably dangerous."[29] Because of this decision the net result of six years of litigation is that injured smokers have renewed opportunity to sue, and manufacturers must prepare for another round of lawsuits.

---

[28]Myron Levin, "Attorneys Disagree on Who Really Won Smoking Case," *Los Angeles Times*, June 15, 1988.

[29]Laurie P. Cohen, "Broader Suits over Cigarettes May Be Possible," *Wall Street Journal*, January 1, 1990.

THE TOBACCO INDUSTRY

Revenues from tobacco products were $35 billion in 1988, and tobacco companies employed more than 350,000 workers. Tobacco also provides an indirect livelihood for another 1.5 million, including tobacco farmers, distributors and retailers, matchbook makers, and perhaps gravediggers. Annually, the industry pays over $10 billion in federal and state taxes and contributes $2 billion to the balance of payments.

Cigarette production is dominated by two large companies: Philip Morris, with 40 percent of the domestic market, and R. J. Reynolds, with 30 percent. The remaining 30 percent of cigarette sales is divided among four other companies—Brown & Williamson, Lorillard, American Brands, and the Liggett Group. All six compete for a dwindling number of customers. As shown in Table 10-1, with the exception of 1984 and 1988, sales have declined every year from 1981 to 1988. Per capita consumption has also dropped steadily since 1963.

Cigarettes, however, are still extremely profitable for all companies selling them. To illustrate, at widely diversified Philip Morris, tobacco brought in 53 percent of 1988 revenues but 81 percent of profits.[30] There are a number of reasons for high profits. Smokers exhibit compulsive behavior, and their regular buying habits cushion cigarette sales from downswings. They also accept regular price increases by the manufacturers, though some price elasticity exists.[31] Cigarettes are simple products, made without high capital investment. The continued market growth of filter cigarettes lowers production costs because filter material is less expensive than tobacco. And tobacco prices have fallen over the past decade because farmers with low labor costs in Brazil and Zimbabwe now compete with American farmers. Ordinarily, an industry blessed with such profitability would attract new entrants. But the antitobacco storm has discouraged other consumer products companies from moving in. This reticence locks in continued high profits.

The industry environment is unique. It mixes threatening social forces with strong economic incentives. Within it, the cigarette companies have adopted broadly similar competitive strategies.[32] Central are these.

---

[30] Amy Dunkin, "Beyond Marlboro Country," *Business Week,* August 8, 1988, p. 57.

[31] It has been estimated that in the United States the price elasticity for adult smokers is -0.42, meaning that every 10 percent price increase for a pack of cigarettes reduces consumption by 4.2 percent. For teenagers, however, price elasticity is -1.4, meaning that every 10 percent price increase reduces consumption by 14 percent. See E. M. Lewit, D. Coate, and M. Grossman, "The Effects of Government Regulation on Teen-Age Smoking," *Journal of Law and Economics,* vol. 24, 1981, and K. E. Warner, "Cigarette Taxation: Doing Good by Doing Well," *Journal of Public Health Policy,* vol. 5, no. 3, 1984.

[32] There are, of course, clear differences in strategy among companies in the industry. These are discussed with much conceptual insight by Robert H. Miles in *Coffin Nails and Corporate Strategies.* Englewood Cliffs, N.J.: Prentice-Hall, 1982. In particular, Miles distinguishes between four distinctive product and market strategies—prospector, analyzer, defender, and reactor. See pp. 102–107.

Development of New Products

Playing on consumer health anxiety, companies introduced new low-tar and -nicotine brands following the surgeon general's report in 1964. In the early 1980s the industry abandoned its one-tier pricing structure, and several companies introduced discounted "generic" brands to counter price and tax increases. Today discount brands such as Doral, Cambridge, and Malibu account for over 11 percent of industry sales. Cigarettes with less sidestream smoke, thin cigarettes, and cigarettes with flavored smoke have been designed to appeal to women.

Sales to Foreign Markets

Though the American market falters, worldwide demand for cigarettes is growing, particularly in developing countries, where smoking is on the increase. Between 1985 and 1988 cigarette exports by U.S. companies rose from 59 billion to 112 billion.[33] Although only about 30 percent of Americans smoke, there are dozens of countries where more than 50 percent of the population smokes and where there are fewer restrictions on advertising and promotional practices. Recent export gains are due in part to the fall of trade barriers in some Asian countries such as Japan, where U.S. brands now have a 12 percent market share. American cigarettes have a reputation for quality and flavor which spurs their sale, and in some poorer countries they are status symbols.

Diversification

Since cigarette earnings generate a lot of cash, the manufacturers have sought out acquisitions in diversified businesses. Philip Morris, for instance, generated an average of $1.6 billion in cash annually during the 1980s and acquired a wide range of consumer products businesses, including Miller Beer, Kraft, and General Foods. Diversification cushions the company against a possible disaster in the troubled tobacco business. In the late 1980s the pace of diversification slowed and profits declined as the companies plowed income into the reduction of debt from earlier acquisitions.

Public Relations Efforts to Counter Antismoking Trends

The industry fights a persistent social and political movement directed at banning its core business. Cigarettes have been called killers and tobacco executives accused of murder by overwrought critics. Each year since 1985 over 500 bills have been introduced in state legislatures and the Congress to restrict

---

[33]Tom Graves, "Tobacco: Industry Adapts to Falling Demand," *Standard & Poor's Industry Surveys,* vol. I. New York: Standard & Poor's Corporation, April 1989, p. F38.

smoking or tobacco marketing in some way. A major goal of the tobacco companies is to maintain their image of legitimacy, defined as the rightful possession and use of power. In the past, public relations efforts focused on denial that smoking was proved to cause disease. Today, however, the overwhelming bulk of medical studies incriminates cigarettes as disease agents. So the industry has emphasized other public relations approaches. Lately, for instance, it has promoted a libertarian argument that smokers have rights which are being infringed by antismoking zealots.

Since surveys have shown that blue-collar workers and blacks are more likely to be smokers, the companies have tried to make allies of them. The Tobacco Institute and five labor unions published a booklet explaining that employers who introduced smoking restrictions might be circumventing the need for substantial air quality improvements in the workplace.[34] And the industry has funded black causes. Brown & Williamson, for example, sponsors the Kool Achiever's Award for people who work to improve inner-city areas. Large contributions are made to the United Negro College Fund and groups such as the National Black Caucus of State Legislators. When the New York City Council debated smoking bans in 1987, Hazel Dukes, president of the New York National Association for the Advancement of Colored People, was an outspoken opponent. She said smoking ordinances in the workplace were racist because white executives could smoke in their private offices; the rank and file, including most minority workers, could not smoke in common areas. The tobacco companies are also among the most generous benefactors of charitable and cultural causes. Philip Morris, for instance, is one of the country's largest sponsors of exhibits in art museums.

Promotion and Advertising

Tobacco marketers are thought to be exceptionally resourceful owing to the difficulty of their task, and they have created state-of-the-art sales campaigns. Each year they spend approximately $2.4 billion on advertising (roughly three times the amount spent on alcoholic beverage advertising). They fill magazines, newspapers, and billboards with well-researched appeals to the multiple motivations of smokers. They are adept at targeting population groups with high percentages of smokers, such as blacks and Hispanics, and groups in which the incidence of smoking is falling most slowly, such as blue-collar workers and women. About one-third of annual expenditures go to newspaper, magazine, transit, and point-of-sale ads. Another third is tied up in promotional activities, including sponsoring sports events (such as Philip Morris's Virginia Slims women's tennis tournaments) and handing out free cigarettes. The rest goes to a miscellaneous range of actions such as direct mailings and the production of videotapes.

[34]Myron Levin, "Big Tobacco Buying New Friendships," *Los Angeles Times*, May 22, 1988.

THE BATTLE OVER TOBACCO ADVERTISING

The attack on tobacco today mainly takes the form of proposals to restrict or ban advertising. Federal law already bans broadcast advertising, but antismoking forces want to go further. In Congress, bills to restrict tobacco ads have adopted three basic approaches.

1 Enact a restrictive format for advertisements. Illustrative is a 1989 bill by Representative Tom Luken (D-Ohio) requiring cigarette ads to be all text, with no pictures. These so-called "tombstone ads" would have no pictures, models, slogans, or colors. Cigarette makers would be unable to make emotional appeals with words and images.

2 Allow states and cities to adopt restrictions. Current law, based on 1969 legislation, permits only federal regulation of tobacco ads. But a 1989 bill introduced by Senator Edward Kennedy (D-Mass.) would end federal preemption and expose industry to a welter of restrictions and challenges. This approach avoids a ban and does not affect advertisements in national newspapers and magazines.

3 Enact a partial or total ban. Although it would be possible to prohibit ads in some media, such as magazines, while permitting them in others, most legislative proposals have advocated a blanket ban on all forms of advertising and promotion. Three bills before Congress in 1990 would end all media ads as well as free samples (for giveaways), sponsorship of sports events, and other marketing techniques. The Kennedy bill, mentioned above, would prohibit sponsorship of sports events such as Philip Morris's Virginia Slims tennis tournaments.

The Case against Tobacco Advertising

The attack on cigarette advertising includes these basic points.

For one thing, say the critics, smoking is harmful to consumers, and advertising increases the consumption of tobacco products. Since the early 1960s, studies have shown a relationship between smoking and illness. In 1990 Dr. Louis W. Sullivan, secretary of health and human services, estimated that smoking-related diseases cost the nation $52 billion a year in lost productivity, health-care expenses, and higher insurance premiums.[35] Other dangers exist also, including the 2,500 annual fire deaths that result from careless smoking. Advertising that depicts smoking as an attractive, worthwhile pastime encourages people to assume big health risks.

Second, tobacco ads are designed to recruit smokers in certain segments of society. Although smoking is in overall decline, certain population groups—blacks, Hispanics, blue-collar workers, women, youth, and the less educated—have a higher percentage of smokers. These groups are targeted by cig-

---

[35] "Smoking: All Clear (Cough, Cough)," *Los Angeles Times,* February 25, 1990.

arette makers seeking growth segments, but critics object to targeting because of the implication that industry is creating victims. Here is how targeting works with some of these groups.

Blacks and Hispanics The number of black and Latino smokers continues to rise. Cigarettes are heavily advertised in minority magazines and on billboards in minority communities. Rio, Dorado, and L&M Superior are special brands introduced for Hispanic smokers. About 75 percent of blacks smoke mentholated brands such as Kool, Newport, and Salem. Early in 1990 R. J. Reynolds tried to launch a new mentholated brand named Uptown to compensate for market share losses in its Salem brand, which was deemed too heavily mentholated for many black smokers. It was openly stated by the company that Uptown targeted blacks. Ads featured black couples in urban scenes. But the brand was withdrawn under fire from Health and Human Services Secretary Sullivan, who said: "Uptown's message is more disease, more suffering and more death for a group already bearing more than its share of smoking-related illness and mortality."[36]

Women Smoking rates are declining among women, but more slowly than for men. Moreover, young women start smoking in greater numbers than young men. Virginia Slims, introduced in the 1960s by Philip Morris, was the first female cigarette to be a big hit. It now leads among all "female" brands, with a market share of 3 percent. To attract women, marketers have used new cigarette production technologies to make slim and ultraslim brands (Capri and Superslims), flavored smokes (Chelsea and Spring Lemon Lights), and decorated cigarettes in packs with pastel colors, flowers, and other feminine touches (Newport Stripes 100s and Eve). Marketing themes targeting women, according to the head of a cigarette account at an ad agency, "try to tap the emerging independence and self-fulfillment of women, to make smoking a badge to express that."[37]

Youth Advertisers also target young people, and the age at which smoking begins has fallen—about 90 percent of smokers adopted the habit before the age of twenty-one. Also, brand loyalty for cigarettes is higher than for any other major consumer product; 70 percent remain faithful to one brand.[38] Therefore, attracting a beginning smoker pays long-term dividends.

The industry has a voluntary code of advertising principles requiring that ads not "appear in publications directed primarily to those under 21 years of age" and that models in cigarette ads not "appear to be under 25 years of

---

[36]James R. Schiffman, "After Uptown, Are Some Niches Out?" *Wall Street Journal*, January 22, 1990.

[37]Anonymous quotation in Peter Waldman, "Tobacco Firms Try Soft, Feminine Sell," *Wall Street Journal*, December 19, 1989.

[38]Ronald Alsop, "Brand Loyalty Is Rarely Blind Loyalty," *Wall Street Journal*, October 19, 1989, p. B1.

age," yet many ads show young-looking models. And there are frequent ads in magazines such as *Hot Rod, Rolling Stone,* and *National Lampoon,* which attract teenage readers. Of course, young models may not be necessary to attract teenagers to smoking. As one critic notes: "That 14-year-old models aren't used in these ads is irrelevant; eighth graders don't smoke cigarettes in order to look like eighth graders."[39] One study of adolescents' recall of tobacco ads found that out of their thirteen favorite magazines, only two (*Seventeen* and *Boys Life*) did not have cigarette ads.[40]

A third and related concern of the critics is that ads concocted with this type of marketing research are redolent with deception. Tobacco ads employ cleverly constructed life-style themes which associate a baleful product with suc-

---

THE VOLUNTARY ADVERTISING CODE OF CIGARETTE MANUFACTURERS

These advertising principles apply to all forms of advertising—including vehicle decals, posters, pamphlets, matchbook covers, and point-of-purchase materials—in the United States, Puerto Rico, and U.S. territorial possessions.

1 No advertising shall appear in publications directed primarily to those under 21 years of age, including school, college or university media (such as athletic, theatrical or other programs), comic books or comic supplements.
2 No one depicted in cigarette advertising shall be or appear to be under 25 years of age.
3 Cigarette advertising shall not suggest that smoking is essential to social prominence, distinction, success or sexual attraction, nor shall it picture a person smoking in an exaggerated manner.
4 Cigarette advertising may picture attractive, healthy looking persons provided there is no suggestion their attractiveness and good health are due to cigarette smoking.

5 Cigarette advertising shall not depict as a smoker anyone who is or has been well known as an athlete, nor shall it show any smoker participating in, or obviously just having participated in, a physical activity requiring stamina or athletic conditioning beyond that of normal recreation.
6 No sports or celebrity testimonials shall be used or those of others who would have special appeal to persons under 21 years of age.
7 Persons who engage in sampling shall refuse to give a sample to any person whom they know to be under 21 years of age or who, without reasonable identification to the contrary, appears to be less than 21 years of age.
8 Sampling shall not be conducted in any public place within two blocks of any centers of youth activities, such as playgrounds, schools, college campuses, or fraternity or sorority houses.
9 Persons who engage in sampling shall not urge any adult 21 years of age or over to accept a sample if the adult declines or refuses to accept such sample.

---

[39]David Owen, "The Cigarette Companies: How They Get Away with Murder, Part II," *Washington Monthly,* March 1985, p. 53.
[40]Paul M. Fischer, John W. Richards, Earl J. Berman, and Dean M. Krugman, "Recall and Eye Tracking Study of Adolescents Viewing Tobacco Advertisements," *Journal of the American Medical Association,* January 6, 1989, p. 86.

cess, adventure, romance, status, fun, and masculinity or femininity. The depiction of the quintessentially macho Marlboro cowboy or the rebellious, liberated Virginia Slims woman is geared to satisfying strong emotional needs in targeted personality types. Cigarettes are mundane physical objects, but advertising endows them with potent psychological magic. Thus an awkward male adolescent—or a middle-aged man—may smoke cigarettes to seek the aura of strength, male sensuality, and peer acceptance exemplified by the Marlboro man. The ads, in addition, imply that healthy, robust people smoke, thereby undermining health warning labels.

Tobacco Companies Defend Their Ads

The battle is joined by cigarette manufacturers. First, they argue that although they are extremely concerned about possible adverse health effects from smoking, the evidence to date does not prove that smoking causes cancer and other diseases. Their point is a precise, technical one about the nature of proof in scientific inquiry. Although epidemiological studies show a *relation* between smoking and lung cancer, they do not prove that smoking was the *cause* of that lung cancer. Rather, they simply show an association between the two. The exact mechanism of cancer causation is not yet definitively explained by science. Until it is, the tobacco companies argue that other factors known to be associated with cancer, including everything from genes to smog, may have initiated the disease process in smokers.

The literature on the health effects of smoking is vast. There are thousands of epidemiological, clinical, and laboratory studies. Like a clever judo opponent, the industry turns this massive body of work against its opponents, asking why, in over 15,000 studies, smoking has never been proved to cause cancer. Why has a mechanism of causation not been identified? Inevitably there is also bickering about methodology and the validity of various findings, as in every other scientific field. Perhaps inevitably, some studies show no relation between smoking and cancer. For example, in a series of Scandinavian studies of identical twins, one of whom smoked while the other did not, the smokers did not differ from the nonsmokers in the incidence of any illnesses, including lung cancer.[41] The evidence on the addictive nature of tobacco use is also ambiguous, say the tobacco companies.

Moreover, even where research shows smokers to be at greater risk for certain pathologies, that extra risk may be small. In 1988 the American Council of Life Insurance released actuarial tables showing how insurance companies calculated annual deaths per 1,000 insured persons. At age thirty-five, 2.63 smokers died compared with 1.69 nonsmokers—a difference of less than 1 in 1,000 and a slight risk, indeed. At age sixty-five, 36 smokers died for every 21 non-

---

[41]U.S. Senate, *Hearings before the Committee on Labor and Human Resources,* "Smoking Prevention Health and Education Act of 1983." Testimony of Hans J. Eysenck, May 6, 1983, p. 317.

smokers, an extra risk for smokers of only 15 out of 1,000.[42] As one analyst of cancer studies has noted, "every study cited in support of the statement that 'cigarette smoking causes cancer' reveals that a smoker is thoroughly unlikely to get cancer—only that he is statistically more likely to get it than a nonsmoker."[43] Data introduced as evidence in the *Cipollone* trial showed that the lifetime risk of contracting lung cancer for someone who initiates smoking as a teenager is low. Only 2 in every 100 women and 5 of every 100 men will be victimized by the disease.

In response to the charge that their marketing is designed to snare new, young smokers, the tobacco companies argue that this is not so. There is no question that children and teenagers have access to tobacco products. Twelve states have no minimum age for tobacco sales, and thirteen set the age lower than eighteen. Underage buying is heavy in states with age limits. In a study in Massachusetts, where it is illegal to sell cigarettes to anyone under age eighteen, researchers sent an eleven-year-old girl to 100 stores to buy cigarettes. She was not disguised to appear older and was told to be honest about her age if asked. She was successful in purchasing cigarettes in 75 percent of the establishments.[44] Similar results in other studies show that the social value of protecting children and teens from tobacco is weak.

The companies, however, say that they do not target this group in marketing efforts. "The simple fact is, we don't target our advertising to appeal to young people," says a Reynolds executive.[45] Research indicates that advertising ranks low among the factors leading teenagers to initiate smoking. For example, in studies of college students who smoked or used smokeless tobacco, the influence of advertising ranked ninth and eighth, respectively, out of ten factors leading to the decision to initiate tobacco use.[46] In these and other studies, the most important factors were peer pressure, tobacco use by parents and siblings, and personality variables such as rebelliousness and extroversion. Advertising is designed to encourage brand switching and get out information to smokers about new products.

Tobacco companies also reject the argument that ads toy unfairly with emotional needs. Numerous surveys indicate that 90 percent or more of both teenagers and adults believe that cigarette smoking is harmful to health and that 99

---

[42]Bob Dunn, "Why Your Life Insurance May Rate a Second Look," *Business Week,* May 30, 1988, p. 105.

[43]B. Bruce-Briggs, "The Health Police Are Blowing Smoke," *Fortune,* April 25, 1988, p. 350.

[44]Joseph R. DiFranza, Billy D. Norwood, Donald W. Garner, and Joe B. Tye, "Legislative Efforts to Protect Children from Tobacco," *Journal of the American Medical Association,* June 26, 1987, p. 3387. For similar research findings see David G. Altman, Valodi Foster, Lolly Rasenick-Douss, and Joe B. Tye, "Reducing the Illegal Sale of Cigarettes to Minors," *Journal of the American Medical Association,* January 6, 1989, p. 80.

[45]Bruce Horovitz, "Cigarette Ads: A Matter of Conscience," *Los Angeles Times,* May 2, 1989.

[46]U.S. House of Representatives, *Hearings before the Subcommittee on Health and the Environment of the Committee on Energy and Commerce,* "Tobacco Issues," July 26, 1985. Statement of John P. Foreyt, pp. 448 and 450.

percent are aware of the charge that it is dangerous.[47] Thus, they freely choose risk exposure. Cigarettes are not marketed differently than other products, and the ads are manipulative only in the sense that any ad copy tries to incorporate positive associations from life experience into product presentation. Millions see tobacco ads daily but do not become smokers. No research or statistics indicate that consumers are tricked by tobacco advertising, so the burden of proof still rests with those who would restrict it. Many factors aside from advertising influence buying decisions, including previous experience with the product, opinions of relatives and friends, and information from other sources such as churches, government, and schools. There also exists widespread skepticism toward ad content. In short, advertising is not a disquieting, powerful determiner of behavior, but it does play an important, if limited, role in informing consumers.

Finally, the tobacco companies point out that there is little hard evidence that advertising increases consumption of tobacco or that its elimination would result in declining consumption. The removal of cigarette ads from the broadcast media in 1971 was followed by years of increased consumption. Studies of European countries such as Sweden and Norway, where restrictions have been placed on advertising, show that advertising restraint generally is not followed by lowered consumption.[48] Extensive research shows no statistically significant correlation between expenditures for cigarette advertising and subsequent sales.[49] The removal of ads would only harm consumers by depriving industry of a competitive weapon and lessening the amount of information available about cigarettes. In countries with ad bans, where low-tar and -nicotine cigarettes cannot be publicized, a lower percentage of smokers buy filtered cigarettes. And some opponents of an ad ban argue that it would release the $2 billion a year spent on advertising to the earnings column on corporate balance sheets, thereby giving tobacco companies windfall profits without cutting consumption much.

WOULD A TOBACCO ADVERTISING BAN BE CONSTITUTIONAL?

Proposals for banning or restricting tobacco product advertisements raise important constitutional issues. The First Amendment protects speech from government-imposed restrictions, but courts have distinguished *political*

---

[47]For the first figure see George Gallup, "Smoking Level Declines as More Perceive Health Hazard," *The Gallup Poll*, August 31, 1981. For the second figure, see *Hearings before the Subcommittee on Transportation, Tourism, and Hazardous Materials of the Committee on Energy and Commerce*, "Cigarettes: Advertising, Testing, and Liability," June 8, 1988. Statement of Gerald M. Goldhaber, p. 442.

[48]*Tobacco Advertising Bans and Consumption in 16 Countries*. New York: International Advertising Association, 1983.

[49]For an overview see *Reducing the Health Consequences of Smoking: 25 Years of Progress. A Report of the Surgeon General*. Rockville, Md.: U.S. Department of Health and Human Services, Publication (CDC) 89-8411, 1989, pp. 503–504.

MARKETING RESTRICTIONS IN FOREIGN COUNTRIES

About twenty-five countries have enacted laws banning all cigarette advertising. More than a dozen countries, including the United States, have partial bans. Here is a sampling of approaches.

Canada

All advertising and promotion of tobacco is prohibited. Tobacco companies are barred from using brand names when sponsoring sports events, so they have set up subsidiaries named after their popular cigarette brands, and the subsidiaries are sponsors. Most magazines sold in Canada come from the United States without censorship of cigarette ads. The result? After the ad ban, American brands began selling better at the expense of Canadian competitors.

China

No warning labels are required. Broadcast, cinema, and newspaper ads are banned. Limited advertising in magazines is permitted, but permission for use of ad copy must be obtained from the government. Point-of-sale advertising is permitted at foreign currency outlets.

France

Broadcast advertising is prohibited. A small quota of newspaper and magazine ads is allowed each brand. Each pack must contain this notice: "Abuse of Smoking is Dangerous." Because of permissive attitudes about smoking in French society, the laws are circumvented. Warning labels on cigarette packs are printed in tiny letters. Cigarette manufacturers sell matches in boxes that look identical to cigarette boxes and carry cigarette brand names. Then the match brands are advertised in the print media. Other products, from lighters to boots, are advertised with cigarette brand names.

Hong Kong

Cigarette packages and print ads must include the words "cigarette smoking is hazardous to your health." Television and radio ads are prohibited. In print ads the use of celebrities and models under twenty-one is prohibited, as are testimonials by athletes. Certain themes are proscribed. For example, tobacco cannot be depicted as "indispensable for success."

Iceland

Most advertising is banned. Manufacturers must label all tobacco products with one of six pictures: blackened lungs, a bedridden patient, a pregnant woman, a diseased heart, an inflamed throat and nose, or a child. Stores may not display cigarettes.

Ireland

Three rotating health warnings are required on packages and print ads. Broadcast ads are banned. Print ads must have a plain background with one color to prevent the creation of subliminal images and preclude the association of tobacco products with other objects and activities. Reduced tar and nicotine content may not be presented as beneficial. Manufacturers may not sponsor sports events whose participants are mainly under eighteen years of age.

Japan

The words "For the Sake of Health, Let's Be Careful about Excessive Smoking" must appear on cigarette packs. Television ads are permitted only for new brands and must cease three years after introduction. Ads may be broadcast only in heavily populated areas and are prohibited from 6:00 p.m. to 8:45 p.m. No promotional activity is allowed which would encourage women to smoke, and women cannot be pictured smoking.[50]

---

[50]In Japan, early 1980s figures showed that 63 percent of men smoked, but only 12 percent of women. Susan Motley, "Burning the South: U.S. Tobacco Companies in the Third World," *Multinational Monitor,* July/August 1987, p. 9.

speech from *commercial* speech. The former is defined as speech in the broad marketplace of ideas, encompassing political, scientific, and artistic expression, and is closely protected. The latter refers to advertisements and other speech designed to stimulate business transactions and has received less protection. In both areas of speech, however, the general principle adopted by the courts to test restrictions is that the right of speech must be balanced against society's need to maintain the general welfare. The right of free speech is assumed to be a fundamental barrier against the growth of tyranny and is not tampered with or restricted lightly. So the courts ordinarily do not permit censorship of speech unless it poses a grave threat to public welfare, as it would, for example, if a speaker posed the threat of imminent violence or a writer published classified military secrets in wartime.

With respect to commercial speech, however, various restrictions have been permitted. For example, advertisements for securities offerings may appear only in the austere format of a legal notice, and, of course, cigarette and snuff advertising has been barred from television and radio. These are not total bans, of course, only restrictions. Total suppression of commercial speech about legal tobacco products, as called for in several bills now before Congress, raises major constitutional questions. Would the courts approve it?

In the case of *Central Hudson Gas & Electric Corp.* v. *Public Service Commission* in 1980, the Supreme Court struck down a New York regulation banning advertising by public utilities, a law that was intended to help conserve energy.[51] In the *Central Hudson* case the Court developed its current theory of commercial speech. Justice Lewis F. Powell, writing for the majority, set forth a four-pronged test for determining when commercial speech could be restricted.

First, the advertisement in question should promote a lawful product or activity and must be accurate. If an ad is misleading or suggests illegal activity, it does not merit protection. Second, the government interest in restricting the particular commercial speech must be substantial, not trivial or unimportant. Third, the regulation or advertising restriction clearly must further the interest of the government. In other words, it should definitely help the government reach a public-policy goal. Fourth, the suppression of commercial speech must not be more extensive than is necessary to achieve the government's purpose. Any advertising ban passed by Congress would, no doubt, be challenged by industry and would have to pass this test.[52]

EVALUATING TOBACCO ADVERTISING

In ethical theory rights and duties are linked. Hence, advertisers who receive First Amendment protection for their sales pitches must exercise their privi-

---

[51]447 U.S. 557.

[52]In 1986 proponents of an advertising ban were given heart by the Supreme Court's decision in *Posadas de Puerto Rico Associates* v. *Tourism Company of Puerto Rico* (54 LW 4960) allowing the Puerto Rican government to ban casino advertising.

lege in an ethically responsible way. At a minimum, advertisers have these general ethical duties:

1 The duty to respect life.
2 The duty to tell the truth and to make honest claims.
3 The duty to accept responsibility for the consequences of their advertisements.
4 The duty to work for positive societal impact and to avoid doing harm. This includes the duty to protect the public against the growth of excessive cynicism. Also, ads should not undermine societal values.
5 The duty to respect and preserve the free will of consumers making buying decisions.

This list of basic duties is derived from a review of discussions of advertising in the literature of business ethics.[53] In an evaluation of cigarette ads to determine whether they pass the test of meeting these duties, one consideration is the intentions of those who produce them. This is discussed in the following section.

THE PUZZLE OF TOBACCO COMPANY EXECUTIVES

Pulitzer prize–winning author William Styron tells of meeting the chief executive officer of a tobacco company at a commencement exercise. "Unfiltered cigarettes of the brand he manufactured never left his lips," reported Styron. "His complexion was sallow—no, waxen—bags hung haggardly beneath his eyes; his lips had a violet, cyanotic hue. His end of the conversation was interrupted by thick, croupy coughs." When the executive called the surgeon general a son of a bitch and his report a plot, Styron challenged him, saying that the report "made a good case." "There's not an iota of truth in the entire book," retorted the executive, "and you're very gullible if you buy any of its cheap line of garbage."[54] He turned his back on Styron, and they never spoke again.

There are so many other examples of tobacco industry executives who appear genuinely sincere in their views that automatic skepticism of their attitudes seems inappropriate. Hammish Maxwell, chairman of Philip Morris, says: "Of course we're concerned about smoking and health and the public's perception of the issue. But I have no feelings of guilt, no trouble sleeping at night."[55] The president of the Liggett Group, K. v. R. Dey, Jr., gave this

---

[53]Robert L. Arrington, "Advertising and Behavior Control," *Journal of Business Ethics,* February 1982; Gerald F. Cavanagh and Arthur F. McGovern. *Ethical Dilemmas in the Modern Corporation.* Englewood Cliffs, N.J.: Prentice-Hall, 1988, chap. 5; Roger Crisp, "Persuasive Advertising, Autonomy, and the Creation of Desire," *Journal of Business Ethics,* July 1987; Michael R. Hyman and Richard Tansey, "The Ethics of Psychoactive Ads," *Journal of Business Ethics,* January 1990; and Manuel G. Velasquez. *Business Ethics: Concepts and Cases.* 2d ed. Englewood Cliffs, N.J.: Prentice-Hall, 1988, pp. 290–300.

[54]In "Cigarette Ads and the Press: A Symposium," *The Nation,* March 7, 1987, pp. 285–86.

[55]In Alan Farnham, "His Own Best Customer," *Fortune,* August 3, 1987, p. 44.

dogged testimony in Congress in answer to questions posed by Representative Thomas Luken (D-Ohio) in 1988.

Mr. Luken: You are head of Liggett & Myers, right?
Mr. Dey: Yes sir.
Mr. Luken: You have been in that office for a long time?
Mr. Dey: Since 1977, as I stated in my opening remarks.
Mr. Luken: And you spent millions and millions of dollars on research?
Mr. Dey: Considerable amount, yes sir.
Mr. Luken: Have you ever advised the public, have you ever published anything, has Liggett & Myers ever published anything that stated that smoking cigarettes causes health problems, including cancer?
Mr. Dey: No. We do not support that. It has not been established cigarette smoking causes lung cancer or any other disease in humans.
Mr. Luken: That is your opinion?
Mr. Dey: That is our position in our company, and my opinion, yes sir.

Mr. Luken: The Surgeon General says cigarette smoking is killing more than 300,000 citizens each year. . . . Don't you believe there is some basis for saying that there is a relationship between smoking and lung cancer?
Mr. Dey: I disagree with the number. The computations are based upon assumptions that I don't agree with.

Mr. Luken: You are playing with the lives of millions of Americans.
Mr. Dey: We have a legal product and we comply with the rules and regulations.
Mr. Luken: You have a legal product which is killing, according to the overwhelming testimony and the Surgeon General of the United States, over 300,000 Americans a year. . . . Members of Congress have repeatedly said if we could ban it, we would, but the problem is there are 55 million people who are hooked on it.
Mr. Dey: I don't agree with your comment that they are hooked on it. . . .
Mr. Luken: You disagree with the Surgeon General.
Mr. Dey: The Congress of the United States put a very comprehensive bill together in 1965 and it has been amended. We adhere to and we live by, and Congress in its own way has established the rules and regulations that we live with, and I think that is sufficient, and we are going along very smoothly.
Mr. Luken: I do respect you, Mr. Dey, and other individuals in the industry. I don't respect what the industry does.[56]

In this passage Dey attempts to protect himself from criticism by asserting that cigarette sales are legal. This argument, popular in the tobacco industry, has been criticized by scholars as "ethically indefensible" because "it pre-

[56]U.S. House of Representatives, *Hearings,* "Cigarettes: Advertising, Testing, and Liability," op. cit., June 29, 1988, pp. 495–502.

sumes that all actions that are unethical have been prohibited by law."[57] Are tobacco executives acting unethically? For executives like Dey the answer hinges on whether they are being truthful. Do they believe what they say? Are they lying to the public? to themselves? Simply put, a lie is a false statement made with the intent to deceive. So for Dey to be lying to Congress two conditions would need to be met: (1) he must know that his statements are false, and (2) he must deliberately intend them to deceive Representative Luken.

In his book *Merchants of Death,* industry critic Larry C. White attributes the views of tobacco executives to the workings of cognitive dissonance, or the inner turmoil arising when a person holds incompatible beliefs simultaneously. "To be a normal law-abiding businessperson and to know that your product is the number one preventable cause of death in your country has got to produce cognitive dissonance," writes White.[58] Tobacco executives, over the course of long careers, may resolve inner conflicts by denying the hazards of smoking. In fact, denial could be quite genuine and essential to long-term emotional health. To the extent that people who create tobacco advertising are controlling anxiety in this fashion, the charge of intentional deception and outright lying is mitigated.

CONCLUSION

While advertising restrictions are debated, sales of cigarettes in the United States continue to drop. The cigarette companies are finding it harder to place ads. Already, over thirty magazines no longer accept tobacco advertising, including *Good Housekeeping, National Geographic,* and *Reader's Digest.* The debate in Congress and society is complex, involving medical, religious, and ethical aspects. But in the end, two factors will be most important in resolving the issue of advertising restrictions. The first is the relative political strength of the economic interests versus the political strength of reform groups. The second is the ultimate determination of the constitutionality of any restrictions on commercial speech that may be enacted.

SOME QUESTIONS

Many questions are raised by the foregoing discussion. Among the most important are these:

1 Should cigarette advertising and promotion be further restricted? The public is well aware of the dangers posed by smoking, so is it necessary for the government to further regulate industry practice?

2 If further regulation is appropriate, what kind is preferable?

---

[57]Cavanagh and McGovern, op. cit., pp. 94–95.
[58]New York: Beech Tree Books, 1988, p. 187.

3 Would a ban on broadcast advertising for cigarettes be constitutional? Apply the four-pronged test set forth by the Supreme Court in the *Central Hudson* case to reach a conclusion.

4 What is your opinion of cigarette ads?

- Are certain ads misleading? Which ones? What is misleading about them?
- Are intentionally persuasive ads powerful enough to unknowingly manipulate consumers? Or are their blandishments a trivial part of modern American culture that everyone can cope with?
- Do tobacco companies that fight for their right to advertise generally fulfill their corresponding ethical duty to be informative and honest?
- In a broad sense, what social values are upheld by cigarette ads? Are any important values undermined?

5 Given the existing social, political, economic, and scientific and technological forces in their environment, what strategies and actions make sense for cigarette manufacturers today?

THE KKR–RJR NABISCO BLOCKBUSTER LEVERAGED BUYOUT*

Richard Joshua Reynolds left his father's Virginia tobacco farm in 1875 to build a factory in Winston, North Carolina. The factory cost $2,400, covered less area than today's tennis court, and employed two regular assistants and occasional seasonal helpers. Chewing tobaccos were the only products made in the early years of the company. In 1907 he introduced Prince Albert pipe tobacco, which soon became a top-selling brand, and it still is today. A year later he introduced the Camel brand cigarette, which became an instant best-seller, and it still is to this day.

This little company became RJR Nabisco, Inc. (RJR), the nineteenth largest industrial corporation in the United States in 1988, as measured by sales of $16.9 billion. Profits amounted to almost $1.4 billion, and the company employed 120,000 people around the world. On November 30, 1988, RJR was bought by Kohlberg Kravis Roberts & Co. (KKR) for $25.1 billion in a leveraged buyout (LBO).

This was by far the largest corporate buyout in U.S. history and one of the most controversial. It was the pinnacle of a frenzied era of corporate takeovers with the use of so-called "junk bonds" in leveraged buyouts (LBOs). Since then the wave of corporate LBO takeovers has somewhat subsided, but the basic issues remain. They encompass fundamental questions of corporate governance, business ethics, managerial motivations, corporate economic stability, and employee and community welfare.

*By George A. Steiner, Harry and Elsa Kunin Professor of Business and Society and professor of management emeritus, UCLA.

WHAT IS AN LBO?

The acronym *LBO* is used to describe a variety of transactions concerned with mergers and acquisitions among corporations. *Leverage* refers to the use of bonds or debt to pay for the common stock of a company, rather than the use of cash or the sale of more common stock. Leverage, therefore, refers to the employment of debt as distinct from equity (or common stock) to acquire a company. Most corporate acquisitions today are leveraged to some extent, but not all. Some may be accomplished solely by the use of cash or the exchange of stock. For example, Grand Metropolitan, a British beverage and food company, acquired Pillsbury, a major U.S. food company, in 1989 for $5.7 billion in cash. Bristol-Myers, a pharmaceutical company, acquired Squibb, another pharmaceutical company, in 1989 for an exchange of stock valued at $12.7 billion.

LBOs are a form of corporate *takeover*. A takeover may be arranged by only the managers of a company, or by the managers with outside partners, or only by an outside buyout specialist. The common, or ownership, stock of the company is acquired and retired.

The takeover may be friendly or hostile. All parties agree in a friendly takeover. A hostile one takes place when an unwanted suitor buys up enough stock to control the company. This usually involves a *tender offer* in which the suitor, often called a *raider* and sometimes worse names, offers to buy stock on the market at a fixed price for a specific period of time.

Leveraged buyouts may result in a company "going private." In such a case, all the stock is bought and then retired, and none exists on the market. Or a company may merge with another corporation and keep the same name, or it may get a different name. Or the company may continue with the same name but have a different set of top managers and owners.[1] Among the 400 largest nonpublic companies compiled by *Forbes* magazine in 1987, 25 percent became private between 1980 and 1987. Some of them were among our largest companies, such as R. H. Macy, Borg-Warner, and Owens-Illinois. The chart in Figure 11-1 shows how a typical LBO takes place.

The KKR-RJR story began with RJR management's interest in buying the company, as the chart shows, but it wound up almost a hostile takeover so far as the chief executive officer of RJR was concerned. The reader must know,

---

[1]This is the meaning of *leverage* used in this study. The word, however, has other meanings. It is often used to refer to transactions undertaken to recapitalize or restructure the financial arrangements of a corporation. For more elaborate definitions see Carolyn Kay Brancato and Kevin F. Winch. *Leveraged Buyouts and the Pot of Gold: Trends, Public Policy, and Case Studies,* Report prepared by the Economics Division of the Congressional Research Service for the Subcommittee on Oversight and Investigations of the Committee on Energy and Commerce, U.S. House of Representatives. Washington, D.C.: U.S. Government Printing Office, December 1987. For references on mergers, acquisitions, and leveraged buyouts see, for example, Robert S. Kirk, *Corporate Mergers and Acquisitions: Selected References, 1986–1989,* and Robert Howe, *Leveraged Buyouts: Selected References, 1987–1989,* Washington, D.C.: Congressional Research Service, Library of Congress, February 1989.

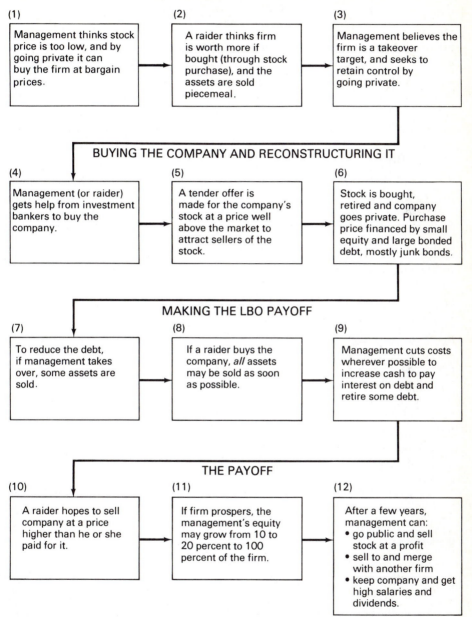

MOTIVATIONS FOR STARTING LBOS

(1)
Management thinks stock price is too low, and by going private it can buy the firm at bargain prices.

(2)
A raider thinks firm is worth more if bought (through stock purchase), and the assets are sold piecemeal.

(3)
Management believes the firm is a takeover target, and seeks to retain control by going private.

BUYING THE COMPANY AND RECONSTRUCTURING IT

(4)
Management (or raider) gets help from investment bankers to buy the company.

(5)
A tender offer is made for the company's stock at a price well above the market to attract sellers of the stock.

(6)
Stock is bought, retired and company goes private. Purchase price financed by small equity and large bonded debt, mostly junk bonds.

MAKING THE LBO PAYOFF

(7)
To reduce the debt, if management takes over, some assets are sold.

(8)
If a raider buys the company, *all* assets may be sold as soon as possible.

(9)
Management cuts costs wherever possible to increase cash to pay interest on debt and retire some debt.

THE PAYOFF

(10)
A raider hopes to sell company at a price higher than he or she paid for it.

(11)
If firm prospers, the management's equity may grow from 10 to 20 percent to 100 percent of the firm.

(12)
After a few years, management can:
- go public and sell stock at a profit
- sell to and merge with another firm
- keep company and get high salaries and dividends.

FIGURE 11-1
How LBOs work.

however, that while the basic elements of all LBOs are much the same as depicted in the chart, in many respects each case can differ.

THE GROWTH OF MERGERS AND ACQUISITIONS

LBOs like that of KKR-RJR should be considered as a part of a broader American merger and acquisition history. The United States has seen four major waves of corporate mergers, and each one involved different motivations, methods of financing, and combinations of companies.

The first wave took place from about 1893 to 1904. This wave was marked by huge combinations of firms in the same industry, such as steel, oil, and shipping. The second wave took place from about 1925 to 1929. In this wave companies that were combined produced a product from raw materials to finished goods. Also, many combinations were of a conglomerate nature, or were aggregations of companies in different lines of business. A third wave took place in the 1960s and 1970s and was dominated by conglomerate mergers. The fourth wave began around 1980 and continues to this day, although the pace has declined since 1988. This wave was marked by LBOs of both a hostile and friendly nature.

The LBO as a corporate combination device is not new. In 1901 the financier J. P. Morgan brought together a number of companies to form the United States Steel Corporation for $1.4 billion (about $23 billion in today's prices). Bonds were sold, backed by the assets of the acquired companies, to finance the deal. This method was used to finance many combinations over the years, but the use of cash and the exchange of equity securities were also used extensively.

As defined above, LBOs are not new. What is new that has raised such a ruckus in business, political, academic, and community circles? What is new are significant differences between recent LBOs and those of the past. There are three significant differences. First are the motivations of the takeover. Second is the magnitude of dollars involved in takeovers. And third are the methods of financing and the huge profits frequently generated for those taking over a company.

Motivations

Takeovers can be divided into two categories on the basis of motivations. In the first category, synergistic takeovers, the motivational force is the prospect of benefits flowing to both firms involved in the takeover. The second category is what might be called entrepreneurial profit-driven takeovers. There are two subgroups in this classification. One is based on the idea that existing management is inefficient and new management will improve corporate performance, profits, and stock price. The second is based upon a simple assumption, as shown in Figure 11-1: that the parts when sold are worth more than the whole.

In the past and still today the majority of mergers and acquisitions are in the first category. There are many reasons for one company wishing to acquire another, such as the need for a new technology, a marketing skill, an engineering capability, a new product line, or special research competence. Or a company may calculate that in order to grow it is cheaper to acquire another firm than to build new facilities.

From about 1984 and into the 1990s more and more takeovers have been motivated by a desire on the part of the initiators to make a lot of money quickly. Although the total number of LBOs and the dollar amounts involved are small compared with all mergers and acquisitions, they raise serious issues about corporate America.

Magnitude of LBO Dollar Volume

IDD Information and Services, a source of merger and acquisition data, says that the transaction value of all mergers and acquisitions in 1984, the first year of creditable comparison with LBOs, was $106.7 billion. There were 1,477 reported for that year. By 1988 the total value had risen to $309.9 billion, and 3,666 transactions were reported for that year. During these years LBOs increased from $13.4 billion in valuation with 105 companies involved to $37 billion in 1988 with 20 companies involved. The 1988 figures do not include the $25.1 billion KKR-RJR deal, which was consummated in 1989.[2] Since 1988 the dollar volume of takeovers and the number of takeovers have declined.

Methods of Financing and Huge Profits

A major feature of current LBOs is the heavy use of so-called "junk bonds" to finance them. These bonds pay interest from 3 to 5 percent over that of high-grade corporate bonds, giving them a yield of 13 to 18 percent. The high interest rate, of course, represents high risk, and the adjective *junk* is a wordplay on their lower quality. The use of lower-grade securities in corporate finance certainly is not new. What is new is their concentrated use in takeovers, which results in what many consider to be excessively heavy debt loads. Junk bonds outstanding grew from about $15 billion in 1980 to about $200 billion in 1990. In 1988 about 25 percent of all new corporate bond issues were junk bonds.[3]

As shown above, the number of individual transactions has declined while the total valuation of individual LBOs has increased. The KKR takeover was about four times as large as the largest prior LBO, which was the takeover of Federated Department Stores by Campeau Corp., a Canadian company, for $6.6 billion. The next largest takeover to go private involved Beatrice Cos. for $6.2 billion.

---

[2]Different authorities have different numbers for these transactions because there are various ways to define terms. We think that the numbers given, however, are consistent with one another and within the "ballpark" range of what really has taken place.

[3]Telephone conversation with Martin S. Fridson of Morgan Stanley. For a detailed discussion of junk bonds see Kevin F. Winch. *Junk Bonds: 1988 Status Report*. Washington, D.C.: Congressional Research Service, Library of Congress, 1988.

Such large numbers result in substantial fees to investment bankers, lawyers, and consultants who are involved in the LBO. Later we will present the estimated fees received in the KKR-RJR LBO.

Some acquiring companies may intend to take over a firm and sell assets for quick profit. For example, Metromedia, Inc., went private in 1984 for $1.1 billion. By early 1987 it had raised five times that amount by liquidating assets for a total of $6.5 billion.

Some LBOs are made with a view of restructuring a company to be sold later at a profit. For example, The Leslie Fay Companies, makers of women's apparel, went private in 1982 for $58 million and then went public in 1986 for $521 million.

In 1986 the management of Safeway Stores, Inc., joined a KKR group of investors in an LBO that took the company private. In 1990 they sold 10 percent of the company (but none of their own shares) to the public. The price they received valued their own shares at more than four times their original cash investment, and they still own a majority interest in the company.

Some corporate raiders are attracted to takeovers for what has been called "greenmail" payments. "Greenmail" is paid when a company buys the stock accumulated by a raider at a premium price to get the raider to stop the takeover attempt. Raiders often claim that they really want to take over a company and run it more efficiently, but actually their hidden agenda often is "greenmail" or dismantlement for their profit. Someone correctly commented: "The objective of the typical raider is not to save the fort, but to dismantle it." British raider Sir James Goldsmith, who has profited substantially in a number of his forays, says that takeovers are "for the public good, but that is not why I do it. I do it to make money."[4]

Perhaps the bitterest complaints about LBOs are directed at such practices. William Simon, former secretary of the U.S. Treasury, was asked what he thought about greenmail. He replied:

> Greenmail is nothing more than extortion by pinstripe bandits. It is a calculated raid of corporate assets, not for the purpose of creating a stronger, more productive, more profitable company, but simply for a quick killing. I don't claim that greenmailing is illegal, but I think it is immoral and a disgrace to U.S. business. There's no stronger proponent of competitive free enterprise capitalism than Bill Simon, but I believe deeply that no economic system can long survive if it is separated from a sense of morality, justice, and fair play.[5]

Why Heavily Leveraged Buyouts in Recent Years?

There is no simple answer to this question, but a number of significant phenomena help to explain it. In no order of importance the following reasons are given:

---

[4]Stewart Toy, "The Raiders," *Business Week*, March 4, 1985, p. 81.
[5]Quoted in *Business and Society Review*, Fall 1985, p. 19.

• The stock of a company is perceived to be undervalued, and financial entrepreneurs see an opportunity to profit by an LBO.

• The tax codes give an advantage to bonded indebtedness over stock because the interest is tax-deductible, while dividends on stock are not.

• New federal government antitrust policy, especially in the Reagan administration, winked at mergers which heretofore would have been declared illegal and prohibited.

• Huge pools of cash have grown, and the managers of them are pressured to show above-average short-term gains (for example, in pension funds, insurance companies, and money market funds). They thus are attracted to high-yielding junk bonds. See Figure 11-2.

• The skill of investment bankers in tapping these large pools of cash to buy junk bonds must not be underestimated.

• The economy has been growing with stability in the period from 1983 to this writing (summer 1989).

• Finally, the large fees paid to advisers of takeover entrepreneurs stimulate the search for likely takeover candidates and aggressive action in pursuing them. Since fees can amount to as much as 6 percent of the takeover price, the dollar value of fees can be large. Also, the fees are paid up front, or as soon as the transaction is completed.

PUTTING RJR "IN PLAY"[6]

It was customary for F. Ross Johnson, president and CEO of RJR, to invite board members to dinner the evening before a scheduled board meeting. At such a dinner on October 19, 1988, Johnson announced that he was thinking about leading a leveraged buyout of the company, but he said he would not pursue it if the board thought it unwise for him to do so. From all accounts the board was stunned with the proposal but did not object. In an interview later, Charles E. Hugel, chairman of Combustion Engineering and chairman of the RJR board, said: "We came to the conclusion that shareholders would be best served by a short-term gain."[7]

Hugel had brought to the dinner meeting Peter Atkins, a partner in the New York law firm of Skadden, Arps, Slate, Meagher & Flom. Atkins advised the board that Johnson's proposal was, in legal parlance, a material one and that a press release about it was mandatory immediately. The announcement was made, and in the words of Wall Street, RJR was "in play."

---

[6]Part of the language of LBOs is that of the gambler. Companies that are involved in management LBOs or are targets of others are said to be "in play." People engaged in a takeover are called "players." Some of them are called "major players." The potential rewards and risks equation is spoken of as "high stakes." As noted previously, and as will be noted later, there are other words peculiar to current takeovers. Some of them follow the language of combat, such as "raider" and "white knight."

[7]John Helyar and Bryan Burrough, "RJR Nabisco Board Asserts Independence in Buy-out Decisions," *Wall Street Journal*, November 1, 1988.

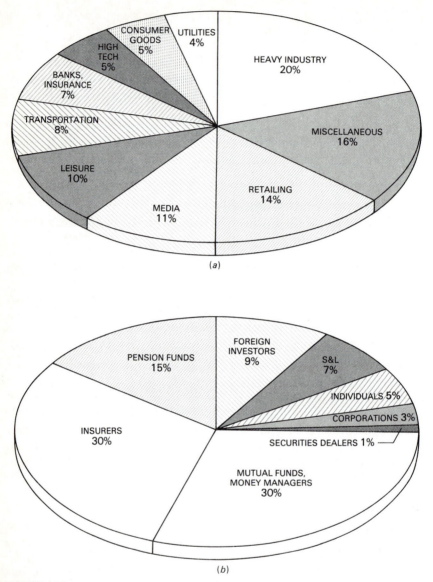

FIGURE 11-2
Who has issued and who has bought junk bonds? (a) Junk bonds outstanding as of the end of 1988; (b) purchasers of junk bonds as of the end of 1988. (*Source: David Zigas and Larry Light, "Don't Put Away the Smelling Salts Yet,"* Business Week, *October 2, 1989, pp. 92–93.*)

While Johnson's proposal may have surprised the board, it had been brewing in his mind for some time. It was triggered by his conviction that the stock was worth much more than it was selling for on the market. As CEO and a large stockholder he believed he should do something to revive the price.

At a board planning meeting in March 1988 Johnson first began to work on the problem. A number of proposals were examined. One was to buy another food company, but at the time these companies were selling at a higher price than he wanted to pay. He studied a joint venture with another food company, but that, too, was rejected. He considered RJR going into the open market to buy back company shares on the assumption that a smaller number of shares outstanding would mean higher per share dividends and hence higher stock prices. But that and a number of other suggestions were rejected. He raised the annual dividend 15 percent in July, but the stock price did not move. He was frustrated.

Prior to the stock market crash in 1987 Johnson was playing golf with Donald Kelly, who had worked with KKR on the Beatrice buyout, and Ira Harris, an investment banker. Kelly suggested that Johnson think about taking RJR private. They thought they should have dinner with Henry Kravis of KKR, an expert in LBOs. At the dinner they all discussed an LBO, but Johnson was not in favor of it at the time, since the stock then was selling for around $70 a share. Shortly thereafter the stock plummeted to the low $50s, and the LBO idea was revived in Johnson's mind.

Johnson had a rapid career rise in RJR. He was president of Standard Brands, producer of Planters nuts and Baby Ruth candy bars, when it merged with Nabisco in 1981. Four years later, as Nabisco president, he sold the company to RJR for $4.9 billion and soon became president of the merged companies. Born in Winnipeg, Manitoba, Canada, Johnson became a tough, direct, no-nonsense "can-do" manager. At the same time he was generous with executive expense accounts. He also believed that a person should have fun running a business. He is a fashionable dresser and is described by some associates as a "charmer" and by others as ruthless in dealing with employees when he is displeased. He lives regally among three houses filled with valuable artworks. In his career he has bought and sold companies without agonizing over decisions. Throughout, he has had, in the words of one viewer, "an uncanny ability to end up on top."[8]

THE BIDDING FOR RJR

What began as a friendly bidding process wound up as a rancorous, bitter, and exhausting takeover battle between RJR management, led by Johnson, and KKR, led by Kravis. Johnson made his first tentative estimate of what his idea of a proper LBO price would be at the October dinner meeting with the board. He suggested $75 a share. Hugel said any acceptable LBO price had to be well over the highest price of $71 yet recorded for the stock. Johnson may have thought he had a deal, because following the announcement the next day after

---

[8]Jonathan Peterson, "Winning Streak Ends for RJR's J. Ross Johnson," *Los Angeles Times,* December 2, 1988; and Sandra L. Kirsch, "They Cleaned Our Clock," *Fortune,* January 2, 1989.

the board meeting he said "now we've got to go find $17 million."[9] Four days later KKR put in a bid of $90 a share, which totaled $20.7 billion. KKR had for some time been evaluating RJR, and so it had information at hand upon which to base its bid. Following these announcements RJR stock began to soar in price.

On October 25 Peter A. Cohen of Shearson Lehman Hutton, Johnson's investment banker, met with Kravis for breakfast to try to work out an agreement by which KKR and RJR management would jointly buy out RJR. Many different approaches were discussed, and intensive meetings went on for some time. Disagreement among the investment bankers for the two sides, however, ended the talks. Aside from the question of who would be the lead banker and make the most money, there was personal animosity between the banking groups.

Johnson's group raised its bid on November 3 to $92 a share, or $21.16 billion. The special board committee set up to evaluate bids then had two bids before it. The board felt, however, that neither one was bona fide, since neither group had paid commitment fees for financing. The committee then decided to establish ground rules for additional bidding (including the use of sealed bids to discourage alliances between groups) and to set a deadline of November 18 for final bids. It also said that any bid for the company not following its ground rules would be considered hostile.

Despite spirited bidding by KKR and the RJR management, the two sides again came to a tentative agreement for a joint offer on a fifty-fifty basis. Under the plan the sides would have equal control of the company, and Johnson would continue to run the company with more autonomy than executives in other KKR-financed businesses.[10] But again the talks failed.

Negotiations before the November 18 deadline were feverish. KKR asked the special committee for equal access to crucial financial information which RJR had. The board agreed, and Kravis, with his partner George Roberts, met with RJR officials. They claimed later that they had not been given correct information. The Johnson group denied this and countered with the assertion that KKR had an informant on the RJR board who tipped off KKR about the Johnson bid. That was denied. On November 18, KKR raised its bid to $94, and Johnson bid $100.

In the meantime, The First Boston Group said it was considering an offer of $23.8 to $26.8 billion, which amounted to between $105 and $118 per share. Because the special board committee would not have enough time to evaluate properly this bid before the November 18 deadline, it extended the deadline to November 29. First Boston had trouble finding funding and later withdrew its bid.

On November 29, KKR had on the table an offer of $106 per share, and

[9]Ibid, Kirsch, p. 73.
[10]Bryan Burrough and John Helyar, "RJR's Management Offers $21.16 Billion for Concern after Talks with KKR Fail," *Wall Street Journal*, April 27, 1989.

Johnson's bid was $101. Both were a combination of cash and securities. Johnson learned details of the KKR bid and asked to appear before the RJR board, which he did in the morning of November 30, to have a revised offer of $108 considered. Later that day Johnson was asked to make one last, and definitely the final, bid. He offered $112 in cash and securities, but an evaluation by the board's bankers concluded that offer was fairly valued at $109. Later in the evening the KKR group was given a last chance to bid. Its final offer was also $109.

The bidding was closed, and shortly thereafter Kravis was named the winner for $25.1 billion.[11]

There was no exuberant celebration in the KKR camp. They were exhausted after many days and nights of negotiating. For weeks Kravis said he would awaken in the middle of the night and wrestle with questions about the RJR deal. In the process he said he lost eight pounds. "It's just the greatest diet," he said.[12]

In the last few hours of the bidding process acrimonious accusations flew from both camps. Lawyers penned strong and often vitriolic letters to the board. Charges were made of misleading statements, double-dealings, and leaked information. One observer commented: "The spectacle underscored the RJR Nabisco battle's reputation for producing some of the most-brazen displays of ego and hubris in Wall Street history, and soiled an auction process whose handlers had hoped would serve as a model of orderliness for the public, corporate America and a Congress that increasingly is becoming wary of big takeovers."[13]

WHY KKR WON AND JOHNSON LOST

In the last frenzied hours of the bidding to meet the November 18 deadline, Johnson thought he had won, but the First Boston bid led the board to postpone the deadline. Then, again, in the last hours of the final, third wave of bidding, he thought he had won. When the results were announced, he thought his bid was about the same as that of KKR and that his past friendly relationships with the board would carry the day for him and his associates. But that did not happen. Why? The reasons why will always remain a matter of speculation, but there are a number of factors which observers say are quite convincing.

First, Johnson made a mistake in setting his first offer at $75 a share. Kravis commented later that at the time he thought the price was too low, hence his interest in bidding higher. He said he could not tell whether at the price Johnson set he really wanted to put the company up for sale or own it. "If the

[11]*RJR Nabisco, Inc. Notice of Special Meeting of Stockholders to Be Held Thursday, April 27, 1989.*
[12]Michael O'Neill, "Greed Really Turns Me Off," *Fortune,* January 2, 1989.
[13]Bryan Burrough, "KKR Wins Bidding War for RJR with Offer Totaling $25.07 Billion," *Wall Street Journal,* December 1, 1988.

latter," he said, "the one thing we were very certain of was that the management group was stealing the company."[14] Some members of the board thought the same thing, and Johnson lost some of their goodwill as a result.

On November 5 *The New York Times* published an article that gave some of the details of the compensation package contained in Johnson's bid. For a modest equity in RJR a small management group could wind up owning a large part of the company, worth well over a billion dollars.[15] Johnson said this number was much too high, and anyway, he assumed that the suggested compensation package was negotiable.

Despite these disclaimers the label of "greed" stuck to Johnson throughout the negotiations. Directors were also offended because they had to learn through the press about the "sweet deals" proposed for Johnson and his small management group.[16] Other events also peeved and angered board members. For example, they were offended when KKR and Johnson began public brawling over a possible joint bid. So, the high goodwill Johnson had with the board before October 19, 1988, gradually eroded. One special committee member commented: "There's no substitute for trust and no excuse for surprises between management and the board."[17]

The board gave the KKR bid higher grades than the Johnson bid because KKR promised to keep as many food companies as it could, whereas the Johnson group planned to sell all the food companies. This group was tagged "bust-up artists" because it wanted to sell so much of the company to reduce the debt to be incurred in the LBO.[18] Furthermore, Kravis promised to be especially considerate of employee interests.

THE ROLE OF THE RJR NABISCO BOARD OF DIRECTORS

Service on the RJR board prior to October 19, 1988, appeared to many observers to be comfortable and well paid, to offer a chance to visit with corporate peers, to provide access to perks such as the company airplane, and to involve little work. The board was composed of RJR officers and outside directors handpicked by Johnson. He was sensitive to their interests and expected them to support him. He is reported to have said: " . . . if I'm there for them, they'll be there for me."[19] As it turned out, of course, the board did not support him.

A special committee of outside directors was selected to administer the bidding process, evaluate the bids, and make recommendations to the full board.

---

[14]O'Neill, op. cit., p. 70.

[15]James Sterngold, "Nabisco Executives to Take Huge Gains in Their Buyout," *The New York Times,* November 5, 1988.

[16]John Helyar and Bryan Burrough, "Nobody's Tool: RJR Nabisco Board Asserts Independence in Buy-out Decisions," *Wall Street Journal,* November 8, 1988.

[17]Bill Saporito, "How Ross Johnson Blew the Buyout," *Fortune,* April 24, 1989.

[18]Ibid. The food companies included such well-known names as Planters nuts, Baby Ruth and Butterfinger candies, Life Savers, Oreo biscuits, and Del Monte—literally hundreds of food products.

[19]Helyar and Burrough, op. cit.

Aside from Hugel the board members were Martin S. Davis, CEO of Gulf & Western; Albert L. Butler, Jr., a Winston-Salem businessman; William S. Anderson, the former chairman of NCR Corp.; and John Macomber, the former chairman of Celanese. This board hired a large staff of legal and investment advisers.

Throughout the process the board displayed independence of thought and gave careful attention to vital issues—corporate and public—surrounding its responsibilities. This demeanor is in sharp contrast to the day when directors rubber-stamped management decisions. Today more and more board members try to avoid even the perception of favoring management's interests over those of stockholders and other stakeholders in the enterprise. This attention is due to legal decisions as well as widespread surveillance of corporate actions by public interest groups and corporate investors. There are still boards whose directors go along with management without dissent, but the trend is in the reverse direction, especially among larger companies.

Today, says George Jarrell, in takeover situations, boards are obligated to do a number of things:

• They must set up special committees of outside directors to evaluate bids and make recommendations to the full board of directors.
• The committee should hire independent advisers to help it evaluate bids.
• The committee should spend an appropriate amount of time evaluating the bids.
• The committee should avoid negotiating with but one bidder and try to start an auction with several bidders.[20]

The RJR board met these standards and more. It was careful to get the best legal and financial advice to be sure that all pertinent laws, regulations, and court decisions were followed. It reflected broad concerns about the social responsibilities of corporations in seeking to balance the interests of the principal stakeholders in the enterprise. It sought to be impartial in its decisions with respect to the bidders.

WHO AND WHAT IS KKR?

KKR was formed in 1976 when Jerome Kohlberg and two professionals, Kravis and Roberts, at Bear Stearns & Co., left to set up Kohlberg, Kravis and Roberts. They began with an investment of $23 million. Their first major LBO valued at $1 billion came in 1984. In that same year the firm stunned Wall Street with a bid of $12 billion for Gulf Oil. That bid fell through when Chevron became a "white knight" (a company asked by a target company's management to save the target company from a raider by buying it out) and acquired

---

[20]Paul Richter and Jonathan Peterson, "RJR Deal May Set New Standards for Outside Directors," *Los Angeles Times*, December 3, 1988.

Gulf for $14.3 billion. But the pace did not slacken, and between 1985 and 1989 KKR engineered four of the ten largest corporate acquisitions.[21]

Today, KKR is probably the largest private company in the United States. It controls, through corporate partnerships, companies with revenues over $50 billion, a level matching the revenues of such giants as IBM and General Electric.

Until recent years the policy of KKR was to pursue only friendly buyouts. In these transactions KKR helped managers of targeted companies to acquire their own companies. But as stock prices rose, competition by other investment bankers increased, and the number of large potential buyout prospects declined, KKR become more combative. Kohlberg did not share this aggressive posture and left KKR in 1988 to form his own company, Kohlberg & Company.

KKR's policy is to enter a partnership arrangement with the management of a company interested in going private. KKR finances the deal with its own and borrowed funds. The policy includes giving the managers substantial autonomy to run their company, and they are expected to improve the cash flow so that the company can be sold back either to management or to the general public at a substantial profit. In 1988 there were twenty-six companies owned by KKR in partnership with managers of other companies. The KKR percentage of ownership was less than 50 in only five companies. Ownership for most of the others was in the range of 80 to 90 percent.[22]

The firm has tapped billions of dollars from investors to be put in blind investment pools (these investors, called "passive," authorize KKR to invest for them, or to buy for them bonds and other securities involved in the buyouts). If sufficient funds are not available from this source, bonds are sold to other investors. KKR has had no trouble in tapping virtually unlimited funds for its investment pools because it has rewarded investors. Passive investors have received returns of 40 to 50 percent annually. Bondholders have received interest payments at rates in excess of those of high-grade corporate bonds.[23]

At age forty-four, Kravis enjoys a socially active and opulent life-style. He owns four palatial residences and possesses an expensive art collection. He is a philanthropist, having donated $10 million to the Metropolitan Museum of Art in New York City for a wing built in his name and $10 million to Mount Sinai Medical Center for the Kravis Women's and Children's Center.

Roberts (age forty-five and a cousin of Kravis's) runs the firm's San Francisco office. He maintains a low profile. In an interview with *Fortune* magazine, Kravis said his working relationships with Roberts were phenomenal. He said they talk with each other at least once a day and make decisions together.

---

[21]Christopher Farrell, Gary Weiss, David Zigas, Mark Vamos, and Scott Ticer, "King Henry," *Business Week*, November 14, 1988.

[22]Bill Sing, "Big, Bigger, Biggest," *Los Angeles Times*, December 3, 1988.

[23]Farrell et. al., op. cit.

"If one of us feels very strongly about not doing something, we don't do it," he said.[24]

WHO WON AND WHO LOST IN THE KKR-RJR DEAL?

Since the focus in this study is on the KKR LBO, the following estimate is presented to explain briefly who won and who lost in that deal. It can also serve as a point of departure for the wider analysis of major issues raised by LBOs that follows.

SIGNIFICANT MAJOR ISSUES RAISED BY LBOs

In the examination of issues that are front and center in today's debates about LBOs, two points of perspective should be noted. First, it is worth repeating that no two LBOs are exactly alike, and hard data about them is difficult to find. Second, qualified experts have diametrically opposed views about LBOs in general and with respect to major issues swirling about them. For example, so far as LBOs in general are concerned, John Creedon, president of Metropolitan Life, says: "What is being done threatens the very basis of our capitalistic system."[25] On the other hand there are many strong defenders of LBOs who claim that they strengthen the capitalistic system. Indeed, the bulk of the academic economic literature on the subject looks upon LBOs as a natural and beneficial operation of the free market system which promotes efficiency to the benefit of society.[26]

Are LBOs Fair to Major Stakeholders of the Corporations Involved?

Stockholders No one disputes the fact that shareholders of a target company usually receive a significant premium for their stock when an LBO is consummated. Michael Jensen summarized the results of more than a dozen studies and concluded from them that shareholders who surrendered their stock in successful takeovers profited with a premium of 30 percent.[27]

It is frequently argued that the premium paid for the stock in tender offers

---

[24]O'Neill, op. cit. See also Farrell, et. al., op. cit.

[25]John Greenwald, "Where's the Limit?" *Time,* December 5, 1988.

[26]For brief surveys of economic literature on the subject see, for example, Murray L. Weidenbaum, "Strategies for Responding to Corporate Takeovers," and Richard E. Cook, "What the Economics Literature Has to Say about Takeovers," in Murray L. Weidenbaum and Kenneth W. Chilton, eds. *Public Policy toward Corporate Takeovers.* New Brunswick, N.J.: Transaction Books, 1988. See also Thomas M. Humbert. *Ten Myths about Leveraged Buyouts.* Washington, D.C.: The Heritage Foundation, 1989, and Michael Jensen, "Takeovers: Folklore and Science," *Harvard Business Review,* November–December 1984. For a summary of differing views and for additional references see *Corporate Takeovers: Public Policy and Implications for the Economy and Corporate Governance.* Report from the chairman of the Subcommittee on Telecommunications, Consumer Protection, and Finance of the Committee on Energy and Commerce, U.S. House of Representatives, Washington, D.C.: U.S. Government Printing Office, December 1986.

[27]Jensen, op. cit.

ONE PLAYER'S GAIN IS ANOTHER'S PAIN

In a buyout as gigantic as RJR Nabisco's, which could cost from $21 billion to $27 billion, even the smallest pieces of the action will translate into tidy fortunes. The deal may generate some hefty losses as well.

Shareholders. $8 billion to $14 billion in profits

Before Oct. 20, when the public first learned that the food-and-tobacco company was in play, RJR's 225 million shares traded at $56 each. RJR's new owners will pay from $94 to $118 a share to buy the conglomerate.

New owners. $2 billion or more

The new stakeholders, a group that may range in size from a small core of investors to a large number of employees, will have a slice of equity that could grow from $200 million to more than $2 billion if the restructured company is successful.

LBO investors. A 40% annual yield

Returns on leveraged-buyout funds managed by firms like Kohlberg Kravis Roberts have been astronomical, compared with other investments. Their performance has attracted money from sources including the Coca-Cola pension fund and the Hartford insurance company.

Investment bankers. $300 million to $350 million

Firms such as Shearson Lehman Hutton and Drexel Burnham Lambert receive substantial fees for helping bidders put their proposals together and financing their deals. An individual partner might earn $1 million to $2 million.

Commercial banks. $170 million or more

Whatever cannot be financed through junk bonds must be borrowed from banks, which impose an up-front fee of 1.4% on such risky loans in addition to substantial interest charges.

Lawyers. $100 million to $200 million

A battery of merger-and-acquisition experts are paid for their advice on how contracts should be worded and whether the deals are legal.

Junk-bond holders. A 14.5% annual return

These investors assume the greatest risk. If the newly acquired company goes bankrupt, they are the last to be repaid.

Corporate bondholders. (− $1 billion)

RJR's $5 billion in highly rated corporate bonds became far riskier as soon as management announced its plans to borrow $16 billion more for an LBO. Their market value dropped 20%.

U.S. taxpayers. (− $2 billion to −$5 billion)

At first the Government will reap a windfall as RJR shareholders pay capital-gains taxes on their stock-sale profits. However, the Government is likely to lose money in the long run because interest payments on corporate debt—and an RJR buyout will create a whopping pile of it—are tax deductible.

Source: John Greenwald, Richard Hornik, William McWhirter, and Frederick Ungeheuer, "Where's the Limit?" *Time*, December 5, 1988, p. 70.

indicates that the bidder believes the company will be more efficient and therefore more profitably managed. Others deny this and assert that many takeovers by corporate raiders are done because the companies will be made more profitable by such factors as tax benefits, sales of assets, firing of employees, cuts in employee wages, and the sharp reduction of other costs. For every case in which an LBO resulted in greater corporate efficiency, one can point to the breakup of a company to make money. Saul P. Steinberg threatened a take-over of Walt Disney Productions in 1984 but failed. (Nevertheless, Disney paid him $325 million for his stock to make him go away. This reportedly netted Steinberg a $60 million profit.) Edwin D. Okun, a Disney spokesperson, said that the attack prompted changes in management which "set the place afire." He added: "At the lowest hour of the attack someone told me good might come of all this. I thought he was crazy. Now I think he was a visionary."[28] (If Steinberg had held his stock instead of selling it to Disney for what many called greenmail, it today would be worth more than twice the price he received.) On the other hand, Beatrice was taken over in a leveraged buyout with the purpose of selling off assets for profit. Beatrice was bought for $6.2 billion in April 1986, and by September 1987 its completed and pending sales of separate units amounted to $8.8 to $10.8 billion.[29] Today it is a much smaller and less profitable company.

David Ruder, chairman of the Securities and Exchange Commission, said his staff calculated that more than $20 billion in premiums was paid to stock-holders in going-private transactions during 1980–87.[30] Alan Greenspan, chairman of the Federal Reserve Board, told the Congress that reconstructuring (meaning the refinancing of balance sheets that brings changes in ownership and firm identity) of all kinds produced paper gains for shareholders of $200 to $500 billion or more from 1982 through 1988.[31]

It must be pointed out, however, that shareholders can lose even when they sell for a profit. They lose if directors accept a price which is less than the true value of the company. Shareholders can lose also when executives buy them out and then make much more when they break up a company and go public.

What about the stockholders of acquiring companies? Studies show modest or negative gains for them. Karen Fowler and Dennis Schmidt found that on the average "accounting and investor returns decrease significantly in the four years after acquisition activity compared with their levels in the four years before such activity."[32] This data is for all mergers. The data for LBOs alone may be different but we do not have such data. Some stockholders of acquiring companies (KKR, for instance) have profited handsomely.

What about stockholders of firms where the takeover bid failed? Richard Ruback studied thirty-three such firms and found that shareholders received abnormal returns of 31 percent with the initial announcement of the bidding.

[28]Leslie Wayne, "Costs of Escaping a Takeover," *The New York Times*, January 20, 1986.

[29]Carolyn Kay and Kevin F. Winch. *Leveraged Buyouts and the Pot of Gold: Trends, Public Policy, and Case Studies*. Report prepared by the Economics Division of the Congressional Research Service for the House Subcommittee on Energy and Commerce, 100th Cong., 2d Sess., Washington, D.C.: Government Printing Office, 1987.

[30]David S. Ruder, "Statement before the House Committee on Ways and Means Concerning Leveraged Buyouts," January 31, 1989.

[31]Alan Greenspan, "Statement to the Committee on Ways and Means," U.S. House of Representatives, February 2, 1989.

[32]Karen L. Fowler and Dennis R. Schmidt, "Tender Offers, Acquisitions, and Subsequent Performance in Manufacturing Firms," *Academy of Management Journal*, December 1988, p. 972.

At the time of the termination announcement, however, the losses were about 10 percent. These losses did not completely offset the gains from the initial announcement. In the next three years there was little change in stock price.[33]

Jensen says that he considers shareholders to be the most important constituency of the modern corporation and that their interests "must be held paramount when discussing the current wave of acquisitions and mergers."[34] John Smale, chief executive of Proctor & Gamble, disagrees in these words: "Pursuit of optimum value for the shareholders is an important obligation. . . . But it should not be the primary obligation. The primary obligation of management and of a board of directors should be to the corporation and its successful continuation. Through the successful continuation of the enterprise, the corporation furthers the interests of all of its constituencies."[35] By "successful continuation" he means a well-managed company in the best sense of the term—high-quality products at low cost; appropriate investment in facilities, research, product improvement, and the training and nurturing of employees; and a strong balance sheet.

Bondholders   When RJR bond prices fell after the takeover announcement, Metropolitan Life sued RJR in New York State court, charging that its LBO plan enriches a few at the expense of the bondholders. Its holding of $360 million in bonds fell 20 percent in value. The fall in price was due to the huge increase in debt which would be incurred to complete the takeover. That would raise the ratio of debt to stockholder equity (called the debt/equity ratio), and a rise in debt relative to equity increases the risk of default and brings about a lower safety rating and price for bonds. As new debt, especially lower-quality debt (for example, junk bonds), is added to old debt, the value of old debt declines. Highly leveraged buyouts, therefore, inevitably penalize old bondholders of target companies.[36]

As the volume of junk bonds has risen sharply, the safety ratings of old bonds have dropped, and bondholders have lost billions of dollars. Such losses in LBOs raise serious issues. Is this fair to old bondholders? Do boards of directors owe bondholders a fiduciary responsibility in LBOs? If so, what is it? Should courts of law award damages to bondholders in case of such losses? Should courts of law strengthen the legal rights of bondholders? How can bondholders protect themselves from such losses?

Employees   The experience of employees in takeovers is mixed. In some cases employees are treated shabbily and discharged with little or no notice.

---

[33]Richard S. Ruback, "Do Target Shareholders Lose in Unsuccessful Control Contests?" in Alan J. Auerbach, ed. *Corporate Takeovers: Causes and Consequences*. Chicago: University of Chicago Press, 1988.

[34]Jensen, op. cit., p. 110.

[35]John G. Smale, "Corporate Takeovers," speech at J. L. Kellogg Graduate School of Management, Northwestern University, Chicago, Ill., February 7, 1989.

[36]Morey W. McDaniel, "Bondholders and Stockholders," *Journal of Corporate Law*, December 1987.

This experience is found especially in cases where corporate raiders have been successful in acquiring a company and then proceed quickly to cut costs and sell off assets to get cash to pay off the bonds sold to finance the takeover.[37] Some buyouts may have been motivated, at least in part, by an intent to abrogate rules governing employee earnings and benefits as a method to cut costs.

On the other hand, there are cases where employee rights are honored. In the KKR-RJR LBO, for example, the merger agreement provided that salaried and nonunion hourly pay rates will not be reduced and will be increased annually at not less than 4 percent or the consumer price index. All current severance plans, policies, and benefits will be honored. The merger agreement also specified that when businesses are sold, the seller must assume responsibility for providing these protections.[38]

Should employees of all takeover companies be protected as specified in the KKR-RJR merger agreement? What is fair treatment of employees in LBOs? Serious restrictions on the merging and consolidation of corporations set by tough requirements for the treatment of employees, other than laws now in force, would seriously restrain the process. This, in turn, would reduce the flexibility and innovation with which assets are employed. This, in turn, in the long run, would weaken the ability of corporations to operate to the optimum benefit of all concerned, including the employees. On the other hand, great opposition exists to giving a free hand to corporate raiders who have in mind only the breaking up of a company to make a quick profit.

Communities As with workers, there have been many instances of complete indifference by takeover managers to the impact on local communities of worker layoffs or plant closings resulting from LBOs. Even in Winston-Salem, North Carolina, the former headquarters of RJR, where many of the residents were made instant millionaires by the takeover, there was much unhappiness with the LBO. The reasons were many, but fundamentally they lay in the fact that an old way of life would be disrupted. As one reporter found: "Despite their quick riches, (they) despise what is taking place. Many would rather that the proposed transaction would go away."[39]

Dealing with the adverse impacts of takeovers on local communities raises the same sort of questions of fairness as with employees. Concerns about these issues may be best dealt with not by more confining regulations but by an enhancement of an ethos of social responsibility in managers, supplemented by a few regulations that provide better public policy guidance for takeover transactions.

Do LBOs Stimulate Managers to Greater Efficiency?

One of the main arguments used to justify hostile takeovers in recent years is that managers of the target company are not operating it efficiently. They need

---

[37]Kirk Victor, "What about the Workers?" *National Journal*, February 18, 1989.
[38]*RJR Nabisco, Inc. Notice of Special Meeting of Stockholders*, op. cit.
[39]Robert E. Dallos, "Tobacco City's Old Retainers Oppose Buyout," *Los Angeles Times*, December 1, 1988.

a stimulus, it is said, to do better or be replaced by new management. A vital free enterprise system, it is asserted, needs new prods to stodgy management. These managers must be activated to create innovations in the efficient rearrangement of assets, to exert constant pressure to cut costs, and to give continuous forceful management attention to better overall performance.[40]

The performance of companies taken over or merged has been mixed. Harold S. Geneen became the chief executive of ITT in 1959 and, through about 350 mergers and acquisitions, built a small company into one of the most profitable and largest in the United States. On the other hand, many mergers and acquisitions have not been successful. For example, R. H. Macy & Co. had revenues of $4.4 billion in the year ending in August 1985 and net income of $189 million. It was taken over by its management, and the profit turned into a loss.

The longer-range record of managerial performance is also mixed. F. M. Scherer and David Ravenscraft studied 6,000 mergers occurring between 1960 and 1975 and concluded: "Although individual exceptions existed, our statistical materials provided no support for the assertion that acquired unit operating efficiency rises on average after acquisition."[41] Unfortunately, this study cannot be extended to the present because comparable data is not available. During this period, 46.6 percent of acquisitions consummated ended in divestiture.[42] W. T. Grim & Co. calculated that for every 100 mergers between 1980 and 1987, 37.5 were divested.[43] Throughout the period 1960 to 1987, many of the divested companies or divisions were profitable but for one reason or another did not fit into the owning company's needs. Other divestitures were made because the divisions were not performing as required.

There is powerful motivation for managers to improve performance after a takeover engineered by or with them. To begin with, the managers after the LBO will typically own a much larger piece of stock equity, and they are, therefore, managing their own business, not that of others. The huge debt usually incurred in the LBO puts great pressure on them to increase the cash flow in order to pay interest and principal on the debt. Then, too, as will be described in detail later, the tax deductibility of interest raises profits higher than would have been the case if the bonds had not been issued. Costs are cut throughout the organization. As one wag observed: "It is remarkable how

---

[40]This is the main motivation, says T. Boone Pickens, a major raider, of his takeover attacks. See his speech, "Takeovers and Mergers: A Function of the Free Market," in *The Diary of Alpha Kappa Psi,* September 1986; and his autobiography, *Boone.* Boston: Houghton Mifflin Company, 1987.

[41]Quoted in F. M. Scherer, "Testimony before the Committee on Ways and Means, U.S. House of Representatives, U.S. Congress," March 14, 1989. Details of the study are in F. M. Scherer and David J. Ravenscraft. *Mergers, Sell-offs, and Economic Efficiency.* Washington, D.C.: Brookings Institution, 1987. Profits are only one measure of performance. As noted in the above survey, short-term profits can be raised by cost cutting, which can jeopardize future corporate performance. Other measures of performance include productivity, training of people, product quality, innovation, managerial strategy capabilities, market standing, and adaptability to changing environmental forces.

[42]Scherer, op. cit.

[43]Ibid.

quickly a management gets rid of its company airplane when it takes over the firm.'' Altogether, there is high incentive to cut fat and maybe go even deeper into muscle and bone.

We do not have comprehensive reliable data about firms that have gone private through LBOs for the simple reason that they need not publicize their financial results. There are a few studies, however, of these firms. One study of seventy-six such companies concluded that for the average company, operating income as a percentage of assets improved relative to prerestructuring figures by 1.8 percentage points in the year after reconstructing and by 5.6 percentage points in the second year after restructuring.[44] These are not remarkable numbers.

Critics of LBOs say that after the takeover all expenditures that are postponable are likely to be cut out of budgets. One is spending for research and development (R&D). The National Science Foundation (NSF), which monitors R&D spending, studied twenty-four firms (for the period 1984, 1985, and 1986) that were involved in LBOs and mergers. The R&D expenditures of these companies before the takeover or merger were 20 percent of all U.S. company R&D expenditures. The NSF found that after the takeover or merger there was a drop of 5.8 percent in R&D spending in current dollars and an 8.3 percent decline in real terms. In contrast, the remaining top 200 R&D-performing companies reported a 5.4 percent increase in R&D spending in the same period. This is a worrisome trend, says the NSF.[45]

Not to worry, say the proponents of LBOs: there are offsets. They assert that the reduction may be due to many causes. R&D that takes too long to commercialize may be cut, but research on the core business is maintained. Or R&D is reduced by centralizing heretofore decentralized research with no loss of effectiveness, it is asserted. Despite such rationale there is widespread fear that reduced research and development is eroding our competitive position in the world.[46]

The Greed Factor

The drive to get rich is a powerful motivator. At what point does a publicly acceptable vigorous drive for wealth become antisocial greed? Many believe the line was crossed in the KKR-RJR LBO, especially by Ross Johnson.

Eyebrows were raised when the compensation package Johnson prescribed for himself and six other executives in the first bid was made public. This group was to invest $20 million to acquire 8.5 percent of the company. If financial goals were met (a prospect well within the capability of RJR), the

---

[44]Ibid.

[45]Erich Bloch, ''Testimony before the House Ways and Means Committee, U.S. Congress,'' March 14, 1989.

[46]Cindy Skrzychi, ''One Thing LBO Doesn't Stand for Is 'Looking Down the Road,''' *Washington Post National Weekly Edition*, January 1, 1989.

group's stake would rise to 20 percent of the company and would be worth $2.5 billion in five years. At the same time, the group would be paid $18 million a year and share a bonus pool of $20 million a year. "It was ugly," one investment banker said.[47] Johnson sought to soften the charge of greed by later saying that the rewards would be shared by about 15,000 workers.

When Johnson resigned from the firm after losing the bid, he reportedly left with a "golden parachute" containing pay, stock, and other benefits of $53.8 million.[48] (Golden parachutes are special compensation agreements conferring generous severance and benefit payments on managers in the event the company changes hands and they lose their jobs.)

Many people also attached the label of greed to investment bankers, lawyers, and banks for what many considered to be excessive fees, figures for which were given above. We discussed previously greenmail and other types of greed accompanying some hostile takeovers. It is said that because the dollars involved in many LBOs are large, and the fees are fixed percentages of the dollar buyout price, the fees will also be large in dollar terms. Others say there is much logic in reducing the percentage of fees to total cost as the total dollars involved increase in the LBOs.

Should CEOs Be Involved in LBOs?

The interests of managers and stockholders can and often do conflict in merger and takeover transactions. There is no conflict in cases where acquisitions are made for sound business reasons. In instances where managers decide to initiate an LBO of their companies, however, conflicts can arise. Richard Trevenet, a management efficiency consultant, lamented as follows: "Managers have an incentive to under-perform before a buyout. Records of dramatic turnarounds after an LBO raise a troubling question. Why were these managers unable to accomplish these feats before the LBO? Shareholders bear all the costs, but not the rewards of the turnaround."[49]

When managers seek to take over their companies, they are both buyers trying to get the best deal for themselves and sellers who should be representing the best interests of the stakeholders. However, if they can get the investment bankers and their board of directors to agree, they can extract large rewards for themselves in a successful buyout. Both situations generate conflicts.

In the case of a hostile takeover, the top managers of the target company can lose much if the takeover is successful—their jobs, their talents, and skills which are unique to the company. To combat such threats, managers try all

---

[47]Judith H. Dobryzynski, "Was RJR's Ross Johnson Too Greedy for His Own Good?" *Business Week*, November 21, 1988, p. 95.

[48]John A. Byrne, "Is the Boss Getting Paid Too Much?" *Business Week*, May 1, 1989.

[49]Quoted in Greenwald, op. cit.

sorts of things to discourage raiders, such as selling off strategic divisions, incurring huge indebtedness, or distributing stock at bargain prices to employees or present shareholders. These methods do frighten off raiders, but they also often adversely affect shareholders. Threatened managers may succeed in getting their boards of directors to give them generous parachutes.

In defense of CEO involvement in LBOs it is said that some companies will perform better in private hands. For example, in private hands managers are relieved of market pressures to enhance short-term earnings. They then can plan better for long-range operations.

Impact of LBOs on Managers

As noted previously, justification for takeover attempts is often made on the grounds that many managers in large corporations own a small percentage of outstanding stock and do not work as hard as they would if they owned the business. It is asserted that they have become lax and inefficient and so new management is needed. But this is a highly simplified response to corporate governance. Nicholas Brady, secretary of the Treasury, commented on this point as follows:

> I find it difficult to accept . . . that LBOs and the psychology that feeds them are a sensible form of corporate governance. As the pace and scope of LBO activity have grown, I fear we are reaching a point where management is simply not disciplined toward more productive investment, but is robbed of any ability to pursue policies not in step with current market attitudes. In particular, to the extent markets become preoccupied with current earning and cash flow, managers lose the flexibility to pursue long-term investment strategies.[50]

But there are instances where the threat of takeover has resulted in improved management. Illustrative is the case of Walt Disney Productions cited earlier.

Do Taxpayers Subsidize LBOs?

There is no doubt that the answer to this question, as noted earlier, is affirmative. For example, operating income for RJR in 1988 was $2.85 billion. It is estimated that interest charges (which are tax deductible) on $5 billion of existing debt plus new debt of $16 to $18 billion to finance the LBO will consume all or virtually all of the 1989 operating profit. Thus, income tax would not be owed in 1989. Macy's paid $206 million in taxes the last year before its 1986 LBO but got a refund of $32 million in 1988.[51]

---

[50]Nicholas F. Brady, "Testimony before the Committee on Ways and Means," U.S. House of Representatives, January 31, 1989.

[51]For an elaboration of this and other ways in which the tax codes encourage LBOs see Martin Feldstein, "Excess Debt and Unbalanced Investment: The Case for a Cashflow Business Tax," testimony before the Committee on Ways and Means, Congress of the United States, January 31, 1989.

The use of tax-deductible junk bonds in LBOs, however, creates more of a redistribution of wealth than a net drain on the U.S. Treasury, at least in the first few years after a takeover. It is not unreasonable to conclude that because of interest deductions, over the next two or three years the Treasury will lose $1 billion in its RJR tax account. But it will find at the end of that period of time that it will have received at least $2 billion more than if the company had remained as it was in 1988.

This can result, of course, from taxes generated by the LBO. One major source of Treasury income from the RJR deal is capital gains. The merger agreement provided for the acquisition of 165,509,015 shares of common stock (74 percent of stock outstanding, with the remainder exchanged for other securities) at $109 per share. Assuming that the shareholders bought their stock at an average price of $56 (an unlikely event) and sold it at $109 at the time of agreement, the taxable gain would be $53. At a capital gains tax rate of 28 percent, the Treasury would stand to get $2.457 billion. Those financial institutions receiving the huge fees mentioned previously must pay their business taxes at the rate of 34 percent. Add to this the taxes paid by those who receive interest on the bonds issued, plus income taxes paid on RJR employee severance income, as well as taxes for other transactions, and it is apparent that over a few years the Treasury will receive more than the initial tax loss.[52] Most of this tax revenue is one-time receipts. After a few years the Treasury might lose substantial revenues because of the tax-deductible interest.

DO LBOs AND HUGE JUNK BOND DEBT ENDANGER THE ECONOMY?

Some observers see junk bond debt as a relatively small part of total corporate debt and are unconcerned about it. Others view it as a time bomb that will explode, with disastrous results in an economic recession. Important issues in this debate are as follows.

Some Important Results of High Junk Bond Debt and Growing LBOs

When the level of total outstanding junk bond debt of about $200 billion is related to total nonfinancial corporate debt of $2.1 trillion (as of March 1990), junk bonds—at 9.5 percent of the total—do not seem of major significance.[53] When related to the total nonfinancial par value of corporate bonds of $881.8 billion (as of March 1989), however, junk bonds—at 18.2 percent of the total— assume more importance. The significance of junk bonds, however, has many other dimensions.

---

[52]John Paul Newport, Jr., "Why the IRS Might Love Those LBOs," *Fortune,* December 5, 1988.
[53]Telephone conversation with Flow of Funds Section of the Federal Reserve Board, Washington, D.C.

Junk bonds, as noted previously, replace equity in the financing of LBOs. This has resulted in a withdrawal of some $500 billion in equity from the financial markets since 1983. The rise in debt and withdrawal of equity have resulted in an increase in the ratio of capital debt to equity for all industry. The ratio of all corporate debt to the market value of stockholder equity is high today relative to historical standards. For LBOs a ratio of $1 of stockholder equity to $9 of debt is not uncommon. As a result, companies must use large amounts of earnings to pay interest on debt, and if earnings are insufficient to pay interest and principal, default and possibly bankruptcy will follow.

The ability of corporations to cover interest payments on debt has declined. A measure of a company's ability to service its debt is net interest expense to cash flow. This index deteriorated in 1989 and has continued to deteriorate to the present time in 1990 (spring). A number of companies with high leverage have sought bankruptcy protection; among them are some very large companies, such as Compeau Corp. Compeau borrowed $11 billion to buy Allied and Federated Store Groups, could not pay interest on the debt, and filed for bankruptcy in January 1990. At this writing a number of other firms are on shaky ground. In 1990, partly reflecting thinner coverage of interest (the difference between cash flow and interest charges), the price of junk bonds generally has dropped 20 to 25 percent on the open market. The razor-thin margin in many buyout companies is worrisome. Unfortunately, we have only spotty data about these companies.

Do LBOs Threaten to Deepen Recessions?

Fears have been expressed that the debt structure and the consequences of high debt will turn a mild recession into a much deeper one. The fear is that if the economy weakens and sales of heavily leveraged companies fall, those companies will default on the bonds and in turn create a wave of financial troubles among holders of the bonds. While there is cause for concern in these views, there are a few offsetting factors to be considered.

First, a large share of the value of LBOs is concentrated in relatively mature, stable, and noncyclical industries such as nondurable manufacturing, retailing, and services. These industries are less affected by economic business cycles than, say, automobiles or construction, and they have generally strong cash flows. Thus, there is less risk of default on their debts than in some other industries. But there are exceptions. Note Compeau Corp.

Second, Greenspan pointed out that lenders to LBO takeovers in large part "can easily absorb losses without major systemic consequences."[54] He has in mind mutual funds, pension funds, insurance companies, and the like, which usually maintain diversified portfolios. Of course, if any of these institutions

---

[54]Greenspan, op. cit.

have high portions of assets in junk bonds, they are vulnerable to large losses. Greenspan says, however, that the Federal Reserve is "concerned about the increasing share of restructuring loans made by banks. Massive failures of these loans could have broader ramifications."[55] William Seidman, chairman of the Federal Deposit Insurance Corporation, has concluded, however, that "at this time . . . banks are managing their LBO financing risks prudently. We do not perceive any serious threat posed by such financing to the banking industry."[56]

What can one conclude? Clearly, the stability of junk bonds has not been tested in a business downturn. It is impossible to appraise the risks. Much depends upon which firms default, the total face value of the defaulted bonds, which financial institutions have large loans outstanding, who holds the junk bonds, and the seriousness of the economic downturn that occurs.

Benjamin Friedman believes that the Federal Reserve Bank has such intolerance of economic contractions and consequent potential financial disaster that in the event of a likely recession it will pursue an expansionary monetary policy to support the economy.[57] This may happen, but we should not bank on it.

Looking to the longer-range future, there is cause for concern in the prevalence of LBOs. Brady expressed this worry in these words:

> I have a growing feeling that we are headed in the wrong direction when so much of our young talent and the nation's financial resources are aimed at financial engineering while the rest of the world is laying the foundation for the future. We have always done best in this country when our savings have been used to create new jobs, new products, and new services at lower prices. LBOs produce fundamental changes in the financial structures of this country's corporations. They, in turn, raise basic questions about our economic future, whether we will continue to grow and create jobs and whether we will remain competitive.[58]

WHAT SHOULD BE DONE, IF ANYTHING, TO REGULATE LBOs?

Radically different positions are taken in answer to this question. At one extreme, it is asserted that there is no problem and that, therefore, no action should be taken. Indeed, it is asserted, LBOs are good things for society because they stimulate greater efficiency in corporate operations. At the other extreme are many who assert that the takeover problems are so serious that tough new legislation is required to curb LBOs.

---

[55]Ibid.

[56]William L. Seidman, "The Impact of Highly Leveraged Transactions upon the Banking Industry," testimony before the Committee on Ways and Means, U.S. House of Representatives, January 31, 1989.

[57]Benjamin M. Friedman, "Testimony before the Committee on Ways and Means," U.S. House of Representatives, January 31, 1989.

[58]Brady, op. cit.

In between these extremes are other views. For example, some say there are problems with takeovers, but they are relatively unimportant in the total merger picture, and so no actions should be taken. Some say that in time the problems will go away as natural market forces operate and the economy expands. Others say that the core problems can be solved by changes in the tax codes or the stiffening of regulations by federal agencies concerned with financial markets.

The most often proposed congressional action is to eliminate double taxation of dividends. This can be accomplished simply by giving individuals a tax credit for dividends received or for taxes paid by corporations on dividends paid out. If this were done, it would eliminate a major advantage of junk bonds over equities and dampen enthusiasm for the use of such bonds in takeovers. This proposal, however, creates serious problems. One is that according to the Internal Revenue Service, the loss to the Treasury would be $20 to $25 billion a year. In light of federal budgetary problems this loss could not be tolerated.

Another popular suggestion is to eliminate the tax deductibility of corporate debt. If done, this would indeed chill the demand for bonds to finance LBOs. However, here, too, serious problems would arise. If the disallowance were applied to presently outstanding debt, it would bankrupt a number of companies which are now barely able to cover their interest costs. If the regulation applied only to interest on new debt and all outstanding indebtedness was excluded, new companies and expanding companies would be placed at a major competitive disadvantage. Also, since such restrictions would not apply to foreign companies, and since most foreign governments permit the tax deductibility of interest, our companies would be at a disadvantage in foreign competition.

To equalize the costs of bonds and dividends to companies, the suggestion has been made to treat a portion of junk bond interest the same as dividends. This proposal is based on this idea: Since interest rates on junk bonds are so high, it indicates that part of the bonds is more like stocks; therefore, the interest on that part should be taxed the same as dividends on stocks. One problem with this proposal concerns the definition of what is tax-deductible and what is taxable. Also, the ingenuity of investment bankers would soon create instruments to avoid the tax.

There are suggestions that guidelines be set forth to address all sorts of abuses perceived in takeovers. Such guidelines include assurances that managements will act in the best interests of shareholders, that there will be adequate disclosure of relevant information throughout the takeover process, that raiders will be inhibited from extracting greenmail, and that bondholders will be protected from loss.[59]

---

[59]See Rand V. Araskog. *The ITT Wars*. New York: Henry Holt, 1989. This book presents the inside story of a major takeover attempt at ITT and its failure, plus details of recommended changes in the law to combat raiders. See also Araskog's article "How I Fought Off the Raiders," *Fortune,* February 27, 1989.

We now have in force a mountain of laws and regulations covering every major aspect of takeover transactions, whether friendly or hostile. Federal and state laws and regulations govern the formation of corporations, the issuance and trading of corporate securities, the duties and responsibilities of managers to stockholders and other stakeholders, and the dissolution of companies. These rules are effective in covering the most egregious abuses. However, more can be done, and the heads of government agencies testify repeatedly before Congress that they are constantly addressing the problems of takeovers and issuing new regulations.

In addition, corporate managements have developed many "poison pills" to repel unwanted takeovers. For example, Indiana passed a law, upheld by the U.S. Supreme Court,[60] that bars an unfriendly suitor who buys 20 percent or more of the stock from voting the shares until approved by a majority of the company's stockholders, excluding inside directors and officers.[61]

So, what to do? Considerable care should be taken in passing new laws in this area. The vast majority of mergers and acquisitions are made for legitimate economic and financial purposes. The areas of controversy noted in this survey deserve attention, but remedies for perceived problems need to be formulated cautiously. The problems are cause for concern, but we need much more information about the long-run consequences of takeovers. Until the need for radical regulatory change is apparent, there is much in existing laws that we can rely on to correct abuses.

EPILOGUE

"The king is dead. Long live the king." This statement is often used in royalty succession. Immediately after the announcement that KKR had bought RJR, signs appeared in Winston-Salem reading: "Good-bye Ross. Hello KKR." Johnson was the subject of rancorous jokes and doggerel, but he expressed no outward bitterness. In February 1989, following a few months of transition, he pulled his golden parachute and sent each of the directors a dozen roses with a note: "Congratulations on a great job. The stockholders won." But very few people thanked Johnson, even when hundreds of millions of dollars gushed into Winston-Salem pockets to pay for the stock sold to KKR.[62]

Kravis named Louis V. Gerstner, Jr., a former top executive of American Express, to be the chief executive of RJR Nabisco. Gerstner immediately set forth a tough program to cut costs, sell assets, reassess products to improve profitability, replace executives who left or were leaving, and lift efficiency

---

[60]*CTS Corp.* vs. *Dynamics Corp. of America*, 55 LW 4478 (1987).

[61]For details of methods used by managers to repel hostile takeovers see Murray L. Weidenbaum, "Strategies for Responding to Corporate Takeovers," op. cit.

[62]Bryan Burrough and John Helyar. *Barbarians at the Gate: The Fall of RJR Nabisco,* New York, Harper & Row, 1990, pp. 504 and 507. This is a detailed, fascinating account of the KKR-RJR takeover by two *Wall Street Journal* reporters who observed the affair from its beginning.

throughout the company. For example, workers were laid off, the "smoke-less" Premier cigarette was discontinued, RJR headquarters were moved to New York City, and the sale of assets was begun. Chun King was the first to be sold, for $52 million. Then in quick order came the sale of corporate air-planes, the Scandinavian food unit, Del Monte Tropical Fruit, the Del Monte Food canned foods unit, and many more, aggregating by mid-1990 over $5.6 billion.

Total 1989 sales of RJR were $12.8 billion, compared with a comparable fig-ure of $12.6 billion in 1988. Net income from continuing operations, however, registered a large loss of $1.1 billion in 1989, compared with a profit of $1.4 billion in 1988. The loss reflected the heavy merger-related costs and charges for discontinuing Premier cigarettes. Forecasts of future cash flows, however, indicate that the margin between available cash and interest charges on RJR's huge debt will be comfortable.

In 1990 a number of events depressed the junk bond market and LBO fi-nancing. On January 26 Standard & Poor's Corporation and Moody's Inves-tors Service, the two leading agencies that evaluate bonds, lowered RJR bonds to "speculative rating," two to three notches below investment grade. Some RJR bonds dropped as much as 20 percent in value within a few days. This, plus other events, led to a general decline in the broad junk bond market and a serious drop in the availability of financing for LBOs.

A major depressing factor in the junk bond market was the bankruptcy of Drexel Burnham Lambert Inc. in February 1990. Drexel was a major player in the development and volume of junk bond financing in the 1980s, and it served as a powerful stabilizing force in that market. Drexel had grown from a small, second-tier firm in 1980 with total underwriting of about $1.4 billion to a giant with underwriting of $61.6 billion in 1986. The next few years saw a decline, but in 1989 the firm still underwrote $42 billion of junk bonds.[63]

In mid-1986 U.S. Attorney Rudolph Giuliani charged Dennis Levine, a top Drexel executive, with violating insider-trading laws. Levine acknowledged his guilt and pointed a finger at Ivan Boesky, a major Drexel client, who later pleaded guilty and served a prison sentence, as did Levine. Charges against Drexel were settled when the firm agreed to pay $650 million in fines to the federal government.

Then, Michael R. Milken was charged with almost 100 counts of insider-trading violations and other crimes. He was the leader of Drexel's growth and the most prominent mover in the junk bond market. His resignation from the firm in late 1988 was devastating to Drexel and the junk bond market. These events set in motion a chain of forces that led to a cash crunch at Drexel, and it filed for bankruptcy.

Drexel's troubles were not lamented on Wall Street. Indeed, a Louis Harris

---

[63]Kathleen Kerwin, "After Drexel," *Business Week,* February 26, 1990.

poll in March 1990 of 404 executives revealed that they thought Drexel's actions in junk bonds and LBOs were bad for corporations and the United States, and they were not sorry to see Drexel go.[64] The bankruptcy of Drexel served—symbolically, at least—to stamp an end to the wild LBOs of the 1980s. The bankruptcy of Drexel was devastating to the employees of the firm but had no serious impact on either Wall Street or the general economy. The LBO mania of the 1980s is not likely to return soon, if ever, but both hostile and friendly LBOs will continue.

It is appropriate to conclude with the final comment of Bryan Burrough and John Helyar in their book *Barbarians at the Gate*.

> The founders of both RJR and Nabisco would have utterly failed to understand what had happened to their companies. In the mind's eye, it is not so hard to see R. J. Reynolds and Adolphus Green wandering through the carnage of the LBO war. They would turn to each other, occasionally, to ask puzzled questions. Why did these people care so much about what came out of their computers and so little about what came out of their factories? And last: What did all this have to do with doing business?[65]

QUESTIONS

1 What is an LBO? What is new about today's LBOs?

2 Do you believe that the label "greed" attached to Ross Johnson was justified in the RJR bidding?

3 Why did KKR win the bidding?

4 Did the RJR board of directors act responsibly to all stakeholders of the company?

5 Who wins and who loses in the typical LBO?

6 What are the major arguments for and against LBOs?

7 Should CEOs engage in LBOs for their companies?

8 Today there is pressure on the U.S. Congress to regulate LBOs, particularly the use of junk bonds in financing them. Do you believe legislation is required to do so? If not, why? If yes, what would you recommend? In your response, distinguish between hostile and friendly LBOs.

[64]*Business Week*/Harris Poll, *Business Week*, March 12, 1990.
[65]Burrough and Helyar, op. cit., p. 515.

UNREST OVER CORPORATE INVOLVEMENT IN SOUTH AFRICA

This is the story of a scenic but troubled country, the Republic of South Africa. The writer of a travelogue once described it this way:

> South Africa is a land of great and often stunning contrasts; of fertile green valleys and harsh near-desert conditions; of rugged mountains and endless silver beaches along two oceans; of hot summers and cold winter conditions; of bustling twentieth-century cities and settlements of hovels; of great wealth and bitter poverty; of dynamic growth and artificial restrictions to growth; of freedom for some and denial of basic human rights for the majority.[1]

One other "stunning contrast" deserves mention—the contrast between the goals of American corporations, which want to do business in South Africa, and the goals of activist critics, who want disinvestment. For corporations, profits in South Africa can be high (even though average returns have declined in recent years). Critics, however, contend that American firms add legitimacy to an official government policy of racial discrimination known as apartheid (literally, "separateness" or "segregation").[2]

A series of discriminatory laws enacted by the white South African government prescribes a policy of separate but equal development for the four officially recognized racial categories in the population of 34.3 million. The population includes:

---

[1]Gill, Garb, ed. *Traveler's Guide to Central and Southern Africa*. London: IC Magazines Ltd., 1981, p. 152.

[2]M. S. B. Kritzinger et al. *Groot Woordeboek*. Pretoria: J. L. Van Schaik, 1970.

• *25.5 million black Africans:* The blacks are composed of ten major ethnic groups, including Zulu, Xhosa, North and South Sotho, Tswana, Shangaan, Swazi, North and South Ndebele, and Venda. Non-Africans often believe that South African blacks are homogeneous, but some animosities exist among these native groups, and each is composed of many separate tribes. The most cohesive group, the Venda, has twenty-seven distinct tribes. Cultural differences exist among the various black ethnic groups, and four main African languages are spoken.

• *4.9 million whites:* One-third of the South African white population is an English-speaking people of British descent, and two-thirds are Afrikaners, or descendants of the white pioneers who settled the South African interior in much the same way that European immigrants settled the American frontier. The Boers were a mixture of Dutch, French Huguenots who left Europe to escape religious persecution, Germans, and English. A language called Afrikaans developed during the colonization period; it is a unique evolution of Dutch mixed with the tongues of other settlers. Today, Afrikaans is the official language of South Africa. The white population, including a large Jewish community, is of European origin, whereas, of course, the black population is African.

• *3 million coloureds: Coloured* is an official term denoting those of mixed race. Most coloureds trace their ancestry from the intermarriage of early male Dutch settlers in the Cape province with women of the indigenous, brown-skinned San and Khoikhoi natives. A great shortage of white European women in the early settlement years led to frequent interracial marriage. Today, most of the coloureds still live in the Cape Town area.

• *884,000 Asians:* The Asian community consists mainly of Indians who are concentrated in the province of Natal. They were originally brought to the country in the 1870s as indentured servants to work on sugar plantations because African men could not be induced to labor in cane fields. This category includes Chinese also.

THE SAGA OF SOUTH AFRICA

To understand South African society today, it is essential to know its colorful and humanly costly history. The original inhabitants of the area were tribes of hunters and gatherers. By 1652, when the Netherlands (Dutch) East India Company established the first permanent white settlement in Cape Town, some of these tribes had developed agricultural and cattle-raising cultures.

Early Dutch settlers established a fort at Cape Town in 1652 to provision ships passing around the Cape of Good Hope. Soon the Dutch began to trade with the native population, and a few hardy employees of the Netherlands East India Company were given free land by the company to farm and raise stock. These were the first Dutch pioneers, known as Boers (literally, "farmers"). It was at this time that the first policies of racial segregation were es-

The African continent. Note the location of South Africa at the bottom.

tablished. By 1658 there were 113 slaves in the colony, and the number grew over the years. These slaves were imported from elsewhere in Africa, for the Dutch East India Company had forbidden the enslavement of local residents at Cape Town. The slaves were strictly disciplined and punished for misdeeds by facial branding; having the nose, ears, or hands cut off; spending their remaining lifetime in chains; or execution. Owing to fears of an uprising, slaves of two different owners were prohibited from talking together, and when they traveled, slaves had to carry passes signed by their owner. The Dutch killed native Africans who opposed them and hunted local cattle-herding tribesmen for sport. After a brief war with these tribesmen in 1658 the Dutch confined them to the use of specific paths in and around the Cape Town colony.

The parallel between these hoary racial policies and existing apartheid laws is unmistakable. Many modern apartheid laws have historical precedent in the early years of Dutch settlement on the Cape. It is doubtful that these first immigrants held strong racial prejudices. Their initial intention was to civilize the African tribes and convert them to the strict Calvinist theology of the Dutch

Reformed Church.[3] In the 1650s Jan Van Riebeeck, the first governor of the colony, took an African girl into his household, and when she was old enough, he married her to a Dutch surgeon stationed in the colony. But kindly intentions were soon overwhelmed by the passions of competition for land with the natives and dread of slave uprisings. Within a generation there existed in the colony a mixture of slaves, half-castes, detribalized natives, and Europeans much like the population of twentieth-century South Africa, and rudimentary legal methods of ensuring white dominance, the precursors of modern apartheid laws, quickly appeared.

Creating a Nation

The settlers gradually expanded from their small enclave, displacing Africans in the area, who were not allowed title to land or political rights in the new white community. It is important to note that native African cultures in an iron-age stage of cultural development had been thrown in contact with European cultures in the early stages of industrial development. The Europeans possessed a military technology that was far superior to the primitive warfare styles of the Africans, and when resistance was encountered, the Dutch settlers massacred opponents with modern firearms. As the Boers expanded to settle new lands in the interior, they fought frequent battles with African peoples. Generally, there were few casualties for the settlers and many for the Africans.

To this day, white South Africans celebrate Covenant Day on December 16, in recognition of the Battle of Blood River in 1838, when 12,000 Zulu warriors attacked 500 Boer settlers who had fortified their position by circling wagons. After two hours of headlong assault, in which the Africans' short spears were matched against the Europeans' large-caliber muskets and three cannon firing grapeshot, 3,000 Zulus were killed. A Boer chaplin in the party observed that on the open plain to the east "the Kaffirs lay on the ground like pumpkins on a rich soil that has borne a large crop."[4] And so many had fallen in the nearby Ncome River that its current reddened with their blood, hence the name of the battle. The Boers had blistered hands from hot rifle barrels, and three had spear wounds, but none were killed.[5] Being fervent Calvinists, they took this

---

[3]This is the view of A. Theodore Wirgman in *The History of the English Church and People in South Africa*. London: Longmans, Green, and Co., 1895, p. 18. Wirgman also notes, however, that "the stern Calivinism of the Dutch Reformed faith did not tend to produce a tolerant type of Christianity" (p. 19).

[4]The chaplain was Sarel Cilliers, who is quoted in Dougie Oakes, ed. *Illustrated History of South Africa*. Pleasantville, N.Y.: Reader's Digest Association, 1989, p. 119.

[5]On later occasions Zulu armies were formidable opponents. In the Zulu War of 1879, for example, a Zulu force attacked veteran troops of the British colonial army at Isandlwana in Natal province, killing 1,300 men and leaving few survivors. This war ended in British victory, but there was heavy loss of life on both sides. In was precipitated by the fears of white settlers in Natal that powerful Zulu tribes to the north might attack them, though there was never any Zulu provocation. The war was one more manifestation of white anxiety over the sheer mass of blacks displaced and abused by predatory conquests. See Robert B. Edgerton. *Like Lions They Fought*. New York: The Free Press, 1988, and Donald R. Morris. *The Washing of Spears*. Rev. ed. London: Jonathan Cape, 1986.

as a sign that God favored the cause of white supremacy in South Africa. "The word of the Lord was fulfilled," said the chaplain.[6] Covenant Day is still a national holiday and an occasion for reaffirmation of this belief.

With the defeat of the Dutch by the British in the Napoleonic Wars, South Africa suddenly came under British rule. Boer settlers were angered when the British imposed new taxes and freed their slaves. They responded by trekking farther into the interior to establish two independent republics. Conflict between the rebellious Boers and the British culminated with the victory of the British in the bitter Anglo-Boer War of 1899 to 1902. But Boer opposition was so strong that following their battlefield victory, the British nonetheless conceded self-government to the territory known as South Africa and its stubborn white settlers. At first, the government was dominated by whites of English origin, but in elections in 1948, the National Party, representing the Boer heritage, achieved an electoral victory. Since 1948, the political interests of the Afrikaners (as the descendants of the Boers now call themselves) have been dominant.

The Afrikaner Ideology

Over the years of their struggles with native Africans and the British, the Afrikaners developed a cohesive ideology. They believed that their group, the descendants of the Boer farmers who fought to settle the land, was predestined by God to rule. Afrikaner values also held that whites were culturally superior to blacks, coloureds, and Asians. Afrikaners believed that the races could not be expected to live in harmony because of vast social and cultural differences. Clerics of the Dutch Reformed Church found confirmation of these beliefs in the Bible. An example of biblical verse interpreted to support the Afrikaner racial ideology is in the second chapter of Acts:

> And when the day of Pentecost was fully come, they were all in accord in one place. And suddenly there came a sound from heaven as of a rushing, mighty wind, and it filled all the house where they were sitting. . . . And they were all filled with the Holy Ghost, and began to speak with other tongues as the spirit gave them utterance . . . every man heard them speak in his own language. [Verses 1–6]

This passage was interpreted to mean that God had made all men brothers but divided them into many groups such as the ethnic groups in South Africa. Further on, in Acts 17:26, the Bible states that God also determined for "all nations of men . . . the bounds of their habitation." This was read as meaning that God willed the races to be kept separate and distinct to maintain their diversity. Other passages also were thought to confirm that apartheid corresponded to biblical teaching.[7]

---

[6]Oakes, loc. cit.

[7]The development of church doctrine is deftly described in a passage from James A. Michener's historical novel of South Africa, *The Covenant*. New York: Fawcett Crest Books, 1980, pp. 969–72. This sweeping work also brings the rest of South Africa's historical development to life.

In 1986 the Dutch Reformed Church officially stated that apartheid is a mistake, that previous

Over time the Afrikaner elite developed a fierce in-group loyalty, that led it to adopt a tone of secretiveness and cultural arrogance. During World War II a pro-Nazi group of Afrikaners called the *Ossewabrandwag* openly supported Adolph Hitler and the ideology expressed in *Mein Kampf.*[8] In 1940, Rev. Koot Vorster, a leader in the Dutch Reformed Church and brother of future Prime Minister John Vorster, said in a speech:

> Hitler's *Mein Kampf* shows the way to greatness—the path of South Africa. Hitler gave the Germans a calling. He gave them a fanaticism which causes them to stand back for no one. We must follow this example because only by such holy fanaticism can the Afrikaner nation achieve its calling.[9]

The *Ossewabrandwag* claimed 400,000 members during the 1940s, including activists who went on to hold top government posts for the National Party in later decades. It had a military wing called the *Stormjaers* (storm troopers), whose members conducted terrorist acts against Jews during World War II, but these acts were broadly condemned in white society, and perpetrators were jailed when caught. In 1939 the South African parliament declared war on Nazi Germany over the strong dissent of the Afrikaner-dominated National Party. A largely voluntary force of South African troops fought for the Allies in North Africa and Italy, but popular sympathy for Germany remained strong during the war years.

Erecting the Legal Framework of Apartheid

After the war the Afrikaners ascended to power with the electoral victory of their National Party in 1948. Soon, the Afrikaner racial ideology was translated into apartheid laws that established the framework of a racially segregated society. It was a far-reaching experiment in social engineering. Some laws set up a system of "petty apartheid" that resembled the old Jim Crow laws in the American South. In this system restaurants, hotels, train stations, post offices, rest rooms, and other public facilities were segregated. Interracial sexual acts and marriages were prohibited.

Other laws, however, set up a continuing and repressive system of "grand apartheid." At the center of the scheme were laws prohibiting black Africans from voting. This restricted suffrage permitted rule by a small, white minority. A complicated web of forty-three pass laws controlled the movements of blacks within the country. They were required to carry passbooks identifying them as black, were forbidden to live or remain overnight in white areas, and

---

exegesis was incorrect, and that racism was a sin. This announcement caused about 30,000 conservative whites in the congregation to break away and form a new white-only church. In 1989 the church issued a new statement declaring apartheid itself a sin and confessing guilt at helping justify the system for forty years.

[8]The original English edition was published in New York by Stackpool Sons in 1939.

[9]In Oakes, op. cit., p. 349.

were required to register with employers if they took jobs away from tribal homelands.

These homelands, which are separate territories within the borders of the Republic of South Africa, were established under a series of laws dating from 1951. Their purpose is to deflect black demands for political rights. In the homelands blacks are permitted to vote, elect black officials, and exercise considerable self-determination free of guidance by the white South African government. Blacks are assigned citizenship in one of these homelands on the basis of their tribal designation, and once they are in residence, they are no longer citizens of South Africa. Since 1976 millions of blacks have been forcibly moved to homelands, their houses and towns elsewhere bulldozed to the ground behind them.

There are ten homelands in scattered locations, and they constitute only 13 percent of South African territory. They are not on the most fertile, valuable, or desirable land, but by 1989 approximately 11 million black South Africans lived in them. Four homelands are declared to be officially independent nation-states, although their constitutions prohibit armed forces, and no country aside from South Africa has granted official diplomatic recognition.[10] They do not have self-sufficient economies and receive over $1 billion a year in support from South Africa.

Other apartheid laws barred blacks from holding certain managerial and professional positions. And to firm the grip of apartheid, a series of enactments allowed the South African police to prohibit assemblies, outlaw black opposition organizations, and detain suspected opponents of apartheid—all without standards of evidence as rigorous as in the United States.

The Society behind Apartheid

The society that these laws created was one of extreme prejudice. A color bar was present in virtually all aspects of everyday life, down to the most mundane. Most facilities were segregated. Whites ate in restaurants, while non-whites were barred or bought food from windows in the back to be eaten away from the premises. Stewardesses on South African Airlines flights marked linen and blankets used by non-Europeans with special red tags so they would not be cleaned with the rest and could be sent for "special hygienic processes and dry cleaning." Cutlery, glasses, and dishes were also washed separately.

Museums, zoological gardens, and parks were not easily segregated, so in large cities nonwhites were permitted to visit them only on one or two days of the week. Elsewhere, such facilities were often closed entirely to nonwhites. In theaters special sections of seats were roped off for them. Blacks were not allowed to be performers, musicians, or athletes where whites were also in-

---

[10]The four independent homelands—or Bantustans, as they are sometimes called—are Transkei, Bophuthatswana, Venda, and Ciskei. The other six are Gazankulu, KaNgwane, KwaNdebele, KwaZulu, Lebowa, and Qwa-Qwa.

volved. Foreign films showing social interaction between whites and nonwhites could not be shown. Separate Dutch Reformed Churches were started for nonwhites. Even cemeteries were segregated, leading an anthropologist studying South African culture to remark: "It is outside the scope of the social scientist to inquire into events beyond that point, but there seems little doubt that many South African whites would be greatly put out to find no colour-bar in Heaven."[11]

In addition, the Afrikaans language developed words and usages that confirmed white superiority. Nonwhites addressed whites as "Mr.," "Miss," or "Mrs." followed by their surnames. Whites ignored these distinctions and referred to blacks by their first names or by derogatory terms such as "boy." The Afrikaans language contained distinctive words for whites and nonwhites not found in English. For example, the word for a coloured boy was *klonkie,* whereas a white boy was denoted by the word *seun.* A coloured woman of any age was referred to by the word *meid,* whereas a white girl was a *meisie.* Naturally, these distinctions were slightly derogatory.

Whites and nonwhites did not mix much, but when they did, manners and customs reflected white superiority. Whites rarely shook hands with nonwhites upon introduction. White men did not step aside for black or coloured women, did not rise when they approached, and did not relinquish their seats to them.

Authorities were greatly troubled in enforcing apartheid laws strictly, because objective criteria about racial classification were not always present. Sometimes people would contest their classification in a nonwhite category. A common method used to resolve these disputes was to place a comb in the person's hair to see if it would stay or fall. Blacks were presumed to have thicker hair than whites, so a falling comb might mean reclassification. At other times people were asked to roll up their sleeves so that bureaucrats could examine skin color. Citizens were encouraged to tattle on nonwhites who tried to pass as white. In one such case a South African judge found a Roman Catholic priest guilty of violating the Prohibition of Mixed Marriages Act. This priest had married a white man and a white-appearing woman, but subsequent investigation revealed that three of her four grandparents were officially registered as coloured at birth. Although the woman had associated only with whites, she was found to be "slightly Coloured" and her marriage illegal.

Apartheid was not only a legal system, it was also a way of life based on long-standing forms of social segregation which had characterized South African society for centuries.

LIVING WITH APARTHEID

During the 1950s and 1960s the government suppressed black opposition and proceeded with the forced relocation of millions of blacks to segregated areas.

---

[11]Sheila Patterson. *Colour and Culture in South Africa.* London: Routledge and Kegan Paul Ltd., 1953, p. 125.

Official criticism from other governments was muted, although civil rights activists worldwide were hostile. In the 1970s, however, the philosophy of black consciousness central to civil rights movements in other nations took hold among blacks in South Africa. New feelings of black pride created racial tensions that boiled over in bloody riots in 1976 in the black township of Soweto. There, South African police violently crushed demonstrations, and hundreds of Africans were killed.

After the Soweto riots internal unrest continued for nearly two years, fomented by the activities of a black opposition group, the African National Congress (ANC). This group had been banned by the white regime, but a military arm called the *Umkhonto we Sizwe* conducted raids in the country from guerilla bases in neighboring countries. News media broadcast the turmoil around the world. Naturally, this stiffened criticism of the regime, but the lasting significance of these events was that they hurt the economy. Investors and banks feared a black revolution, and growth in the South African economy slowed. Stock prices fell, foreign bank loans were harder to get, and unemployment rose. Other countries threatened economic sanctions, and when a deep recession occurred, the Afrikaner business elite pressured the government to mitigate black unrest by reforming apartheid laws.

In 1978 a new prime minister, P. W. Botha, was elected, and he initiated policies designed to control unrest. Somewhat immodestly, he referred to these policies as a "Total Strategy." Simplified, the Total Strategy had two prongs: (1) military suppression of the ANC and (2) cosmetic reform of the apartheid system to placate blacks and world opinion. To implement the first prong the South African army began a series of raids across the border into black African nations which harbored ANC camps. These raids met with success and continued for many years.

To implement the second, Botha made a series of token changes that relaxed enforcement of apartheid restrictions. Segregated facilities disappeared in cities. Black trade unions were permitted; the prohibition against mixed marriages was repealed; business districts, hotels, restaurants, and cinemas were integrated; the pass laws were revised so that passbooks were no longer required of blacks; and job restrictions for blacks were abolished. But Botha steered well clear of apartheid's core—disenfranchisement of the huge African majority. He did advocate some power sharing with Indians and coloureds. In 1984, he implemented a new constitution that gave the vote to coloured and Asian citizens, who could elect separate, advisory parliaments to represent their racial categories. Blacks, however, were given no vote and no parliament. Only whites, of course, voted for members of the dominating white parliament.

Many blacks were enraged by their exclusion from power sharing in the new constitution. On September 3, 1984, the day it went into effect, nine people were killed when violence broke out in the black township of Sharpeville. Antiapartheid activists then incited riots in other areas. Soon violence spread to black urban townships throughout the country. Many blacks died at the hands of South African police, and black gangs roamed the townships, killing blacks who had served on the town councils set up as part of Botha's reform scheme. World condemnation of the white regime grew. Finally, in July 1985, Botha declared a state of emergency, giving police sweeping powers to detain black agitators. Over 5,000 were arrested in the next two months. The government banned antiapartheid organizations, including some formed by liberal whites. News coverage was suppressed. Camera crews, for example, were denied entry to areas of civil disobedience. This did not stop the violence, but the outside world saw less of it. The state of emergency continued until 1990.

For much of the 1980s a stalemate existed between the white government and its opponents. The government was unable to achieve group harmony through reforms that preserved the essence of apartheid. The ANC was never able to start a real revolution. It conducted guerilla raids, sabotage, car bombings, and worldwide political opposition. But white military and police forces were too strong, and many blacks were economically well off and not inclined to fight.

As this stalemate dragged on and international economic sanctions braked the economy, white South Africans increasingly realized that the apartheid system had failed as a political solution for governing diverse population groups. In 1990 a new South African President, F. W. de Klerk, took dramatic actions. He lifted a ban on black political demonstrations; lifted bans on sixty antiapartheid groups, including the violence-prone African National Congress and the South African Communist party; integrated beaches and rescinded the law that segregated many public facilities; freed prominent political prisoners, including Nelson Mandela, a long-imprisoned revolutionary of mythic stature to blacks; and called on the African National Congress and other groups to join in negotiations to shape a new, as yet undefined, South African system. What de Klerk did not do was abolish the main apartheid laws.

WHY DO THE AFRIKANERS CLING TO APARTHEID?

To opponents, the racist social disorder of apartheid can no more be cured by reform than cancer can be cured by a bandage. Many Americans, who take for granted civil and political rights for minorities, find apartheid an inconceivable anachronism. Why do white South Africans retain it in the face of world opprobrium?

Hard-line Afrikaners argue that they conquered and colonized the territory now comprising South Africa and have a legal right to rule. The apartheid system, they say, is the best solution for governing a nation of such diverse inhabitants. Democracy cannot work in a multiracial, fragmented society like South Africa; it works best in a homogeneous political culture, they say, and is not workable where unusually vast differences in language, religion, cultural heritage, education, and race exist. It is also argued that the system is less repressive than other African governments. Blacks in South Africa have a higher economic standard of living than blacks in other African countries. And blacks throughout the African continent have suffered under impoverished black leadership in newly independent black nations.

A black takeover of the government in South Africa, particularly under precipitous or violent circumstances, could lead to a repetition of the experience in other black African states released from colonial domination. That experience has often included civil war between tribal groups, decaying infrastructures, declining industrial output, and declining agricultural output. Many black African nations are not only poorly run but brutally repressive as well. Such situations arise where no pluralist tradition exists and ageless tribal rivalries reassert themselves within modern parliamentary frameworks. Soon opposition parties and rival tribes are viciously repressed by the dominant tribe.

This can lead to bloodshed. African tribal groups coming into political power have murdered traditional enemies, committing heinous crimes that dwarf the detention of black activists by South African police. In Burundi, for example, the ruling Watusi government massacred 200,000 Hutsus in a three-month period in 1972.[12] Violence continued, and in 1988 over 50,000 Hutsu refugees fled the country.[13] In Zimbabwe, formerly white-ruled Rhodesia, members of the dominant Shona tribe have waged a genocidal war against their historic enemies, the Ndebele, since independence in 1979. In Uganda, Amnesty International has estimated that over 500,000 blacks have been killed by Idi Amin and successor regimes. And in the Central African Republic, President Bokassa slaughtered rival tribesmen, kept parts of their bodies in his refrigerator, and ate them.

South African whites fear the emergence of virulent tribalism in their nation. In South African history, the Zulu tribe has twice emerged as dominant, once to be defeated by the Boers and a second time by the British. Today, the Zulus are the largest black ethnic group and number 6 million. They might again emerge as a dominant tribe under their strong leader, Chief Mangosuthu Gatsha Buthelezi. In an interview, former President P. W. Botha was once asked why the white government consistently ruled out reforms giving blacks the vote in democratic elections. He answered:

> Because the winner-takes-all principle makes no provision for the protection of minority groups and will lead, in my opinion, to what has happened elsewhere in Africa—a one-party state and eventually dictatorship and domination by one group over the others. . . .
>
> You know, there are two very important elements in our population. One is the Zulus. They form a strong minority amongst the black people, the strongest one. And the Afrikaner forms the strongest white minority. Both the Zulus and the Afrikaners have no other country to go to and must find a way to live together without destroying each other's heritage and ideals and way of life.[14]

It is clear that whites are reluctant to permit black suffrage because they envision chaotic government at best or dictatorship and violent repression at

---

[12]David Lamb. *The Africans*. New York: Random House, 1982.

[13]U.S. Department of State, Bureau of Public Affairs. *Human Rights Issues in Africa*. Current Policy No. 1148. Washington, D.C.: Department of State, March 1989, p. 1.

[14]P. W. Botha, "Interview: 'We Must Find a Way to Live Together,'" *U.S. News & World Report*, May 26, 1986, p. 29.

worst. Rioting and agitation in the black townships after 1984 fed such fears. Black gangs roamed lawlessly, killing former leaders who had cooperated with whites. One callous form of execution utilized "necklaces," or old rubber tires filled with gasoline. The tires were forced over the victims' heads, trapping their arms at their sides, and then lit. After "necklacing" became widespread, Winnie Mandela, the activist wife of Nelson Mandela, former leader of the ANC, incited blacks with these words:

> We work in the white man's kitchen. We bring up the white man's children. We could have killed them at any time we wanted to. Together, hand-in-hand with our sticks and our matches, with our necklaces, we shall liberate this country.[15]

Recently a conservative Afrikaner openly voiced the fear that such statements create among whites. "Ask a black leader what he would do if he took over this country and he will say all whites will have to be killed. But you ask, what about the ones who want integration? 'He's white, we'll also kill him.'"[16]

Such fears explain much white opposition to reform.

THE SOUTH AFRICAN ECONOMY

South Africa, which had a GNP of $63 billion in 1989, is the most industrialized country on the African continent. The economy is based on a variant of free-enterprise capitalism in which there is heavy government ownership of vital industries. Steel mills, oil refineries, chemical plants, electric utilities, radio and television stations, airlines, railroads, and defense plants are directed by government agencies that work with private management firms. The government provides many incentives for foreign investors.

Blacks in South Africa may own businesses, join labor unions, and serve in the police and army. But the unemployment rate for blacks ranges from 20 percent to 40 percent, compared to a rate of only 2 percent for whites in most years. Income is, of course, unevenly distributed. In 1987 the average monthly wage of blacks in manufacturing was $293 compared to $1,070 for whites.[17] Many blacks live in shantytowns, while whites enjoy one of the world's highest living standards. Nevertheless, average black incomes exceed those of workers in other African nations. Blacks from neighboring countries press to get in and the South African economy employs over 1,000,000 migrant workers, who tolerate white repression for the high wages they can earn.

The economy suffered a severe recession in the mid-1980s and limped through the rest of the decade with an annual growth rate of only 2.5 percent, well below the 5 percent estimated as necessary to create enough new jobs to match work-force growth in a country with a fast-rising black population. Un-

[15]In Oakes, op. cit., p. 480.
[16]In "The South African Experience: A Renaissance Perspective." U.S. Senate, *Hearings before the Committee on Foreign Relations*, "United States Policy toward South Africa," 100th Cong., 2d Sess., June 22–24, 1988, p. 677.
[17]The Africa Fund, "South Africa Fact Sheet," November, 1988, p. 2.

less the economy picks up, unemployment for blacks may be as high as 50 to 60 percent after the year 2000.[18]

Despite its sluggishness, however, South Africa remains the industrial powerhouse among neighboring African countries. Sub-Saharan Africa, a region of 45 countries, has suffered dramatic economic declines in recent years. During the decade of the 1980s the total gross domestic product of these countries declined by over 20 percent, making it roughly equivalent to the GNP of tiny Belgium, a European country with less than 2 percent of the population and less than 1 percent of the land mass of these African nations. During this decade, foreign aid declined and total private investment ceased to grow. In this deeply troubled region infrastructures have decayed to the point where private companies frequently need to have their own water supplies and set up short-wave radios for outside contact because telephones are unreliable. Mass markets for modern consumer products do not exist.

Because sub-Saharan states are mired in this economic morass, trade with nearby South Africa is vital. Even though the South African economy is troubled (its GNP is roughly half that of Spain and less than that of Hungary) it is a titan next to neighboring economies. Although only one black African nation, Malawi, extends formal diplomatic recognition to South Africa, only one nation, tiny Guinea Bissau, refuses to trade with it. Trade between South Africa and black African nations exceeds $1.5 billion a year, and South Africa provides railroad rolling stock, wheat, corn, electricity, and gasoline in large quantities to its neighbors. As the economies of sub-Saharan African countries have stagnated they have turned more and more openly to South Africa for trade and private capital. And for some nations economic dependence is near total. When South Africa imposed an economic embargo on Lesotho in 1986 to force expulsion of ANC guerilla operations its government toppled in one week. Over 60 percent of neighboring Zimbabwe's imports and exports are with South Africa.

U.S. CORPORATIONS IN SOUTH AFRICA

South Africa welcomes American multinationals, and in 1990 about 125 U.S. firms had direct investment there. Some of the largest are Caltex (a partnership of Chevron and Texaco), Goodyear, Colgate-Palmolive, and Johnson & Johnson. About 5,000 others have trading arrangements, such as distributorships. Coca-Cola, Ford, and IBM, for example, sell their products through licensing arrangements with businesses owned entirely by South Africans and have no employees or assets in the country. Total direct foreign investment by U.S. companies is about 6 percent of the total capital invested in South Africa and about 18 percent of all foreign investment there.[19] This is a far smaller

---

[18]John A. Marcum, "Africa: A Continent Adrift," *Foreign Affairs,* vol. 68, no. 1, 1988/89, p. 173.

[19]David Brock, "Pondering the Cost of Sanctions," *Insight,* July 14, 1986.

commitment than that of British companies, other European companies, and Japanese companies. (In order to court Japanese business, incidentally, South Africans classify Japanese businessmen as "honorary whites" rather than Asians and allow them to use white facilities and move freely in white areas without harassment.) U.S. firms employ 120,000 black African workers— about 2 percent of the black labor force.

In 1950, direct foreign investment by U.S. firms was $140 million. Today it stands at $1.6 billion, down from a high of $2.63 billion in 1982, according to U.S. Commerce Department estimates. This is less than one half of 1 percent of all U.S. foreign direct investment. The figure does not include bank loans (which totaled $3 billion in 1987), stock held by U.S. citizens (in the range of $4 to $6 billion), or indirect ownership of South African companies through wholly owned subsidiaries of U.S. firms on foreign soil. Total U.S. economic involvement, then, is far greater than the $1.6 billion figure.

ECONOMIC SANCTIONS ARE APPLIED

As conditions in South Africa deteriorated in 1985, the debate about policy with respect to U.S. corporations and trade became polarized. All sides wanted apartheid ended, and two paths to this goal each had strong support.

Antiapartheid groups called for *principled disengagement,* requiring U.S. corporations to end investment in and trade with South Africa. Disinvestment would end direct tax subsidy and symbolic corporate support for apartheid. Trade sanctions would destabilize the South African economy, weakening white support for apartheid and leading to negotiations for democracy with nonwhites.

Corporations and the Reagan administration, on the other hand, called for *constructive engagement,* a policy which encouraged U.S. firms to stay in South Africa as a means of building leverage to pressure a recalcitrant Afrikaner class for reform.[20] The companies argued that they were a progressive force improving the life of all races. The Department of State favored the presence of U.S. corporations to increase diplomatic influence. South Africa has always been seen as an important strategic ally in world politics because it is the major source of a number of strategic minerals, and its location on the southern tip of the African continent gives it control of the oil sea lane from the Persian Gulf, through which the bulk of the Western world's oil supply passes.

But in 1986 Congress passed the Comprehensive Anti-Apartheid Act to re-

---

[20]The two best explanations of constructive engagement as a national policy are Chester A. Crocker, "South Africa: Strategy for Change," *Foreign Affairs,* vol. 59, no. 2, winter 1980/81, and Ronald Reagan's single public statement, "U.S. Economic Relations with South Africa: Apartheid, Some Solutions," speech delivered to the American people, Washington, D.C., July 22, 1986 (in *Vital Speeches of the Day,* August 15, 1986). The term *constructive engagement* subsequently fell into official disuse, but it still characterizes a distinctive policy approach standing in contrast to approaches that advocate severing economic relations.

strict economic involvement with South Africa. President Reagan vetoed it, but large majorities in both the House and Senate overrode his veto, and it became law.[21] Its major provisions are as follows:

• New investment by U.S. corporations is limited to firms owned by black South Africans, reinvestment of profits, and purchase of South African stock market shares.
• Some trade with South Africa is prohibited. Export of crude oil, petroleum products, munitions, nuclear materials, and nuclear technology is banned. Import of uranium, coal, textiles, iron, steel, arms, ammunition, military vehicles, agricultural products, food, and Krugerrand gold coins is banned.
• South African aircraft are prohibited from landing in the United States and no airline may schedule a direct flight from the United States to South Africa.
• U.S. government aid for social projects and victims of apartheid in South Africa is increased.
• Support for any country or organization that countenances "necklacing" is prohibited.
• The president is to enlist the aid of other countries to develop multilateral sanctions if apartheid does not end.
• The act shall cease to be enforced when four of the following five conditions are met.

  1 Nelson Mandela, the ANC leader, is released from prison.
  2 The state of emergency is repealed.
  3 Militant antiapartheid groups are again legalized.
  4 Apartheid laws regulating where blacks may live and work are repealed.
  5 The government starts serious negotiations with black leaders to end apartheid.

This law was followed the next year by a budget act amendment which ended the practice of allowing U.S. corporations to deduct taxes paid to the South African government from their U.S. income taxes.[22] Together, these laws constitute the strongest economic sanctions of any country. But other countries have similar laws. Five other countries—Japan, West Germany, Italy, France, and Canada—prohibit new corporate investment, and the Euro-

---

[21]Pub.L. 99-440; 22 U.S.C. Secs. 5001–5116 (Supp. IV 1986). The vote in the House was 313 to 83; the vote in the Senate was 78 to 21. The large majorities were formed by a coalition of groups in Congress, each with different motives. They included the Congressional Black Caucus, which supports black causes; young Republican conservatives trying to attract black support for the GOP; a bloc of Democrats who were afraid to vote against the bill in an election year; and moderate Republicans, who wanted to shape a new alternative to presidential policy. See Michael Clough, "Southern Africa: Challenges and Choices," *Foreign Affairs*, vol. 66, no. 5, summer 1988, pp. 1071–72.
[22]Section 10231, Part IV, Title X of the Omnibus Budget Reconciliation Act of 1987. Pub.L. 100–203.

pean Economic Community asks for voluntary restraint.[23] These countries, and others, also restrict a range of trade activities similar to that in the U.S. law but generally not as extensive.

Have sanctions hurt the South African economy? The government has been reluctant to concede it, but the economy has been sluggish. After 1987 economic growth slowed; inflation, unemployment, and interest rates rose. A 1988 study by the General Accounting Office stated that world sanctions were causing massive trade problems for South Africa, reducing both imports and exports. The fall in imports was slight, but exports were cut by 7 percent.[24] A 1990 study estimated that world sanctions had cost South Africa $32 to $40 billion, including $11 billion in net capital outflows and $4 billion in lost export revenues.[25] And to evade the ban on oil shipments by OPEC countries and other nations, South Africa, by its own admission, has to pay a premium of $2 billion each year for oil.[26] Growth of the economy slowed to only 0.8 percent in 1989.[27]

Sanctions have not crippled the South African economy, but evidence indicates that they have created trouble. More comprehensive sanctions, of course, could mean deep trouble. One recent study suggests that concerted action by six nations—the United States, Great Britain, West Germany, Japan, France, and Switzerland—would virtually exclude South Africa from the world economy and collapse its internal economy.[28]

THE ARGUMENT FOR U.S. CORPORATE INVESTMENT

American corporations have resisted disinvestment pressure and make a number of arguments.

First, American companies are committed to ending apartheid and act as a liberal force in the country. Indeed, there is a long record of corporate responsibility. In the 1960s companies such as IBM and General Motors defied the law to integrate their employee cafeterias and put blacks in supervisory posi-

---

[23]For a discussion of sanctions by European countries see Martin Holland, "Disinvestment, Sanctions, and the European Community's Code of Conduct in South Africa," *African Affairs*, October 1989. In 1990 Britain elected to unilaterally lift its embargo on new investment after failing to persuade other European Community nations to do the same.

[24]Allan I. Mendelowitz. *U.S. Sanctions against South Africa.* Washington, D.C.: General Accounting Office, June 24, 1988, p. 15.

[25]William Claiborne, "South Africa's Quiet Revolution," *Washington Post National Weekly Edition*, January 22–28, 1990, p. 24.

[26]*Questions and Answers on South Africa Sanctions.* New York: The Africa Fund, 1989, p. 3.

[27]Penter Junker, "A Land 'Suffocating' from Apartheid," *World Press Review*, April 1990, p. 13.

[28]*Research into Global Structures, Development, and Crisis.* Munich: Starnberger Institute, 1988. The nations would have to prevent banks from rolling over loans; ban the import of mining products, capital goods, and security products; and ban their own multinationals from banking, mining, and energy production in South Africa. See also Marcum, op. cit., who suggests that multilateral sanctions such as an international air embargo or bans on critical industrial chemicals or machinery might have a "sharp psychological or strategic impact" (p. 176).

tions. After 1977 up to 130 companies followed a set of guidelines for social responsibility drawn up by the Reverend Leon Sullivan, a black director of General Motors. These principles, called the Sullivan Principles, were as follows:

1 Nonsegregation of the races in all eating, comfort, and work facilities
2 Equal and fair employment policies for all workers
3 Equal pay for equal work
4 Initiation of training programs to bring blacks into supervisory, administrative, clerical, and technical employment
5 Recruitment and training of minorities for management and supervisory positions
6 Improvements in the quality of life for minorities outside the work environment in areas such as housing, health, transportation, schooling, and recreation

Every year American firms spent millions on training, education, housing, health care, and other benefits for blacks to fulfill their duties as signatories to the Sullivan Principles. There was an annual report prepared by an independent consulting firm, Arthur D. Little, which rated companies on their compliance with the guidelines.

Although Rev. Sullivan abandoned the principles which bear his name in 1987 and called for a complete withdrawal of U.S. corporations, companies still in South Africa adhere to a similar set of principles today.[29]

American firms have also needled the South African government about racial policies. In 1985, President P. W. Botha and his cabinet met with the heads of 200 leading corporations in South Africa, who demanded that blacks receive full political and social rights. In August 1985, Mobil published newspaper ads in South Africa, headlined "There Is a Better Way," which called for a "new non-racial democracy" and a "South Africa without apartheid." A network of U.S. companies has set up legal aid centers in black townships to advise South Africans of their rights. In 1986 General Motors created a stir by offering to pay the legal fees of any employee arrested for trespass on a whites-

---

[29]The evolution of the Sullivan Principles is described in Karen Paul, "Corporate Social Monitoring in South Africa: A Decade of Achievement, an Uncertain Future," *Journal of Business Ethics,* June 1989.

The revised statement of Principles commits signatory companies to:

(*1*) Eliminating laws and customs that impede social and political justice. (*2*) Increasing the number of blacks, coloureds, and Asians in management and supervisory positions. (*3*) Initiating and developing training programs that prepare blacks, coloureds, and Asians in substantial numbers for supervisory, administrative, clerical, and technical jobs. (*4*) Improving the quality of employees' lives outside the work environment by devoting corporate resources to the improvement of housing, transportation, schooling, recreation, and heath facilities. (*5*) Providing equal and fair employment practices for all employees. (*6*) Assuring that the pay system is applied to all employees without regard to race or ethnic origin. (*7*) Desegregating all eating, comfort, locker room, and work facilities.

only beach near its Port Elizabeth plant. Many of the most outspoken companies have left, of course, including General Motors.

When U.S. firms leave South Africa, they seldom close down operations completely. Rather, assets are sold to local managers, South African companies, or other foreign companies. In most cases American brands or products continue to be sold by the new owners through licensing, distribution, or franchise arrangements. Two examples are Coca-Cola and General Motors.

Coca-Cola elected to leave South Africa late in 1986, when the Southern Christian Leadership Conference threatened a black consumer boycott if the company was still there on Martin Luther King's birthday, January 15, 1987. It sold its interests to white-owned Amalgamated Beverage Industries, the country's largest soft-drink bottler, which continues to distribute Coca-Cola brands under a licensing agreement. General Motors left South Africa in 1986, having sold its subsidiary to its white South African managers. The subsidiary was renamed Delta Motors, but it continues to manufacture GM cars and trucks under license. Sales increased from 24,000 vehicles in 1986 to 40,000 in 1988. Conservative whites, who had refused to buy GM cars owing to GM's stand on Port Elizabeth's beaches, returned as customers, and Delta Motors also began to sell cars to the South African military and police, a market closed to GM.

Amalgamated Beverage sold 11 percent of its shares to employees and merchants who sell Coke; Delta Motors hired more new black workers as sales jumped. But other new South African owners have been less generous to nonwhites than the U.S. firms they replace. The new white owners do not fear American pressure groups or subscribe to the Statement of Principles. They contribute less to nonwhite community groups, education, and training.[30]

Second, American firms argue that apartheid will end sooner in a climate of economic growth than in a climate of constriction. Blacks have borne the greatest burden under U.S. sanctions. Thousands of black workers have been laid off in industries hurt by the law, such as coal mining, agriculture, and iron and steel. The vast majority of public opinion polls in South Africa show large majorities of blacks opposed to trade boycotts and the pullout of foreign companies. In a typical poll 1,478 urban blacks were asked "Should the outside world apply an economic boycott against South Africa or not?" Only 10 percent favored a boycott.[31] Black self-interest was forcefully stated by James Nycoya, president of the South African Black Taxi Association, in testimony before a congressional committee: "I ask you to hear our voices . . . before you decide what is good for us. Before you decide that black children must go hungry so you can be on the right side of history."[32]

---

[30]Jim Jones, "Aftermath of the Exodus," *U.S. News & World Report*, May 1, 1989, p. 50.

[31]Donald W. Caldwell, "Attitudes in South Africa," *Public Opinion*, January/February 1988, p. 55. For another summary and assessment of these polls see Meg Voorhes. *Black South Africans' Attitudes on Sanctions and Disinvestment*. Washington, D.C.: Investor Responsibility Research Center, June 1988.

[32]In "Statement of Mobil Oil Corporation," in *Hearings before the Committee on Foreign Relations*, op. cit., p. 521.

Sanctions not only adversely impact nonwhites but also may stiffen white resistance to reforms. Historically, Afrikaners have had a "circle the wagons" mentality. Economic stagnation resulting from an effective trade boycott would not provide a fertile base for the growth of a healthy democracy. One scholar sets forth the following scenario of change following sanctions.

> Let us assume that comprehensive sanctions were imposed against South Africa, and achieved their desired result. They severely damage the economy, starving it of avenues for export, needed imports and external financial support. Among the whites, the importance and influence of the business class decreases. The white community is forced back to exclusive reliance upon the political-military establishment. In the black community, unemployment rises, the power of the black trade unions atrophies. Desperation feeds violence, with leadership passing into the hands of the best organized forces of violence. . . . [L]et's assume that eventually a combination of economic deprivation and the pressures of a mounting civil war bring the whites to the negotiating table.
>
> . . .[T]his is likely to take a generation (20–30 years), and destroy much of the country's infrastructure. . . . As a result of negotiations black leaders move into the positions of political leadership.
>
> This would be the end of apartheid—but would any elements of stable democracy exist?[33]

Finally, American companies argue that disinvestment pressures subordinate corporate policy to the goals of activists, church groups, and minority shareholders who sponsor get-out-of-South Africa stockholder proposals. And if Congress passes a law requiring disinvestment by a specific date, it might be unconstitutional. American firms faced with a withdrawal deadline might be unable to sell property at market value. The Fifth Amendment to the Constitution states that property shall not be taken "for public use without just compensation." In the case of *Armstrong* v. *United States,* the Supreme Court ruled that the government may not "force some people alone to bear public burdens which, in all fairness and justice, should be borne by the public as a whole."[34] Stockholders of companies could challenge a disinvestment law on these grounds or sue for compensation. In any case, sale prices might be a windfall for white South Africans, some of whom have already become millionaires in buyouts of American assets.

THE ARGUMENT AGAINST U.S. INVESTMENT

In the United States, as in other countries, a strong antiapartheid movement exists. One early success of this movement came as long ago as 1971, when

---

[33]Alan L. Keyes, "Sanctions or Empowerment: The Choice between War and Freedom in South Africa," in U.S. House of Representatives, "Proposed Economic Sanctions against South Africa," *Hearings before the Committee on Foreign Affairs,* 100th Cong., 2d Sess., March 23, 1988, pp. 368–69.

[34]364 U.S. 49 (1960). See also *Lutheran Evangelical Church* v. *Los Angeles County,* 107 S.Ct. 2378 (1987), in which the Court held that if government legislation renders privately held property worthless, the "taking" clause requires compensation to the property holder.

Polaroid stopped distributing film in South Africa because of pressure from black employees who objected to its sale for use in taking photographs for government-required black identification. Since then the movement has gained strength.

Critics object to the role that American corporations play in supporting the South African government and economy. Although U.S. corporations are a liberalizing influence and generally follow enlightened employment practices, their presence buttresses a racist regime. In a commencement address at Hunter College, Archbishop Desmond M. Tutu, a black South African, addressed U.S. corporations' defense of their presence in these uncompromising terms:

> I would be more impressed with those who made no bones about the reason they remain in South Africa and said honestly, "We are concerned for our profits," instead of the baloney that the businesses are there for our benefit. We don't want you there. Please do us a favor: Get out and come back when we have a democratic and just South Africa. . . .
>
> It is true that many foreign corporations in South Africa have introduced improvements for their black staff. . . . American companies, especially, have begun to speak out more forthrightly against apartheid than has been their wont, and they would be the first to admit that they got a considerable jog to their consciences from the disinvestment campaign.
>
> There has been progress, but we do not want apartheid ameliorated or improved. We do not want apartheid made comfortable. We want it dismantled.[35]

There are many ways that U.S. corporations support the South African economy. For example, Caltex processes oil for South Africa, and Fluor Corporation has built three coal-to-oil conversion plants that give the nation considerable energy independence. Babcock and Wilcox, Combustion Engineering, and General Electric have built nuclear reactors. IBM, Unisys, and Control Data supply most of the computers used in South Africa; IBM 370 computers, for example, were once used by the Interior Department in Pretoria to maintain the population registry in which whites, coloureds, and Asians are classified.[36]

Activists emphasize three techniques for applying pressure to U.S. corporations. First, they have lobbied all levels of government for laws that restrict investment and trade. At the federal level passage of the Comprehensive Anti-Apartheid Act in 1986 was a great victory. Over sixty-five city, county, and state governments have passed laws prohibiting investment of government funds in corporations still operating in South Africa. These laws vary in scope but commonly prohibit pension fund investments in the stock of these companies and purchases or bids by them for government contracts. The laws vary in defining when companies are "South Africa–free." Michigan, for example, has

---

[35]Desmond M. Tutu, "Sanctions against Apartheid: Which Side Are You On?" *The Corporate Examiner,* vol. 15, no. 5, 1986.

[36]Richard Leonard, "Hardware, Software and Ingenuity for Apartheid: U.S. Computer Companies in South Africa," *The Corporate Examiner,* vol. 18, no. 1, 1989.

a strict law that required the sale of $16 billion in state pension fund investments in GM and Ford stock because although both firms sold their physical assets in South Africa, they maintained licensing agreements. Some embarrassment ensued because the companies are the state's two largest employers. Under a similar law in New Jersey, however, GM and Ford met the criteria of withdrawal. Share divestment can also be expensive. After passage of its law in 1985, New Jersey calculated a cost of $330 to $515 million in broker fees and lost profits for purging its $20 billion state pension fund.[37]

Second, activists have introduced shareholder resolutions calling for disinvestment at the annual meetings of companies still operating in South Africa. Rules of the Securities and Exchange Commission permit stockholders owning at least $1,000 in stock for a year to introduce these resolutions. If they pass, they are binding on management. Since the early 1970s there have been hundreds of such resolutions. None have passed, and most get less than 10 percent of the vote, but some have gotten over 25 percent. Few publicly held corporations can escape such resolutions today. They put corporations on the defensive and increase the "hassle factor" of a South African presence. Virtually all resolutions are sponsored by church investors, who have set up an organization in New York, the Interfaith Center on Corporate Responsibility, to coordinate their activities. Its membership includes 200 Roman Catholic orders and dioceses and 14 Protestant denominations.

And third, activists have initiated consumer boycotts. The most extensive is a boycott against Royal/Dutch Shell, whose South African subsidiary supplies oil to consumers and to the police and military. A boycott of Shell USA has been supported by the American Baptist churches, the Church of Christ, the United Methodist church, Unitarians, and many Roman Catholic orders. The churches ask members to stop purchasing Shell products and have adopted the slogan "Don't Shell Out for Apartheid." Since 1986 Shell has faced a worldwide boycott of its products, as well as picketing of gas stations, demonstrations at corporate offices, the burning of Shell credit cards at rallies, and the firebombing of two gas stations in the Netherlands. Consumers may also practice selective buying to withdraw support from other companies remaining in South Africa. A guide entitled *Rating America's Corporate Conscience,* published by a group opposed to apartheid, promotes "shopping for a better world."[38] It lists brands of companies in South Africa that buyers may wish to avoid.

ETHICAL PERSPECTIVES ON APARTHEID

There are two distinct ethical questions in the debate over business involvement with South Africa. First, is apartheid ethical? This question does not gen-

---

[37]James A. White, "Divestment Proves Costly and Hard," *Wall Street Journal,* February 22, 1989.
[38]Steven D. Lydenberg, Alice Tepper Marlin, Sean O'Brien Strub, and the Council on Economic Priorities. Reading, Mass.: Addison-Wesley, 1986.

erate disagreement. All voices in the policy debate concede that a system of racial segregation which denies fundamental rights and distributes the benefits and burdens of society on the basis of skin color violates core ethical norms in the American value system. The second question is more difficult. Is it ethical to do business in and with South Africa? This question generates heated disagreement, and the answer differs according to a person's ethical perspective.

Corporate critics who advocate disengagement believe that economic transactions with South Africa are unethical. They give priority to ethical theories of human rights. These theories hold that human beings have a unique dignity entitling them to respectful treatment by others. The apartheid system violates basic rights of freedom and self-determination. For that reason alone it is unethical. It matters not that nonwhites are more prosperous than in some other African nations. A system built on the wholesale deprivation of rights cannot be condoned, even if it results in some benefits for citizens. By analogy, a nation that used slavery would be evil, even if the economy was productive. The blacks in South Africa would be better off living in freedom under miserable economic conditions rather than existing in thrall to bigoted Afrikaners under apartheid. Rights violations in South Africa are so egregious that groups in the United States are justified in intervening in the policies of a foreign government to force correction. As Senator Paul Simon (D-Illinois) once noted, "We cannot sit silently. What we did in the 1930s when Hitler had institutional racism was we issued little pious sermons, but we did nothing to exert our economic muscle. We can't repeat that mistake."[39]

Corporate managers and opponents of trade sanctions, on the other hand, are utilitarians. The utilitarian ethic is the product of a school of English philosophers who believed that the most ethical course of action in any situation was the alternative that maximized pleasure for all parties and minimized pain.[40] On the basis of this theory, the good and bad consequences of doing business under apartheid must be carefully calculated. And when they are, the benefits (pleasures) exceed the costs (pains). Therefore, more good is done by staying involved than by withdrawing, and American corporations should remain as liberalizing influences, even though apartheid is wrong. Furthermore, citizens of the United States have no right to decide that since their ethical sensibilities are hurt, black South Africans should endure economic hardship. As former Prime Minister Botha once pointed out, there is much hypocrisy in the U.S. call for sanctions.

> . . .racial tensions pervade all levels of American life. You have a huge and growing underclass, and over 30 million are living below the poverty line in the richest country in the world. Three times as many blacks as whites live in abject poverty. So it

---

[39]In *Hearings before the Committee on Foreign Relations*, "United States Policy toward South Africa," op. cit., June 23, 1988, p. 123.

[40]See, for example, Jeremy Bentham. *An Introduction to the Principles of Morals and Legislation.* New York: Oxford University Press, 1948 (originally published in 1789), and John Stuart Mill. *Utilitarianism.* New York: New American Library, 1962 (originally published in 1863).

would seem that people who live in glass houses still enjoy pelting South Africa with stones.[41]

The two sides in the South Africa debate disagree over both facts and ethical theories. Both policies, principled disengagement and constructive engagement, may result in a mixture of good and bad consequences. The ethical priorities and approaches of participants determine their choices.

APARTHEID AT THE CROSSROADS?

What change will take place in South Africa? Both whites and blacks have set forth proposals for a new society.

President de Klerk and his National Party revealed the outlines of a new "dispensation" that might be acceptable to whites in a National Party platform statement made public prior to elections in 1989. His vision is one of a system in which blacks share power but do not dominate whites. How can this be accomplished? Only if black demands for a democratic system with one-person, one-vote majority rule are rejected. Then, the National Party favors a system in which all racial groups have guaranteed rights. One such group right would be the freedom to choose a communal life-style. For example, if whites chose to live in geographic or occupational segregation from blacks, they would have the right to do so. Blacks would not participate in the new government as a single mass but would be divided into ten tribal groups, each with group participation rights. In addition to the other traditional groups—whites, coloureds, and Asians—an "open group" of people unwilling to be classified would also exist. All population groups would decide their own affairs through self-government, and issues of common interest would be decided through a consensus process in which all groups participate. Where consensus could not be reached, a judicial body would act as a referee. No group, of course, would be allowed to dominate the white group.

The African National Congress has set forth much different guidelines for a new constitution. It would set up a multiparty democracy in a unitary state with universal suffrage for members of all races. There would be a bill of rights enforceable by an independent judiciary. Although private property rights would be recognized, the ANC has called for wider government ownership of industry, extensive redistribution of land, and a radical redistribution of wealth from whites to blacks to compensate for years of unfair deprivation. Many blacks associate the current capitalist economy with apartheid and are suspicious of its merits.

Whites are opposed to one-person, one-vote majority rule in a unitary government; they fear that this will guarantee not democracy but, rather, the tyranny of the black majority over the white minority. Blacks, on the other hand, are unwilling to accept the group-rights concept proposed by de Klerk. The

[41]In Peter Younghusband, "Shades of Gray in Conflict of Color," *Insight,* April 4, 1988, p. 38.

African National Congress believes that a strong central government will be necessary to implement income redistribution and other programs. And the ANC has always rejected the concept of a federation of groups or states within South African territory because it is opposed to legitimizing the homelands policy of the white government.[42]

White-driven reform efforts in South Africa are calculated to reduce international and domestic pressures by presenting the appearance of movement toward a negotiated end to apartheid. Yet the end has not yet arrived. In the country's 1989 parliamentary elections a large majority of moderate and conservative whites voted for parties with platforms that would preserve some aspects of apartheid.[43] As a pessimistic analyst notes, "The outlook for South Africa is change but no solution."[44] Others are more optimistic. De Klerk has been praised for moving boldly and creating a real, constructive opportunity for change. One diplomat has called him the "Gorbachev of southern Africa."[45]

It is a time of change. Policies in both countries are fluid, and South Africa is at a crossroads. The National Party may choose to permit true democratic reforms. Or it may continue to resist inexorable historical forces. Barring violent civil war, which is unlikely, a set of political reforms acceptable to both blacks and whites will eventually be negotiated in South Africa. But this lies in the future.

In the meantime, the pressure is on American corporations to exit South Africa. In 1990 a 57 percent majority of the American public favored continued withdrawal.[46] The following questions, then, are inviting. First, what are the outlines of a negotiated resolution of the apartheid issue which would be acceptable to all races in South Africa? What kind of new society would be both ethically and politically acceptable? Second, what is your assessment of the positive and negative aspects of corporate involvement in South Africa? On balance, do you favor continued corporate involvement? If you believe that companies should remain there, under what conditions would you favor economic disengagement? Third, is it unethical to make profits in foreign countries where public policy is contrary to American ethics and not democratically determined? Fourth, should managers of American firms advocate political change in foreign countries where they do business? And fifth, if you favor withdrawal of U.S. firms, what conditions should be met before they are allowed to return?

---

[42]Chris Erasmus, "The ANC Positions," *World Press Review*, April 1990, p. 15.

[43]In the September 6, 1989, elections 48 percent of whites voted for the National Party and 31 percent for the Conservative Party, a reactionary party that takes a hard line on preserving apartheid. Only 21 percent voted for the Democratic party, a leftist party committed to ending apartheid. For a discussion of the election see Raymond Bonner, "Choices," *The New Yorker*, December 25, 1989.

[44]Bruce W. Nelan, "Changes in South Africa," *Foreign Affairs*, vol. 69, no. 1, 1989/90, p. 151.

[45]Former British Foreign Secretary David Owen, quoted in David B. Ottaway, "De Klerk: South Africa's Gorbachev?" *Washington Post National Weekly Edition*, February 19–25, 1990.

[46]An NBC News–*Wall Street Journal* poll reported in "Opinion Outlook: Sanctioning Pretoria," *National Journal*, March 10, 1990, p. 597. Twenty-seven percent favored renewed investment, and 16 percent were "not sure."

UNION CARBIDE AND THE BHOPAL PLANT GAS LEAK

On December 3, 1984, operations went awry at the pesticide-manufacturing plant in Bhopal, India. Rapidly, a sequence of safety procedures and devices failed. Fugitive, lethal vapors crossed the plant boundaries, killing 2,347 and seriously injuring 30,000 to 40,000 more.

The gas leak was said to be the worst industrial disaster ever. It put enormous pressure on the management of Union Carbide and reverberated throughout international society. Industry critics were galvanized. "Like Auschwitz and Hiroshima," said one, "the catastrophe at Bhopal is a manifestation of something fundamentally wrong in our stewardship of the earth."[1]

This is the story of the gas leak at Bhopal.

UNION CARBIDE BEFORE BHOPAL

In 1984, the year of the tragic events in Bhopal, Union Carbide was the nation's thirty-fifth-largest industrial corporation. The giant firm, which was founded in 1886, had grown from a small dry-cell battery company into the nation's third-largest chemical producer, with a net profit of $199 million on $9.5 billion in sales. It employed 98,366 "Carbiders" at 500 facilities in thirty-seven countries, and foreign sales were 31 percent of total sales. The company had a variety of product lines, including petrochemicals, industrial gases, welding equipment, popular consumer products—such as Prestone antifreeze,

---

[1]David Weir. *The Bhopal Syndrome.* San Francisco: Sierra Club Books, 1987, p. xii.

Eveready batteries, Glad bags, and Simoniz wax—and high-technology products and services for the electronics, aerospace, and chemical industries.

Although it was the third-largest U.S. chemical producer, Carbide ranked only sixteenth in profitability. Its petrochemical sales were 28 percent of total sales in 1984 but only 23 percent of operating profits; Carbide, a low-cost producer of petrochemicals such as ethylene, had been slow to divert its resources to more profitable business lines. To make matters worse, the entire chemical industry had been in a slump for several years. In addition, new Saudi Arabian petrochemical plants were coming on line in 1985 and 1986. Chemical companies worldwide now faced competition from those Saudi plants, which had access to low-cost raw materials. In anticipation of Saudi production, chemical manufacturers the world over were reducing capacity. Hence, by 1984, Carbide's strategy was to emphasize growth segments in its other operating divisions.

Union Carbide had a reputation as a socially and environmentally concerned company; a 1983 *Fortune* magazine survey ranked Carbide in the upper half of the chemical industry for environmental responsibility. In 1977, Carbide added Russell E. Train, former head of the EPA, to its board of directors and shortly thereafter set up a corporate department of health, safety, and environmental affairs.

UNION CARBIDE'S PLANT IN BHOPAL

Union Carbide first incorporated in India in 1934, when it began to make batteries there. It operates through an Indian subsidiary in which it owns a 50.9 percent majority interest and Indian investors, a 49.1 percent minority interest. Among Indian investors, the Indian government predominates. Through a set of investment firms operating under the Public Financial Institutions, it owns roughly half the 49.1 percent minority interest. This jointly owned subsidiary, named Union Carbide India Ltd. (UCIL), trades its shares on the Bombay Stock Exchange and is operated entirely by Indians. In 1984, UCIL had fourteen plants and 9,000 employees, including 120 at the Bhopal plant in central India. Although UCIL contributed less than 2 percent to Carbide's revenues, it was the fifteenth-largest in sales among all Indian companies in 1984. Most of its business was from the sales of Eveready batteries.

Union Carbide elected to build a pesticide plant in Bhopal in 1969. At that time, there was a growing demand in India and throughout Asia for pesticides, due to the burgeoning "green revolution," a type of planned agriculture that requires intensive use of pesticides and fertilizers in the cultivation of special strains of food crops such as wheat, rice, and corn. Although pesticides may be misused and pose some risk, they have great social value as well. Without pesticides, there is no question that damage to crops, losses in food storage, and toxic mold growth in food supplies would mean the loss of many lives from starvation and food poisoning in developing countries like India. It has been estimated that pesticide use increases India's annual crop yield by about

10 percent—enough to feed roughly 70 million people. In India, about half the nation's population of 750 million lives below a minimum caloric intake established as a poverty line by the government. The chances of an Indian dying from starvation are astronomically greater than those of dying from pesticide poisoning or a Bhopal-type disaster.

In the early 1970s, the small Bhopal plant made pesticides from chemicals imported to the site. The plant was supported by the government of the city of Bhopal and the state of Madhya Pradesh, which reduced the plant's taxes as an incentive. In 1975, however, UCIL was pressured by the Indian government to reduce its imports. The company proposed to manufacture methyl isocyanate (MIC) at the plant rather than ship it in from Carbide facilities outside the country.

Methyl isocyanate, CH_3NCO, is a colorless liquid with a sharp odor. It is used in the production of foams and polyurethane plastics. At the Bhopal plant, however, MIC was used as an intermediate chemical in pesticide manufacture. It was not a final product. Rather, MIC molecules were created and then reacted with other synthetic organic chemicals to produce uniquely shaped molecules that interfere with the natural chemistry of insect nervous systems and thus act as chemical weapons within pests. The two pesticides made by an MIC reaction process at Bhopal, with the trade names Sevin and Temik, are carbamate pesticides that disable a critical enzyme in the nervous systems of pests, leading to convulsions and deaths.[2]

In 1975, Carbide received a permit from the Ministry of Industry in New Delhi to build a methyl isocyanate unit at the Bhopal plant. Two months before this permit was issued, the city of Bhopal had enacted a development plan that required the relocation of dangerous industries to an industrial zone 15 miles outside the city. Pursuant to the plan, M. N. Buch, the Bhopal city administrator, tried to relocate the UCIL pesticide plant and convert the site to use for housing and light commercial activity. This effort failed for reasons that are unclear, and Buch was shortly thereafter transferred to forestry duties elsewhere.

Between 1975 and 1980, the MIC unit was constructed from a design package provided by Union Carbide's engineering group in the United States. Detailed design work was done by an Indian subsidiary of a London firm, Humphreys & Glasgow Pvt. Ltd. The unit was built by local labor using Indian equipment and supplies. The reason for such heavy Indian involvement with

---

[2]Sevin molecules are absorbed into the body of an insect and interfere with the normal cholinergic function during the chemical transmission of nervous impulses in the synaptic gap between axon and dendrite. Normally, nerve impulses are transmitted across the gap by secretion, diffusion, and chemoreception of acetylcholine, after which the acetylcholine is hydrolyzed in a reaction with its substrate, cholinesterase. Sevin molecules, however, have an active site that occupies the receptor site in cholinesterase. Acetylcholine is not hydrolyzed, and the insect suffers disruption of its nervous system and, hence, of every organ in its body. The key to the effectiveness of Sevin is the active site on the molecule. When MIC is reacted with 1-naphthol, a molecule with this active site is created. That is why MIC was present in large quantities at the Bhopal plant.

the plant was an Indian law, the Foreign Exchange Regulation Act of 1973, which requires foreign multinationals to share technology and use Indian resources.

In 1980, the project was finished, and the MIC unit began operation. During construction, large, unplanned slums and shantytowns called *jhuggis* had grown up near the plant, peopled mainly by manual laborers. Of course, the plant had become far more dangerous, for it now manufactured the basic chemical ingredients of pesticides rather than simply making them from shipped-in ingredients. One step in the manufacture of MIC, for example, involves the production of phosgene, the lethal "mustard gas" used in World War I.

In 1981, a phosgene gas leak at the Bhopal plant killed one worker, and a crusading Indian journalist wrote a series of articles about the plant and its potential dangers to the population. No one heeded these articles. In 1982, a second phosgene leak forced the temporary evacuation of some surrounding slum areas. Also in 1982, a safety survey of the plant by three Carbide engineers from the United States cited approximately fifty safety defects, most of them minor, and noted "no situation involving imminent danger or requiring immediate correction."[3] Subsequently, all suggested changes in safety systems and procedures were made (except the replacement of one troublesome valve outside the accident area). Worker safety and environmental inspections of the plant were carried out by the Department of Labor in Madhya Pradesh. The agency had only fifteen factory inspectors to cover 8,000 plants and had a record of lax enforcement.[4] This was in keeping with the generally low commitment to pollution control in India by regulators at all levels.

A recent downturn in the Indian economy and stiff competition from other pesticide firms marketing newer, less expensive products had caused the Bhopal plant to lose money for three years in a row. As revenues fell, the plant's budgets were cut, and it had been necessary to defer some maintenance, lessen the rigor of training programs, and lay off some workers. At the time of the accident, the MIC unit was operating with a reduced crew of six workers per shift rather than the normal crew of twelve—a condition some process-design engineers thought unsafe.

UNION CARBIDE'S RELATIONSHIP WITH THE BHOPAL PLANT

The Bhopal pesticide plant fit into the Union Carbide management hierarchy as depicted in the organization chart in Figure 13-1. Although some Americans had staffed the plant and had conducted safety inspections in the early years, Carbide turned the plant completely over to Indian personnel after 1982. It did

---

[3]L. A. Kail, J. M. Poulson, and C. S. Tyson. *Operational Safety Survey, CO/MIC/Sevin Units, Union Carbide India Ltd., Bhopal Plant.* South Charleston, W.Va.: Union Carbide Corporation, July 28, 1982, p. 1.

[4]Sheila Jasanoff, "Managing India's Environment," *Environment*, October, 1986, p. 33.

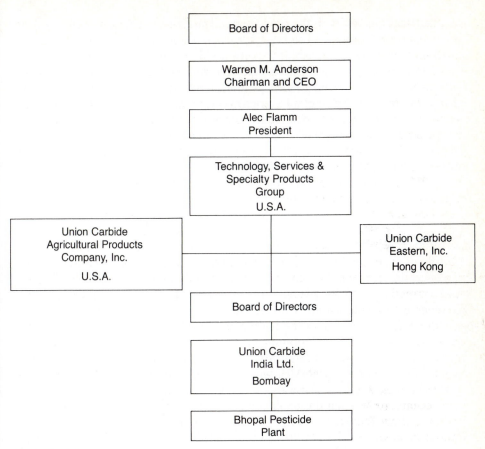

FIGURE 13-1
Union Carbide's organization structure as related to the Bhopal plant.

so under government pressure to increase the self-sufficiency of Indian industry. Plant safety inspections after 1982 were the responsibility of the Indian subsidiary, UCIL. At the time of the accident, therefore, line responsibility for the day-to-day operations and safety of the plant rested with the plant manager, an Indian employee of UCIL. The plant operated with a great deal of autonomy. But Union Carbide had majority ownership of UCIL; in addition, it was represented by five members on the UCIL board of directors, four from Union Carbide Eastern, Inc., and the fifth from the international headquarters group. The Bhopal plant was also in close contact with the management of Union Carbide Agricultural Products Company, Inc., which was Carbide's arm for the production and marketing of pesticides.

Top management at Union Carbide's Danbury, Connecticut, headquarters received monthly reports from the Bhopal plant and approved major financial, maintenance, and personnel decisions. Carbide engineers also provided UCIL and the Bhopal plant with the processing manual on MIC that was supposed to guide plant operations.

In the reporting relationship, Union Carbide's top management in Connecticut had ultimate, formal responsibility for the operation of the Bhopal plant. Shortly after the accident, Chairman Warren M. Anderson stated in interviews that Carbide accepted "moral responsibility" for the tragedy. Nevertheless, the Bhopal plant was but one of hundreds of sites worldwide in which the company had an equity interest. For this reason and because of the vast physical distance separating the two sites, Carbide's U.S. management team delegated considerable authority over operations to UCIL's management team on the spot. The exact nature of this shared authority remains unclear, since the gas victims' claims have never come to trial.

THE GAS LEAK

On the evening of December 2, 1984, storage tank 610, one of three storage tanks at the MIC unit, was filled with 11,290 gallons of MIC. The tank, which had a capacity of 15,000 gallons, was a partly buried, stainless steel, pressurized vessel. The purpose of Tank 610 was to store large batches of MIC. MIC was produced elsewhere at the plant and routed through pipes into Tank 610. At an appropriate time operators in a control room would open and close valves to move 1-ton batches of MIC through a transfer pipe to the area where pesticides were made.[5] The MIC would then be converted to Sevin (or Temik).

At about 9:30 p.m., a supervisor ordered Rehman Khan, an operator in the MIC complex, to unclog four filter valves near the MIC production area by washing them out with water. Khan connected a water hose to the piping above the clogged valves but neglected to insert a slip blind above the point of water entry. A slip blind is a simple device that seals lines to prevent water leakage into adjacent pipes. This action violated instructions in the MIC processing manual, the technical manual which sets forth procedures established by the chemical engineers who set up the plant.

Either because of this careless washing procedure or because of the introduction of water elsewhere, 120 to 240 gallons of water entered Tank 610, initiating a powerful exothermic (heat-building) reaction. Initially, operators were unaware that the reaction was proceeding that night. At 10:30, tank pressure was logged at 2 pounds per square inch. Then, at 10:45, a new shift came on duty. At 11:30 p.m., a new operator in the MIC control room noticed that the

---

[5]Some other companies used a different production process to make carbamate pesticides in which MIC was manufactured in small amounts and then immediately reacted to produce the pesticide. The advantage? Storage of large batches of MIC was unnecessary. After the accident, Carbide was criticized for using a production process that required storage of tens of thousands of gallons of MIC for long periods. Some process chemists thought it was particularly inappropriate to use the method in a less developed country lacking experience with high-risk production technologies.

pressure in Tank 610 was 10 pounds per square inch, but the operator was unconcerned because this was within tolerable limits, the gauges were often wrong, and he did not read the log to discover that the pressure was five times greater than it had been one hour earlier.

As the reaction continued, the temperature in Tank 610 rose. Unfortunately, the refrigeration units that cooled the tanks had been shut down for five months as an economy measure. Had the tanks been refrigerated, as the MIC processing manual required, the heat buildup from the reaction with the water might have taken place over several days instead of several hours.

As pressure built in the tank, a leak developed. At about 11:30, workers smelled MIC, and their eyes watered. At 11:45, one operator spotted a small, yellowish drip of MIC from some high piping and informed his supervisor. The supervisor suggested fixing the leak after a tea break scheduled for 12:15 a.m. on December 3.

At 12:40, the tea break ended. But by this time a gauge in the control room showed that the pressure in Tank 610 was 40 pounds per square inch. It rose in a short time to 55 pounds per square inch, the top of the scale. A glance at the tank temperature gauge brought more bad news: the MIC was vaporizing at 77°F, 36° higher than the safety limit specified in the MIC processing manual. After reading the gauges, an operator ran out to look at Tank 610. He felt heat radiating from the tank and heard the concrete over it cracking. Within seconds, a pressure-release valve opened, and a white cloud of deadly MIC vapor shot into the atmosphere with a screech.

Operators back in the control room turned a switch to activate the vent gas scrubber, a safety device designed to neutralize any escaped toxic gases from the MIC unit by circulating them through a caustic soda solution. The scrubber, however, failed to operate because it had been shut down for maintenance. A subsequent investigation established that even if the scrubber had been on-line that night, it was not designed to handle the temperature and pressure reached by the MIC in the tank and would have been quickly overwhelmed. A flare tower designed to burn off toxic gases before they escaped into the atmosphere was also off-line; it had been disassembled for maintenance, and an elbow joint was missing. Another emergency measure, the transferring of MIC from Tank 610 to one of two other storage tanks, was impossible as well, because both of those tanks were full or nearly so. This situation also violated procedures in the MIC processing manual, which called for leaving one tank empty as a safety measure.

At about 1:00 a.m., an operator turned on an alarm to warn workers of danger from escaping gas. The plant superintendent, who had arrived in the control room, directed that a water spray be turned on the escaping MIC vapor to knock it down, but this had little effect. At this time, most workers in the plant ran in panic, ignoring four parked buses, which they were supposed to drive through the surrounding area to begin the evacuation of residents. Only two workers stayed in the MIC control room. They shared the only available ox-

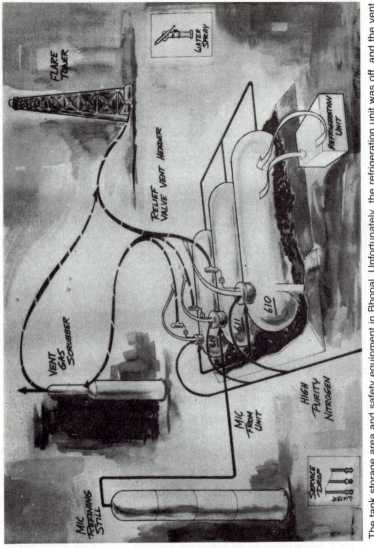

The tank storage area and safety equipment in Bhopal. Unfortunately, the refrigeration unit was off, and the vent gas scrubber, flare tower, and water spray failed to prevent disaster. The service drop in the lower left corner is a likely route of entry for the water that caused the reaction. (*Photo used courtesy of Union Carbide.*)

ygen mask when the room filled with MIC vapor. Finally, at about 2:30 a.m., the pressure in the tank dropped, the leaking safety valve resealed, and the MIC leak stopped.

Over a two-hour period, roughly 10,000 gallons, or about 90 percent, of the MIC in Tank 610 vaporized and blew out in a white cloud. The cloud spread for miles across the sleeping city. That night the wind was calm and the temperature was about 60°F, and so the heavy chemical mist lingered just above the ground. The gas attacked people in the streets and seeped into their homes. Those who panicked and ran into the night air suffered higher doses of toxic vapor. Because MIC is so reactive with water, simply breathing through a wet cloth would have saved many lives. But people lacked this simple knowledge. Unprotected animals met the same fate as humans. Trees were stripped of leaves. As word of the gas leak spread, crowds of Bhopal residents fled the city, including many of the relatively affluent suburbanites who owned cars. The poor in the slums and shantytowns near the plant were left to bear the brunt of misfortune.

As the poisonous cloud blanketed its victims, MIC, a very active compound, reacted with water in their eyes. This reaction created heat, which burned corneal cells, rendering them opaque. Residents with cloudy, burning eyes staggered into aid stations, permanently or temporarily blind.

Many victims suffered shortness of breath, coughing fits, inflammation of the respiratory tract, and chemical pneumonia. In the lungs, MIC molecules reacted with moist tissues, causing chemical burns. Fluid oozed from seared lung tissue and pooled, causing a condition called pulmonary edema, and many victims literally drowned in their own secretions. If they did not suffocate from edema, chemical burns destroyed sheets of cells that facilitate the exchange of gases in breathing and the clearing of foreign matter from the lungs. In survivors, the burned tissue eventually healed but was covered with a tough protein substance called fibrin, which created areas of pulmonary fibrosis that diminished breathing capacity. The injured were also in great danger of developing respiratory infections as they recovered.

There is no known antidote for MIC exposure. Treatment consisted of the administration of oxygen, mechanical ventilation of the lungs, the use of diuretics to maintain fluid balance, and the short-term use of steroids to decrease lung inflammation. The use of sedatives and painkillers was an adjunct treatment. Often, however, doctors were helpless. Unfortunately, many residents of the slums around the plant were already in poor health from living in poverty; they suffered from malnutrition, tuberculosis, and a variety of infections. These chronic conditions exacerbated the effects of MIC injury.

How many died at Bhopal? The Indian government issued 1,450 death certificates, but many families built funeral pyres without consulting local authorities. The local police department estimated 1,900 deaths. Bhopal's mayor said 3,000. Other Indian officials suggested a toll as high as 7,000 to 10,000. Finally, in November 1986, the Indian government established an official death toll of 2,347. About 200,000 of Bhopal's roughly 700,000 residents were exposed to the gas, and the government estimates that 30,000 to 40,000 were seriously injured.[6] Victims continue to die in hospitals from gas-related injuries long after exposure, and visitors to Bhopal describe sounds of coughing and wheezing wherever people congregate.

UNION CARBIDE REACTS

Unprecedented management problems faced Warren M. Anderson, age sixty-three, chairman and CEO of Union Carbide. Awakened early in the morning on Monday, December 3, Anderson rushed to Carbide's Danbury, Connecticut, headquarters and learned of the rising death toll. In the early morning hours, when the extent of the disaster was evident, an emergency meeting of a senior management committee was held. The committee sent emergency medical supplies, respirators, and oxygen (Carbide products), as well as an American doctor with extensive knowledge of MIC, to Bhopal.

The next day, Tuesday, December 4, Carbide dispatched a team of technical experts to examine the plant and find out what had happened. Production of MIC was halted immediately at Carbide's plant in Institute, West Virginia. A press conference was held. Staff members were pulled from other duties to work in corporate communications and return phone calls. On Thursday, Anderson himself departed for India. He went both as a symbol of top-level commitment and as an on-the-scene crisis manager. Only two phone lines into Bhopal were operative, and it was proving difficult to get information in Danbury about events there. Upon arriving in Bhopal, Anderson was arrested, charged with criminal negligence, briefly detained in the guest house at the Bhopal plant, flown to New Delhi, and then asked to leave the country. Later, he would be charged with homicide.

With worldwide attention focused on Bhopal, Carbide held daily press conferences. It released copies of the 1982 safety survey of the Bhopal plant. Anderson made two videotapes telling employees to bear up, and 500 copies of each were dispatched to plants around the world. Christmas parties were canceled. Flags at Carbide facilities were flown at half-mast. All of Carbide's nearly 100,000 employees observed a moment of silence for the victims. Many employees contributed to a relief fund. Carbide gave $1 million to an emergency relief fund and offered to turn its guest house in Bhopal into an orphan-

---

[6]Many Bhopal residents have reported injuries other than to the respiratory tract and eyes, including ulcers, colitis, memory loss, hysteria, and birth defects. See Mark Fineman, "Bhopal—Death Won't Leave City," *Los Angeles Times,* March 13, 1989. But there is no evidence that MIC had other target organs, and animal tests show minimal or no effects on fertility, reproduction, and immune defense mechanisms. See, for example, Ernest E. McConnell et al., "Toxicity of Methyl Isocyanate," *Environmental Science and Technology,* vol. 21, no. 2, 1987. Hence, reports of excessive numbers of birth defects among Bhopal residents are suspect. Psychological problems such as depression are common, and evidence suggests that MIC impairment of the lungs is not reversible.

Death and injury tolls continued to mount after 1984. In 1989 the Indian government published an official death toll of 3,415 and said that 60,000 living victims were seriously impaired.

age. Both companies also contributed to a victims medical care research program at Hamidia University Hospital in Bhopal. Months later, Carbide offered another $5 million to the state of Madhya Pradesh, but the money was refused because Indian politicians thought they would appear to be in collusion with the company. The political climate was so hostile that anything associated with Carbide was reviled. Later, when the government discovered that Union Carbide had set up a training school in Bhopal, the facility was torn down with bulldozers.

In the days following the disaster, Anderson assumed full responsibility for management problems and events related to Bhopal. Alec Flamm, president and chief operating officer of Carbide, assumed full responsibility for normal business operations. A five-member board of directors committee, chaired by former EPA head Russell E. Train, was set up to oversee the management response to Bhopal-related issues.

Investor confidence in Carbide was shaken. Carbide's stock fell from about $49 at the time of the disaster to a low of $32.75. As lawsuits were filed on behalf of the victims, with a potential payout exceeding Carbide's net worth, Standard & Poor's, a rater of securities, lowered Carbide's debt rating, an action that made it more difficult and costly for the company to raise money. Anderson, as spokesperson for Carbide, had to undertake the delicate task of assuring investors that the company would continue to make profits while appearing not to show callous disregard for the human tragedy in Bhopal.

LAWSUITS AGAINST CARBIDE

No sooner had the MIC vapor cleared than American attorneys arrived in Bhopal to seek litigants for damage claims against Union Carbide. They walked the shantytown streets, signing up plaintiffs. Names of potential litigants were sold for profit. These events, said a *Wall Street Journal* editorial, were "a second tragedy."[7]

The American lawyers who rushed to Bhopal defended their actions by making three points. First, if multinational corporations could be tried in U.S. courts, a single global liability standard would exist to promote safety. Second, big awards by juries, such as the recent ones against the Manville Corporation and the A. H. Robins Company, act as effective curbs on corporate irresponsibility. And third, after the disaster, these lawyers kept the victims on center stage so that their plight was not forgotten.

Shortly after the MIC leak, the Indian government paid settlements of about $800 to the families of those who died. A program of smaller awards to injury victims was undertaken, but it was not completed because of administrative problems. Union Carbide offered a settlement of $300 million to the Indian

---

[7]"Bhopal's Best Hope," August 12, 1985, p. 16.

government. Acceptance would have meant immediate aid to victims and surviving family members, but the government rejected the offer as inadequate.

On December 7, just four days after the gas leak, the first lawsuit against Carbide was filed in a federal district court in West Virginia.[8] American lawyers, who altogether represented an astronomical $50 billion in damage claims against Carbide, sought to have the Bhopal victims' cases tried in U.S. courts. There they could seek large punitive damages and profit from the American contingency-fee system, under which they could claim a percentage of the ultimate awards to their Indian clients. They were not licensed to practice law in India and could not try the cases there. By February 1985, 145 suits involving approximately 200,000 Indian plaintiffs were consolidated for trial in the U.S. District Court for the Southern District of New York.[9] The suits were brought there because Union Carbide is chartered by the state of New York.

But on March 29, 1985, before the American lawyers could make much headway, the Indian Parliament enacted the Bhopal Gas Leak Disaster (Processing of Claims) Act ("Bhopal Act"), which gave India the exclusive right to represent Indian plaintiffs in India or any other nation.[10] A week later, India filed a suit on behalf of the victims in the New York court. In this suit India was represented by an attorney from a Minneapolis law firm.

Was the Indian government entitled to sole representation of victims? Did the Bhopal Act disqualify American lawyers? These questions would be decided by District Court Judge John Keenan. Soon Union Carbide's lawyers filed a motion to dismiss the cases on the grounds of *forum non conveniens*. This is a legal principle which allows a court to decline jurisdiction of a case when an alternative trial forum is more convenient. Carbide argued that it would be more reasonable to try the cases in India. After all, witnesses, records, and evidence at the plant were there. In addition, Indian law was probably applicable, language barriers would be less formidable, and travel costs would be reduced.

Unargued were other enormous advantages for Union Carbide in moving the cases to India. Compensation for the value of a life in Indian courts was typically infinitesimal compared with awards in American courts. Average annual income was about $28,000 in the United States in 1985 but only $300 in India and $170 in the Bhopal area.[11] Indian courts rarely awarded more than $10,000 for a wrongful death, and the families of Indians killed by buses usually received $100 to $200. By contrast, in American courts there have been hundreds of awards exceeding $1,000,000. Also, Indian courts were notorious for delays and procedural complications that could work in favor of Union Carbide. The Carbide motion put the Indian government in the embarrassing

---

[8]*Dawani et al.* v. *Union Carbide Corp.*, S.D.W.Va. (84–2479).

[9]601 F.Supp. 1035 (J.P.M.D.L. 1985).

[10]Indian Parliament Act. No. 21 of 1985, *entered into force* Feb. 20, 1985, GAZETTE OF INDIA (EXTRAORDINARY), pt. 2, sec. 2, March 29, 1985.

[11]James Flanigan, "Bhopal a Hard Lesson in Value of Safety Rules," *Los Angeles Times,* February 15, 1989.

position of having to argue that fairer and speedier compensation to victims would result from trial in the American venue.

Shortly before Judge Keenan was to rule on Union Carbide's motion, the company offered $350 million to settle the 487,000 existing claims filed by that time. The American lawyers, fearing that Judge Keenan would send the cases to India, rushed to accept Carbide's money. The Indian government, however, refused the offer as inadequate.

On May 12, 1986, Judge Keenan ruled that the cases should be heard in India. This was a victory for Carbide. The American lawyers lost any chance of compensation for their efforts to represent the victims. In his opinion, Judge Keenan showed no sympathy for them. "Suffice it to say," he wrote, "that those members of the American bar who travelled the 8,200 miles to Bhopal [in the days immediately following the tragedy] did little to better the American image in the Third World—or anywhere else."[12] As for the government of India, Judge Keenan said that it faced a challenge. He wrote:

> In the Court's view, to retain the litigation in this forum, as plaintiffs request, would be yet another example of imperialism, another situation in which an established sovereign inflicted its rules, its standards and values on a developing nation. This Court declines to play such a role. The Union of India is a world power in 1986, and its courts have the proven capacity to mete out fair and equal justice. To deprive the Indian judiciary of this opportunity to stand tall before the world and to pass judgment on behalf of its own people would be to revive a history of subservience and subjugation from which India has emerged. India and its people can and must vindicate their claims before the independent and legitimate judiciary created there since the Independence of 1947.[13]

On September 9, 1986, the Indian government filed a suit on behalf of the victims in the District Court of Bhopal. It sought a judgment of $3.3 billion against Union Carbide. It argued that Carbide, while engaged in the hazardous act of making pesticides, had breached duties to (*a*) protect the environment, (*b*) protect human life, (*c*) utilize effective safety practices in the handling of MIC, and (*d*) inform Indian authorities of the full risks of carbamate pesticide manufacture. Thus began a second round of legal fencing.

IN THE AFTERMATH

In the weeks following the Bhopal tragedy, there was a strong backlash against Union Carbide, the chemical industry, and multinational corporations. This

---

[12]*In re Union Carbide Corporation Gas Plant Disaster at Bhopal, India in December, 1984,* 634 F.Supp. 844 (S.D.N.Y. 1986).

[13]634 F.Supp. 867. Judge Keenan's opinion was upheld on appeal to the U.S. Court of Appeals, Second Circuit, on January 14, 1987. The appeals court did, however, strike several procedural conditions that Judge Keenan had imposed on Union Carbide related to discovery, parallel jurisdiction, and satisfaction of eventual judgment. Left intact was an order that Union Carbide waive defenses based on the statute of limitations. Nos. 86–7517, 86–7589, 86–7637. In October 1987 the U.S. Supreme Court, without comment, let the judgment stand.

was perhaps unfair, because the record of safety in the chemical industry is generally excellent. Nonetheless, the world reacted. Townspeople in Livingston, Scotland, rejected plans for a new Union Carbide plant for blending industrial gases. A judge in Brazil banned imports of MIC. Protesters demonstrated at Union Carbide plants worldwide. At home, the American public was cynical about Carbide's actions. A *Business Week*/Louis Harris poll in mid-December 1984 reported that only 48 percent of the public gave a rating of "good" to Carbide for "its overall reaction to the disaster;" only 36 percent gave a "good" rating for "telling the truth about what happened in India."[14]

Early in 1985, a number of safety-oriented bills were introduced in Congress. The National Transportation Safety Board raised federal standards for shipping toxic chemicals. Chemical companies reviewed their safety controls. Insurance companies made liability policies covering industrial risk more restrictive and more expensive. And many states and cities passed "right-to-know" laws requiring chemical plants to reveal listings of dangerous chemicals on their premises.[15] For its part, Carbide resumed production of MIC at its Institute, West Virginia, plant but ended shipments of MIC from that plant to its Woodbine, Georgia, pesticide-formulation plant. Instead, it shipped aldicarb, a less volatile chemical produced further down the pesticide-production process stream. The company made costly improvements in the safety systems of the Institute MIC unit and pledged $120 million in new safety and environmental expenditures.

CARBIDE FACES DIFFICULT TIMES

Unfortunately for Carbide, disaster soon struck again, neutralizing whatever public relations gains had been made by its careful responses to the Bhopal crisis. On August 11, 1985, a 200-yard-wide cloud of yellowish gas escaped from the Institute plant and sent 135 nearby West Virginia residents to the hospital. The next morning, a picture on the front page of *The New York Times* showed paramedics taking small children to the hospital on stretchers. The unlucky 135 received hospital treatment for burning eyes, breathing difficulty, and other pulmonary complications, but the injuries were not serious. The escaped gas was not MIC, but analysis showed it to be composed of other chemicals that could have been fatal in larger doses. Carbide once again suspended production at Institute pending an investigation. That investigation related a series of human and procedural errors leading directly to the toxic discharge. Another $88.2 million in lawsuits was filed against Carbide, and in April 1986,

---

[14]Stewart Jackson and Harris Collingwood, "*Business Week*/Harris Poll: Is an Antibusiness Backlash Building?" *Business Week*, July 20, 1987.

[15]The first of these was New Jersey's Toxic Catastrophe Prevention Act, which was signed into law on January 8, 1986. The law became known as the "Bhopal bill" and required chemical companies to register hazardous substances such as MIC, to do formal studies of risks posed by their plants, and to take specific steps to reduce risks. The federal government later passed a similar law, the Emergency Planning and Community Right-to-Know Act of 1986.

OSHA fined the company $1.4 million for "conscious, overt, and willful" safety violations at the Institute plant. At the time, this was the largest OSHA fine ever imposed.

In addition to dealing with problems caused by gas leaks, Carbide had to fight for its independence when, in August 1985—the same month as the Institute, West Virginia, gas leak—GAF Corporation announced that it was accumulating Carbide shares for a possible takeover bid. In December, this takeover effort materialized. In a month-long war of wills, Carbide successfully repelled GAF, but only at the cost of taking on enormous new debt to buy back 55 percent of its outstanding shares. In 1986, after the takeover battle, Carbide's debt-to-capitalization ratio exceeded 80 percent. This huge debt load had to be reduced, because interest payments were crippling. So in 1986, Carbide sold $3.5 billion worth of assets, including its most popular consumer brands—Eveready batteries, Glad bags, and Prestone antifreeze. The company also sold more than a dozen other businesses and by 1987 had restructured into three tightly focused business groups—chemicals and plastics, industrial gases, and carbon products.

Its chairman, Robert D. Kennedy, said that restructuring was "like walking into a pet shop, opening all the bird cages and letting the birds fly out."[16] But, he added, the old conglomerate structure had been unwieldy; diversification had gone too far. The old Carbide had suffered from internal culture clashes, an imbalance between cash-hungry and cash-generating businesses, and the lack of a clear strategic mission. Of the new Carbide, Kennedy said: "We make decisions faster, things happen faster, we're more open to new thinking and new ideas, are less a multi-culture company and more a company with a coherent view of ourselves and our markets."[17] Cost cutting and layoffs had made the remaining businesses leaner. By 1988 Carbide's payroll had dropped to 43,000 from its pre-Bhopal high of 98,000. The revamped Carbide performed well. Earnings and net profit rose substantially from 1987 to 1988.[18]

INVESTIGATIONS INTO THE CAUSE OF THE MIC LEAK

In the days following the disaster there was worldwide interest in pinning down the precise cause of the gas leak. A team of reporters from the *The New York Times* visited Bhopal and interviewed plant workers. Their six-week investigation led to the publication of lengthy newspaper accounts which concluded that the accident was caused by a large volume of water entering Tank 610 and reacting with the MIC.[19] The water entered because the operator who

---

[16]"Strategic Planning," *Vital Speeches of the Day,* August 1, 1987, p. 624.

[17]Ibid., p. 626.

[18]Carbide's sales in 1987 were $6.9 billion and increased to $7.3 billion in 1988 (compared with $9.5 billion in 1984). The net profit was $285 million in 1987 and rose to $355 million in 1988 (compared with $364 million in 1984).

[19]Stuart Diamond, "The Bhopal Disaster: How It Happened," *The New York Times,* January 28, 1985; Thomas J. Lueck, "Carbide Says Inquiry Showed Errors but Is Incomplete," *The New*

had washed out filter valves earlier in the evening had violated procedure and failed to use a slip blind. So water from the hose simply backed up and eventually flowed about 400 feet into the MIC storage tank. The *Times* account was widely accepted as authoritative, and this theory, called the "water-washing theory," gained wide currency. Media audiences found a plausible explanation that satisfied their curiosity.

Immediately after the accident, Union Carbide rushed a team of investigators to Bhopal, including scientists, chemical engineers, attorneys, and accident investigation experts from the independent consulting firm of Arthur D. Little. But the team was severely hampered by lack of cooperation from Indian authorities, who were under political pressure from anti-Carbide protest groups and anti-American public feeling in the wake of the tragedy. It was denied access to plant records and blocked from interviews with workers by the Indian Central Bureau of Investigation, which was conducting a criminal inquiry into the incident. In accident investigation, early debriefing of witnesses is critical because over time memories of minor details fade and stories tend to alter and harden.[20] But Carbide was denied this advantage and was unable, in the short run, to counter the image of inept management and blundering projected in the *The New York Times* stories.

The Carbide investigative team was, however, given access to Tank 610 and took a number of core samples from the residue in the bottom. These samples were sent to the United States and analyzed. Over 500 experimental chemical reactions were undertaken to explain the chemistry of the residue material. In March 1985, Union Carbide finally released its first report of the accident. The short (25-page) Carbide report concluded that the accident had been caused by the entry of water into the tank, but it did not accept the water-washing theory. It stated that "the source of the water is unknown" but focused attention on the possibility of entry through misconnection of a water line at a utility station near the tank.[21]

Utility stations (or "service drops," as they are sometimes called) are located throughout chemical plants and provide needed services. Typically, they contain headers for compressed air, water, nitrogen, and steam—all essential

---

York Times, January 28, 1985; Stuart Diamond, "The Disaster in Bhopal: Workers Recall Horror," *The New York Times,* January 30, 1985; and Robert Reinhold, "Disaster in Bhopal: Where Does Blame Lie?" *The New York Times,* January 31, 1985.

[20]Ted S. Ferry. *Modern Accident Investigation and Analysis,* 2d ed. New York: John Wiley & Sons, 1988, p. 32. According to Ferry: "Witnesses are strongly influenced by each other and by the news media. When given time to talk to or listen to others who have seen the event they may change their story. They can listen to a TV news account and alter their story to support the media account. A witness may not understand what he has seen and, innocently, to explain things in his own mind, will change his story. This can happen unconsciously and without any intent to deceive. Several hours later or the next day he may have a different story to tell and believe it himself. Witnesses can also forget. A witness may not remember some events, particularly if they do not confirm what he has come to believe he saw or heard. ... Some witnesses are hostile and, given time, may change their story to hurt the company or protect a friend" (p. 32).

[21]*Bhopal Methyl Isocyanate Incident Investigation Team Report.* Danbury, Conn.: Union Carbide Corporation, March 1985, p. i.

for chemical plant operations. At the utility station near Tank 610, the nitrogen and water lines are located together. The Carbide investigation team hypothesized that if a worker had deliberately or accidentally connected piping leading to Tank 610 with the water line at the service drop, the resulting flow could account for an amount of water sufficient to cause the reaction. Carbide investigators rejected the water-washing hypothesis for several reasons. The piping system was designed to prevent water contamination. Valves between the filter valves being washed and Tank 610 were found closed after the accident. And the amount of water contamination required to create the reaction—1,000 to 2,000 pounds—was too great to be explained by valve leakage.

The Carbide report contradicted the water-washing theory, but within nine months an investigation sponsored by the Indian government embraced it once again. This study, made by Indian scientists and engineers, stated that the entry of water into Tank 610 was the cause of the accident and that water had gotten into the tank as a result of an improper water-washing procedure.[22]

There matters stood until December 1985, when Judge Keenan ordered the Indian government to give Carbide access to plant records and the names of workers. This order corrected an unfairness in the litigation process in which the government of India was suing Carbide, while simultaneously barring Carbide from access to critical evidence that might prove its innocence. Carbide renewed its investigation.

What ensued is a remarkable detective story. A team of interviewers began work in January 1986. Among them were Nawser Parakh, a former engineer at the Bhopal plant who had been popular with the workers; Ashok S. Kalelkar, a consultant from Arthur D. Little; and Paul Doyle, a New York attorney leading Carbide's litigation effort. At first, they had trouble finding former workers. Many had left Bhopal. The plant had been closed for over one year, and they had scattered to find new jobs. The team members interviewed landlords and relatives, but sometimes there were no forwarding addresses. Their search extended to far corners of India and beyond. Once, they traveled in 90° heat to a small town in Nepal just to interview a tea boy named V. Mani. They found that their subject was the wrong V. Mani (the right V. Mani was never located). They were hampered by poor telephone service and lack of cooperation from workers who did not want to talk. The strong value attached to politeness in Indian culture frustrated investigators too. Reticent workers politely made interview appointments and then failed to keep them. But politeness also worked to the advantage of the team, for when interviews were finally held, the subjects tried hard to please their questioners.

The team was tenacious. Former workers were sometimes tricked into

---

[22]*Report on Scientific Studies on the Release Factors Related to Bhopal Toxic Gas Leakage.* Bombay: Indian Council of Scientific and Industrial Research, December 1985. The report suggested another possible route for water entry into Tank 610: backflow from the vent gas scrubber. As evidence, the report cited high concentrations of sodium in the residue of Tank 610, which would indicate that water had mixed with the caustic soda in the scrubber prior to entry.

opening the door. Nawser Parakh would ring a doorbell while other team members stayed out of sight and the American-looking Doyle slumped in a car seat. When the subject answered the door, team members would suddenly spring up. Once, the team members constructed an elaborate ruse involving a marriage proposal to trick an important witness into coming home. Agents of the Central Bureau of Investigation followed the Carbide team, eavesdropping on phone conversations and debriefing employees.

Over seventy interviews, plus a careful examination of plant records and physical evidence, led the investigators to conclude that the cause of the gas leak was sabotage by a disgruntled employee, who intentionally hooked up a water hose to Tank 610. Furthermore, Carbide alleged a cover-up among plant employees. Interviews and evidence at the plant indicated that MIC operators had known about the introduction of water, but in the postdisaster atmosphere of arrests and criminal sanctions they denied knowledge of causation.

Here is the Carbide explanation of how water entered Tank 610. It begins by discrediting the water-washing theory in three ways. First, experiments showed that it was impossible for a water hose to provide the necessary hydraulic head to push water up a 10.4-foot rise from the area the employee was washing to the inlet on Tank 610. Second, maintenance records showed that an intermediate valve was closed before the accident, and a postaccident inspection found that it was still closed. And third, for water to have reached the tank, a large reservoir of piping had to be filled first. About 4,500 pounds of water would have been required, but when the Central Bureau of Investigation drilled a tap into this area in February 1985, it was bone-dry. Had water entered through this route, some would have remained. There was not a drop.

Here is the sequence of events on the night of December 2–3 that Carbide substitutes for the water-washing theory. At 10:20 p.m. the pressure gauge on Tank 610 read 2 pounds per square inch. This meant that no water had yet entered the tank and no reaction had begun. At 10:45 p.m. the regularly scheduled shift change occurred. Shift changes take half an hour, and the MIC storage area would have been deserted. At this time an operator who had been angry for several days about his failure to get a promotion stole into the area. He unscrewed the local pressure gauge on Tank 610, hooked up a rubber water hose, and turned the water on. Five minutes would have sufficed to do this. Carbide claims to know the name of this person but has never revealed it.

Why did he do it? Carbide speculates that his intention was simply to ruin the MIC batch in the tank. Some acts of sabotage had occurred from time to time at the Bhopal plant. It is doubtful that this worker realized how toxic MIC vapor is or intended any loss of life. The interviews had revealed that the workers thought of MIC chiefly as a lacrimator, or a chemical that produces tearing; they did not regard it as a lethal hazard. Indeed, there had been no prior experience with fatalities from the release of vaporized MIC, and after the venting of Tank 610 into the air, operators in the MIC control room felt some relief. They believed the threat had passed and informed town authorities that there was no danger to life.

After entry, the water began to react with MIC in the tank to create carbon dioxide, which began escaping from the vent gas scrubber by 11:30 to 11:45 p.m. Some operators smelled the pungent odor and reported it to supervisors, who sprayed water from a fire hose into the structure around the scrubber mechanism and then went on a tea break in the main canteen.

A few minutes after midnight MIC operators noted a strong pressure rise in Tank 610. Walking to the tank, they found the hose connected and removed it; then they asked the supervisors to come back from their tea break to deal with the situation. The supervisors rushed back. They tried to prevent a catastrophic pressure rise by draining water from Tank 610. Between 12:15 and 12:30 a.m., just minutes before the major gas release, they transferred about one metric ton of MIC from Tank 610 to a holding tank in the Sevin manufacturing area. Water is heavier than MIC, and the transfer was accomplished through a drain in the bottom of Tank 610; thus, the supervisors hoped to remove all the water. They failed. At 12:45 a.m. the gas leak occurred.

Union Carbide investigators had physical evidence to support this scenario. After the accident the local-pressure-gauge hole on Tank 610 was still open, and no plug had been inserted as would have been normal if the gauge had been removed for normal maintenance. When written records for the MIC unit were examined, a crude drawing of the hose connection was found on the back of one page from that night's log book. Also, operators outside the MIC unit told the investigation team that MIC operators had told them about the hose connection that night.

Log entries in the MIC unit had been falsified, causing the Carbide team to conclude that the operators had engaged in a crude cover-up. The major falsification was an attempt to hide the transfer of MIC from Tank 610 to the Sevin production area. The operators on duty that night made clumsy efforts to show that the transfer had come from Tank 611 instead and had been done more than an hour earlier, before the shift change. But the entries were out of chronological sequence and were in the handwriting of operators who did not come on until the night shift. Further, analysis of the contents of the MIC transferred into the Sevin area showed it to be contaminated with reaction by-products. The MIC in Tank 611, from which the operators claimed to have made the transfer, was found to be on-specification and untainted. The transfer had to have come from Tank 610.

Why did the supervisors and operators attempt a cover-up? One Carbide investigator has written this explanation.

> Not knowing if the attempted transfer had exacerbated the incident, or whether they could have otherwise prevented it, or whether they would be blamed for not having notified plant management earlier, those involved decided on a cover-up. They altered logs that morning and thereafter to disguise their involvement. As is not uncommon in many such incidents, the reflexive tendency to cover up simply took over.[23]

[23] Ashok S. Kalelkar, "Investigation of Large-Magnitude Incidents: Bhopal as a Case Study," paper presented at The Institution of Chemical Engineers Conference on Preventing Major Chemical Accidents, London, England, May 1988, p. 27.

This theory of deliberate sabotage was the centerpiece of Carbide's legal defense. The Indian government made no public comment on Carbide's investigation, but Srinivason Varadarajan, the lead investigator in the 1985 study by the Indian Council of Scientific and Industrial Research, commented: "We have other evidence showing the likelihood that water came in by the water washing. I don't think we'll have any difficulty showing it."[24] And some observers noted that the sabotage theory failed to mitigate management responsibility for equipment failures and procedures that were inadequate to contain the MIC reaction.

THE TRYING COURSE OF THE LAWSUITS

In the meantime, the Indian government's civil suit against Carbide in the Bhopal District Court had a rocky start. The government could not keep a presiding judge on the bench. The first judge, R. M. Rastogi, was transferred for reasons not made public. His replacement, K. S. Srivastav, was injured in a car crash and resigned. A third judge, G. S. Patel, resigned when it was discovered from a computerized list that he was a plaintiff in a suit against Carbide. By February 1987 a fourth judge, M. W. Deo, had just been assigned to the case. He would not be the last.

In addition to the disruption of frequent judicial changes, Carbide had to combat forceful and sometimes disconcerting legal moves by the Indian government. In its suit the government of India sued only Union Carbide Corporation, the American corporation, and not Union Carbide India Ltd., the Indian corporation. At issue in the suit was the responsibility of the parent corporation for a majority-owned subsidiary. The traditional concept of parent corporation legal responsibility is that parent corporations are not liable for acts or omissions of subsidiaries "except in instances such as fraud or where the affairs of the two corporations are intermingled to the point that one is the alter ego of the other."[25] But in its suit the Indian government advanced a novel theory of "multinational enterprise liability" that departed from established precedent. The government argued as follows:

> Key management personnel of multinationals exercise a closely-held power which is neither restricted by national boundaries nor effectively controlled by international law. The complex corporate structure of the multinational, with networks of subsidiaries and divisions, makes it exceedingly difficult or even impossible to pinpoint responsibility for the damage caused by the enterprise to discrete corporate units or individuals. In reality, there is but one entity, the monolithic multinational, which is responsible for the design, development and dissemination of information and tech-

---

[24]Wil Lepkowski, "Union Carbide Presses Bhopal Sabotage Theory," *Chemical & Engineering News,* July 4, 1988, p. 11.

[25]Robert A. Butler, "Claims against a Parent Corporation from the Perspective of In-House Counsel," paper presented to the Practising Law Institute Program on the theme "Responsibility of the Corporate Parent for Activities of a Subsidiary," New York, June 10, 1988, p. 1.

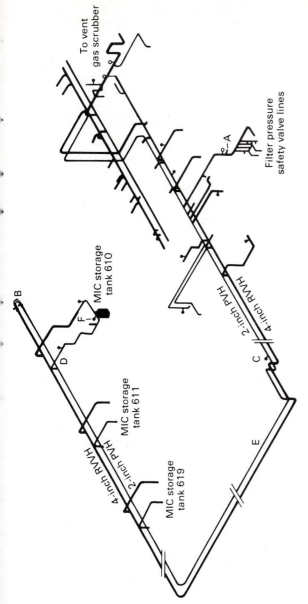

To vent
gas scrubber

Filter pressure
safety valve lines

B

MIC storage
tank 610

F

D

2-inch PVH

4-inch RVVH

C

2-inch PVH

4-inch RVVH

E

MIC storage
tank 611

MIC storage
tank 619

A

According to water-washing theory of Indian government, water was introduced through a hose into bleeder A at filter pressure safety valve lines. As hose kept running, water proceeded through leaking valve in that area and rose up into the relief valve vent header line (RVVH). It took a turn at the jumper line, B, and moved into the process vent header line (PVH), filling it in the reverse direction all the way to the slip blind, C. When PVH was completely filled, water rose at line D and proceeded into MIC storage tank 610. On Feb. 8, 1985, two months after the leak, India's Central Bureau of Investigation drilled a hole in the PVH line at point E to drain any water left in the line. No water emerged. Carbide says this fact alone disproves the water-washing theory. The fact that various valves in the pathway to the tank were closed also disproves the theory, according to Carbide. Carbide espouses an alternate theory: The company says it has proof that water was introduced by a "disgruntled employee" who removed pressure gauge F, attached a hose to the open piping, and ran water into the MIC tank. Gas then escaped through a rupture disk and proceeded through the RVVH and out the vent gas scrubber.

315

nology worldwide, acting through a forged network of interlocking directors, common operating systems, global distribution and marketing systems, financial and other controls.[26]

This was a theory beyond precedent both in the law of either country and in international law.[27] Then, in March 1987, the Indian Supreme Court issued a bizarre ruling which created a new legal principle of absolute liability for a hazardous activity. The *Mehta* v. *Union of India* case arose when a fertilizer plant owned by an Indian company, Shri Ram Foods & Fertilizer Industries Ltd., released a mixture of sulfuric acid and sulfur trioxide which killed one person and injured several more.[28] Chief Justice P. N. Bhagwati wrote the opinion, on the day before he retired, holding that "where an enterprise is engaged in a hazardous or inherently dangerous activity and harm results to anyone on account of an accident in the operation of such hazardous or inherently dangerous activity resulting, for example, in escape of toxic gas the enterprise is strictly and absolutely liable to compensate all those who are affected by the accident. ...."[29] He added that absolute liability was not mitigated by malicious acts of individuals. And he ruled that compensation to victims should be based on the ability of the corporation to pay, not on the traditional grounds of the victim's income. "The larger and more prosperous the enterprise," he wrote, "the greater must be the amount of compensation."[30]

This decision was a knife in Carbide's ribs. It would vitiate Carbide's defense against breach of duty, a defense based on proof of an unpreventable, deliberate act of sabotage. *Mehta* would even have ruled out an act of God as a defense. Judge Bhagwati later denied having Carbide in mind when he wrote his decision, but few believed him. A Carbide lawyer called the *Mehta* ruling "extreme and without precedent in the entire world."[31]

Throughout 1987 Union Carbide appeared willing to settle. In November, it offered a settlement of $496.2 million in ten years of installments. But two deadlines for settlement set up by the Bhopal court passed without agreement. In December, perhaps hoping to put more pressure on Carbide, the Bhopal Criminal Court filed homicide charges against Warren Anderson, who had re-

---

[26]Ibid., pp. 2–3.

[27]The United Nations Draft Code of Conduct on Transnational Corporations, however, applies to all subsidiaries of transnationals. It requires transnationals, *inter alia*, to protect the environment and restore it after damage, to supply full information on risky technologies to local authorities, and to promote high standards of environmental protection (secs. 41–43). The logic for applying these standards to both parent corporations and subsidiaries is the same as that used by the Indian government in support of the theory of "multinational enterprise liability," namely that the affairs of parent and subsidiary are linked in a system of common ownership, decision making, and policy formulation. Y. K. Tyagi and Armin Rosencranz, "Some International Law Aspects of the Bhopal Disaster," *Social Science and Medicine*, vol. 27, no. 10, p. 1108.

[28]*M. C. Mehta and Anr.* v. *Union of India & Ors.*, Writ petition (civil), No. 12739 (1985). Decided March 10, 1987.

[29]Butler, op. cit., p. 4.

[30]Ibid., p. 5.

[31]Matt Miller, "Carbide's Bhopal Case May Be Hurt by Ruling in India's Supreme Court," *Wall Street Journal*, March 11, 1987.

tired as chairman more than a year earlier. Arrest warrants were soon issued, but lawyers advised Anderson that the Bhopal court had no jurisdiction. No attempt to arrest him was ever made.

Two weeks later, Judge Deo of the Bhopal District Court dealt Carbide an outrageous blow. He ruled that because of delays in legal proceedings, Carbide had to pay victims of the gas leak $270 million in interim relief even before the trial began. This amounted to punishment before legal proceedings to establish Carbide's liability. "It was like a kangaroo court," a lawyer said later.[32] The ruling so outraged Carbide's attorneys that they filed a motion for Judge Deo's dismissal along with their appeal. Judge Deo's ruling survived one appeal, but in August 1988 the High Court in Madhya Pradesh overruled interim compensation and disqualified Judge Deo for the appearance of bias against Carbide. Judge Nirmal K. Jain replaced him as the fifth presiding magistrate in the case.

At last, on February 14, 1989, a settlement was reached. Carbide agreed to pay $470 million. In return, India dropped all pending lawsuits and indemnified Carbide and its officers against any further legal action. Carbide's insurers paid approximately $200 million. The *Washington Post* estimated that Carbide had already paid over $100 million in legal fees since 1984.[33] Carbide was pleased with the settlement. It was affordable and required only a $0.50-per-share charge against 1988 profits of $5.31 a share. And it may avoid litigation into the twenty-first century. The case was a festering political sore for Indian Prime Minister Rajiv Gandhi, who feared that opposition candidates in the next general election would pillory him for his failure to force Carbide into paying restitution. Thus, the Indian government was anxious to settle.

Victims' groups such as the Bhopal Poison Gas Struggle Front were upset. Some estimated the needs of Bhopal victims in the billions of dollars, and many Indians had demanded a harsher punishment for the American company. Shortly after the settlement was announced, victims of the gas leak gathered outside Union Carbide offices in New Delhi, shouting "Killer Carbide, quit India." About fifty stormed the offices, breaking windows and furniture. In Parliament, opponents of Prime Minister Gandhi walked out upon learning of the settlement. And newspapers around the country ran pictures and stories of the victims and their miseries.

The settlement has been appealed by victims' groups on technicalities. They argue, for example, that it was illegal for the government to represent victims because that violated the right of victims to choose their own lawyers. In June the Indian Supreme Court agreed to hear oral arguments challenging the settlement, belying its finality.

Because the case has not come to trial, the water-washing theory and the

---

[32]Malcolm Gladwell, "Union Carbide's Costly Lesson in Bhopal," *Washington Post National Weekly Edition,* February 27–March 5, 1989, p. 20.

[33]Malcolm Gladwell, "Bhopal's Final Chapter," *Washington Post National Weekly Edition,* February 20–26, 1989.

sabotage theory have never clashed in a legal forum. The world does not know which would be more persuasive to a jury.

WHAT DOES BHOPAL MEAN?

"Most of us," Warren Anderson once said, "believe that in one way or another Bhopal will be with Union Carbide and our people for as long as the company is around."[34] It will be remembered for a long time. It is an incident that has left a legacy of issues.[35]

BHOPAL: A CHRONOLOGY

1969	Bhopal pesticide plant constructed.	1985 (Dec.)	Report of India's official investigation of disaster supports water-washing theory.
1975	License for MIC manufacture at Bhopal granted by India's Ministry of Industry.	1986 (May)	Carbide offers $350 million settlement to victims. American lawyers accept; Indian
1980	MIC production begins.		government refuses.
1982	Last safety inspection by Americans.	1986 (May)	Judge Keenan rules that all cases must be heard in In-
1984 (Dec. 3)	Water entry in Tank 610 leads to heat reaction and major MIC leak.		dia on grounds of *forum non conveniens*.
1985 (Dec. 7)	First lawsuit against Carbide filed in a U.S. court.	1986 (Sept.)	India brings $3.3 billion suit against Carbide in Bhopal District Court.
1985 (Jan.)	*New York Times* article introduces the water-washing theory.	1987 (Nov.)	Carbide settlement offer of $496.2 million is rejected.
1985 (March)	Union Carbide releases a report on the accident based on analysis of residue in Tank 610.	1987 (Dec.)	Bhopal District Court orders Carbide to pay $270 million in "interim relief" to victims.
1985 (March)	India enacts the Bhopal Gas Leak Disaster Act, which gives it exclusive right to represent Indian victims in the United States.	1988 (May)	Carbide permits A. D. Little consultant to deliver a paper at a London conference detailing its sabotage theory.
1985 (Aug.)	Chemical leak at Institute plant.	1989 (Feb.)	Carbide and India reach settlement of $470 million.
1985 (Dec.)	GAF Corporation begins hostile takeover bid.		

---

[34]"Remarks," at the International Conference on Industrial Crisis Management, New York University, September 5, 1986, p. 1.

[35]A number of books have been written about Bhopal. In addition to Weir, op. cit., see Larry Everest. *Behind the Poison Cloud: Union Carbide's Bhopal Massacre*. Chicago: Banner Press, 1985; Paul Shrivastava. *Bhopal: Anatomy of a Crisis*. Cambridge, Mass.: Ballinger, 1987; and Sidney C. Suffrin. *Bhopal: Its Setting, Responsibility and Challenge*. Delhi: Ajanta Publications,

Foremost is the question of who was responsible. How should blame be apportioned among the parties involved, including Union Carbide senior management, UCIL managers, operators in the MIC unit, governments in India that issued permits and provided incentives for the plant, slum dwellers who moved into illegal settlements near the plant, Indian environmental and safety inspectors, and others? Do you believe that a U.S. multinational should accept responsibility for the actions of an overseas affiliate managed by foreign nationals?

Some other fundamental issues are raised by these questions.

- Did Union Carbide handle the crisis well? No other company has ever been faced with a like situation. How would you grade Carbide's performance?
- Were victims compensated fairly? How well did the legal system work in compensating victims? Was it fair to compensate them at a lower level owing to their poverty, or should the settlement have been higher in recognition of Carbide's ability to pay?
- Does Bhopal represent an unacceptably heavy reliance on high-risk industrial activity? It is only one incident in a string of unsettling environmental disasters, including the reactor failures at Three Mile Island and Chernoble and the huge Alaskan oil spill. These incidents and others stem from the dangers inherent in certain production technologies. Future Bhopals are probably inevitable. Is something wrong with modern industry?

1985. For a concise analysis of major issues see S. Prakash Sethi, "Inhuman Errors and Industrial Crisis," *Columbia Journal of World Business,* spring 1987.

INDEX